New Tribalisms

The Resurgence of Race and Ethnicity

Edited by

Michael W. Hughey

Professor of Sociology
Moorhead State University
Minnesota

First published 1998 by
MACMILLAN PRESS LTD
Houndmills, Basingstoke, Hampshire RG21 6XS
and London
Companies and representatives
throughout the world

ISBN 0–333–66665–8 hardcover
ISBN 0–333–66666–6 paperback

A catalogue record for this book is available
from the British Library.

This book is printed on paper suitable for recycling and
made from fully managed and sustained forest sources.

10 9 8 7 6 5 4 3 2 1
07 06 05 04 03 02 01 00 99 98

Printed and bound in Great Britain by
Antony Rowe Ltd, Chippenham, Wiltshire

NEW TRIBALISMS

MAIN TRENDS OF THE MODERN WORLD

General Editors: Robert Jackall and Arthur J. Vidich

New Tribalisms: The Resurgence of Race and Ethnicity
Edited by Michael W. Hughey

Propaganda
Edited by Robert Jackall

Metropolis: Center and Symbol of Our Times
Edited by Philip Kasinitz

Social Movements: Critiques, Concepts, Case-Studies
Edited by Stanford M. Lyman

Science and the Quest for Reality
Edited by Alfred I. Tauber

The New Middle Classes: Life-Styles, Status Claims and Political Orientations
Edited by Arthur J. Vidich

Contents

Series Preface

Main Trends of the Modern World is a series of books analyzing the main trends and the social psychology of our times. Each volume in the series brings together readings from social analysts who first identified a decisive institutional trend and from writers who explore its social and psychological effects in contemporary society.

The series works in the classical tradition of social theory. In this view, theory is the historically informed framing of intellectual problems about concrete social issues and the resolution of those problems through the analysis of empirical data. Theory is not, therefore, the study of the history of ideas about society, nor the abstract, ahistorical modeling of social realities, nor, as in some quarters, pure speculation often of an ideological sort unchecked by empirical reality. Theory is meaningful only when it illuminates the specific features, origins, and animating impetus of particular institutions, showing how these institutions shape experience and are linked to the social order as a whole.

Social analysts such as Karl Marx, Max Weber, Émile Durkheim, Sigmund Freud, Georg Simmel, Thorstein Veblen and George Herbert Mead, whose works we now consider classics, never consciously set out to construct paradigms, models or abstract theories of society. Instead they investigated concrete social phenomena such as the decline of feudal society and the emergence of industrial capitalism, the growth of bureaucracy, the consequences of the accelerating specialization of labor, the significance of religion in a scientific and secular age, the formation of self and the moral foundations of modern society, and the on-going rationalization of modern life. The continuing resonance of their ideas suggests the firmness of their grasp of deep-rooted structural trends in Western industrial society.

Later European and American social thinkers, deeply indebted though they were to the intellectual frameworks produced by the remarkable men who preceded them, faced a social order marked by increasing disarray, one that required fresh intellectual approaches. The social, cultural and intellectual watershed was, of course, the Great War and its aftermath. The world's first total war ravaged a whole generation of youth. In Europe it sowed the seeds of revolution, militarism, totalitarianism, fascism and state socialism; in both

Europe and America it signaled the age of mass propaganda. On both continents the aftermath of the war brought economic and political turmoil, cultural frenzies, widespread disenchantment and disillusionment, and social movements of every hue and description that led eventually to the convulsions of the Second World War. These later social thinkers grappled with issues such as:

- The deepening bureaucratization of all social spheres and the ascendance of the new middle classes.
- The collapse of old religious theodicies that once gave meaning to life and the emergence of complex social psychologies of individuals and masses in a rationalized world.
- The riddles posed by modern art and culture.
- The emergence of mass communications and propaganda as well as the manufacture of cultural dreamworlds of various sorts.
- War, militarism and the advent of totalitarianism, fascism and state socialism.
- The deepening irrational consequences and moral implications of the thoroughgoing rationalization of all life spheres.

Emil Lederer, Hans Speier, Joseph Schumpeter, Kenneth Burke, Robert MacIver, Harold Lasswell, Walter Lippmann, Robert Park, W. I. Thomas, Florian Znaniecki, George Orwell, Hannah Arendt, Herbert Blumer and Hans H. Gerth are only a few of the men and women who carried forward the theoretical attitude of the great classical thinkers in the course of working on the pressing issues of their own day. In this tradition, social theory means confronting head-on the social realities of one's own times, trying to explain both the main structural drift of institutions as well as the social psychologies of individuals, groups and classes.

What then are the major structural trends and individual experiences of our own epoch? Four major trends come immediately to mind, each with profound ramifications for individuals. We pose these as groups of research problems.

BUREAUCRACY AS THE ORGANIZATIONAL FORM OF MODERNITY

- What are the social and psychological consequences of living and working in a society dominated by mass administered bureaucratic

structures? How do mass bureaucratic structures affect the private
lives of the men and women exposed to their influences?

• What is the structure and meaning of work in a bureaucratic
society? In particular, how does bureaucracy shape moral consciousness? What are the organizational roots of the collapse of
traditional notions of accountability in our society?
• What is the relationship between leaders and followers in a society
dominated by a bureaucratic ethos? What are the changing roles of
intellectuals, whether in the academy or public life, in defining,
legitimating, challenging or serving the social order?

THE TECHNOLOGIES OF MASS COMMUNICATION AND
THE MANAGEMENT OF MASS SOCIETY

• What role do public relations, advertising and bureaucratized
social research play in shaping the public opinions and private
attitudes of the masses?
• What is the relationship between individuals' direct life experiences
(with, for example, family, friends, occupations, sex and marriage)
and the definitions that the mass media suggest for these individual
experiences? What illusions and myths now sustain the social
order? What are the ascendant forms of this-worldly salvation in
our time?
• What are the different origins, dynamics and consequences of
modern political, social and cultural mass movements with their
alternative visions of justice and morality?
• What social, economic and cultural trends have made many great
metropolises, once the epitomes of civilization and still the centers
and symbols of modern life, into new wildernesses?

THE ON-GOING SOCIAL TRANSFORMATIONS OF
CAPITALISM

• What are the prospects for a transformed capitalism in a post-
Marxist, post-Keynesian era?
• How has the emergence of large bureaucratic organizations in
every sector of the social order transformed the middle classes?
• What is the social and political psychology of these new middle
classes?

- What transformations of the class and status structure have been precipitated by America's changing industrial order?
- What are the social, cultural and historical roots of the pervasive criminal violence in contemporary American society? What social factors have fostered the breakdown of traditional mechanisms of social control and the emergence of violence as a primary means for effecting individual or group goals?

THE CLASH BETWEEN WORLDVIEWS AND VALUES, OLD AND NEW

- How has science, particularly in its bureaucratized form, transformed the liberal doctrines of natural rights, individual rights and concomitant conceptions of the human person, including notions of life and death?
- How have the old middle classes come to terms with mass bureaucratic institutions and the subsequent emergence of new classes and status groups? What social forces continue to prompt the framing of complicated social issues in terms of primal antagonisms of kith, kin, blood, color, soil, gender and sexual orientation?
- What are the roots of the pervasive irrationalities evident at virtually every level of our society, despite our Enlightenment legacy of reason and rationality and our embrace of at least functional rationality in our organizational apparatus? To what extent is individual and mass irrationality generated precisely by formally rational bureaucratic structures?

In short, the modern epoch is undergoing social transformations every bit as dramatic as the transition from feudalism to industrial capitalism. The very complexity of the contemporary world impedes fixed social scientific understanding. Moreover we may lack the language and concepts necessary to provide coherent analyses of some emerging features of our social order. Nonetheless this series tries to identify and analyze the major trends of modern times. With an historical awareness of the great intellectual work of the past and with a dispassionate attitude toward contemporary social realities, the series tries to fashion grounded, specific images of our world in the hope that future thinkers will find these more useful than speculation or prophecy.

Each volume in this series addresses one major trend. The book in hand analyzes the foundations and implications of the resurgence of ethical and racial identifications and loyalties in contemporary societies.

ROBERT JACKALL
ARTHUR J. VIDICH

Introduction
Michael W. Hughey

Social thinkers in the 20th century devoted their attention primarily to issues of economic class. The great experiments of this century with communism and welfare state liberalism were intended to rationally manage the problems associated with class inequalities, either by softening the inequities created by capitalism or by attempting to eliminate class altogether. In this focus, the more primordial bonds of racial, ethnic, and nationalist loyalties and identities were often regarded as irrational anachronisms that would either be submerged under the imposed orthodoxy of communism or, more benignly, dissolved within the liberal frameworks of constitutional democracies. Yet, today, communism is nearly dead, liberalism is on the wane, and the older ethno-racial tribalisms, as well as some newly invented ones, have seemingly everywhere broken through our illusions of a rationally manageable world to find expression in chauvinistic nationalisms, "multiculturalist" ideologies, vicious civil wars, "ethnic cleansing" of whole regions, intensified racial and ethnic strife, a resurgence of racism, prejudice, scapegoating, hate groups, and nativism in almost all societies, and new group-based challenges to the individualistic focus of Western liberalism. It appears increasingly likely that as the 20th century draws to a close it will bequeath an urgent preoccupation with these new tribalisms to its successor.

This volume will approach this issue with a twofold purpose: to examine some of the conceptions of racial and ethnic pluralism raised earlier in this century, particularly in the United States, which has confronted issues of diversity for most of its history, and which, as a result, has produced a broad range of scholarly literature on the topic, and; to explore some of the causes, implications, and possible outcomes of resurgent tribalisms in the contemporary United States and other areas of the world.

The very terms "race" and "ethnicity" have never been as unambiguous as our common sense understandings have often led us to believe. Historically, both have generally been understood as biological categories, and even today demagogic political leaders routinely evoke images of racial brotherhood and mystic communities of blood to create solidarity and intensified support among their followers.

1

Even in the more dispassionate realm of scholarship, it was only in this century that race and ethnicity came to be understood as social rather than biological phenomena.

In different ways, the essays in Part I make significant contributions to this understanding. Max Weber points out in Chapter 1 that inherited physical traits as such play no significant part in ethnic relations. The decisive issue, he argues, is "monopolistic closure" of the group, which can originate around a focus on any cultural or physical traits. These traits subsequently become the basis for group members' "subjective belief in their common descent," a belief that comes to be invested with a sense of group honor and which is nurtured especially by the political community. Yet, even after carefully delineating its origins and meaning, Weber regards "ethnic group" as a concept too nebulous for use in sociological analysis.

As Herbert Blumer makes clear in Chapter 2, however, analytic clarity is not required for those who embrace race and/or ethnicity as a decisive aspect of personal identity or as a foundation of political and social action. Blumer points out that race (and ethnic) prejudice emerges out of the ongoing relations between groups, and especially from shifts in a group's sense of its social position relative to that of the other group or groups. In particular, the real or imagined social ascent of the subordinate group is perceived by dominant group members as an indication of their own decline, or as a diminution of their group's honor, resulting in an intensification of prejudicial attitudes toward the offending group, often combined with actions designed to restore it to its rightful "place." In this sense, for Blumer prejudice is a kind of defensive reaction on the part of a dominant group to a perceived threat to its status and prerogatives within the social hierarchy. Blumer's concluding discussion of the social processes by which dominant groups construct their images of themselves and other groups offers a framework for an analysis not only of prejudice as such but for the upsurge of ethnic nationalism throughout the world today.

In "Beyond Reason: The Nature of the Ethnonational Bond" (Chapter 3), Walker Connor underscores the theoretical points made by Weber and Blumer by giving them a more empirical focus. Examining the speeches and proclamations of ethnonational spokesmen, Connor demonstrates that the psychosocial core of ethnonational identity is *the belief* of a people in their shared origin and evolution. The intensity of this belief and the degree of the group's psychological investment in it largely determine how susceptible the group is to political manipulation by leaders who evoke images of blood, family, forefathers, homeland – what Weber referred to as the "irrationality of blood." Since, as Connor points out, the sources of ethnonationalism are non-rational and emotional, it may not be readily subject to rational management even by those who would exploit it.

As the world's first modern polyglot nation, the United States has wrestled throughout most of its history with issues of racial and ethnic pluralism. It is therefore to be expected that the problems and issues associated with the resurgence of tribal identities lead almost inevitably to a re-examination of the American experience.

The history of racial and ethnic pluralism in the United States can only be understood with reference to the cultural assumptions and expectations of its historically dominant white Anglo-Protestant groups. As the first European settlers in the New World, these groups invested their own cultural values into the development and operating rationales of American political, economic, and social institutions; they established the basic patterns of "traditional" American culture. Inasmuch as it embodied their cultural styles, standards, and values, Anglo-Protestants tended to regard America as "theirs." This sense of proprietary ownership posed no special problems at a time when Anglo-Protestant dominance was unchallenged and even unquestioned. Later, however, as other groups began to press their claims for membership rights in the political community and for shares of available social resources, America's dominant groups found it necessary to seriously confront the ambiguities of and contradictions between their inclusive ideology of liberalism and their exclusive proprietary claim to the nation.

Part II opens with three essays that bring very different emphases to an examination of the sources and implications of the contradiction between American ideals and practices.

In his classic discussion of "An American Dilemma" (Chapter 4) written in the 1940s, Gunnar Myrdal insisted that liberal, universalistic ideals constitute the authentic contents of the "American Creed," and that these represent "higher" values than the "lower," merely local and particularistic values of racism, prejudice, and exclusion. On the basis of this premise, Myrdal confidently predicted that America's liberal ideals would ultimately win out to provide the foundations of a truly inclusive American brotherhood.

Taking issue with Myrdal, I argue in "Americanism and Its Discontents: Protestantism, Nativism, and Political Heresy in America" (Chapter 5) that the exclusive emphases and proprietary "ownership" of American society are equally authentic features of the Anglo-Protestant cultural heritage. I locate the origin of these notions in the convenantal social organization of the Puritans, and point to their subsequent transmutation into secular political ideas and conceptions. America's dominant groups, I suggest, merged the two sides of their cultural heritage into "a normative conception of the political community that was at once democratic and exclusive, universalistic and restrictive, tolerant and discriminatory." The practical implications of this political conception are demonstrated mainly with reference to nativist reactions to ideological subversion, but they are equally applicable to the social organization of racial and ethnic pluralism.

In practice, the uneasy relationship between America's liberal ideals and exclusive practices was given shape and substance by judicial interpretation. As the ultimate arbiter of the permissible, the United States Supreme Court constructed the legal framework for the social organization of American race and ethnic relations. In his essay "The Race Question and Liberalism: Casuistries in American Constitutional Law" (Chapter 6), Stanford M. Lyman traces out the legal interpretations, sophistries, and justifications by which the Court has sought to square the universalist and restrictive sides of the American political heritage. Examining the judicial treatment of blacks, Chinese, Japanese, Armenians, Burmese, Syrians, Arabs, East Indians, Puerto Ricans and other groups, Lyman demonstrates that the Court in effect created "a condition of permanent alienage" for virtually all non-Caucasian groups. Lyman takes issue in particular with those apologists who would absolve political and economic liberalism of any responsibility for contemporary racial inequality, especially the persistence of the urban black "underclass," and who attribute it instead to character defects instilled by the pre-liberal structures of slavery. As Lyman's legal review demonstrates, "prejudices of race and culture have gone hand-in-hand with the development of modern industrial society." Noting the continuing conflict between the United States's liberal ideals and racial practices, he offers a defense of affirmative action programs as a reasonable way for the nation to achieve its constitutional principles.

The "color line," as W.E.B. DuBois called it,[1] has always posed the greatest test of American liberalism. For the most part, historically non-white peoples have mainly experienced the more exclusive and restrictive emphases of America's political culture. The experience of white ethnics, by contrast, has been more mixed. For them, the simultaneous emphases on inclusion and exclusion found expression primarily in the ideal of assimilation. Although with significant exceptions, membership in the political community was extended to most groups, but it was conditional upon their ability to "melt" or conform to the Anglo-Protestant cultural pattern. American social thinkers understood the requirement and process of assimilation in different ways but, at least until the early part of this century, few seriously questioned it as a normative ideal or goal of race and ethnic relations. For example, in their separate works, Gunnar Myrdal and Talcott Parsons[2] viewed assimilation as an eventual product of the alchemy of political and economic liberalism. Robert E. Park[3] anticipated that it would represent the evolutionary outcome of cultural contacts. Even the celebrated image of America as a "melting pot" that would ultimately produce a new cultural amalgam – "the American, this new man" in Crévecoeur's well-known phrase[4] – was not generally understood by dominant groups as implying that they too would be mixed into the pot as one ingredient among many. Others would melt; Anglo-Protestants would serve as the mold into which they would be poured.

Despite their differences in conception, all of these images of assimilation were grounded in an obvious historical reality. America represented freedom and opportunity for most of the "huddled masses" who immigrated to its shores, and most eagerly strove to shed their Old World customs in return for what they viewed as the privileges and prospects of becoming Americans. To be sure, Anglo-Protestants were occasionally aggressive and insistent in pushing some groups toward Anglo-conformity, but heavy handed pressures were seldom necessary. For most immigrants, to assimilate and become an American entailed nothing but gain. Most wanted very much to assimilate to the dominant culture, and most did precisely that.

Later, however, during the early middle part of the 20th century, some groups – especially Jewish intellectuals – began to reject the cultural standardization required by assimilationists. Asserting that ethnicity is a fundamental feature of the self, Horace Kallen[5] argued that economic and political assimilation should proceed but that cultural heritages should be preserved as a source of energy and creativity in American life. Kallen's conception of "cultural plural-ism" offered an image of American society as a federation of distinct ethnic cultures within a tolerant democratic context. This image also proved attractive to some cosmopolitan "native" intellectuals such as Randolph Bourne, who advocated the encouragement of dual

citizenship and a "trans-national" American society.[6] Almost completely neglected in these conceptions of American pluralism, and even
more neglected in practice, were blacks, Indians, and Asians, whose
visible racial differences marked them as "unassimilable" and in some
way as unqualified for full membership in the society.

This traditional pattern of American racial and ethnic pluralism
was upset by the Civil Rights movement early in the second half of
this century. At that time, as the cultural unity of white Anglo-
Protestants was eroding due to a broader institutional transformation
of American life, black Americans began pressing their claims for
economic and political inclusion, but in a way that initiated a reorganization of race and ethnic relations. Essentially blacks – and later,
other minority groups – successfully claimed the benefits of inclusion
on the basis of racial identity itself. To counter the lingering effects of
their past exclusion, group identities (race, gender, some ethnicities)
were legally accepted as important criteria for the distribution of
political, economic, educational, and other resources, as institutionalized in affirmative action guidelines, minority set-aside programs,
enrollment targets, and other minority preference programs. This
situation has helped to create opportunities for racial and ethnic
leaders who can cultivate power and privilege by appealing to group
loyalties and reinforcing group boundaries. Even as this has led to
greater politicization and polarization of racial and ethnic groups, it
has made possible, and perhaps necessary, the creation of new group-
based coalitions to defend, advance, or challenge the existing distribution of spoils and the ethno-racial criteria on which it is based. In
effect, the resulting arrangement constitutes a new framework of
ethno-racial pluralism in America.

In "The New American Pluralism: Racial and Ethnic Sodalities and
Their Sociological Implications" (Chapter 7), Arthur J. Vidich and I
examine some of the sources, features, and political and social implications of this new ethno-racial system, focusing especially on the
extraordinarily complex reactions by and transmutations of ethno-
racial identities and communities as they have creatively adapted to a
fluid American context. We construct a conception of ethnicity in the
contemporary United States that takes into account characteristics of
the cultures of origin, different times of arrival for and within various
groups, and differences in the starting points for various groups both
in terms of their social psychology at the time of arrival and in terms
of changing social, political, economic, and cultural developments in
the United States.

According to Howard Winant in Chapter 8, the new pluralism originated in the inconsistent emphases of the Civil Rights movement. The Civil Rights movement successfully gained legal guarantees of formal equality for members of all groups, but also resulted in the further "racialization" of the society – understood as the extension of racial meanings to groups, practices, and relationships not previously understood in racial terms – and led to an intensification of racial consciousness on the part of all groups. Heightened racial awareness, and especially the elevation of ethno-racial identity into a strategic political device, has worked to broaden the boundaries of some groups, consolidating previously distinct ethnic identities into a single pan-ethnic category and sometimes even creating wholly new ethno-racial types.[7]

Winant notes that despite, or perhaps because of, the ongoing American preoccupation with and sensitivity to racial matters, the United States currently lacks a "clear and consensual racial order" to replace the system of legal segregation overturned by the Civil Rights movement. The absence of such a dominant normative framework provides opportunities and incentives for interested parties to put forth new conceptions and ideological articulations of what the emerging ethno-racial order should be. By far the most prominent of these conceptions, at present, is that of multiculturalism. As currently expressed, multiculturalism is not simply an extension of the older ideal of cultural pluralism. Cultural pluralism advocated a kind of ecumenical framework in which ethno-racial identities would be tolerated and valued as different but still fellow worshipers at the altar of Americanism. Multiculturalism, at least in some versions, so exalts group identities that it offers no program or framework for the integration of groups into a larger unity. So important is the ethno-racial group that, as some critics have charged, no loyalties can transcend it.[8]

Multiculturalism finds expression both as an ideological romanticization and exaltation of minority group identities and as an assertion of minority claims against the traditional Anglo-Protestant majority by virtue of an aggressive devaluation of its culture as inherently oppressive. In pursuit of this agenda, for example, multiculturalists cultivate a linguistic moralism or etiquette of public discourse (one aspect of "political correctness") in which all ethno-racial identities are proclaimed to be equally positive, all valuable and cherished possessions (except for the Anglo-Protestant). Any critical, pejorative, or "insensitive" public references to these identities are quickly condemned by the aggrieved group.

Perhaps the most controversial feature of the multiculturalist agenda is its attempts to revise the historical record and literary canon in ways that are designed to serve the needs, interests, and claims of contemporary ethno-racial groups. Much of this multiculturalist revisionism seeks to overcome what its proponents regard as the "hegemonic" interpretation of history and standards of literary or scholarly worth imposed by dead white European males. It proposes instead a truly multicultural history that emphasizes the achievements and contributions of all peoples. Centered mainly around public school and university curricula, multicultural histories are self-consciously designed to enhance the self-esteem of ethno-racial group members.

In "Multiculturalism and Universalism: A History and Critique" (Chapter 9), John Higham offers both a historical account of the emergence of multiculturalism and a critical commentary on its emphases and agenda. He argues that in nourishing "cultures of endowment" and thereby largely ignoring economic inequalities, multiculturalism undermines its own egalitarian purpose. Its suppression of class identities denies a potentially important ally in the fight for economic and social reform. Higham concludes with an incisive discussion of the dilemmas – some shaped by the lingering residues of universalist ideals – that confront those who would forge multiculturalist ideals into policy.

The ideals and goals of multiculturalism appear to hold little appeal for most white ethnics. By the time of the Civil Rights movement, most white ethnics had already been thoroughly assimilated into the mainstream of American life, retaining few authentic vestiges of their ethnic heritage. Yet, the well defined cultural styles and social supports for personal identity which they sacrificed to assimilation could not easily be replaced within the rootless, commercial, individualistic framework of American society. Partly for this reason, the last two decades have witnessed a resurgence of ethnic identification among whites. However, the ethnicity they reclaim appears to be more symbolic than real, not so much an authentic, deeply felt feature of lived experience as a self-consciously expressive, voluntaristic, and lightly worn aspect of personal identity.[9] Generally lacking authentic cultural content, symbolic ethnicity appears to be primarily a nostalgic reclamation of an ethnic identity already lost.

One implication of the lightness or looseness with which ethnicity is often now worn is that, as an aspect of individual identity, it can be modified, selectively presented, or even abandoned altogether, depending on the situation. Ethnicities in general offer individuals a reservoir or "toolkit"[10] of cultural resources which can be selectively adopted in order to self-consciously fashion situational or even more enduring personal identities.[11] In Chapter 10, Joane Nagel identifies some of the social processes by which ethnic identities and cultures are created and recreated in modern societies, focusing on the formation of collective meaning, the construction of community, and the development of symbolic bases for ethno-racial mobilization.

In her essay "The Costs of a Costless Community" (Chapter 11), Mary C. Waters describes symbolic ethnicity as a kind of compromise between the desire for individuality and a craving for community, enabling an individual to feel personally unique and yet to belong to a presumed primordial group. It is in this way both personally satisfying and psychologically functional. However, contrasting the voluntaristic ethnicity of whites with the more enduring ascribed ethno-racial identities of non-whites, Waters points to a darker side of symbolic ethnicity. The lightness of ethno-racial identity for whites can blind them to the burdensome weight it can have for non-whites in a society that has never achieved its "color blind" ideals, in this way subtly reinforcing racism.

Even as the traditional cultural contents of their ethnicity has faded, white ethnics have begun coalescing into a more generic "white" or "European" identity, partly as a reaction to minority gains, multiculturalist claims, and especially to "reverse discrimination" and other perceived inequities created by the new system of ethno-racial pluralism.[12] Over the past decade and a half, this emergent identification has been nourished and increasingly mobilized for political ends. The Republican Party in particular has strategically played the "race card" to great success as part of its "Southern strategy" to win more white male voters. The potential for racial divisiveness is clearly enhanced by these developments.

Despite struggling throughout its history to resolve its divisive and often contentious problems of ethno-racial pluralism – often, to be sure, in a heavy handed and repressive way – American society has somehow held together. Its diversity has been successfully managed, at least in the sense that the United States has neither been "Balkanized" into contending ethno-racially defined geographic zones nor thrown into enduring civic violence. For this reason alone, the American case has become a renewed object of interest to social thinkers attempting to comprehend the expressions of resurgent tribalisms that have lately surfaced in their own societies and to policy makers seeking ways to manage or in some way come to terms with them.

There is, of course, no shortage of commentators who offer some aspect of the American liberal democratic tradition as a solution to ethno-racial divisions in other parts of the world,[13] in this way extending that aspect of America's historical self-proclaimed mission to be a "city upon a hill," a model for the rest of the world to emulate. In Chapter 12, "Multicultural Foreign Policy," Yossi Shain suggests that some features of the American model are actively "marketed" abroad as domestic ethnic and racial groups increasingly attempt to influence American foreign policy toward their native countries and symbolic homelands. In practice, their efforts often take the form of opposing nondemocratic practices in these countries, as, for example, in the mobilization of the black community against apartheid and in the continuing campaign of Cuban-Americans against the Castro regime. These emphases commit the ethnic and racial groups who are engaged in foreign policy discourse to domestic liberal pluralism. As a result, Shain concludes, to some degree multiculturalist and ethnonational identifications in the United States both advance an ideal of American-style civic culture abroad and reinforce "the values of democracy and pluralism at home."

It may be the case, of course, that the American experience has few or no lessons to offer. Rita Jalali and Seymour Martin Lipset make clear in Chapter 13 that ethnic and racial conflicts throughout the world are rooted in causes and circumstances that are shaped by the specific historical, social, and cultural conflicts in which they emerge. Contrary to expectations, they argue, modernization itself has led to an increase in ethnic consciousness and to enhanced opportunities for ethnic mobilization, but the specific social dynamics of this outcome are heavily influenced by more local and regional circumstances. Generally, for example, race and ethnic relations in Sudan, Nigeria, Sri Lanka, Malaysia and other Third World countries clearly reveal the role of colonial powers in drawing national boundaries, implementing policies that promoted differential treatment of groups, and even creating new categories of identity. Similarly, dissolution of empires, migration patterns of guest workers, and the redrawing of state boundaries in postwar peace settlements have in different ways affected race and ethnic relations in the countries of Europe. While recognizing that the diverse underpinnings of ethnic and racial divisiveness may defeat any efforts to offer general solutions, Jalali and Lipset conclude with a discussion of political structures that have proven somewhat successful in containing it.

Managing ethno-racial conflict through internal political measures is made more difficult by the fact that some of the critical sources of the conflict may be external. In "Ethnic Nationalism: Politics, Ideology, and the World Order" (Chapter 14), Joane Nagel calls attention to broader geopolitical factors that provide support for ethno-racial mobilization and ethnic nationalist movements. For example, she suggests ethnic movements can readily find legitimacy in widely accepted ideological tenets of the international order, such as commitments to self-determination, sovereignty, territorial integrity, representative government, and home rule. Material resources are also often available as global and regional powers provide support to dissident or dominant ethnic groups in a effort to secure or advance their own economic and geopolitical interests. In their Cold War competition for global dominance, the United States and Soviet Union subsidized countless ethnic movements as their proxies around the world. This system of ethnic subsidization was of course undermined by the collapse of the Soviet Union, resulting in new ethnic alliances, instabilities, claims for autonomy, and attempts at state making.

The resurgence of ethno-national and racial tribalisms throughout the world derives partly from the failure of broader political communities to establish and maintain effective integrative anchors for personal identity. According to Robert Wistrich in this book's concluding chapter, in Europe this failure can be traced to the "leveling and homogenizing tendencies of modernity" and, in the formerly communist societies, to a backlash against the totalitarian experience. With no coercive state power to impose social order, and lacking a unifying ideology to knit them together, many Europeans have sought refuge in "a return to history," resurrecting tribal loyalties and identities as well as the ancient grievances, traumas, and hatreds associated with them.

Wistrich's discussion brings to mind Santayana's well known axiom that those who forget the past are condemned to repeat it, but Santayana is here turned on his head. Recent events make clear that those who remember the past, or who recall it only selectively, can also suffer the tragedies of repetition. History is surely our best teacher, but it is also a deep reservoir of our ignorance and hatred, the repository of ancient passions, grievous wrongs, and half-remembered primordial bonds. If the new world order is to avoid another round of Balkanization, nationalist wars, ethnic cleansing, and genocide, it must somehow take to heart one of history's simplest but perhaps most demanding lessons. As Wistrich concludes his essay, even the noblest sentiments of nationalism or racial and ethnic pride "must be balanced by an elementary respect for dignity, solidarity, and universal human rights."

NOTES

1. W. E. B. DuBois, *The Souls of Black Folk* (New York: Fawcett World Library, 1961 [1903]), p. 23.
2. Gunnar Myrdal, *An American Dilemma: The Negro and Modern Democracy* (NY: Harper Collins, 1944). Talcott Parsons, "Full Citizenship for the Negro American? A Sociological Problem," in Talcott Parsons and Kenneth B. Clark (eds), *The Negro American* (Boston: Houghton Mifflin, 1966).
3. Robert E. Park, *Race and Culture* (New York: The Free Press, 1950).
4. J. Hector St John Crévecoeur, *Letters From An American Farmer* (New York: Albert and Charles Bon, 1925). See also Israel Zangwill, *The Melting-Pot* (New York: Macmillan, 1911); Frederick Jackson Turner, *The Frontier in American History* (New York: Henry Holt & Co., 1920).
5. Horace Kallen, *Culture and Democracy in the United States* (New York: Arno Press and the New York Times, 1970 [1924]).
6. Randolph Bourne, "Trans-National America" and "The Jew and Trans-National America," both reprinted in Bourne *The War and the Intellectuals: Collected Essays, 1915–1919*, ed. by Carl Resek (New York: Harper and Row, 1964).
7. Winant refers to Asian-Americans as an example of a newly created ethno-racial identity. Hispanics also constitute an ethnic category forged in the post-Civil Rights era. See Patricia Kolb, "The Development of the Pan-Hispanic Community in the United States," in Michael W. Hughey and Arthur J. Vidich (eds), *The Ethnic Quest for Community: Searching for Roots in the Lonely Crowd* (Greenwich,: CT:JAI Press, 1993).
8. Arthur M. Schlesinger, *The Disuniting of America* (New York: Norton, 1992).
9. See Herbert J. Gans, "Symbolic Ethnicity: The Future of Ethnic Groups and Cultures in America," *Ethnic and Racial Studies*, 2(1) (January 1979) 1–20.
10. See Ann Swidler, "Culture as Action: Symbols and Strategies," *American Sociological Review*, 51 (1986) 273–86.
11. A particularly incisive ethnographic example of this can be found in Carl Kavadlo, "World Rejecting Hedonism of the Working

Classes: Irish and Italians in Queens and Brooklyn," in Michael W. Hughey and Arthur J. Vidich (eds.), *The Ethnic Quest for Community: Searching for Roots in the Lonely Crowd* (Greenwich, CT: JAI Press, 1993).

12.   This shift has been well documented by Waters as well as by Richard Alba, *Ethnic Identity: The Transformation of White America* (New Haven, CT: Yale University Press, 1990).

13.   See, for example, Benjamin R. Barber, "Global Multiculturalism and the American Experiment," *World Policy Journal*, 10(1) (Spring 1993) 47–55.

Part I
Racial and Ethnic Pluralism: Sociological Conceptions

— Weber sees 'ethnicity' & related terms as arising fr. strategies to gain pol. P.

~ In what sense is his Sy in gen. a Sy f pol's? Has a/1 pursued this idea?

— Gd value in seeing social dtg thro' ethnicity — tho' this @ relation to phy. traits — & esp. in terms f e/day conduct. Rel. etc. seen as arising fr pol.

— B/c f so many other factors involved, suggests uselessness f 'ethnicity' for Sy (27) ~ but doesn't he show its value, as a term to organise these facets into a coherent pattern, directed by pol. aims?

1 Ethnic Groups
Max Weber

"RACE" MEMBERSHIP

A ... problematic source of social action is "race identity": common inherited and inheritable traits that actually derive from common descent. Of course, race creates a "group" only when it is subjectively perceived as a common trait: this happens only when a neighborhood or the mere proximity of racially different persons is the basis of joint (mostly political) action, or conversely, when some common experiences of members of the same race are linked to some antagonism against members of an *obviously* different group. The resulting social action is usually merely negative: those who are obviously different are avoided and despised or, conversely, viewed with superstitious awe. Persons who are externally different are simply despised irrespective of what they accomplish or what they are, or they are venerated superstitiously if they are too powerful in the long run. In this case antipathy is the primary and normal reaction. However, this antipathy is shared not just by persons with anthropological similarities, and its extent is by no means determined by the degree of anthropological relatedness; furthermore this antipathy is linked not only to inherited traits but just as much to other visible differences.

If the degree of objective racial difference can be determined, among other things, purely physiologically by establishing whether hybrids reproduce themselves at approximately normal rates, the subjective aspects, the reciprocal racial attraction and repulsion, might be measured by finding out whether sexual relations are preferred or rare between two groups, and whether they are carried on permanently or temporarily and irregularly. In all groups with a developed "ethnic" consciousness the existence or absence of intermarriage (*connubium*) would then be a normal consequence of racial attraction or segregation. Serious research on the sexual attraction and repulsion between different ethnic groups is only incipient, but there is not the slightest doubt that racial factors, that means, common descent, influence the incidence of sexual relations and of marriage, sometimes decisively. However, the existence of several million mulattoes in the United States speaks clearly against the

17

assumption of a "natural" racial antipathy, even among quite different races. Apart from the laws against biracial marriages in the Southern states, sexual relations between the two races are now abhorred by both sides, but this development began only with the Emancipation and resulted from the Negroes' demand for equal civil rights. Hence this abhorrence on the part of the Whites is socially determined by the previously sketched tendency toward the monopolization of social power and honor, a tendency which in this case happens to be linked to race.

The *connubium* itself, that means, the fact that the offspring from a permanent sexual relationship can share in the activities and advantages of the father's political, economic or status group, depends on many circumstances. Under undiminished patriarchal powers, ... the father was free to grant equal rights to his children from slaves. Moreover, the glorification of abduction by the hero made racial mixing a normal event within the ruling strata. However, patriarchal discretion was progressively curtailed with the monopolistic closure, by now familiar to us, of political, status or other groups and with the monopolization of marriage opportunities; these tendencies restricted the *connubium* to the offspring from a permanent sexual union within the given political, religious, economic and status group. This also produced a high incidence of inbreeding. The "endogamy" of a group is probably everywhere a secondary product of such tendencies, if we define it not merely as the fact that a permanent sexual union occurs primarily on the basis of joint membership in some association, but as a process of social action in which only endogamous children are accepted as full members. (The term "sib endogamy" should not be used; there is no such thing unless we want to refer to the levirate marriage and arrangements in which daughters have the right to succession, but these have secondary, religious and political origins.) "Pure" anthropological types are often a secondary consequence of such closure; examples are sects (as in India) as well as pariah peoples, that means, groups that are socially despised yet wanted as neighbors because they have monopolized indispensable skills.

Reasons other than actual racial kinship influence the degree to which blood relationship is taken into account. In the United States the smallest admixture of Negro blood disqualifies a person unconditionally, whereas very considerable admixtures of Indian blood do not. Doubtlessly, it is important that Negroes appear esthetically even more alien than Indians, but it remains very significant that Negroes were slaves and hence disqualified in the status hierarchy. The conventional *connubium* is far less impeded by anthropological differences than by status differences, that means, differences due to socialization and upbringing (*Bildung* in the widest sense of the word). Mere anthropological differences account for little, except in cases of extreme esthetic antipathy.

THE BELIEF IN COMMON ETHNICITY: ITS MULTIPLE SOCIAL ORIGINS AND THEORETICAL AMBIGUITIES

The question of whether conspicuous "racial" differences are based on biological heredity or on tradition is usually of no importance as far as their effect on mutual attraction or repulsion is concerned. This is true of the development of endogamous conjugal groups, and even more so of attraction and repulsion in other kinds of social intercourse, that is, whether all sorts of friendly, companionable, or economic relationships between such groups are established easily and on the footing of mutual trust and respect, or whether such relationships are established with difficulty and with precautions that betray mistrust.

The more or less easy emergence of social circles in the broadest sense of the word (*soziale Verkehrsgemeinschaft*) may be linked to the most superficial features of historically accidental habits just as much as to inherited racial characteristics. That the different custom is not understood in its subjective meaning since the cultural key to it is lacking, is almost as decisive as the peculiarity of the custom as such. But, as we shall soon see, not all repulsion is attributable to the absence of a "consensual group." Differences in the styles of beard and hairdo, clothes, food and eating habits, division of labor between the sexes, and all kinds of other visible differences can, in a given case, give rise to repulsion and contempt, but the actual extent of these differences is irrelevant for the emotional impact, as is illustrated by primitive travel descriptions, the Histories of Herodotus or the older prescientific ethnography. Seen from their positive aspect, however, these differences may give rise to consciousness of kind, which may become as easily the bearer of group relationships. Groups ranging from the household and neighborhood to political and religious communities are usually the bearers of shared customs. All differences of customs can sustain a specific sense of honor or dignity in their practitioners. The original motives or reasons for the inception of "monopolistic closure" of culture > ∴ ?/ts of race (Aal types)

different habits of life are forgotten and the contrasts are then perpetuated as conventions. In this manner, any group can create customs, and it can also effect, in certain circumstances very decisively, the selection of anthropological types. This it can do by providing favorable chances of survival and reproduction for certain hereditary qualities and traits. This holds both for internal assimilation and for external differentiation.

Any cultural trait, no matter how superficial, can serve as a starting point for the familiar tendency to monopolistic closure. However, the universal force of imitation has the general effect of only gradually changing the traditional customs and usages, just as anthropological types are changed only gradually by racial mixing. But if there are sharp boundaries between areas of observable styles of life, they are due to conscious monopolistic closure, which started from small differences that were then cultivated and intensified; or they are due to the peaceful or warlike migrations of groups that previously lived far from each other and had accommodated themselves to their heterogeneous conditions of existence. Similarly, strikingly different racial types, bred in isolation, may live in sharply segregated proximity to one another either because of monopolistic closure or because of migration. We can conclude then that similarity and contrast of physical type and custom, regardless of whether they are biologically inherited or culturally transmitted, are subject to the same conditions of group life, in origin as well as in effectiveness and identical in their potential for group formation. The difference lies partly in the differential instability of type and custom, partly in the fixed (though often unknown) limit to engendering new hereditary qualities. Compared to this, the scope for assimilation of new customs is incomparably greater, although there are considerable variations in the transmissibility of traditions.

Almost any kind of similarity or contrast of physical type and of habits can induce the belief that affinity or disaffinity exists between groups that attract or repel each other. Not every belief in tribal affinity however, is founded on the resemblance of customs or of physical type. But in spite of great variations in this area, such a belief can exist and can develop group- forming powers when it is buttressed by a memory of an actual migration, be it colonization or individual migration. The persistent effect of the old ways and of childhood reminiscences continues as a source of native-country sentiment (*Heimatsgefühl*) among emigrants even when they have become so thoroughly adjusted to the new country that return to their homeland would be intolerable (this being the case of most German-Americans, for example).

In colonies, the attachment to the colonists' homeland survives despite considerable mixing with the inhabitants of the colonial land and despite profound changes in tradition and hereditary type as well. In case of political colonization, the decisive factor is the need for political support. In general, the continuation of relationships created by marriage is important, and so are the market relationships, provided that the "customs" remained unchanged. These market relationships between the homeland and the colony may be very close, as long as the consumer standards remain similar, and especially when colonies are in an almost absolutely alien environment and within an alien political territory.

The belief in group affinity, regardless of whether it has any objective foundation, can have important consequences especially for the formation of a political community. We shall call "ethnic groups" those human groups that entertain a subjective belief in their common descent because of similarities of physical type or of customs or both, or because of memories of colonization and migration; this belief must be important for the propagation of group formation; conversely, it does not matter whether or not an objective blood relationship exists. Ethnic membership (*Gemeinsamkeit*) differs from the kinship group precisely by being a presumed identity, not a group with concrete social action, like the latter. In our sense, ethnic membership does not constitute a group; it only facilitates group formation of any kind, particularly in the political sphere. On the other hand, it is primarily the political community, no matter how artificially organized, that inspires the belief in common ethnicity. This belief tends to persist even after the disintegration of the political community, unless drastic differences in the custom, physical type, or, above all, language exist among its members.

This artificial origin of the belief in common ethnicity follows the pattern of rational association turning into personal relationships. If rationally regulated action is not widespread, almost any association, even the most rational one, creates an overarching communal consciousness; this takes the form of a brotherhood on the basis of the belief in common ethnicity. As late as the Greek city state, even the most arbitrary division of the polis became for the member an association with at least a common cult and often a common fictitious ancestor. The twelve tribes of Israel were subdivisions of a political community, and they alternated in performing certain functions on a monthly basis. The same holds for the Greek tribes (*phylai*) and their subdivisions; the latter, too, were regarded as units of common ethnic descent. It is true that the original division may have been induced by political or actual ethnic differences, but the effect was the same when such a division was made quite rationally and schematically, after the break-up of old groups and relinquishment of local cohesion, as it was done by Cleisthenes. It does not follow, therefore, that the Greek polis was actually or originally a tribal or lineage state, but that ethnic fictions were a sign of the rather low degree of rationalization of Greek political life. Conversely, it is a symptom of the greater rationalization of Rome that its old schematic subdivisions (*curiae*) took on religious importance, with a pretense to ethnic origin, to only a small degree.

The belief in common ethnicity often delimits "social circles," which in turn are not always identical with endogamous connubial groups, for greatly varying numbers of persons may be encompassed by both. Their similarity rests on the belief in a specific "honor" of their members, not shared by the outsiders, that is, the sense of "ethnic honor" (a phenomenon closely related to status honor). These few remarks must suffice at this point. A specialized sociological study of ethnicity would have to make a finer distinction between these concepts than we have done for our limited purposes.

Groups, in turn, can engender sentiments of likeness which will persist even after their demise and will have an "ethnic" connotation. The political community in particular can produce such an effect. But most directly, such an effect is created by the *language group*, which is the bearer of a specific "cultural possession of the masses" (*Massenkulturgut*) and makes mutual understanding (*Verstehen*) possible or easier.

Wherever the memory of the origin of a community by peaceful secession or emigration ("colony," *ver sacrum*, and the like) from a mother community remains for some reason alive, there undoubtedly exists a very specific and often extremely powerful sense of ethnic identity, which is determined by several factors: shared political memories or, even more importantly in early times, persistent ties with the old cult, or the strengthening of kinship and other groups, both in the old and the new community, or other persistent relationships. Where these ties are lacking, or once they cease to exist, the sense of ethnic group membership is absent, regardless of how close the kinship may be.

Apart from the community of language, which may or may not coincide with objective, or subjectively believed, consanguinity, and apart from common religious belief, which is also independent of consanguinity, the ethnic differences that remain are, on the one hand, esthetically conspicuous differences of the physical appearance (as mentioned before) and, on the other hand and of equal weight, the perceptible differences in the *conduct of everyday life*. Of special importance are precisely those items which may otherwise seem to be of small social relevance, since when ethnic differentiation is concerned it is always the conspicuous differences that come into play.

Common language and the ritual regulation of life, as determined by shared religious beliefs, everywhere are conducive to feelings of ethnic affinity, especially since the intelligibility of the behavior of others is the most fundamental presupposition of group formation. But since we shall not consider these two elements in the present context, we ask: what is it that remains? It must be admitted that palpable differences in dialect and differences of religion in themselves do not exclude sentiments of common ethnicity. Next to pronounced differences in the economic way of life, the belief in ethnic affinity has at all times been affected by outward differences in clothes, in the style of housing, food and eating habits, the division of labor between the sexes and between the free and the unfree. That is to say, these things concern one's conception of what is correct and proper and, above all, of what affects the individual's sense of honor and dignity. All those things we shall find later on as objects of specific differences between status groups. The conviction of the excellence of one's own customs and the inferiority of alien ones, a conviction which sustains the sense of ethnic honor, is actually quite analogous to the sense of honor of distinctive status groups.

The sense of ethnic honor is a specific honor of the masses (*Massenehre*), for it is accessible to anybody who belongs to the subjectively believed community of descent. The "poor white trash," that is, the propertyless and, in the absence of job opportunities, very often destitute white inhabitants of the southern states of the United States of America in the period of slavery, were the actual bearers of racial antipathy, which was quite foreign to the planters. This was so because the social honor of the "poor whites" was dependent upon the social *déclassement* of the Negroes.

And behind all ethnic diversities there is somehow naturally the notion of the "chosen people," which is merely a counterpart of status differentiation translated into the plane of horizontal co-existence. The idea of a chosen people derives its popularity from the fact that it can be claimed to an equal degree by any and every member of the

*~ Webo's S₂ concerned w/ Eurasia—
ignorant ≠ social forms in Af & S Amer.

24   *Racial and Ethnic Pluralism*

mutually despising groups, in contrast to status differentiation which always rests on subordination. Consequently, ethnic repulsion may take hold of all conceivable differences among the notions of propriety and transform them into "ethnic conventions."

Beside the previously mentioned elements, which were still more or less closely related to the economic order, conventionalization (a term expounded elsewhere) may take hold of such things as a hairdo or style of beard and the like. The differences thereof have an "ethnically" repulsive effect, because they are thought of as symbols of ethnic membership. Of course, the repulsion is not always based merely on the "symbolic" character of the distinguishing traits. The fact that the Scythian women oiled their hair with butter, which then gave off a rancid odor, while Greek women used perfumed oil to achieve the same purpose, thwarted – according to an ancient report – all attempts at social intercourse between the aristocratic ladies of these two groups. The smell of butter certainly had a more compelling effect than even the most prominent racial differences, or – as far as I could see – the "Negro odor," of which so many fables are told. In general, racial qualities are effective only as limiting factors with regard to the belief in common ethnicity, such as in case of an excessively heterogeneous and esthetically unaccepted physical type; they are not positively group-forming.

Pronounced differences of custom, which play a role equal to that of inherited physical type in the creation of feelings of common ethnicity and notions of kinship, are usually caused, in addition to linguistic and religious differences, by the diverse economic and political conditions of various social groups. If we ignore cases of clear-cut linguistic boundaries and sharply demarcated political or religious communities as a basis of differences of custom – and these in fact are lacking in wide areas of the African and South American continents – then there are only gradual transitions of custom and no immutable ethnic frontiers, except those due to gross geographical differences. The sharp demarcations of areas wherein ethnically relevant customs predominate, which were not conditioned either by political or economic or religious factors, usually came into existence by way of migration or expansion, when groups of people that had previously lived in complete or partial isolation from each other and became accommodated to heterogeneous conditions of existence came to live side by side. As a result, the obvious contrast usually evokes, on both sides, the idea of blood disaffinity (*Blutsfremdheit*), regardless of the objective state of affairs.

It is understandably difficult to determine in general – and even in a concrete individual case – what influence specific ethnic factors (i.e. the belief in a blood relationship, or its opposite, which rests on similarities, or differences, of a person's physical appearance and style of life) have on the formation of a group.

There is no difference between the ethnically relevant customs and customs in general, as far as their effect is concerned. The belief in common descent, in combination with a similarity of customs, is likely to promote the spread of the activities of one part of an ethnic group among the rest, since the awareness of ethnic identity furthers imitation. This is especially true of the propaganda of religious groups.

It is not feasible to go beyond these vague generalizations. The content of joint activities that are possible on an ethnic basis remains indefinite. There is a corresponding ambiguity of concepts denoting ethnically determined action, that means, determined by the belief in blood relationship. Such concepts are *Völkerschaft, Stamm* (tribe), *Volk* (people), each of which is ordinarily used in the sense of an ethnic subdivision of the following one (although the first two may be used in reversed order). Using such terms, one usually implies either the existence of a contemporary political community, no matter how loosely organized, or memories of an extinct political community, such as they are preserved in epic tales and legends; or the existence of a linguistic or dialect group; or, finally, of a religious group. In the past, cults in particular were the typical concomitant of a tribal or *Volk* consciousness. But in the absence of the political community, contemporary or past, the external delimitation of the group was usually indistinct. The cult communities of Germanic tribes, as late as the Burgundian period 6th century AD, were probably rudiments of political communities and therefore pretty well defined. By contrast, the Delphian oracle, the undoubted cultic symbol of Hellenism, also revealed information to the barbarians and accepted their veneration, and it was an organized cult only among some Greek segments, excluding the most powerful cities. The cult as an exponent of ethnic identity is thus generally either a remnant of a largely political community which once existed but was destroyed by disunion and colonization, or it is – as in the case of the Delphian Apollo – a product of a *Kulturgemeinschaft* brought about by other than purely ethnic conditions, but which in turn gives rise to the belief in blood relationship. All history shows how easily political action can give rise to the belief in blood relationship, unless gross differences of anthropological type impede it.

TRIBE AND POLITICAL COMMUNITY: THE DISUTILITY OF THE NOTION OF "ETHNIC GROUP"

The tribe is clearly delimited when it is a subdivision of a polity, which, in fact, often establishes it. In this case, the artificial origin is revealed by the round numbers in which tribes usually appear, for example, the previously mentioned division of the people of Israel into twelve tribes, the three Doric *phylai* and the various *phylai* of the other Hellenes. When a political community was newly established or reorganized, the population was newly divided. Hence the tribe is here a political artifact, even though it soon adopts the whole symbolism of blood-relationship and particularly a tribal cult. Even today it is not rare that political artifacts develop a sense of affinity akin to that of blood relationship. Very schematic constructs such as those states of the United States that were made into squares according to their latitude have a strong sense of identity; it is also not rare that families travel from New York to Richmond to make an expected child a "Virginian."

Such artificiality does not preclude the possibility that the Hellenic *phylai*, for example, were at one time independent and that the polis used them schematically when they were merged into a political association. However, tribes that existed before the *polis* were either identical with the corresponding political groups which were subsequently associated into a *polis*, and in this case they were called *ethnos*, not *phyle*; or, as it probably happened many times, the politically unorganized tribe, as a presumed "blood community", lived from the memory that it once engaged in joint political action, typically a single conquest or defense, and then such political memories constituted the tribe. Thus, the fact that tribal consciousness was primarily formed by common political experiences and not by common descent appears to have been a frequent source of the belief in common ethnicity.

Of course, this was not the only source: common customs may have diverse origins. Ultimately, they derive largely from adaptation to natural conditions and the imitation of neighbors. In practice, however, tribal consciousness usually has a political meaning: in case of military danger or opportunity, it easily provides the basis for joint political action on the part of tribal members or *Volksgenossen* who consider one another as blood relatives. The eruption of a drive to political action is thus one of the major potentialities inherent in the rather ambiguous notions of tribe and people. Such intermittent

political action may easily develop into the moral duty of all members
of tribe or people (*Volk*) to support one another in case of a military
attack, even if there is no corresponding political association; viola-
tors of this solidarity may suffer the fate of the (Germanic, pro-
Roman) sibs of Segestes and Inguiomer – expulsion from the tribal
territory – even if the tribe has no organized government. If the tribe
has reached this stage, it has indeed become a continuous political
community, no matter how inactive in peacetime, and hence unstable,
it may be. However, even under favorable conditions the transition
from the habitual to the customary and therefore obligatory is very
fluid. All in all, the notion of "ethnically" determined social action
subsumes phenomena that a rigorous sociological analysis – as we do
not attempt it here – would have to distinguish carefully: the actual
subjective effect of those customs conditioned by heredity and those
determined by tradition; the differential impact of the varying content
of custom; the influence of common language, religion and political
action, past and present, upon the formation of customs; the extent to
which such factors create attraction and repulsion, and especially the
belief in affinity or disaffinity of blood; the consequences of this belief
for social action in general, and specifically for action on the basis of
shared custom or blood relationship, for diverse sexual relations, and
so on – all of this would have to be studied in detail. It is certain that
in this process the collective term "ethnic" would be abandoned, for it
is unsuitable for a really rigorous analysis. However, we do not pursue
sociology for its own sake and therefore limit ourselves to showing
briefly the diverse factors that are hidden behind this seemingly uniform phenomenon.

The concept of the "ethnic" group, which dissolves if we define our
terms exactly, corresponds in this regard to one of the most vexing,
emotionally charged concepts: the *nation*, as soon as we attempt a
sociological definition.

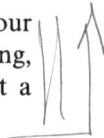

NATIONALITY AND CULTURAL PRESTIGE

The concept of "nationality" shares with that of the "people" (*Volk*) –
in the "ethnic" sense – the vague connotation that whatever is felt to
be distinctively common must derive from common descent. In reality, of course, persons who consider themselves members of the same
nationality are often much less related by common descent than are
persons belonging to different and hostile nationalities. Differences of

nationality may exist even among groups closely related by common descent, merely because they have different religious persuasions, as in the case of Serbs and Croats. The concrete reasons for the belief in joint nationality and for the resulting social action vary greatly.

Today, in the age of language conflicts, a shared common language is pre-eminently considered the normal basis of nationality. Whatever the "nation" means beyond a mere "language group" can be found in the specific objective of its social action, and this can only be the *autonomous polity*. Indeed, "nation state" has become conceptually identical with "state" based on common language. In reality, however, such modern nation states exist next to many others that comprise several language groups, even though these others usually have one official language. A common language is also insufficient in sustaining a sense of national identity (*Nationalgefühl*). Aside from the examples of the Serbs and Croats, this is demonstrated by the Irish, the Swiss and the German-speaking Alsatians; these groups do not consider themselves as members, at least not as full members, of the "nation" associated with their language. Conversely, language differences do not necessarily preclude a sense of joint nationality: The German-speaking Alsatians considered themselves – and most of them still do – as part of the French "nation," even though not in the same sense as French-speaking nationals. Hence there are qualitative degrees of the belief in common nationality.

Many German-speaking Alsatians feel a sense of community with the French because they share certain customs and some of their "sensual culture" (*Sinnenkultur*) and also because of common political experiences. This can be understood by any visitor who walks through the museum in Colmar, which is rich in relics such as tricolors, *pompier* and military helmets, edicts by Louis Philippe and especially memorabilia from the French Revolution; these may appear trivial to the outsider, but they have sentimental value for the Alsatians. This sense of community came into being by virtue of common political and, indirectly, social experiences which are highly valued by the masses as symbols of the destruction of feudalism, and the story of these events takes the place of the heroic legends of primitive peoples. *La grande nation* was the liberator from feudal servitude, she was the bearer of civilization (*Kultur*), her language was *the* civilized language; German appeared as a dialect suitable for everyday communication. Hence the attachment to those who speak the language of civilization is an obvious parallel to the sense of community based on common language, but the two phenomena are not identical; rather, we deal here with an attitude that derives from a partial sharing of the same culture and from shared political experiences.

Until a short time ago most Poles in Upper Silesia had no strongly developed sense of Polish nationality that was antagonistic to the Prussian state, which is based essentially on the German language. The Poles were loyal if passive "Prussians," but they were not "Germans" interested in the existence of the *Reich*; the majority did not feel a conscious or a strong need to segregate themselves from German-speaking fellow citizens. Hence, in this case there was no sense of nationality based on common language, and there was no *Kulturgemeinschaft* in view of the lack of cultural development.

Among the Baltic Germans we find neither much of a sense of nationality amounting to a high valuation of the language bonds with the Germans, nor a desire for political union with the *Reich*; in fact, most of them would abhor such a unification. However, they segregate themselves rigorously from the Slavic environment, and especially from the Russians, primarily because of status considerations and partly because both sides have different customs and cultural values which are mutually unintelligible and disdained. This segregation exists in spite of, and partly because of, the fact that the Baltic Germans are intensely loyal vassals of the Tsar and have been as interested as any "national" Russian (*Nationalrusse*) in the predominance of the Imperial Russian system, which they provide with officials and which in turn maintains their descendants. Hence, here too we do not find any sense of nationality in the modern meaning of the term (oriented toward a common language and culture). The case is similar to that of the purely proletarian Poles: loyalty toward the state is combined with a sense of group identity that is limited to a common language group within this larger community and strongly modified by status factors. Of course, the Baltic Germans are no longer a cohesive status group, even though the differences are not as extreme as within the white population of the American South.

Finally, there are cases for which the term nationality does not seem to be quite fitting; witness the sense of identity shared by the Swiss and the Belgians or the inhabitants of Luxemburg and Liechtenstein. We hesitate to call them "nations," not because of their relative smallness – the Dutch appear to us as a nation – but because these neutralized states have purposively forsaken power. The Swiss are not a nation if we take as criteria common language or common literature and art. Yet they have a strong sense of community despite some recent disintegrative tendencies. This sense of identity is not only sustained by loyalty toward the body politic but also by what are perceived to be common customs (irrespective of actual differences). These customs are largely shaped by the differences in social structure between Switzerland and Germany, but also all other big and hence militaristic powers. Because of the impact of bigness on the internal power structure, it appears to the Swiss that their customs can be preserved only by a separate political existence.

The loyalty of the French Canadians toward the English polity is today determined above all by the deep antipathy against the economic and social structure, and the way of life, of the neighboring United States; hence membership in the Dominion of Canada appears as a guarantee of their own traditions.

This classification could easily be enlarged, as every rigorous sociological investigation would have to do. It turns out that feelings of identity subsumed under the term "national" are not uniform but may derive from diverse sources: differences in the economic and social structure and in the internal power structure, with its impact on the customs, may play a role, but within the German *Reich* customs are very diverse; shared political memories, religion, language and, finally, racial features may be source of the sense of nationality. Racial factors often have a peculiar impact. From the viewpoint of the Whites in the United States, Negroes and Whites are not united by a common sense of nationality, but the Negroes have a sense of American nationality at least by claiming a right to it. On the other hand, the pride of the Swiss in their own distinctiveness, and their willingness to defend it vigorously, is neither qualitatively different nor less widespread than the same attitudes in any "great" and powerful "nation." Time and again we find that the concept "nation" directs us to political power. Hence, the concept seems to refer – if it refers at all to a uniform phenomenon – to a specific kind of pathos which is linked to the idea of a powerful political community of people who share a common language, or religion, or common customs, or political memories; such a state may already exist or it may be desired. The more power is emphasized, the closer appears to be the link between nation and state. This pathetic pride in the power of one's own community, or this longing for it, may be much more widespread in relatively small language groups such as the Hungarians, Czechs or Greeks than in a similar but much larger community such as the Germans 150 years ago, when they were essentially a language group without pretensions to national power.

2 Race Prejudice as a Sense of Group Position

Herbert Blumer

In this paper I am proposing an approach to the study of race prejudice different from that which dominates contemporary scholarly thought on this topic. My thesis is that race prejudice exists basically in a sense of group position rather than in a set of feelings which members of one racial group have toward the members of another racial group. This different way of viewing race prejudice shifts study and analysis from a preoccupation with feelings as lodged in individuals to a concern with the relationship of racial groups. It also shifts scholarly treatment away from individual lines of experience and focuses interest on the collective process by which a racial group comes to define and redefine another racial group. Such shifts, I believe, will yield a more realistic and penetrating understanding of race prejudice.

There can be little question that the rather vast literature on race prejudice is dominated by the idea that such prejudice exists fundamentally as a feeling or set of feelings lodged in the individual. It is usually depicted as consisting of feelings such as antipathy, hostility, hatred, intolerance, and aggressiveness. Accordingly, the task of scientific inquiry becomes two-fold. On one hand, there is a need to identify the feelings which make up race prejudice – to see how they fit together and how they are supported by other psychological elements, such as mythical beliefs. On the other hand, there is need of showing how the feeling complex has come into being. Thus, some scholars trace the complex feelings back chiefly to innate dispositions; some trace it to personality composition, such as authoritarian personality; and others regard the feelings of prejudice as being formed through social experience. However different may be the contentions regarding the make-up of racial prejudice and the way in which it may come into existence, these contentions are alike in locating prejudice in the realm of individual feeling. This is clearly true of the work of psychologists, psychiatrists, and social psychologists, and tends to be predominantly the case in the work of sociologists.

Unfortunately, this customary way of viewing race prejudice over-looks and obscures the fact that race prejudice is fundamentally a matter of relationship between racial groups. A little reflective thought should make this very clear. Race prejudice presupposes, necessarily, that racially prejudiced individuals think of themselves as belonging to a given racial group. It means, also, that they assign to other racial groups those against whom they are prejudiced. Thus, logically and actually, a scheme of racial identification is necessary as a framework for racial prejudice. Moreover, such identification involves the formation of an image or a conception of one's own racial group and of another racial group, inevitably in terms of the relationship of such groups. To fail to see that racial prejudice is a matter (a) of the racial identification made of oneself and of others, and (b) of the way in which the identified groups are conceived in relation to each other, is to miss what is logically and actually basic. One should keep clearly in mind that people necessarily come to identify themselves as belonging to a racial group; such identification is not spontaneous or inevitable but a result of experience. Further, one must realize that the kind of picture which a racial group forms of itself and the kind of picture which it may form of others are similarly products of experience. Hence, such pictures are variable, just as the lines of experience which produce them are variable.

The body of feelings which scholars today are so inclined to regard as constituting the substance of race prejudice is actually a resultant of the way in which given racial groups conceive of themselves and of others. A basic understanding of race prejudice must be sought in the process by which racial groups form images of themselves and of others. This process, as I hope to show, is fundamentally a *collective process*. It operates chiefly through the public media in which individuals who are accepted as the spokesmen of a racial group character-ize publicly another racial group. To characterise another racial group is, by opposition, to define one's own group. This is equivalent to placing the two groups in relation to each other, or defining their positions *vis-à-vis* each other. It is the *sense of social position* emerging from this collective process of characterization which provides the basis of race prejudice. The following discussion will consider import-ant facets of this matter.

I would like to begin by discussing several of the important feelings that enter into race prejudice. This discussion will reveal how fundamentally racial feelings point to and depend on a positional arrangement of the racial groups. In this discussion I will confine myself to such feelings in the case of a dominant racial group.

There are four basic types of feeling that seem to be always present in race prejudice in the dominant group. They are (1) a feeling of superiority, (2) a feeling that the subordinate race is intrinsically different and alien, (3) a feeling of proprietary claim to certain areas of privilege and advantage, and (4) a fear and suspicion that the subordinate race harbors designs on the prerogatives of the dominant race. A few words about each of these four feelings will suffice.

In race prejudice there is a self-assured feeling on the part of the dominant racial group of being naturally superior or better. This is commonly shown in a disparagement of the qualities of the subordinate racial group. Condemnatory or debasing traits, such as laziness, dishonesty, greediness, unreliability, stupidity, deceit and immorality, are usually imputed to it. The second feeling, that the subordinate race is an alien and fundamentally different stock, is likewise always present. "They are not of our kind" is a common way in which this is likely to be expressed. It is this feeling that reflects, justifies, and promotes the social exclusion of the subordinate racial group. The combination of these two feelings of superiority and of distinctiveness can easily give rise to feelings of aversion and even antipathy. But in themselves they do not form prejudice. We have to introduce the third and fourth types of feeling.

The third feeling, the sense of proprietary claim, is of crucial importance. It is the feeling on the part of the dominant group of being entitled to either exclusive or prior rights in many important areas of life. The range of such exclusive or prior claims may be wide, covering the ownership of property such as choice lands and sites; the right to certain jobs, occupations or professions; the claim to certain kinds of industry or lines of business; the claim to certain positions of control and decision-making as in government and law; the right to exclusive membership in given institutions such as schools, churches and recreational institutions; the claim to certain positions of social prestige and to the display of the symbols and accoutrements of these positions; and the claim to certain areas of intimacy and privacy. The feeling of such proprietary claims is exceedingly strong in race prejudice. Again, however, this feeling even in combination with the feeling of superiority and the feeling of distinctiveness does not explain race prejudice. These three feelings are present frequently in societies showing no prejudice, as in certain forms of feudalism, in caste relations, in societies of chiefs and commoners, and under many settled relations of conquerors and conquered. Where claims are solidified into a structure which is accepted or respected by all, there seems to be no group prejudice.

The remaining feeling essential to race prejudice is a fear or apprehension that the subordinate racial group is threatening, or will threaten, the position of the dominant group. Thus, acts or suspected acts that are interpreted as an attack on the natural superiority of the dominant group, or an intrusion into their sphere of group exclusiveness, or an encroachment on their area of proprietary claim are crucial in arousing and fashioning race prejudice. These acts mean "getting out of place."

It should be clear that these four basic feelings of race prejudice definitely refer to a positional arrangement of the racial groups. The feeling of superiority places the subordinate people *below*; the feeling of alienation places them *beyond*; the feeling of proprietary claim excludes them from the prerogatives of position; and the fear of encroachment is an emotional recoil from the endangering of group position. As these features suggest, the positional relation of the two racial groups is crucial in race prejudice. The dominant group is not concerned with the subordinate group as such but it is deeply concerned with its position *vis-à-vis* the subordinate group. This is epitomized in the key and universal expression that a given race is all right in "its place." The sense of group position is the very heart of the relation of the dominant to the subordinate group. It supplies the dominant group with its framework of perception, its standard of judgment, its patterns of sensitivity, and its emotional proclivities.

It is important to recognize that this sense of group position transcends the feelings of the individual members of the dominant group, giving such members a common orientation that is not otherwise to be found in separate feelings and views. There is likely to be considerable difference between the ways in which the individual members of the dominant group think and feel about the subordinate group. Some may feel bitter and hostile, with strong antipathies, with an exalted sense of superiority and with a lot of spite; others may have charitable and protective feelings, marked by a sense of piety and tinctured by benevolence; others may be condescending and reflect mild contempt; and others may be disposed to politeness and considerateness with no feelings of truculence. These are only a few of many different patterns of feeling to be found among members of the dominant racial group. What gives a common dimension to them is a sense of the social position of their group. Whether the members be humane or callous, cultured or unlettered, liberal or reactionary, powerful or impotent, arrogant or humble, rich or poor, honorable or dishonorable – all are led, by virtue of sharing the sense of group position, to similar individual positions.

The sense of group position is a general kind of orientation. It is a general feeling without being reducible to specific feelings like hatred, hostility or antipathy. It is also a general understanding without being composed of any set of specific beliefs. On the social psychological side it cannot be equated to a sense of social status as ordinarily conceived, for it refers not merely to vertical positioning but to many other lines of position independent of the vertical dimension. Sociologically it is not a mere reflection of the objective relations between racial groups. Rather, it stands for "what ought to be" rather than for "what is." It is a sense of where the two racial groups *belong*.

In its own way, the sense of group position is a norm and imperative – indeed a very powerful one. It guides, incites, cows, and coerces. It should be borne in mind that this sense of group position stands for and involves a fundamental kind of group affiliation for the members of the dominant racial group. To the extent they recognize or feel themselves as belonging to that group they will automatically come under the influence of the sense of position held by that group. Thus, even though given individual members may have personal views and feelings different from the sense of group position, they will have to conjure with the sense of group position held by their racial group. If the sense of position is strong, to act contrary to it is to risk a feeling of self-alienation and to face the possibility of ostracism. I am trying to suggest, accordingly, that the locus of race prejudice is not in the area of individual feeling but in the definition of the respective positions of the racial groups.

The source of race prejudice lies in a felt challenge to this sense of group position. The challenge, one must recognize, may come in many different ways. It may be in the form of an affront to feelings of group superiority; it may be in the form of attempts at familiarity or transgressing the boundary line of group exclusiveness; it may be in the form of encroachment at countless points of proprietary claim; it may be a challenge to power and privilege; it may take the form of economic competition. Race prejudice is a defensive reaction to such challenging of the sense of group position. It consists of the disturbed feelings, usually of marked hostility, that are thereby aroused. As such, race prejudice is a protective device. It functions, however shortsightedly, to preserve the integrity and the position of the dominant group.

It is crucially important to recognize that the sense of group position is not a mere summation of the feelings of position such as might be developed independently by separate individuals as they come to compare themselves with given individuals of the subordinate race. The sense of group position refers to the position of group to group, not to that of individual to individual. Thus, *vis-à-vis* the subordinate racial group the unlettered individual with low status in the dominant racial group has a sense of group position common to that of the elite of his group. By virtue of sharing this sense of position such an individual, despite his low status, feels that members of the subordinate group, however distinguished and accomplished, are somehow inferior, alien, and properly restricted in the area of claims. He forms his conception as a representative of the dominant group; he treats individual members of the subordinate group as representative of that group.

An analysis of how the sense of group position is formed should start with a clear recognition that it is an historical product. It is set originally by conditions of initial contact. Prestige, power, possession of skill, numbers, original self- conceptions, aims, designs and opportunities are a few of the factors that may fashion the original sense of group position. Subsequent experience in the relation of the two racial groups, especially in the area of claims, opportunities and advantages, may mould the sense of group position in many diverse ways. Further, the sense of group position may be intensified or weakened, brought to sharp focus or dulled. It may be deeply entrenched and tenaciously resist change for long periods of time. Or it may never take root. It may undergo quick growth and vigorous expansion, or it may dwindle away through slow-moving erosion. It may be firm or soft, acute or dull, continuous or intermittent. In short, viewed comparatively, the sense of group position is very variable.

However variable its particular career, the sense of group position is clearly formed by a running process in which the dominant racial group is led to define and redefine the subordinate racial group and the relations between them. There are two important aspects of this process of definition that I wish to single out for consideration.

First, the process of definition occurs obviously through complex interaction and communication between the members of the dominant group. Leaders, prestige bearers, officials, group agents, dominant individuals and ordinary laymen present to one another characterizations of the subordinate group and express their feelings and ideas on the relations. Through talk, tales, stories, gossip, anecdotes, messages, pronouncements, news accounts, orations, sermons, preachments and the like definitions are presented and feelings are expressed. In this usually vast and complex interaction separate views run against one another, influence one another, modify each other, incite one another and fuse together in new forms. Correspondingly, feelings which are expressed meet, stimulate each other, feed on each other, intensify each other and emerge in new patterns. Currents of view and currents of feeling come into being; sweeping along to positions of dominance and serving as polar points for the organization of thought and sentiment. If the interaction becomes increasingly circular and reinforcing, devoid of serious inner opposition, such currents grow, fuse and become strengthened. It is through such a process that a collective image of the subordinate group is formed and a sense of group position is set. The evidence of such a process is glaring when one reviews the history of any racial arrangement marked by prejudice.

Such a complex process of mutual interaction with its different lines and degrees of formation gives the lie to the many schemes which would lodge the cause of race prejudice in the make-up of the individual – whether in the form of innate disposition, constitutional make-up, personality structure, or direct personal experience with members of the other race. The collective image and feelings in race prejudice are forged out of a complicated social process in which the individual is himself shaped and organized. The scheme, so popular today, which would trace race prejudice to a so-called authoritarian personality shows a grievous misunderstanding of the simple essentials of the collective process that leads to a sense of group position.

The second important aspect of the process of group definition is that it is necessarily concerned with *an abstract image* of the subordinate racial group. The subordinate racial group is defined as if it were an entity or whole. This entity or whole – like the Negro race, or the Japanese, or the Jews – is necessarily an abstraction, never coming within the perception of any of the senses. While actual encounters are with individuals, the picture formed of the racial group is necessarily of a vast entity which spreads out far beyond such individuals and transcends experience with such individuals. The implications of the fact that the collective image is of an abstract group are of crucial significance. I would like to note four of these implications.

First, the building of the image of the abstract group takes place in the area of the remote and not of the near. It is not the experience with concrete individuals in daily association that gives rise to the definitions of the extended, abstract group. Such immediate experience is usually regulated and orderly. Even where such immediate experience is disrupted the new definitions which are formed are limited to the individuals involved. The collective image of the abstract group grows up not by generalizing from experiences gained in close, first-hand contacts but through the transcending characterizations that are made of the group as an entity. Thus, one must seek the central stream of definition in those areas where the dominant group as such is characterizing the subordinate group as such. This occurs in the "public arena" wherein the spokesmen appear as representatives and agents of the dominant group. The extended public arena is constituted by such things as legislatives assemblies, public meetings, conventions, the press, and the printed word. What goes on in this public arena attracts the attention of large numbers of the dominant group and is felt as the voice and action of the group as such.

Second, the definitions that are forged in the public arena center, obviously, about matters that are felt to be of major importance. Thus, we are led to recognize the crucial role of the "big event" in developing a conception of the subordinate racial group. The happening that seems momentous, that touches deep sentiments, that seems to raise fundamental questions about relations, and that awakens strong feelings of identification with one's racial group is the kind of event that is central in the formation of the racial image. Here, again, we note the relative unimportance of the huge bulk of experiences coming from daily contact with individuals of the subordinate group. It is the events seemingly loaded with great collective significance that are the focal points of the public discussion. The definition of these events is chiefly responsible for the development of a racial image and of the sense of group position. When this public discussion takes the form of a denunciation of the subordinate racial group, signifying that it is unfit and a threat, the discussion becomes particularly potent in shaping the sense of social position.

Third, the major influence in public discussion is exercised by individuals and groups who have the public ear and who are felt to have standing, prestige, authority and power. Intellectual and social elites, public figures of prominence, and leaders of powerful organizations are likely to be the key figures in the formation of the sense of group position and in the characterization of the subordinate group. It is well to note this in view of the not infrequent tendency of students to regard race prejudice as growing out of the multiplicity of experiences and attitudes of the bulk of the people.

Fourth, we also need to perceive the appreciable opportunity that is given to strong interest groups in directing the lines of discussion and setting the interpretations that arise in such discussion. Their self-interests may dictate the kind of position they wish the dominant racial group to enjoy. It may be a position which enables them to retain certain advantages, or even more to gain still greater advantages. Hence, they may be vigorous in seeking to manufacture events to attract public attention and to set lines of issue in such a way as to predetermine interpretations favorable to their interests. The role of strongly organized groups seeking to further special interest is usually central in the formation of collective images of abstract groups. Historical records of major instances of race relations, as in South USA, or in South Africa, or in Europe in the case of the Jew, or on the West Coast in the case of the Japanese show the formidable part played by interest groups in defining the subordinate racial group.

I conclude this highly condensed paper with two further observations that may throw additional light on the relation of the sense of group position to race prejudice. Race prejudice becomes entrenched and tenacious to the extent the prevailing social order is rooted in the sense of social position. This has been true of the historic South in America. In such a social order race prejudice tends to become chronic and impermeable to change. In other places the social order may be affected only to a limited extent by the sense of group position held by the dominant racial group. This I think has been true usually in the case of anti-Semitism in Europe and America. Under these conditions the sense of group position tends to be weaker and more vulnerable. In turn, race prejudice has a much more variable and intermittent career, usually becoming pronounced only as a consequence of grave disorganizing events that allow for the formation of a scapegoat.

This leads me to my final observation which in a measure is an indirect summary. The sense of group position dissolves and race prejudice declines when the process of running definition does not keep abreast of major shifts in the social order. When events touching on relations are not treated as "big events" and hence do not set crucial issues in the arena of public discussion; or when the elite leaders or spokesmen do not define such big events vehemently or

adversely; or where they define them in the direction of racial harmony; or when there is a paucity of strong interest groups seeking to
build up a strong adverse image for special advantage – under such
conditions the sense of group position recedes and race prejudice
declines.

The clear implication of my discussion is that the proper and the
fruitful area in which race prejudice should be studied is the collective
process through which a sense of group position is formed. To seek,
instead, to understand it or to handle it in the arena of individual
feeling and of individual experience seems to me to be clearly
misdirected.

3 Beyond Reason: The Nature of the Ethnonational Bond
Walker Connor

Nationalism, as commonly encountered in the press, television news and even in most scholarly tracts, refers to an emotional attachment to one's state or country and its political institutions – an attachment more properly termed *patriotism*. Nationalism, in correct usage, refers to an emotional attachment to one's people – one's ethnonational group. It is therefore proper to speak of an English, Scottish, or Welsh nationalism, but not of a 'British' nationalism, the latter being a manifestation of patriotism.

When examining the political loyalties of some peoples, the confusing of nationalism and patriotism is not of great significance because the two loyalties reinforce one another. This is so in the case of true nation-states; that is to say, in the case of states in which the borders of an ethnonational group closely coincide with the borders of a state. In a nation-state the populace is essentially ethnically homogeneous.

In such a case, the state is popularly perceived as the agent or political expression of the nation. Loyalty to one's national group (nationalism) and loyalty to one's state (patriotism) merge into a single reinforcing blur in the perceptions of the populace. Thus, Adolph Hitler could make his tragically effective appeals to the German masses in the name of either the nation (the *Volk*) or the state (*Deutschland* or the *Deutsches Reich*). He was able to do so because both triggered identical positive vibrations within the German people. Hitler showed his awareness of this aspect of ethnopsychology even before taking power. As he wrote in *Mein Kampf* (Hitler 1940, p. 595): "We [are] able to imagine a State only to be the living organism of a *Volk* (a nation). Again, then, in such nation-states, nationalism and patriotism reinforce one another.

Most states, however, are not nation-states but multinational states. Of some 180 contemporary states, probably not more than fifteen could qualify as nation-states: Japan, Iceland, the two Koreas, Portugal and a few others.

41

The *multinational state* is therefore easily the most common form of country. It contains at least two statistically and/or politically significant groups. In 40 per cent of all states there are five or more such groups. A few states, such as Nigeria (and parenthetically the former Soviet Union), contain more than one hundred groups. Perhaps the most startling statistic is that in nearly one-third of all states (31 per cent), the largest national group is not even a majority. (This is true of newly independent Kazakhstan and nearly true of Latvia). Ethnic heterogeneity and *not* homogeneity is therefore the rule. Even in a multinational state, the same tendency that we noted in the case of nation-states – the tendency to perceive the state as an extension of one's own national group – is often true in the case of what the Germans term a *Staatvolk* (a people who are culturally, and politically pre-eminent in a state, even though other groups are present in significant numbers). There is a tendency on the part of such a people to equate the entire country with their own ethnic homeland and, as in the case of a people in an ethnically homogeneous state, to perceive the state as the political expression of their particular ethnic group.

Thus, many Englishmen have a tendency to use the term *England* to describe the entire country, and *English* to describe all the people therein. A relatively recent illustration of both was offered by David Loviband, in the *Sunday Telegraph* (London, 15 October 1989). Referring to the then current debate concerning the number of British passports to be granted to Hong Kong residents prior to the Colony's reannexation by Beijing, he noted what he called the "profound foreignness of the Hong Kong people" and then continued:

> The prospect of an unprecedented influx of Chinese immigrants obliges us to consider whether the pernicious doctrine of multi-racialism has so debilitated the English that they have lost their voice and no longer think of themselves as the only possessors of England. *Barely a generation ago these islands were occupied by a single people.* Thirty years on and the English have become "the white section of the community".

How strange Cornish, Irish, Manx, Scottish and Welsh people must feel to be informed that prior to 1960 the British Isles were populated solely by the English. Similarly, to an Englishman the words of "There'll always be an England" inspire a fused sense of nationalism and patriotism. Yet Englishmen seldom appreciate that the words of "There'll always be an England" fail to inspire a similar sentiment in

the Scots and other non-English peoples. On the contrary, the words
are, of course, a reminder to those non-English people that they live in
a multinational state dominated by Englishmen.

Similarly, references over the years by ethnic Russians to the entire
Soviet Union as Russia or Mother Russia – a practice, incidentally, to
which Gorbachev was not immune – did nothing to increase the
patriotic feelings of Armenians, Georgians, Jews, Lithuanians, Ukrainians, and the other approximately one hundred non-Russian peoples
who populated the former USSR. On the contrary, it irritated their
nationalist sensitivities.

The point, then, is that nationalism and patriotism are *not* synonymous. As noted, for national groups, such as the Japanese, who
possess their own ethnically homogeneous state, and for *Staatvolk*,
such as the French, the fact that nationalism and patriotism are two
different phenomena is of little consequence. Again, such groups are
the exception. As a consequence, for most people the sense of loyalty
to one's nation and to one's state do not coincide: they often compete
for the allegiance of the individual.

For example, a Basque or Catalan nationalism has often been in
conflict with a Spanish patriotism; a Tibetan nationalism with a
Chinese patriotism; a Flemish nationalism with a Belgian patriotism;
a Corsican nationalism with a French patriotism; a Kashmiri nationalism with an Indian patriotism; a Quebec nationalism with a Canadian patriotism. The list could be lengthened several times over.
Nationalism and patriotism are vitally different phenomena and
should not be confused through the careless use of language.

We know from the comparative study of nationalism that when the
two loyalties are perceived as being in irreconcilable conflict – that is
to say, when people feel they must choose between them – nationalism
customarily proves the more potent. One of history's most vivid
illustrations of the relative strength of these two loyalties is the very
recent case of the Soviet Union, wherein a beleaguered Soviet President Gorbachev only belatedly discovered that a sense of loyalty
to the Union of Soviet Socialist Republics (what, for seventy years
had been termed Soviet patriotism) was no match for the sense of
nationalism demonstrated by nearly all the peoples of the former
Soviet Union, including even the Russian nation. Obviously, events
within what, until recently, was known as the Federal Republic of
Yugoslavia certify that Albanian, Bosnian, Croatian and Slovene
nationalism has each proved itself to be far more potent than a
Yugoslav patriotism.

To understand why nationalism customarily proves to be a much more powerful force than patriotism, it is necessary to take a closer look at national consciousness and national sentiment. What, for example, is the nature of the bond that both unites all Poles and differentiates them from the remainder of humanity?

Until quite recently it was the vogue among prominent writers on nationalism to stress the tangible characteristics of a nation. The nation was defined as a community of people characterized by a common language, territory, religion, and the like.

Probing the nation would be a far easier task if it could be explained in terms of such tangible criteria. How much simpler it would be if adopting the Polish language, living within Poland, and adhering to Roman Catholicism were sufficient to define membership in the Polish nation – were sufficient to make one a Pole. However, there are Germans, Lithuanians, and Ukrainians who meet these criteria but who do not consider themselves Polish and are not considered Polish by their Polish fellow citizens.

Objective criteria, in and by themselves, are therefore insufficient to determine whether or not a group constitutes a nation. The essence of the nation is a psychological bond that joins a people and differentiates it, in the subconscious conviction of its members, from all non-members in a most vital way.

With very few exceptions, authorities have shied away from describing the nation as a kinship group and have usually explicitly denied any kinship basis to it. These denials are customarily supported by data showing that most nations do in fact contain several genetic strains. This line of reasoning ignores the dictum that it is not *what is* but *what people perceive as is* which influences attitudes and behavior. A subconscious belief in the group's separate origin and evolution is an important ingredient of national psychology.

In ignoring or denying the sense of kinship that infuses the nation, scholars have been blind to that which has been thoroughly apparent to nationalist leaders. In sharpest contrast with most academic analysts of nationalism, those who have successfully mobilized nations have understood that at the core of ethnopsychology is the sense of shared blood, and they have not hesitated to appeal to it. Consequently, nationalistic speeches and proclamations tend to be more fruitful areas for research into the emotional/psychological nature of nationalism than are scholarly works. Too often such speeches and proclamations have been precipitously dismissed as propaganda in which the leadership did not truly believe. Nationalism is a mass phenomenon, and the degree to which its inciters are true believers does not affect its reality. The question is not the sincerity of the propagandist, but the nature of the mass instinct to which he or she appeals.

Consider, then, Bismarck's famous exhortation to the Germans, spread at the time throughout more than thirty sovereign entities, urging them to unite in a single state: "Germans, think with your blood!" Adolph Hitler's repeated appeals to the ethnic purity of the German nation (*Volk*) are notorious. To take but a single example. In a 1938 speech in Konigsburg (now Kaliningrad, part of the Russian Republic), Hitler declared (1942, p. 1438):

> In Germany today we enjoy the consciousness of belonging to a community, a consciousness which is far stronger than that created by political or economic interests. That community is conditioned by the fact of a blood-relationship. Man to-day refuses any longer to be separated from the life of his national group; to that he clings with a resolute affection. He will bear extreme distress and misery, but he desires to remain with his national group. [It is this noble passion which alone can raise man above thoughts of gain and profit.] Blood binds more firmly than business.

Although it may be tempting to pass off such allusions to the blood-bond as the exaggerations of a demagogue and zealot, what should not be forgotten is that it was precisely through such allusions that Hitler was able to gain the intense, unquestioning devotion of the best educated, the most literate nation in Europe. As earlier noted, it is not the leader but the mass instinct to which he or she appeals that interests us. By appealing to common blood, Hitler was able to wrap himself in the mantle of German nationalism – to become the personification of the nation in German eyes.

It is ironic that Benito Mussolini, to whom Hitler was indebted for the inspiration behind numerous nationalistic motifs, should have come to power in a state characterized by significant ethnic heterogeneity. His task was therefore far more difficult: if he were to mobilize all segments of the population through nationalistic appeals, he must first convince the Lombards, Venetians, Florentines, Neapolitans, Calabrians, Sardinians, Sicilians *et al.* of their consanguinity. To this end, the local vernaculars were outlawed, and state propaganda seldom passed up the opportunity to emphasize a common Italian ancestry. As but one example, the following is an extract from a manifesto promulgated throughout all of Italy in 1938 (as cited in Delzell 1970, pp. 193–94):

The root of differences among peoples and nations is to be found in differences of race. If Italians differ from Frenchmen, Germans, Turks, Greeks, etc., this is not just because they possess a different language and different history, but because their racial development is different.... A pure "Italian race" is already in existence. This pronouncement [rests] on the very pure blood tie that unites presentday Italians... This ancient purity of blood is the Italian nation's greatest title of nobility.

Nationalistic appeals to ethnic purity were fully consonant, of course, with fascist dogma. More surprising is that Marxist-Leninist leaders, despite the philosophical incompatibility between communism and nationalism, should feel compelled to resort to nationalistic appeals to gain the support of the masses. Both Marx and Lenin, while insisting that nationalism was a bourgeois ideology that must be anathema to all communists, none the less appreciated its influence on the masses. They not only condoned but recommended appealing to it as a means of taking power. Even with this background, however, it appears strange to encounter Mao Tse-tung, when appealing for support from the Chinese masses, referring to the Chinese Communist Party *not* as "the vanguard of the proletariat," but as "the vanguard of the Chinese nation and the Chinese people" (Brandt *et al.* 1952, p. 260). The Chinese communists in Mao's propaganda became "part of the Great Chinese nation, flesh of its flesh and blood of its blood" (Mao Tse-tung 1975, p. 209).

In another proclamation (Brandt *et al.* 1952, p. 245), Mao appealed directly to the family ties deriving from a single common ancestor:

Beloved Compatriots! The Central Committee of the Chinese Communist Party respectfully and most sincerely issues the following manifesto to all fathers, brothers, aunts, and sisters throughout the country: [W]e know that in order to transform this glorious future into a new China, independent, free, and happy, all our fellow countrymen, every single zealous descendent of Huang-ti[1] must determinedly and relentlessly participate in the concerted struggle.

Ho Chi Minh, the father of the Vietnamese communist movement, also appealed to common ancestors and made use of terms connoting familial relationships, when courting the support of the masses. For example, in 1946 he stated:

Compatriots in the South and the Southern part of Central Viet-Nam! The North, Center, and South are part and parcel of

Viet-Nam!... We have the same ancestors, we are of the same family, we are all brothers and sisters.... No one can divide the children of the same family. Likewise, no one can divide Viet-Nam (Ho Chi Minh 1967, p. 158).

Democratic leaders have also appealed to a sense of shared blood in order to gain mass support for a course of action. Somewhat paradoxically, the early history of the American people – that human collectivity destined to form the polygenetic immigrant society *par excellence* – offers two noteworthy examples: one involving the decision to separate from Britain, and the other the decision to form a federal union. The explanation for the seeming paradox again lies in what we earlier termed *Staatvolk* psychology. The political élite of the period did not believe that they were leading an ethnically heterogeneous people. Despite the presence of settlers of Dutch, French, German, Irish, Scottish, Welsh – as well as, of course, the presence of native Americans and peoples from Africa (the latter accounted for one in every five persons at the time) – the prevalent élite-held and mass-held self-perception of the American people was that of an ethnically homogeneous people of English descent. As perceived by would-be revolutionary leaders of the time, if popular support for separation from Britain was to be propagated, a major problem to be overcome was the colonists' sense of belonging to a larger English family. Therefore, the framers of the Declaration of Independence apparently concluded that the feeling of transatlantic kinship should be directly confronted and countered in order to ensure popular support for the separation. After itemizing the grievances against the king, the Declaration turned to the transgressions of the branch of the family still in Britain:

Nor have We been wanting in attention to our British brethren.... We have appealed to their native justice and magnanimity, *and we have conjured them by the ties of our common kindred to disavow these usurpations*, which, would inevitably interrupt our connections and correspondence. *They too have been deaf to the voice of justice and of consanguinity*. We must, therefore ... hold them, as we hold the rest of mankind, Enemies in War, in Peace Friends.

In sum, from the American viewpoint, the apostates were "they," not "we." It was "they" who had destroyed the family through faithlessness to the sacred bond between kindred, through having been "deaf to the voice of consanguinity."

Eleven years later, political reformers were trying to entice the population, now spread throughout thirteen essentially independent countries, to adopt a federal constitution. The situation was therefore not unlike that which, as we earlier noted, would face Bismarck nearly a century later: How to appeal to people, strewn throughout a number of states, to join together. Just as Bismarck, one of the authors of the *Federalist Papers* (which were designed to elicit popular support for union) appealed to the popularly held self-perception of the society as an ancestrally related union. In the second of the eighty-five papers, John Jay wrote (Hamilton, Jay and Madison 1937, p. 9):

> With equal pleasure I have as often taken notice, that Providence has been pleased to give this one connected country to one united people – *a people descended from the same ancestors, speaking the same language, professing the same religion*, attached to the same principles of government, very similar in their manners and customs...
> This country and this people seem to have been made for each other, *and it appears as if it was the design of Providence, that an inheritance so proper and convenient for a band of brethren, united to each other by the strongest ties*, should never be split into a number of unsocial jealous, and alien sovereignties.

Jay was saying in effect, we are members of one family and the family should be reunited.

Thus, in the case of the United States, charges of betrayal of an ancestral bond were first used to gain popular support for politically dividing the family, and this was followed years later by appeals to the ancestral bond to bring about the political union of the American section of the family.

Parenthetically, it may be of interest to note that Americans of Anglo-Saxon ancestry (the so-called WASPS) continued to manifest the *Staatvolk* perception that all Americans, or rather "all true Americans," were blood relatives of the English. For example, in a mid-nineteenth century poem, entitled "To Englishmen", John Greenleaf Whittier wrote:

O Englishmen! – in hope and creed,
In blood and tongue our brothers!
We too are heirs of Runnymede;
And Shakespeare's fame and Cromwell's deed
Are not alone our mother's.

. . .

"Thicker than water," in one rill
Through centuries of story
Our Saxon blood has flowed, and still
We share with you its good and ill,
The shadow and the glory.

Paeans to the greatness of the Anglo-Saxon strain said to be inherited by the true Americans were plentiful well into the twentieth century. Fear of diluting or polluting that strain with immigrants of inferior ethnic background underpinned the country's immigration policy until after World War II.

We have so far confined our illustrations mainly to in-state situations. Nevertheless, because political and ethnic borders seldom coincide, appeals in the name of the nation have often jumped state borders. A shared sense of ancestral ties can become intermeshed in foreign policy and raise the issue of divided loyalties if important segments of the group are separated by political borders. Hitler's appeals in the name of the *Volksdeutsche* to all Germans living within Austria, the Sudetenland and Poland are well known. More recently, Albania has claimed the right to act as the protector of Albanians within Yugoslavia on the ground that "the same mother that gave birth to us gave birth to the Albanians in Kosovo, Montenegro, and Macedonia" (King 1973, p. 144); China has proclaimed its right to Taiwan on the ground that "the people of Taiwan are our kith and kin" (*New York Times*, 1 September 1975); the leader of North Korea, Kim II Sung, has declared the need to unify Korea in order to bring about the "integration of our race" (*Atlas* 1976, p. 19). In 1990 those who advised Germans in the Federal Republic of Germany and in the German Democratic Republic to approach most cautiously the question of reuniting the family in one state were no match for the kinship-evoking strategy of Chancellor Helmut Kohl, who appealed successfully for support of immediate unification by employing the disarmingly simple slogan "*Wir sind ein Volk!*" ("We are one nation!").

Unlike most writers on nationalism, then, political leaders of the most diverse ideological strains have been mindful of the common blood component of ethnonational psychology and have not hesitated to appeal to it when seeking popular support. Both the frequency and the record of success of such appeals attest to the fact that nations are indeed characterized by a sense, a feeling, of consanguinity.

Our answer, then, to that often asked question, "What is a nation?" is that it is a group of people who feel that they are ancestrally related.

It is the largest group that can command a person's loyalty because of felt kinship ties; it is, from this perspective, the fully extended family.

The sense of unique descent, of course, need not, and *in nearly all* cases *will not*, accord with factual history. Nearly all nations are the variegated offspring of numerous ethnic strains. It is not chronological or factual history that is the key to the nation, but sentient or felt history. All that is irreducibly required for the existence of a nation is that the members share an intuitive conviction of the group's separate origin and evolution. To aver that one is a member of the Japanese, German, or Thai nation is not merely to identify oneself with the Japanese, German, or Thai people of today, but with that people throughout time. Or rather, given the intuitive conviction that one's nation is unique in its origin, perhaps we should say not *throughout time* but *beyond time*. Logically, such a sense of one's nation's origin must rest on a presumption that somewhere in a hazy, pre-recorded era there existed a Japanese, German, or Thai Adam and Eve. However, logic operates in the realm of the conscious and the rational; convictions concerning the singular origin and evolution of one's nation belong to the realm of the subconscious and the non-rational (note: not *irrational*, but non-rational).

This distinction between reason and the emotional essence of the nation was expressed in a tract written a few years back by a person in solitary confinement within the Soviet Union (Moroz 1974, p. 54). He had just been found guilty of anti-state activities in the name of Ukrainian nationalism. He wrote:

> A nation can exist only where there are people who are prepared to die for it;
> ... Only when its sons believe that their nation is chosen by God and regard their people as his highest creation.
> I know that all people are equal.
> My reason tells me that.
> But at the same time I know that my nation is unique...
> My heart tells me so.
> It is not wise to bring the voices of reason and of emotion to a common denominator.

The dichotomy between the realm of national identity and that of reason has proved vexing to students of nationalism. With the exception of psychologists, people trained in the social sciences tend to be uncomfortable in confronting the non-rational. They are inclined to seek rational explanations for the nation in economic and other "real" forces. National consciousness resists explication in such terms. Indeed, in a strong testament to the difficulty of explicating national consciousness in any terms, Sigmund Freud, who spent so many years exploring and describing what he termed "the unconscious," acknowledged that the emotional sources of national identity defied articulation. After noting that he was Jewish, Freud made clear that his own sense of Jewishness had nothing to do with either religion or national pride. He went on to note that he was "irresistibly" bonded to Jews and Jewishness by "many obscure and emotional forces, *which were the more powerful the less they could be expressed in words*, as well as by a clear consciousness of inner identity, a deep realization of sharing the same psychic structure."[2] Having noted that national identity defied articulation in rational terms, Freud made no attempt to describe further the national bond and the feelings to which it gives rise, but there is no mistaking that the sentiments he was trying to express are the same as those more concisely and enigmatically summed up in the German maxim, *"Blut will zu Blut!,"* a loose translation of which might be "People of the same blood attract!" A nineteenth-century author, Adolph Stocker, expanded on this sentiment (Hayes 1941, p. 258):

> German blood flows in every German body, and the soul is in the blood. When one meets a German brother and not merely a brother from common humanity, there is a certain reaction that does not take place if the brother is not German.

"German" in this passage could, of course, be replaced by English, Russian, Lithuanian, etc. without affecting the passage's validity. Indeed, the thrust of the passage is remarkably similar to the sentiment expressed by a young Chinese nationalist revolutionary (Chen Tiannua) around 1900 (Dikötter 1990, p. 427):

> As the saying goes, a man is not close to people of another family. When two families fight each other, one surely assists one's own family, one definitely does not help the "exterior" family. Common families all descend from one original family: the Han race is one big family. The Yellow Emperor is a great ancestor, all those who are not of the Han race are not the descendants of the Yellow Emperor, they are exterior families. One should definitely not assist them; if one assists them, one lacks a sense of ancestry.

No matter how described – Freud's interior identity and psychic structure, or blood-ties, or chemistry, or soul – it is worth repeating that the national bond is subconscious and emotional rather than conscious and rational in its inspiration. It can be analysed but not explained rationally.

How can we analyse it? It can be at least obliquely analysed by examining the type of catalysts to which it responds, that is to say, by examining the tested techniques for reaching and triggering national responses. How has the non-rational core of the nation been reached and triggered? As we have seen in the case of numerous successful nationalist leaders, not through appeals to *reason* but through appeals to the *emotions* (appeals not to the mind but to the blood).

The non-rational core of the nation has been reached and triggered through national symbols, as historically varied as the Rising Sun, the Swastika and Britannia. Such symbols can speak messages without words to members of the nation, because, as one author has noted: "There is something about such symbols, especially visual ones, which reach the parts rational explanation cannot reach."

The non-rational core has been reached and triggered through nationalist poetry, because the poet is far more adept than the writer of learned tracts at expressing deeply felt emotion, as witness the following words written in 1848 by a Romanian poet to describe the Romanian nation (Tudor 1982, p. 61):

> It is in it that we were born, it is our mother;
> We are men because it reared us;
> We are free because we move in it;
> If we are angered, it soothes our pain with national songs.
> Through it we talk today to our parents who lived thousands of
> years back;
> Through it our descendents and posterity thousands of years later
> will know us.

The non-rational core has been reached and triggered through music popularly perceived as reflecting the nation's particular past or genius; the music may vary in sophistication, embracing the work of composers such as Richard Wagner, as well as folk music.

The core of the nation has been reached and triggered through the use of familial metaphors which can magically transform the mundanely tangible into emotion-laden phantasma: which can, for example, mystically convert what the outsider sees as merely the territory populated by a nation into a motherland or fatherland, the ancestral land, land of our fathers, this sacred soil, land where our fathers died, the native land, the cradle of the nation, and most commonly, the *home* – the *home*land of our particular people – a "Mother Russia," an Armenia, a Deutschland, an England (Engla land: land of the Angles), or a Kurdistan (literally, land of the Kurds). Here is an Uzbek poet referring to Uzbekistan (Connor 1985):

So that my generation would comprehend the Homeland's worth,

Men were always transformed to dust, it seems.
The Homeland is the remains of our forefathers
Who turned into dust for this precious soil.

A spiritual bond between nation and territory is thus touched. As concisely stated in the nineteenth-century German couplet, "*Blut und Boden*," ("Blood and Soil") become mixed in national perceptions.

It is, then, the character of appeals made through and to the senses, not through and to reason, which permit us some knowledge of the subconscious convictions that people tend to harbour concerning their nation. The near universality with which certain images and phrases appear – blood, family, brothers, sisters, mother, forefathers, ancestors, home – and the proven success of such invocations in eliciting massive, popular responses tell us much about the nature of national identity. Yet, again, this line of research does not provide a rational explanation for it.

Rational would-be explanations have been abundant: relative economic deprivation; élite ambitions; rational choice theory; intense transaction flows; the desire of the intelligentsia to convert a "low," subordinate culture into a "high," dominant one; cost-benefit considerations; internal colonialism; a ploy of the bourgeoisie to undermine the class consciousness of the proletariat by obscuring the conflicting class interests within each nation, and by encouraging rivalry among the proletariat of various nations; a somewhat spontaneous mass response to competition for scarce resources. All such theories can be criticized on empirical grounds, but they can be faulted principally on their failure to reflect the emotional depth of national identity: the passions at either extreme of the hate-love continuum which the nation often inspires, and the countless fanatical sacrifices which have been made in its name. As Chateaubriand expressed it nearly 200 years ago (Sulzbach 1943, p. 62): "Men don't allow themselves to be killed for their interests; they allow themselves to be killed for their passions." To phrase it differently: people do not voluntarily die for things that are rational.

The sense of kinship which lies at the heart of national consciousness helps to account for the ugly manifestations of inhumanity that often erupt in the relations among national groups. A chain of such eruptions in the late 1980s found Soviet authorities totally unprepared for the scale of brutality that surfaced in the wake of *perestroika* and *glasnost*, as national groups across the entire southern USSR gave vent to their previously pent-up ethnic enmities.

Such behaviour patterns are hardly unusual. The annual reports of organizations such as Amnesty International offer a dismal recitation of officially condoned oppression of national minorities: Tibetans by Han Chinese; West Bank Arabs by Jews; Kurds by Iraqi Arabs, by Persians, and by Turks; Dinkas and other Nilotic peoples by Sudanese Arabs; Xhosas, Zulus and other black peoples by Afrikaners; Quechuans by Peruvian mestizos; Ndebele by Shonas; Turks by Bulgars; Mayan peoples by Guatemalan mestizos; Kachins, Karens, Mons, and Shans by Burmese. The list could be lengthened. Moreover, as suggested by earlier described events in the Soviet Union, genocidal tendencies towards members of another nation have often surfaced without governmental approval. Recent non-Soviet illustrations of sets of nations who have manifested such tendencies are Xhosa and Zulu, Serb and Croat, Serb and Albanian, Irishman and "Orangeman", Greek and Turk, Sikh and Hindu, Punjabi and Sindhi, Sindhi and Pushtuh, Hutu and Tutsi, Ovambo and Herero, Corsican and Frenchman, Vietnamese and Han, Khmer and Vietnamese, Assamese and Bengali, Malay and Han. Again, the list could be lengthened.

Not all relations among nations are so hate-filled. Popular attitudes held by one nation towards another are often quite positive. Nonetheless, while attitudes towards various other nations may vary across a broad spectrum, the national bond, because it is based upon belief in common descent, ultimately bifurcates humanity into "us" and "them". This propensity towards bifurcating the human race has a long history. Note the simple cause-and-effect relationship between ethnic purity and hatred of all outsiders that Plato has Menexos ascribe to that most cultured and sophisticated of ancient peoples, the Athenians:

The mind of this city is so noble and free and so powerful and healthy *and by nature hating the barbarians because we are pure Hellenes* and not commingled with barbarians. No Pelops or Cadmus or Aegyptus or Danaus or others who are barbarians by nature and Hellenes only by law dwell with us, but we live here as pure Hellenes who are not mixed with barbarians. *Therefore, the city has acquired a real hate of alien nature.*

Because the sense of common kinship does not extend beyond the nation, that sense of compassion to which kinship usually – not always but usually – gives rise is lacking in the relations among national groups. The fault lines that separate nations are deeper and broader than those separating non-kindred groups, and the tremors that follow those fault lines more potentially cataclysmic. What underlies the now commonplace phrase "man's inhumanity to man" is all too often "nation's inhumanity to nation."

Failure on the part of scholars to appreciate the psychological wellsprings of the nation most certainly contributes to the tendency to undervalue the potency of nationalism. As earlier noted, when nationalism and patriotism are perceived as in conflict, it is nationalism that customarily proves itself to be the more powerful allegiance.

This is not to deny that patriotism can be a very powerful sentiment. The state has many effective means for inculcating love of country and love of political institutions – what social scientists collectively term "political socialization." Not the least effective of these is control of public education and, particularly, control over the history courses.

Moreover, even governments of complex multi-ethnic states are free to, and often do, adopt the idiom of nationalism when attempting to inculcate loyalty to the state. From my own primary-school education of many years ago, I recall how we students – many, probably most, of whom were first-, second- or third-generation Americans from highly diverse national backgrounds – were told we shared a common ancestry.

We were programmed to consider Washington, Jefferson, *et al.* as our common "founding fathers." We memorized Lincoln's reminder in the Gettysburg Address that four score and seven years earlier, it was "our Fathers [who had] brought forth upon this continent a new nation." We repetitively sang that very short song, "America," one of whose seven lines reads "land where my fathers died." Yet despite the many advantages that the state has for politically socializing its citizens in patriotic values, patriotism – as evident from the multitude of separatist movements pockmarking the globe – cannot muster the level of emotional commitment that nationalism can. As already noted, loyalty to state and loyalty to nation are not always in conflict, but when they are perceived as being in irreconcilable conflict, nationalism customarily proves to be the more potent.

Again, perhaps the most instructive recent case is that of the Soviet Union, wherein a most comprehensive, intensive, and multigenerational

56 Racial and Ethnic Pluralism

programme to exorcise nationalism and exalt Soviet patriotism has proved remarkably ineffective. Similar programmes throughout Eastern Europe also clearly failed, most glaringly in Yugoslavia. As I noted in a piece twenty-five years ago [Connor 1967, p. 52]: "Political developments since World War II clearly establish that national consciousness is not on the wane as a political force, but is quite definitely in the ascendency."

NOTES

1. Huang-ti was the legendary first emperor of China.
2. The quotation interutilizes translated extracts of Leon Poliakov, *The Aryan Myth* (London: Sussex University Press, 1974, p. 287), and the more clumsy translation in *The Standard Edition of the Complete Psychological Works of Sigmund Freud, Vol. XX (1925–26)* (London: The Hogarth Press, 1959, pp. 273–74).

REFERENCES

ATLAS 1976 (February)
BRANDT, CONRAD et al. 1952 *A Documentary History of Chinese Communism*, London: Allen & Unwin
CONNOR, WALKER 1967 "Self-determination: the new phase," *World Politics*, vol. 20 (October 1967)
—— 1985 "The impact of Homelands upon diasporas," in Gabriel Sheffer (ed.), *Modern Diasporas in International Politics*, London: Croom Helm, pp. 16–46
—— 1987 "Ethnonationalism," in Samuel Huntington and Myron Weiner (eds), *Understanding Political Development*, Boston, MA: Little Brown & Company
DELZELL, CHARLES 1970 *Mediterranean Fascism*, New York: Harper & Row
DIKÖTTER, FRANK 1990 "Group definition and the idea of 'race' in modern China (1793–1949)," *Ethnic and Racial Studies*, vol. 13, no. 3, pp. 420–32
HAMILTON, ALEXANDER, JAY, JOHN and MADISON, JAMES 1937 *The Federalist: A Commentary on the Constitution of the United States*, New York: The Modern Library
HAYES, CARLTON 1941 *A Generation of Materialism, 1871–1900*, New York: Harper & Row
HITLER, ADOLPH 1940 *Mein Kampf*, New York: Reynal & Hitchcock

—— 1942 *The Speeches of Adolph Hitler, April 22-August 1939*, vol. 2, London: Oxford University Press
HO CHI MINH 1967 *On Revolution: Selected Writings 1920–1966* [edited by Bernard Fall], New York: New American Library
KING, ROBERT 1973 *Minorities Under Communism*, Cambridge, MA: Harvard University Press
MAO TSE-TUNG 1975 *Selected Works of Mao Tse-tung, Vol. 2*, Peking: Foreign Languages Press
MOROZ, VALENTINE 1974 *Report from the Beria Reserve*, Chicago: Cataract Press
POLIAKOV, LEON 1974 *The Aryan Myth*, London: Sussex University Press
[THE] STANDARD EDITION OF THE COMPLETE PSYCHOLOGICAL WORKS OF SIGMUND FREUD, VOL. XX (1925–26), London: The Hogarth Press
SULZBACH, WALTER 1943 *National Consciousness*, Washington, DC: American Council on Public Affairs
TUDOR, CORNELIU VADIM 1982 "Humanism, fraternity of national minority policy stressed," *JPRS* 81624 (25 August)

Part II
Resurgent Tribalisms:
Foundations and Implications
of the New American
Pluralism

4 An American Dilemma
Gunnar Myrdal

THE NEGRO PROBLEM AS A MORAL ISSUE

There is a "Negro problem" in the United States and most Americans
are aware of it, although it assumes varying forms and intensity in
different regions of the country and among diverse groups of the
American people. Americans have to react to it, politically as citizens
and, where there are Negroes present in the community, privately as
neighbors.

To the great majority of white Americans the Negro problem has
distinctly negative connotations. It suggests something difficult to
settle and equally difficult to leave alone. It is embarrassing. It
makes for moral uneasiness. The very presence of the Negro in
America; his fate in this country through slavery, Civil War and
Reconstruction; his recent career and his present status; his accommodation; his protest and his aspiration; in fact his entire biological, historical and social existence as a participant American
represent to the ordinary white man in the North as well as in
the South an anomaly in the very structure of American society.
To many, this takes on the proportion of a menace – biological,
economic, social, cultural, and, at times, political. This anxiety may
be mingled with a feeling of individual and collective guilt. A few
see the problem as a challenge to statesmanship. To all it is a
trouble.

These and many other mutually inconsistent attitudes are blended
into none too logical a scheme which, in turn, may be quite inconsistent with the wider personal, moral, religious, and civic sentiments
and ideas of the Americans. Now and then, even the least sophisticated individual becomes aware of his own confusion and the contradiction in his attitudes. Occasionally he may recognize, even if only
for a moment, the incongruence of his state of mind and find it so
intolerable that the whole organization of his moral precepts is shaken. But most people, most of the time, suppress such threats to their
moral integrity together with all of the confusion, the ambiguity, and
inconsistency which lurks in the basement of man's soul. This, however, is rarely accomplished without mental strain. Out of the strain

comes a sense of uneasiness and awkwardness which always seems attached to the Negro problem.

The strain is increased in democratic America by the freedom left open – even in the South, to a considerable extent – for the advocates of the Negro, his rights and welfare. All "pro-Negro" forces in American society, whether organized or not, and irrespective of their wide differences in both strategy and tactics, sense that this is the situation. They all work on the national conscience. They all seek to fix everybody's attention on the suppressed moral conflict. No wonder that they are often regarded as public nuisances, or worse, even when they succeed in getting grudging concessions to Negro rights and welfare.

At this point it must be observed that America, relative to all the other branches of Western civilization, is moralistic and "moral-conscious." The ordinary American is the opposite of a cynic. He is on the average more of a believer and a defender of the faith in humanity than the rest of the Occidentals. It is a relatively important matter to him to be true to his own ideals and to carry them out in actual life. We recognize the American, wherever we meet him, as a practical idealist. Compared with members of other nations of Western civilization, the ordinary American is a rationalistic being, and there are close relations between his moralism and his rationalism. Even romanticism, transcendentalism, and mysticism tend to be, in the American culture, rational, pragmatic and optimistic. American civilization early acquired a flavor of enlightenment which has affected the ordinary American's whole personality and especially his conception of how ideas and ideals ought to "click" together. He has never developed that particular brand of tired mysticism and romanticism which finds delight in the inextricable confusion in the order of things and in ineffectuality of the human mind. He finds such leanings intellectually perverse.

These generalizations might seem venturesome and questionable to the reflective American himself, who, naturally enough, has his attention directed more on the dissimilarities than on the similarities within his culture. What is common is usually not obvious, and it never becomes striking. But to the stranger it is obvious and even striking. In the social sciences, for instance, the American has, more courageously than anywhere else on the globe, started to measure, not only human intelligence, aptitudes, and personality traits, but moral leanings and the "goodness" of communities. This man is a rationalist; he wants intellectual order in his moral set-up; he wants to pursue his own inclinations into their hidden haunts; and he is likely to expose himself and his kind in a most undiplomatic manner.

In hasty strokes we are now depicting the essentials of the American *ethos*. This moralism and rationalism are to many of us – including myself – the glory of the nation, its youthful strength, perhaps the salvation of mankind. The analysis of this "American Creed" and its implications have an important place in our inquiry. While on the one hand, to such a moralistic and rationalistic being as the ordinary American, the Negro problem and his own confused and contradictory attitudes toward it must be disturbing; on the other hand, the very mass of unsettled problems in his heterogeneous and changing culture, and the inherited liberalistic trust that things will ultimately take care of themselves and get settled in one way or another, enable the ordinary American to live on happily, with recognized contradictions around him and within him, in a kind of bright fatalism which is unmatched in the rest of the Western world. This fatalism also belongs to the national *ethos*.

The American Negro problem is a problem in the heart of the American. It is there that the interracial tension has its focus. It is there that the decisive struggle goes on. This is the central viewpoint of this treatise. Though my study includes economic, social, and political race relations, at the bottom our problem is the moral dilemma of the American – the conflict between his moral valuations on various levels of consciousness and generality. The "American Dilemma," referred to in the title of this chapter, is the ever-raging conflict between, on the one hand, the valuations preserved on the general plane which I shall call the "American Creed," where the American thinks, talks, and acts under the influence of high national and Christian precepts, and, on the other hand, the valuations on specific planes of individual and group living, where personal and local interests; economic, social, and sexual jealousies; considerations of community prestige and conformity; group prejudice against particular persons or types of people; and all sorts of miscellaneous wants, impulses, and habits dominate his outlook.

The American philosopher, John Dewey, whose immense influence is to be explained by his rare gift for projecting faithfully the aspirations and possibilities of the culture he was born into, in the maturity of age and wisdom has written a book on *Freedom and Culture*, in which he says:

Anything that obscures the fundamentally moral nature of the social problem is harmful, no matter whether it proceeds from the side of physical or of psychological theory. Any doctrine that eliminates or even obscures the function of choice of values and enlistment of desires and emotions in behalf of those chosen weakens personal responsibility for judgment and for action. It thus helps create the attitudes that welcome and support the totalitarian state.

I shall attempt to follow through Dewey's conception of what a social problem really is.

VALUATIONS AND BELIEFS

The Negro problem in America would be of a different nature and, indeed, would be simpler to handle scientifically, if the moral conflict raged only between valuations held by different persons and groups of persons. The essence of the moral situation is, however, that the conflicting valuations are also held by the same person. *The moral struggle goes on within people and not only between them. As people's valuations are conflicting, behavior normally becomes a moral compromise. There are no homogeneous "attitudes" behind human behavior but a mesh of struggling inclinations, interests, and ideals, some held conscious and some suppressed for long intervals but all active in bending behavior in their direction.*

The unity of a culture consists in the fact that all valuations are mutually shared in some degree. We shall find that even a poor and uneducated white person in some isolated and backward rural region in the Deep South, who is violently prejudiced against the Negro and intent upon depriving him of civic rights and human independence, has also a whole compartment in his valuation sphere housing the entire American Creed of liberty, equality, justice, and fair opportunity for everybody. He is actually also a good Christian and honestly devoted to the ideals of human brotherhood and the Golden Rule. And these more general valuations – more general in the sense that they refer to all human beings – are, to some extent, effective in shaping his behavior. Indeed, it would be impossible to understand why the Negro does not fare worse in some regions of America if it were not constantly kept in mind that behavior is the outcome of a compromise between valuations, among which the equalitarian ideal is one. At the other end, there are few liberals, even in New England, who have not a well-furnished compartment of race prejudice, even if it is usually suppressed from conscious attention. Even the American Negroes share in this community of valuations: they have eagerly imbibed the American Creed and the revolutionary Christian teaching of common brotherhood; under closer study, they usually reveal also that they hold something of the majority prejudice against their own kind and its characteristics.

The intensities and proportions in which these conflicting valuations are present vary considerably from one American to another, and within the same individual, from one situation to another. The cultural unity of the nation consists, however, in the fact that *most Americans have most valuations in common* though they are arranged differently in the sphere of valuations of different individuals and groups and bear different intensity coefficients. This cultural unity is the indispensable basis for discussion between persons and groups. It is the floor upon which the democratic process goes on.

In America as everywhere else people agree, as an abstract proposition, that *the more general valuations – those which refer to man as such and not to any particular group or temporary situation – are morally higher.* These valuations are also given the sanction of religion and national legislation. They are incorporated into the American Creed. The other valuations, which refer to various smaller groups of mankind or to particular occasions, are commonly referred to as "irrational" or "prejudiced," sometimes even by people who express and stress them. They are defended in terms of tradition, expediency or utility.

Trying to defend their behavior to others, and primarily to themselves, people will attempt to conceal the conflict between their different valuations of what is desirable and undesirable, right or wrong, by keeping away some valuations from awareness and by focusing attention on others. For the same opportune purpose, *people will twist and mutilate their beliefs of how social reality actually is.* In my study I encounter whole systems of firmly entrenched popular beliefs concerning the Negro and his relations to the larger society, which are bluntly false and which can only be understood when we remember the opportunistic *ad hoc* purposes they serve. These "popular theories," because of the rationalizing function they serve, are heavily loaded with emotions. But people also want to be rational. Scientific truth-seeking and education are slowly rectifying the beliefs and thereby also influencing the valuations. In a rationalistic civilization it is not only that the beliefs are shaped by the valuations, but also that the valuations depend upon the beliefs...

When we thus choose to view the Negro problem as primarily a moral issue, we are in line with popular thinking. It is as a moral issue that this problem presents itself in the daily life of ordinary people; it is as a moral issue that they brood over it in their thoughtful moments. It is in terms of conflicting moral valuations that it is discussed in church and school, in the family circle, in the workshop, on the street corner, as well as in the press, over the radio, in trade union meetings, in the state legislatures, the Congress and the Supreme Court. The social scientist, in his effort to lay bare concealed truths and to become maximally useful in guiding practical and political action, is prudent when, in the approach to a problem, he sticks as closely as possible to the common man's ideas and formulations, even though he knows that further investigation will carry him into tracts uncharted in the popular consciousness. There is a pragmatic common sense in people's ideas about themselves and their worries, which we cannot afford to miss when we start out to explore social reality. Otherwise we are often too easily distracted by our learned arbitrariness and our pet theories, concepts, and hypotheses, not to mention our barbarous terminology, which we generally are tempted to mistake for something more than mere words. *This study takes its starting point in the ordinary man's own ideas, doctrines, theories and mental constructs.*

In approaching the Negro problem as primarily a moral issue of conflicting valuations, it is not implied, of course, that ours is the prerogative of pronouncing on *a priori* grounds which values are "right" and which are "wrong." In fact, such judgments are out of the realm of social science, and will not be attempted in this inquiry. My investigation will naturally be an analysis *of* morals and not *in* morals. In so far as I make my own judgments of value, they will be based on explicitly stated value premises, selected from among those valuations actually observed as existing in the minds of the white and Negro Americans and tested as to their social and political relevance and significance. My value judgments are thus derived and have no greater validity than the value premises postulated.

A WHITE MAN'S PROBLEM

Although the Negro problem is a moral issue both to Negroes and to whites in America, we shall have to give *primary* attention to what goes on in the minds of white Americans. To explain this direction of interest a general conclusion from my studies needs to be stated a: this point. When I started my inquiry, my preconception was that it had to be focused on the Negro people and their peculiarities. This is understandable since, from a superficial view, Negro Americans, not only in physical appearance, but also in thoughts, feelings, and in manner of life, seemed stranger to me than did white Americans. Furthermore, most of the literature on the Negro problem dealt with the Negroes: their racial and cultural characteristics, their living standards and occupational pursuits, their stratification in social classes, their migration, their family organization, their religion, their illiteracy, delinquency and disease, and so on. But as I proceeded in my studies into the Negro problem, it became increasingly evident that little, if anything, could be scientifically explained in terms of the peculiarities of the Negroes themselves.

As a matter of fact, in their basic human traits the Negroes are inherently not much different from other people. Neither are, incidentally, the white Americans. But Negroes and whites in the United States live in singular human relations with each other. All the circumstances of life – the "environmental" conditions in the broadest meaning of that term – diverge more from the "normal" for the Negroes than for the whites, if only because of the statistical fact that the Negroes are the smaller group. The average Negro must experience many times more of the "abnormal" interracial relations than the average white man in America. The more important fact, however, is that practically all the economic, social, and political power is held by whites. The Negroes do not by far have anything approaching a tenth of the things worth having in America.

It is thus the white majority group that naturally determines the Negro's "place." All my attempts to reach scientific explanations of why the Negroes are what they are and why they live as they do have regularly led to determinants on the white side of the race line. In the practical and political struggles of effecting changes, the views and attitudes of the white Americans are likewise strategic. The Negro's entire life, and, consequently, also his opinions on the Negro problem, are, in the main, to be considered as secondary reactions to more primary pressures from the side of the dominant white majority.

The Negro was brought to America for the sake of the white man's profit. He was kept in slavery for generations in the same interest. A civil war was fought between two regional groups of white Americans. For two years no one wanted Negroes involved in the fighting. Later on some two hundred thousand Negro soldiers fought in the Northern

army, in addition to all the Negro laborers, servants, spies, and help-
ers in both armies. But it was not the Negroes' war. As a result of the
war, which took a toll of some half million killed and many more
wounded, the four million Negro slaves were liberated. Since then the
Negro's "place" in American society has been precarious, uncertain
and changing; he was no longer so necessary and profitable to the
white man as in slavery before the Civil War. In the main, however,
the conflicting and vacillating valuations of the white majority have
been decisive, whether the issue was segregation in the schools,
discrimination with reference to public facilities, equal justice and
protection under the laws, enjoyment of the franchise, or the freedom
to enter a vocation and earn an honest living. The Negro, as a
minority, and a poor and suppressed minority at that, in the final
analysis, has had little other strategy open to him than to play on the
conflicting values held in the white majority group. In so doing, he has
been able to identify his cause with broader issues in American
politics and social life and with moral principles held dear by the
white Americans. This is the situation even today and will remain so
in the foreseeable future. In that sense, "this is a white man's
country."

THE NEGRO COMMUNITY AS A PATHOLOGICAL FORM OF
AN AMERICAN COMMUNITY

The value premise for this section is derived from the American
Creed. America was settled largely by persons who, for one reason
or another, were dissatisfied with conditions in their homelands and
sought new opportunities. Until 1921 the nation welcomed
immigrants almost unreservedly. They came from everywhere and
brought with them a diversity of institutions and cultural patterns.
It was natural that the "melting pot," "Americanization" – or, to use
a more technical term, "assimilation" – became a central element in
the American Creed. To make a homogeneous nation out of diverse
ethnic groups, the immigrants were to abandon their cultural "peculiarities" – or to contribute them to American culture as a whole, as
some would have it – and to take on the cultural forms of America.
There could be diversity, to be sure, but this diversity was not to have
a strictly ethnic basis; individuals should be free to be part of any
community they wished. Ideally, Americanization was to take place
immediately, or, rather, in the five years required to achieve

citizenship. But it was realistically recognized that in some cases it might require two or three generations.

Negroes have been living here for over three hundred years, and practically all of the ancestors of present-day Negroes came to this country more than a hundred years ago. It is probable that, on the average, Negroes have been Americans longer than any immigrant group except the British. They should be well assimilated by now. Negroes, however, together with the Orientals and, to some extent, Indians and Mexicans, have not been allowed to assimilate as have European immigrants. There is intense resistance on the part of the white majority group to biological amalgamation; and the lower caste status of Negroes is rationalized to prevent miscegenation. Negroes have been segregated, and they have developed, or there have been provided for them, separate institutions in many spheres of life, as, for instance, in religion and education. Segregation and discrimination have also in other ways hampered assimilation. Particularly they have steered acculturation so that the Negroes have acquired the norms of lower class people in America.

Negro institutions are, nevertheless, similar to those of the white man. They show little similarity to African institutions. In his cultural traits, the Negro is akin to other Americans. Some peculiarities are even to be characterized as "exaggerations" of American traits. Horace Mann Bond has characterized the American Negro as a "quintessential American." Even the "exaggeration" or intensification of general American traits in American Negro culture is explainable by specific caste pressures. In his allegiances the Negro is characteristically an American. He believes in the American Creed and in other ideals held by most Americans, such as getting ahead in the world, individualism, the importance of education and wealth. He imitates the dominant culture as he sees it and in so far as he can adopt it under his conditions of life. For the most part he is not proud of those things in which he differs from the white American.

True, there has developed recently a glorification of things African, especially in music and art, and there was a back-to-Africa movement after the First World War. But this is a reaction to discrimination from white people, on the one hand, and a result of encouragement from white people, on the other hand. Thus, even the positive movement away from American culture has its source in that culture. Negro race pride and race prejudice serve to fortify the Negro against white superiority. *In practically all its divergences, American Negro culture is not something independent of general American culture. It is a distorted development, or a pathological condition, of the general American culture.* The instability of the Negro family, the inadequacy of educational facilities for Negroes, the emotionalism in the Negro church, the insufficiency and unwholesomeness of Negro recreational activity, the plethora of Negro sociable organizations, the narrowness of interests of the average Negro, the provincialism of his political speculation, the high Negro crime rate, the cultivation of the arts to the neglect of other fields, superstition, personality difficulties, and other characteristic traits are mainly forms of social pathology which, for the most part, are created by the caste pressures.

This can be said positively: *we assume that it is to the advantage of American Negroes as individuals and as a group to become assimilated into American culture, to acquire the traits held in esteem by the dominant white Americans.* This will be the value premise here. I do not imply that white American culture is "higher" than other cultures in an absolute sense. The notion popularized by anthropologists that *all* cultures may be good under the different conditions to which they are adaptations, and that no derogatory association should *a priori* be attached to primitive cultures, is a wholesome antidote to arrogant and erroneous ideas closely bound up with white people's false racial beliefs and their justification of caste. But it does not gainsay my assumption that *here, in America*, American culture is "highest" in the pragmatic sense that adherence to it is practical for any individual or group which is not strong enough to change it.

Also not to be taken in a doctrinal sense is the observation that peculiarities in the Negro community may be characterized as social pathology. As a reaction to adverse and degrading living conditions, the Negroes' culture is taking on some characteristics which are not given a high evaluation in the larger American culture. Occasionally the Negro culture traits are appreciated by the whites. The Negro spirituals – called by James Weldon Johnson, though with some exaggeration, "America's only folk music" – are a case in point.[1]

AMERICA'S OPPORTUNITY

The conquering of color caste in America is America's own innermost desire. This nation early laid down as the moral basis for its existence the principles of equality and liberty. However much Americans have dodged this conviction, they have refused to adjust their laws to their own license. Today, more than ever, they refuse to discuss systematizing their caste order to mutual advantage, apparently because they most seriously mean that caste is wrong and should not be given recognition. They stand warmheartedly against oppression in all the world. When they are reluctantly forced into war, they are compelled to justify their participation to their own conscience by insisting that they are fighting against aggression and for liberty and equality.

America feels itself to be humanity in miniature. When in this crucial time the international leadership passes to America, the great reason for hope is that this country has a national experience of uniting racial and cultural diversities and a national theory, if not a consistent practice, of freedom and equality for all. What America is constantly reaching for is democracy at home and abroad. The main trend in its history is the gradual realization of the American Creed.

In this sense the Negro problem is not only America's greatest failure but also America's incomparably great opportunity for the future. If America should follow its own deepest convictions, its well-being at home would be increased directly. At the same time America's prestige and power abroad would rise immensely. The century-old dream of American patriots, that America should give to the entire world its own freedoms and its own faith, would come true. America can demonstrate that justice, equality and cooperation are possible between white and colored people.

In the present phase of history this is what the world needs to believe. Mankind is sick of fear and disbelief, of pessimism and cynicism. It needs the youthful moralistic optimism of America. But empty declarations only deepen cynicism. Deeds are called for. If America in actual practice could show the world a progressive trend by which the Negro became finally integrated into modern democracy, all mankind would be given faith again – it would have reason to believe that peace, progress and order are feasible. And America would have a spiritual power many times stronger than all her financial and military resources – the power of the trust and support of all good people on earth. *America is free to choose whether the Negro shall remain her liability or become her opportunity.*

NOTES

1. Similar exceptions can be noticed in every lower class culture. There has been, for instance, in most industrial countries in recent decades, a "proletarian" branch of literature, which draws its themes and its inspiration from life in the lower classes. This literature is often, characteristically enough, appreciated more by members of the higher classes than by the proletarians themselves. Generally pastoral romanticism, which has been a part of urban civilization since the time of the ancient Greeks, has idealized lower class life. The tendency is tainted with sentimentality, and this is frequently displayed by people who show a particular interest in Negro culture. Among the radically inclined, this romanticism serves to express their sympathy for the underdog; among conservatives it serves as a rationalization for continuing the inequalities. To Negroes it serves as an expression of their protest and their "race pride." As usual it appeals much more to upper and middle class Negroes than to lower class Negroes. The sentimentality involved in idealizing lower class traits has, of course, nothing to do with scientific observation. The residuum of truth in the tendency is, however, that even if generally the result of adverse living conditions are bad, exceptionally they may be good – "good" and "bad" defined according to our value premise of placing the general American culture "higher."

5 Americanism and Its Discontents: Protestantism, Nativism, and Political Heresy in America
Michael W. Hughey

AN AMERICAN DILEMMA RECONSIDERED

In his celebrated study of *An American Dilemma* in 1944, Swedish social scientist Gunnar Myrdal chastised the American political community for failing to live up to its ideals. Taking the situation of blacks as the paradigmatic case, Myrdal exposed the moral contradiction between the nation's "American Creed," with its commitment to democracy, egalitarianism, and tolerance, and its racist policies and practices. While recognizing the emotional and moral intensity of this contradiction, Myrdal was nonetheless certain that a favorable resolution would be achieved. Whereas racist and segregationist values and practices were grounded in only particularistic and local interests, jealousies, wants, and impulses, the liberal contents of the American Creed were transcendent, universal, and more fundamental. "Americans of all national origins, classes, regions, creeds, and colors," Myrdal wrote, "have something in common: a common *ethos*, a political creed. It is difficult to avoid the judgment that this 'American Creed' is the cement in the structure of this great and disparate nation."[1] As such, this "social ethos" embodied morally higher and more authentic American values than the "lower" and merely "local" racist values that were also held by many Americans. Because of this inherent imbalance between the two competing value systems, Myrdal was convinced that the American dilemma would eventually be resolved in favor of the American Creed and that the authentic ideals of the political community would be restored to their rightful orthodoxy.

In juxtaposing America's "true" and authentic political ideals with what he regarded as only temporary and particularistic aberrations,

Myrdal failed to comprehend the real depth and magnitude of the American dilemma. He rightly identified one side of the dilemma as being framed by political universalism, which emphasizes such cherished notions as government by consent of the governed, egalitarian democracy, universal and inalienable political rights, and an open political system. These political ideals have their roots in the Lockean[2] and Commonwealth[3] ideas that were borrowed by American political thinkers prior to the Revolutionary War and in the democratic-republican ideas transmitted by Puritanism into the political order.[4] They have become celebrated tenets of the nation's political culture. However, Myrdal did not fully recognize that throughout American history these democratic ideals have been interwoven with a different and even opposed, but equally authentic, political tradition. Also originating in Puritanism but undergoing numerous secular permutations and transformations over the years, this tradition asserts that the rights and privileges of democratic citizenship should be extended only to those groups who are in some way qualified to exercise them. Some groups, having arrived earlier and contributed most to the construction of American political institutions, have claimed and exercised the right to oversee their operation, determine the criteria for political inclusion, and reap the benefits thereof. In practice, therefore, democracy has been monopolized by dominant groups who have appropriated its rights and privileges while excluding and discriminating against religious, racial, gender, and ethnic groups.

The historically dominant groups in American society embraced these two divergent political traditions simultaneously, merging them into a normative conception of the political community that was at once democratic and exclusive, universalistic and restrictive, tolerant and discriminatory. The American dilemma is therefore much more profound than Myrdal imagined: it does not represent a struggle between "higher" and "lower" values but rather is contained *within* the nation's most central political and cultural ideals. At the ideological heart of the American political community, both inclusive and exclusive ideals have long coexisted in dynamic tension as equally authentic features of the political culture.

Perhaps because he identified with the dominant Anglo-Protestant political culture, Myrdal did not see that the intolerant and exclusive values and practices he disdained were not simply anomalies in that culture, but fundamental and endemic features of it.[5] More specifically, while he readily acclaimed a connection between the nation's political universalism and its "Christian precepts,"[6] he could not imagine that the racism and intolerance he disdained might also be grounded in America's religious heritage. This paper re-examines the American dilemma at this deeper level by analyzing the religious foundations of the normative conception of the American political community, particularly its exclusive and restrictive emphases. I will be especially concerned to trace out the casuistries and secular trans-mutations of ideas whose origins rested in religion, showing how they have affected both actions and ideals as America's dominant groups have sought to deal with the problems and issues posed by an increasingly diverse society. Simply put, I suggest that values, images, and ideals that originated in Protestantism influence the organization of race, ethnic, religious, and other group relations in America. This chapter will explore and demonstrate some of the dimensions of this religious legacy by taking as a paradigmatic case the episodic history of ideological heresy against Americanism and the nativist reactions to it.

POLITICAL EXPANSION OF THE PURITAN COVENANT

American social and political organization has its origins in the seventeenth-century Puritan ideal of a covenant as a voluntary asso-ciation of qualified saints. The Elect few whom God chose to save from the brimstone entered first into an "invisible covenant" with the Almighty, receiving precious assurance of salvation in return for a pledge to follow God's laws and to actively work for the fulfillment of His will on earth. As part of their obligations to God's service, His Elect extended their private agreements with Him into two further compacts in which they jointly agreed to live together under the laws of God and according to His purposes. The "visible" or church covenant forged brotherly ties and obligations by which the saints vowed to be "knitt together in this worke as one man ... always having before our eyes our Commission and Community,"[7] and established an ecclesiastical authority to which they subjected them-selves. The civil covenant created and empowered government to enforce the godly terms on which their community was based. Church discipline alone might be sufficient to keep the Elect walking the paths of righteousness, but governmental force was needed to restrain and punish the inherent sinfulness of unregenerates. The religious com-munity thus embraced the political one into a theocratic framework.

In every respect, the Puritan covenants were thought to be entirely voluntary. Even unregenerate residents, while they were not parties to the covenant and could not be trusted with the right to vote or hold public office, were considered at liberty to either obey the divinely inspired laws or to live elsewhere.[8] God would coerce none into His service. However, once His Elect had voluntarily pledged their assent to the invisible and social covenants, they were personally and collectively bound by and responsible for upholding their terms. The moral duty of the Elect was thus to uphold the orthodoxy to which they had agreed. At bottom, therefore, Puritan social organization rested upon ideological consensus and active conformity.

The corollary of this consensual unity and commitment to orthodoxy was the Puritans' well known intolerance of any differences they considered threatening or even contrary to the terms of their compacts. In their covenant, as one of its most perceptive analysis put it, inhered "the tribalization of the Puritan spirit," which permitted "no diversity of opinion ... within the tribe."[9] Thus, just as they screened out and rejected any unworthy applicants for church members,[10] so they relied upon their civil magistrates to "not open the Gates for all sorts" but to purge from the community "all the sowre Leven of unsound doctrine."[11] John Winthrop's defense of an Order of the Court that was designed to ensure ideological hegemony within the community reveals both the consensual and exclusive features of the covenant. Since "no man hath right to come into us etc. without our consent," he wrote, " ... then we may lawfully refuse to receive such whose dispositions suite not with ours and whose society (we know) will be hurtful to us."[12] Several Quakers who tested Winthrop's resolve by repeatedly proselytizing in Massachusetts Bay were forcefully banished and, when they persisted, were reluctantly hanged.[13] The consensual community, both civil and religious, was upheld by the elimination of apostates.

Winthrop's theocracy, of course, did not endure. From the outset, secularizing tendencies that were inherent in Puritanism combined with the press of worldly interests to undermine the ability of religion ,to regulate and coordinate civil society. However, even after religion had lost its ability to dominate community life, the covenant ideal continued to provide the basic model for colonial social and political organization. For example, colonial townships, which soon replaced churches as the primary public institution, were based upon the covenant-derived notion of "townsmen together."[14] Until well into the eighteenth century, small towns, while no longer using sainthood as a criteria of admission, nonetheless continued to exercise their taken-for-granted right to prevent undesirables from establishing residence in the community. The first town covenant of Dedham was typical in its resolve "to keepe from us all such as ar contrarye minded. And receave onely such unto us as be such as may be probably of one hearte."[15] Anyone deemed undesirable after already having secured entry into a town was routinely "warned out" – i.e., instructed to leave immediately – and, if necessary, forcibly ejected.[16] Those unwilling or unable to conform to the local norms were privileged to express their deviance elsewhere.

Ultimately, the covenant framework of the Puritans was broadened beyond these early forms. As suggested by such political innovations as the pledge of allegiance and the slogan *"E Pluribus Unum,"* covenant ideals were eventually transmuted into political values and ideals, and, upon independence, invested into the institutional structures and ideological rationales of American government.[17] By this time, of course, membership in the new political covenant had been extended well beyond the tribal boundaries of the various religious establishments, and even beyond the colonial townships, until it embraced the entire national political community. Despite this extension, however, the restrictive as well as consensual features of the original religious covenant were retained, for the American political community through at least the half-century following the Revolutionary War consisted almost exclusively of white Protestants. This group – or more specifically, particular segments of this stratum – inherited from its Puritan ancestors an ideological self-conception that they were in some way a Chosen People, an Elect with a special destiny, the instrument of which would be the American state itself. The Constitution, the charter of their covenant, formalized both their status as a political Elect and their exclusive possession of the national covenant by extending full membership rights to them alone. Only white Protestant men "owned" the American covenant, and as a result they took for granted their right and ability to define its terms, invest their own values into its institutions, regulate its operations, and establish the requirements for entry and membership. America, like the Holy Commonwealth of its Puritan founders, was to be a democracy of the Elect alone.

The full implications of political election were not readily apparent in the late 1700s and early 1800s when the economy was still predominantly agrarian, blacks still slaves, Catholics and Jews still few in number, native Indians still generally considered savages, women still respectful of their place at home and hearth, and immigration from southern Europe and Asia not yet fully underway. Later, however, as these and other groups began to press their claims for political membership and for shares of available social resources, they set in motion major political conflicts which, while not yet fully resolved, have left an enormous and indelible imprint on American social life. Faced with the issues posed by an emerging pluralistic society, America's dominant white Protestant Elect responded in ways that continued to be informed by ideals, values, and conceptions whose origins lay in their religious heritages, and particularly in the conception of America as a covenantal association of the like-minded. The broader historical structure of American race, ethnic, religious, and gender relations is at least in part the product of the incomplete secularization and political transvaluation of indigenous Protestant ideals. The eventual organization of American diversity was forged in the on-going political and economic praxis of the national covenant.

To be sure, the influence of religious ideals and their secular extensions are by no means alone responsible for nor even the most important factors in affecting the character and structure of group relations in America. Clearly, the relationships between dominant and subordinate groups emerged through specific struggles over particular issues that were marked on all sides by concrete economic as well as ideal interests. These economic interests rather than ideals alone have most shaped and determined the contours of American diversity. Still, the background of values, images, and ideals possessed by a people constitute a primary conceptual resource which informs their attempts to organize and make sense of their world. These background ideas and images, or world view, normatively and conceptually "frame" the more specific struggles that are fought out over economic interests, thus providing them with guidance and organizing them into a general pattern.[18] In this sense, our interest is in the general influence exerted by religious ideas and their ideological transmutations as they gave structure and direction to the changing content, structure, and implementation of American conceptions of diversity.

IDEOLOGICAL TERMS OF THE AMERICAN COVENANT: THE NATIONAL FAITH

Americanism was and perhaps still is a creed in a way that Britishism or Frenchism is not. As Tocqueville observed, the American republic exists "without contention, opposition, argument, or proof, being based on a tacit agreement and a sort of *consensus universalis*."[19] On this point, Tocqueville was only lending his greater eloquence to a point also recognized by many others: that for roughly a century after gaining independence, American political and social order rested to a significant and perhaps unique degree upon a self-conscious ideological consensus, or at least upon the majority's fervent belief that such a consensus *should* exist.[20]

In part, the very youth of the "First New Nation" contributed to the majority's insistence upon an ideological affirmation of Americanism. Composed of immigrants from throughout northern Europe and therefore lacking a common cultural past, ancient traditions, or other broad primordial loyalties, the young nation possessed no other cohesive forces that could be tapped as a basis for social order. In part also, its decentralized political and other institutional authority intensified the need for unity on other, ideological grounds. Even the rough equality of the original settlers may have contributed to the ideological consensus by enhancing the authority of public opinion,[21] for, without common traditions, each looked to the other for moral confirmation of one's righteousness. America was a "lonely crowd" from the very beginning.[22]

However, it was the covenant ideals that had been partly secularized and extended into central features of the operating philosophy of American government that made the broadest and most positive contribution to the ideological underpinnings of social and political order. Like the covenants of its Puritan founders, America was presumed to rest upon a voluntary allegiance to its basic political principles, which all were responsible for upholding.[23] The nation was founded upon a creed that, uniquely in America, preceded the establishment of government. Largely as a result, American nationalism has been committed far less to a territorial definition than to America as the embodiment of a national faith.

By the closing decades of the eighteenth century, when the political covenant was formally constituted, the terms of that faith were no longer strictly religious, even though Protestantism remained one of its central features. In the 1740s, the religious enthusiasm of the Great Awakening had undermined the authority and tribal boundaries of the religious establishments and extended a more generic set of religious beliefs and values throughout the colonies, thereby furnishing an initial source of national unity.[24] Even a century later it was still obvious to such foreign observers as Tocqueville and James Bryce that Christianity (by which they meant Protestantism), while not an established religion, nonetheless "reigned without obstacles, by universal consent."[25] By then, however, Protestantism no longer reigned alone, for it had been joined in the American orthodoxy by the republican ideology on which the political covenant was officially founded, as expressed in the Constitution. During the revolutionary and founding generations, such republican ideals as liberty, equality, popular sovereignty, the need for civic virtue, and commitment to the public good were elevated into revered features of the American creed.[26]

In terms of their contributions to America's cultural identity and nationalist faith, it is decisive that Protestantism and republicanism did not simply provide the terms of the ideological consensus on which America's social and political order rested, but they did so in a new combination, as an original ideological compound. These two ideologies were thoroughly intermeshed, forged together into a uniquely American ideological alloy, a conception of national identity, purpose, and destiny that was at once both sacred and secular.

That Protestantism and republicanism should be conflated into "Americanism" is neither surprising nor accidental, for republicanism is at least in part a secular derivative of Calvinist political theory.[27] Indeed, when Horace Bushnell observed in 1835 that "it was Protestantism in religion that created republicanism in government,"[28] he was only succinctly stating a widely shared understanding. But more important to America's Protestant-republican synthesis than the kinship of its constituent ideologies were the casuistic interpretations that located the Republic and its citizens within the larger context of Protestant millennialism and assigned the nation and its political community, its White Protestant Elect, a special role and destiny in sacred history. References to America as a New Israel and to the Puritans as a Chosen People were commonplace in the early colonial settlements. God had sifted the "choice grain" of Europe and sent it to purify His churches, conquer the wilderness, and build a Holy Commonwealth on earth.[29] During the Great Awakening, and particularly as a result of the millennialist expectations raised by its miracles of salvation, America began to appear even more important in God's plans. As Edwards and others interpreted it, America might well be the very seat of God's millennial Kingdom.[30] During the French and Indian Wars in the mid-1700s, the clergy began to view the nature of that Kingdom in terms that were partly political. The wars were interpreted as a cosmic contest between God and Satan. Since Satan's French Papist legions were committed to religious and political tyranny, and certainly sought to enslave God's champions, then surely liberty must be the cause of God.[31] This conception was confirmed again in the war of independence from Britain.[32] Liberty was thus elevated to a sacred status and identified with the Kingdom of God, which in turn was identified with the American Republic. As a result, God's Chosen People were now charged with a political rather than purely spiritual responsibility: to preserve and perhaps extend the sacred cause of liberty and its institutional embodiment, republican government, in order to usher in the millennial Kingdom. The Protestant Republic would be their instrument of world redemption.[33]

Such an awesome responsibility required but one duty of Americans: they had to keep the faith on which their political covenant was founded. Should Americans become lax in safeguarding that faith, their liberties, their republican institutions, and their historic destiny would all forfeited. "The last, best hope on earth," as Abraham Lincoln summarized America's promise, would go unfulfilled. In their awareness of this collective responsibility, Americans in the early nineteenth century were much like their Puritan ancestors, who were constantly instructed to be ever watchful of their brethren for signs of sinfulness and moral depravity, for a broken covenant with God would surely cause Him to "break out in wrathe...(and)... revenged of such a perjured people."[34] Countless Puritan jeremiads combined ominous threats of ruin and divine retribution with exhortations to moral and spiritual regeneration – in effect, a call for the Elect to reaffirm their covenants with God.[35] In the American political community, this sense of joint responsibility for upholding collective ideals not only continued to receive the traditional religious interpretation by the clergy,[36] but also found secular expression and support in republican ideology. Virtue alone – a secularized version of piety and righteousness – was thought to ensure the survival of a republic; corruption, including such secular sins as luxury, greed, and licentiousness, threatened its destruction. Accordingly, in political adaptations of the religious jeremiads, Americans were constantly exhorted to sustain their republican virtues, or else to lose their liberties to tyranny.[37] And the best guardian of republican virtue, most Americans agreed, again demonstrating the conflation of religious and political creeds, was the Protestant religion.[38]

The duty of Americans, then, much like that of the Puritans, was to maintain the consensual faith on which their unity was presumed to rest. This sense of collective responsibility with its combined religious and political supports, accounts not only for the intensity of

Americans' insistence on ideological conformity, but also for their historical sensitivity to any real or imagined threats to the ideological faith on which their political covenant was based.

YE OF LITTLE FAITH: IDEOLOGICAL HERESY IN AMERICA

Not only was it necessary for Americans to be vigilant against the erosion of their own religio-political faith, but they also had to be on guard against the Republic's enemies. Once the new nation was well established, the danger of foreign invasion seemed increasingly unlikely, but a democratic society offered many other opportunities to its foes. In the American mind, the *internal* subversion of its ideals, and thus of its historic promise, has appeared as a very real danger.

The fear of internal enemies, which has periodically swept through American society throughout its history, is due in part to the indistinctness of the American creed itself. The components of Americanism – such as the republican ideals of liberty, equality, and need for civic virtue, and commitment to the public good – have never lent themselves to precise definition. No less an authority than John Adams confirmed the ambiguous nature of republican ideals when, late in his life, he confessed that he had "never understood" what a republic was and that "no other man ever did or ever will."[39] Indeed, much of the political turmoil that took place during Adam's lifetime involved frequent and heated struggles over exactly what republicanism was to mean and how it was to be expressed in specific policies,[40] and it is possible to suggest that similar uncertainties have animated many of the political disputes that have arisen since. Ultimately, the very vagueness of its meaning probably made Americanism more widely acceptable as the national faith. But because Americanism cannot be easily defined in terms of what it is, it has often been defined in terms of what it is not – with reference to those who are presumed to be its enemies.

Since around 1830, the United States has witnessed several episodic waves of nativist reaction against perceived threats to the political covenant and its ideals by groups committed to a contrary or even hostile ideology. Catholics, Mormons, Freemasons, Jews and communists have all, indifferent times and places, been the targets of groups seeking to defend "native" American values, ideals, and institutions against the subversive influence of an alien creed. These "subversive" groups obviously have little in common with one another, either in creed or organization, and so would appear to constitute very different threats to Americanism. Moreover, neither the dangers they represented nor the responses they provoked were ever determined solely by perceived threats to the American faith. Quite diverse material interests were almost always also involved and frequently were paramount. Otherwise, given the relatively constant dominance of the Protestant-republican ideology, we might expect nativism to have been a permanent rather than sporadic feature of American history. However, despite all differences either in the nature of the subversive groups themselves or in the particular interests they challenged, nativists viewed each danger against the ideological backdrop of America's consensual faith, revealing the group in question to be a menace to the entire society rather than to just that portion whose interests it directly threatened. For this reason, the thrusts of nativist responses are remarkably similar throughout American history.[41]

To the nativist mind, for example, each subversive group, despite their many doctrinal differences, appeared to be the very antithesis of America's ideals, institutions, and mission. As one historian has suggested, these groups represented "an inverted image of Jacksonian democracy and the cult of the common man."[42] Not only, for example, was Catholicism a "false religion," but its hierarchical structure presented a clear challenge to America's civil liberties and republican institutions. Democracy and Catholicism, as Edward Beecher warned, "are diametrically opposed; one must and will exterminate the other."[43] The Mormon threat was portrayed in similar terms. As an autocrat, Brigham Young appeared to "outpope the Roman,"[44] while the practice of polygamy was both degrading to womankind[45] and subversive of the "proper" monogamous family. Masons were accused of creating "an empire of itself...that has its own laws paramount to all other laws, its altars and its priests exalted above the religion of the land."[46] "Our government cannot be continued," warned a speaker at the 1830 Anti-Masonic Convention, "without the active, strenuous and constant maintenance of principles directly opposed to those of free-masonry."[47] Jews also, though lacking a centralized ecclesiastical organization, were periodically accused of being disloyal to American ideals and institutions. In his anti-Semitic writings, for example, Henry Adams apparently found Jews to be the chief cause of the decline of everything good in his own American society.[48] Finally, while "godless" communism emerged as the gravest threat to America only in the twentieth century, its hostility to the

American Way was recognized as early as the 1880s. In 1884, an alarmed Richard Ely alerted Americans that communism forcefully "wages war against all that we hold most sacred, and...seeks to abolish those institutions which we hold to be of inestimable value both to the individual and to society."[49] His appraisal has hardly been altered in the subsequent history of American anti-communism. In every case, then, the subversive group is regarded as committed to ideals and practices that are, as nativists have so often called them, un-American.

A second similarity in nativist reactions to these very different groups suggests the "paranoid style" in American politics.[50] Each group was thought to be deliberately subversive of American institutions and ideals, even to the point of involvement in an organized conspiracy to undermine the state and divest Americans of their liberties. Anti-Catholic agitators, for example, were convinced that the Pope had set in motion a secret plot to conquer America for the Catholic faith, the result of which would be to end republican freedoms, establish political and ecclesiastical tyranny,[51] and deny America its historic destiny.[52] In sensationalist exposés, such nativist spokesmen as Samuel F. B. Morse and Lyman Beecher issued fervent warnings in the 1830s that the Pope's indoctrinated legions were already busy organizing to subvert the ballot and urged all liberty-loving Protestants to unite against Catholic schools and office-holders and against lenient immigration laws.[53] In the 1850s, a sharp increase in Catholic numbers and political participation sparked new fears of a Catholic conspiracy and inspired the formation of the Know-Nothing Party – a major political force at the time – to beat back the Roman threat.[54] Mormons were similarly "dazzled...with the vision of an earthly empire"[55] and, it seemed, were busily constructing it in the West. Likewise, in secret and arcane rituals, Masons swore allegiance "to laws not recognized by our constitution...laws cruel and abominable,"[56] and pledged to help fellow Masons rise politically by subverting the democratic process.[57] Perhaps the most grandiose conspiracy has been attributed to Jews. American anti-Semitism seems to have stemmed far less from religious sources than from the economic stereotype of the parasitic Shylock. Extreme but not uncommon versions of this stereotype described a vast, international Jewish conspiracy, the aim of which was to gain control of the economy and, through it, the state. Indeed, as Henry Ford and other prominent anti-Semites tirelessly charged, the Elders of Zion had launched an insidious plot to conquer the entire world.[58] Rural and small town folk newly subjected to the mysterious and uncontrollable vagaries of the national market seem to have been especially receptive to the specter of an ominous conspiracy of Jewish financiers in Eastern cities parasitically appropriating the fruits of their hard work.[59] Finally, the red scares of the twentieth century were largely inspired by a fear that well-organized communists were stealthily infiltrating American institutions, quietly seizing key positions, and gradually taking control of the government.[60] During the post-war Americanism of 1919–20, Attorney General A. Mitchell Palmer, who thought communism to be the corrupt creed of "criminal aliens,"[61] considered the threat of internal subversion serious enough to order the arrest and detention of thousands of suspicious aliens, over 200 of whom were subsequently deported.[62] The fear that communists were seeking to bury America from within intensified again during the Second World War and the Cold War years.

To the American nativist, members of these groups were often committed to their subversive principles not by voluntary and knowledgeable consent, but by ignorance, gullibility, and a false sense of loyalty. Frequently they were portrayed as the unwitting victims of a colossal hoax or mass delusion. Given all the information, nativists seemed to think, no rational human being would ever consciously choose tyranny over liberty or autocracy over republicanism. Catholics, for example, were typically portrayed as "too ignorant to act at all for themselves," the products of centuries of "habitual subjection" to priestly depotism.[63] Masons often were not aware of the injunctions to which they swore until it was too late.[64] And reminiscent of the "communist dupes" of the twentieth century, radical participants in the Haymarket Affair were described as "hypnotized ... by the plausible sophisms and the inflammatory writings of unscrupulous men bent on notoriety.... As boys are led astray by yellow-covered literature, these poor fools were crazed by Anarchistic vaporings."[65] To the nativist mind, the reliance of these groups upon the fear, superstition, and ignorance of their members partly accounted for their secretive nature. Not one of these groups would submit their aims and ideals to the test of open discussion, from which "real" Americans assumed truth would emerge.[66] In fact, the presumed insulation of these groups from the controlling force of public opinion – the sole moral arbiter in American society[67] – further fueled nativist suspicions of subversive conspiracies.

Finally, not only did nativists tend to view each subversive group in strikingly similar terms, shaping each into an almost identical Great

Enemy of American ideals, but clearly their reactions to these groups were greatly disproportionate to any real threat they posed. For example, what nativists were willing to believe about these groups – for example, that Catholic confessionals were routinely used for purposes of seduction, that Mormon divines had mastered the mysteries of Animal Magnetism, that nunneries were actually nothing more than "legalized brothels," etc.[68] – suggests very strong anxieties, uncertainties, and fears. The rhetorical excess to which the protectors of Americanism resorted in describing their foes – references to Masonry as a "blood-stained institution"[69] or to Jews as "Monstrous Shylocks"[70] are among the milder examples – appear to calmer minds as wildly imaginative and fanciful at best. And the lengths to which nativists sometimes went to repress their subversive enemies – the burning of Catholic churches and convents,[71] the massacre of Mormon families, unjust execution and harassment of communists, etc. – rank among the darker chapters in American history.

These typical features of the nativist reaction may be generally understood in terms of an aspect of social psychology that derives from America's covenant framework, and especially from its insistence that ideological consensus and conformity form the primary basis of political and social order. Precisely because American unity rests so heavily upon voluntary allegiance to its ideals, and because those ideals were acknowledged to be fragile and vulnerable to corruption, Americans were rarely able to attain the security of taking their ideals for granted. American nationalism has always been something of an artificial creed – or a genuine faith – in that it was assented to by conscious choice rather than being assumed unreflectively. It is surely this self-consciousness of belief, for example, that accounts for the "irritable patriotism" that so annoyed Tocqueville and other visitors to nineteenth century America. Lacking the secure taken-for-grantedness or authenticity of belief that comes only from long-standing habits of mind or from traditional usage, Americans in the 1830s felt "a duty to defend anything criticized there."[72] As this sort of self-conscious defensiveness indicates, Americans embraced their political faith with varying degrees of uncertainty, anxiety, and insecurity. In general, it is this insecurity or self-consciousness of belief that made America's dominant groups so sensitive to ideological heresy, and which enabled them to magnify even small challenges to their ideals into vast subversive conspiracies.

Thus considered, nativist opposition to "un-American" groups offered participants an opportunity to soothe their psychological anxiety and to gain a degree of moral certainty in American nationalism. Nativism sealed a secure sense of ideological commitment or unconditional loyalty by forging it in the heat of action. It also allowed Americans to affirm to themselves and others the fundamental rightness of their ideals. To denounce other groups for their un-American creeds was at the same time to assert the validity and authenticity of their own. In a sense, then, participation in nativist activities constituted a public demonstration or active testimonial of one's faith in the American Way, and therefore served as a kind of secular sanctification – a patriotic work that could be taken as a sign of one's own political Election. Nativism thus provided America's dominant groups with a way of gaining confidence in their own politically Elect status, with a psychological confirmation of their ideological self-conception. In general, these psychological factors suggest why all ideologically heretical groups, however different, were shaped by nativists into similar Great Enemies: the social-psychological functions of the Enemy were at least as important as any specific threat it posed to particular interests.

Finally, nativism supplied Americans with negative rites of social cohesion, which enabled them to collectively reaffirm and regenerate their own political ideals in opposition to those of their enemies, and thus to renew the bonds of their own unity. Indeed, it was only through the example of the Enemy, the negative image of Americanism, that those ideals could be made vivid and concrete. The existence of the Enemy gave substance to a creed that was not explicitly definable in its own terms. Hatred of the Enemy provided a focus for Americanism, and thus a focus for a community of believers, a unity of the secular self-righteous. Nativism constituted a social exaltation of the "native" values and ideals, and thus of the ideological consensus on which the political covenant was founded and on which American political and social order was presumed to rest.

None of these nativist reactions required any substantial alterations in the ideological or organizational terms of the political covenant. Catholics, Masons, Mormons, Jews, and communists all appeared, at various times, to pose direct threats to the underlying "faith" on which the political community was based, and the nativist reaction to these groups emerged from squarely within the traditions, rhetorics, and meanings of Protestant-republicanism. In the last third of the nineteenth century, however, as Darwinian notions grew more pervasive and influential, a different sort of challenge to the ideals and promise of America appeared increasingly ominous. In addition to the subversive conspiracies of ideological heretics, the mindless biological deficiencies of some groups now also threatened to undermine both the nation's sacred institutions and the politically Elect white Protestant groups who were responsible for their creation and maintenance. In response to this threat of biological un-Americanism, the nation's leading ideologists redefined the terms of their consensual faith. In effect, America's institutions and way of life were redefined as a racial responsibility. Political Election in the American covenant would now be claimed as the exclusive possession of the Anglo-Saxon "race."

American nativism continues to find political expression. During the period of America's claim to participate in the company of Europe's world empires, nativism took the form of white American supremacy over Filipinos, Cubans, Puerto Ricans, and Asiatics. After World War II, America's response to the alleged threat of communism led it to a claim of ideological superiority that downplayed racism in service to a politico-economic ethnocentrism. The end of the Cold War, acclaimed as a triumph of liberal capitalism over Marxist communism, re-opens the question of domestic nativism, which has found expression in the use of the "race card" in the Helms senatorial and Bush presidential campaigns of 1988, and most recently in the campaign rhetoric of Buchanan and Duke as they seek the Republican nomination for the 1992 presidential race. The collapse of America's great external enemy, the "Evil Empire" against which Americanism could be easily defined, again raises the issue of what Americanism is to mean, and of what form of political community will express it.

NOTES

1. Gunnar Myrdal, with the assistance of Richard Sterner and Arnold Rose, *An American Dilemma: The Negro Problem and Modern Democracy* (New York: Harper and Brothers, 1944), p. 3. Also see the discussion of Myrdal's work in Chapter IV of Stanford M. Lyman, *The Black American in Sociological Thought: A Failure of Perspective* (New York: Capricorn Books, 1972).
2. John P. Diggins, *The Lost Soul of American Politics: Virtue, Self-Interest, and the Foundations of Liberalism* (New York: Basic Books, 1984), has recently reasserted the primacy of Locke and of liberalism generally in influencing the construction of American government. Many contemporary

historians have questioned the judgment of previous generations of historians, who saw Locke as very nearly the only intellectual and ideological source for America's political founders, and have instead asserted the influence of the English Commonwealth tradition. Diggins disparages the influence of the latter in returning Locke to his former prominence, but he as well as some Commonwealth historians have tended to overlook some similarities between these two ideological sources, and have neglected the extent to which both ideological frameworks have parallels in the theology of indigenous American Puritanism. For example, see Michael W. Hughey, "The National Covenant: Protestantism and the Creation of the American State," *State, Culture, and Society*, Vol. 1, No. 1, Fall 1984; 113–156.

3.   The literature on the Commonwealth tradition and its influence on the American founders has grown vast over the past few decades. Some of the most important works in this literature include: Bernard Bailyn, *The Ideological Origins of the American Revolution* (Cambridge: Harvard University Press, 1967); Bailyn, *The Origins of American Politics* (New York: Vintage, 1968); Pauline Maier, *From Resistance to Revolution: Colonial Radicals and the Development of American Opposition to Britain, 1765–1776* (New York: Vintage, 1972); Pocock, J. G. A., "Machiavelli, Harrington, and English Political Ideologies in the Eighteenth Century," *William and Mary Quarterly*, 3rd Ser., 22 (1965); 549–83; Pocock, *The Machiavellian Moment: Florentine Political Thought and the Atlantic Republican Tradition* (Princeton, NJ: Princeton University Press, 1975); Caroline Robbins, *The Eighteenth Century Commonwealthman* (Cambridge: Harvard University Press, 1961); Gordon S. Wood, *The Creation of the American Republic, 1776–1787* (New York: Norton, 1969).

4.   See Hughey, *op. cit.* for a discussion of how the political ideas inherent in Puritanism found secular expression in the organization of American government.

5.   It may be that Myrdal's critique was so warmly received by the dominant culture with which he identified because it affirmed the higher authenticity of the ideal against the practices that contradicted it, thus absolving the dominant culture of responsibility and offering the hope of an ultimate solution. This hope has always prevented many Americans from accepting the full and intractable reality of the problem.

6.   The universalistic side of the American dilemma, Myrdal wrote, is defined by "the valuations preserved on the general plane which we shall call the 'American Creed,' where the American thinks, talks, and acts under the influence of high national and Christian precepts...." In Myrdal, *op. cit.*, p. xlvii.

7.   John Winthrop's "A Model of Christian Charity," from which this quote is taken, is generally regarded as the best articulation of the covenant ideal in the literature of American Puritanism. Winthrop's sermon is reprinted in Perry Miller and Thomas H. Johnson (eds.), *The Puritans: A Sourcebook of Their Writings* (New York: Harper and Row), Vol. 1, p. 198.

8. "I dare take upon me," Nathaniel Ward preached, "to be the Herauld of New-England so farre, as to proclaim to the world, in the name of our Colony, that all Familists, Antinomians, Anabaptists, and other Enthusiasts, shall have free Liberty to keep away from us, and such as will come to be gone as far as they can, the sooner the better.
    Secondly, I dare averre, that God doth no where in his word tolerated Christian States, to give Tolerations to such adversaries of his Truth, if they have power in their hands to suppress them." See Ward's "The Simple Cobler of Aggawam" in *ibid.*, p. 227.

9. Alan Simpson, *Puritanism in Old and New England* (Chicago: University of Chicago Press, 1955), p. 24.

10. Max Weber examined the institutional dynamics and implications of this screening process in his essay "The Protestant Sects and the Spirit of Capitalism," reprinted in Hans Gerth and C. Wright Mills (eds.), *From Max Weber* (New York: Oxford University Press, 1946). The specific criteria used to separate sheep from goats in New England is discussed by Edmund S. Morgan, *Visible Saints: The History of a Puritan Idea* (Ithaca: Cornell University Press, 1963), pp. 36–44.

11. J. Franklin Jameson (ed.), *Johnson's Wonder Working Providence, 1628–1651* (New York: Original Narratives of Early American History, 1910), pp. 28–32. Reprinted in Robert T. Handy (ed.), *Religion in the American Experience* (New York: Harper and Row, 1972), pp. 3–6.

12. John Winthrop, "A Declaration in Defense of an Order of Court Made in May, 1637." Reprinted in Edmund S. Morgan (ed.), *Puritan Political Ideas, 1558–1794* (Indianapolis: Bobbs-Merrill, 1965), pp. 144–149.

13. See Herbert W. Schneider, *The Puritan Mind* (Ann Arbor: University of Michigan Press, 1958), pp. 67–73.

14. See the excellent discussion by Michael Zuckerman, "The Social Context of Democracy in Massachusetts," *William and Mary Quarterly* 25, 3rd Series (October 1968), pp. 523–544. Also see his *Peaceable Kingdoms: New England Towns in the Eighteenth Century* (New York: Knopf, 1970).

15. Quoted in Zuckerman, 1968, *Ibid.*, p. 536.

16. Josiah Benton, *Warning Out in New England* (Boston: W. B. Clarke Company, 1911) provides the most comprehensive treatment of this practice, but some discussion of it is also found in Zuckerman, 1968, *op. cit.*

17. These connections are elaborated in Hughey, *op. cit.*

18. Max Weber's well known conception of this same idea is perhaps more elegant: "Not ideas, but material and ideal interests, directly govern men's conduct. Yet very frequently the 'world images' that have been created by 'ideas' have, like switchmen, determined the tracks along which action has been pushed by the dynamic of interest." See Weber's, "The Social Psychology of the World Religions" in Gerth and Mills, *op. cit.*, p. 280.

19. Alexis de Tocqueville, *Democracy in America* (Garden City, New York: Anchor, 1969), p. 398.

20. For example, James Fenimore Cooper, *Notions of the Americans, Vol. II* (New York: Frederick Ungar Publishing Co., pp. 108–109), avowed

that "I have never seen a nation so much alike in my life, as the people of the United States." Many contemporary historians have also recognized the broad agreement of post-revolutionary Americans on political principles. See, for example, John Higham, "Hanging Together: Divergent Unities in American History," *Journal of American History*, Vol. 61 (1974), pp. 5–28; Sidney Mead, "Abraham Lincoln's 'Last, Best Hope of Earth': The American Dream of Destiny and Democracy," *Church History*, XXII (March 1954), pp. 3–16; Sacvan Bercovitch, *The American Jeremiad* (Madison: University of Wisconsin Press, 1978); and Donald G. Mathews, "The Second Great Awakening as an Organizing Process, 1780–1830," *American Quarterly*. XXI (1969); pp. 23–43.

21. This, of course, is Tocqueville's, *op. cit.*, p. 435, argument. "In times of equality," he suggested, "men, being so like each other, have no confidence in others, but this same likeness leads them to place almost unlimited confidence in the judgment of the public. For they think it not unreasonable that, all having the same means of knowledge, truth will be found on the side of the majority."

22. David Riesman, *et al., The Lonely Crowd* (New Haven: Yale University Press, 1950).

23. It is perhaps partly due to this almost complete reliance on ideological conformity to preserve American unity that disputes between Federalists and Jeffersonians were so vituperative. The contending parties appear as factious sectarians who, while agreeing on most basic principles, are unable to tolerate deviations from what each perceives to be the True Faith on which the nation was presumed to be founded. See John Howe, Jr., "Republican Thought and the Political Violence of the 1790s." *American Quarterly* 19 (1967), pp. 147–165; and Richard Buel, Jr., *Securing the Revolution: Ideology in American Politics, 1789–1915* (Ithaca: Cornell University Press, 1972). To be sure, of course, neither the bitterness of their disputes nor the substantive issues over which they fought were entirely ideological. Vital political and economic interests were also at stake, for the struggle was ultimately to determine which faction would appropriate control of the political covenant.

24. On the unifying role of the Awakening, see Alan Heimert, *Religion and the American Mind: From the Great Awakening to the Revolution* (Cambridge: Harvard University Press, 1966), pp. 139–148; William McLoughlin, "The Role of Religion in the Revolution: Liberty of Conscience and Cultural Cohesion in the New Nation," in Stephen G. Kurtz and James H. Hutson (eds.), *Essays on the American Revolution* (Chapel Hill, NC: University of North Carolina Press, 1973), p. 198; H. Richard Niebuhr, *The Kingdom of God in America* (New York: Harper & Row, 1959), p. 126.

25. See James Bryce, *The American Commonwealth*, Vol. II (Philadelphia: J. D. Morris, 1906). The quotation is from Tocqueville, *op. cit.*, p. 292. Tocqueville's judgment, incidentally, was confirmed several times in the 19th century by the courts, the established arbiters of the political covenant. In 1811, Chief Justice Kent of the New York Supreme Court sustained the conviction of blasphemy against a man named

Ruggles on the grounds that "we are a Christian people, and the morality of the country is deeply engrafted upon Christianity." Cited in Mark De Wolfe Howe, *The Garden and the Wilderness: Religion and Government in American Constitutional History* (Chicago: University of Chicago Press, 1965), pp. 28–29. As late as 1892, Justice Brewer of the United States Supreme Court announced that "this is a Christian nation" (*Church of the Holy Trinity v. United States*, 143 U.S. 457, 471; 1892).

26. See Wood, *op. cit.*, 1969, Chapter 2.
27. Hughey, 1984.
28. Horace Bushnell, *Crisis of the Church* (Hartford, 1835). Quoted in J. R. Pole, *The Pursuit of Equality in American History* (Berkeley: University of California Press, 1978), p. 89. Also see William Gribbin, "Republican Religion and the American Churches in the Early National Period," *The Historian*, 35 (1972), pp. 61–74.
29. This is an obvious paraphrase of the famous passage in William Stoughton's election sermon: "God sifted a whole Nation that he might send choice Grain over into this wilderness." From "New England's True Interest" (1670), reprinted in Perry Miller and Thomas H. Johnson (eds.), *The Puritans: A Sourcebook of Their Writings* (New York: Harper and Row, 1963), 243–246.
30. Jonathan Edwards, "Some Thoughts Concerning the Present Revival of Religion in New England," in *The Works of President Edwards, IV* (New York: S. Converse, 1830), pp. 128–133. Relevant portions are also reprinted in Conrad Cherry (ed.), *God's New Israel* (Englewood Cliffs, NJ: Prentice-Hall, 1971), pp. 55–59.
31. Outstanding discussions of the casuistries by which the clergy incorporated liberty into the context of Protestant millenialism are contained in two works by Nathan O. Hatch: *The Sacred Cause of Liberty: Republican Thought and the Millennium in Revolutionary New England* (New Haven: Yale University Press, 1977); and "The Origins of Civil Millennialism in America: New England Clergymen, War With France, and the Revolution," *William and Mary Quarterly*, 31, 3rd Ser. (1974).
32. Ibid.
33. The secularization of Protestant millennialism into American nationalism is too well known and well documented to require greater elaboration here. See, for example, Ernest Lee Tuveson, *Redeemer Nation: The Idea of America's Millennial Role* (Chicago: University of Chicago Press, 1968); Hatch, 1977, *op. cit.*; Russel B. Nye, *The Almost Chosen People: Essays in the History of American Ideas*, (East Lansing, MI: Michigan State University Press, 1966); Yehoshua Arieli, *Individualism and Nationalism in American Ideology* (1964); James Maclear, "The Republic and the Millennium," in John H. Mulder and John F. Wilson (eds.), *Religion in American History: Interpretive Essays* (Englewood Cliffs, NJ: Prentice Hall, 1978); Christopher Beam, "Millennialism and American Nationalism, 1740–1800," *Journal of Presbyterian History*, Vol. 54 (1976).
34. Winthrop, "A Model of Christian Charity" (1630), reprinted in Miller and Johnson, *op. cit.*, p. 198.

35. On the Puritan jeremiad, see Perry Miller, *The New England Mind: From Colony to Province* (Cambridge: Belknap Press of Harvard University Press, 1953), especially Chapters 1 and 2. Sacvan Bercovitch, *op. cit.*, while differing with Miller on the nature of the jeremiad – regarding it to be an expression of optimism as much as lamentation – traces its political and cultural transformation.
36. See Gribben, *op. cit.*
37. John Adams captured both the covenant framework and sense of American responsibility in his defense of the Constitution. "The people of America," he wrote, "have now the best opportunity and the greatest trust in their hands that Providence ever committed to so small a number since the transgression of the first pair; if they betray their trust their guilt will merit even greater punishment than other nations have suffered and the indignation of Heaven." From Adams's *A Defense of the Constitutions of the United States of America (1787–1788)*, quoted in Bercovitch, *op. cit.*, p. 135.
38. That Protestantism alone could save the American people and preserve their republican institutions was a primary motivating sentiment behind the organized evangelical movements of the mid-nineteenth century. For a detailed discussion of these movements and their aims, see Peter Dobkin Hall, *The Organization of American Culture, 1700–1900: Private Institutions, Elites, and the Origins of American Nationality* (New York: New York University Press, 1984); Charles C. Cole, *The Social Ideas of the Northern Evangelists, 1820–1860* (New York: Octagon Books, 1954); Charles I. Foster, *An Errand of Mercy: The Evangelical United Front, 1790–1837* (Chapel Hill: University of North Carolina Press, 1960); Clifford S. Griffin, *Their Brothers' Keepers: Moral Stewardship in the United States*, 1800–1865 (New Brunswick, NJ: Rutgers University Press, 1960); Clifford S. Griffin, "Religious Benevolence as Social Control, 1815–1860," *Mississippi Valley Historical Review*, XLIV, 1857–1958, pp. 423–444; Lois Banner, "Religious Benevolence as Social Control: A Critique," *Journal of American History*, LX (June 1973), pp. 23–41; Richard Lyle Power, "A Crusade to Extend Yankee Culture, 1820–1865," *New England Quarterly*, XIII (1940), pp. 638–653; Timothy L. Smith, "Righteousness and Hope: Christian Holiness and the Millennial Vision in America, 1800–1900," *American Quarterly*, 31, 1 (Spring 1979), pp. 21–45.
39. Quoted in Wood, *op. cit.*, 1969, p. 48.
40. See John R. Howe, *op. cit.*
41. That nativism has in fact been a sporadic rather than permanent feature of American history is clearly demonstrated by historians of the subject. See, for example, Ray Alan Billington, *The Protestant Crusade, 1800–1860: A Study of the Origins of American Nativism* (Gloucester, MA: Peter Smith, 1973) for a concentration on anti-Catholicism. An excellent work that deals with all forms of American nativism is John Higham. *Strangers in the Land: Patterns of American Nativism, 1860–1925* (New York: Atheneum, 1978).

42.   See David Brion Davis, "Some Themes of Counter-Subversion: An Analysis of Anti-Masonic, Anti-Catholic, and Anti-Mormon Literature," *Mississippi Valley Historical Review*, XLVII (September 1960), p. 208. Davis's comments were made with reference only to Masons, Mormons, and Catholics, but they fit the stereotypes of Jews and communists equally well.

43.   Edward Beecher, *The Papal Conspiracy Exposed, and Protestantism Defended in the Light of Reason, History, and Scripture* (Boston, 1855), p. 29. Quoted in Davis, *Ibid.*, p. 212.

Lest these sentiments be regarded as quaint relics of a previous century or as merely the thoughts of an unenlightened moralist, consider the views of Talcott Parsons, writing in 1940:

". . . in general the Anglo-Saxon Protestant traditions supply the solidest foundations for this kind of loyalty [i.e., resistance to subversive influences] . . . [Those who do not possess] the strong Anglo-Saxon tradition of responsibility in the affairs of the community . . . are . . apt to be particularly pliable material in the hands of any strong leadership which is able to exploit their characteristics and position."

Parsons further suggested that some religions, such as Catholicism and Lutheranism, predispose their members toward disloyalty: Due to the "authoritarian element in the basic structure of the Catholic Church . . . individual self-reliance and valuation of freedom" could be weakened. Those with "Lutheran background . . . are apt to be partial to political authoritarianism and old-fashioned legitimist conservations." These comments are quoted from Parson's unpublished "Memorandum for Council on Democracy" by William Buxton, *Talcott Parsons and the Capitalist Nation-State* (Toronto: University of Toronto Press, 1975), p. 100. Also see Arthur J. Vidich, "State, Society and Calvinism: Parsons and Merton as Seen From Abroad," *The International Journal of Politics, Culture, and Society*, Vol. 2, No. 1 (Fall 1988), pp. 109–125.

44.   The comment is by Josiah Strong, *Our Country*. Edited by Jurgen Herbst (Cambridge, MA: Belknap Press of Harvard University Press, 1963), p. 109.

45.   This charge was also leveled at Catholicism and Masonry. See, for example, David Brion Davis, "Some Ideological Functions of Prejudice in Ante-Bellum America," *American Quarterly*, XV (Summer 1963).

46.   Speech by Samuel W. Dexter, *The Proceedings of the United States Anti-Masonic Convention* (New York, 1830). Reprinted in David Brion Davis (ed.), *The Fear of Conspiracy: Images of Un-American Subversion from the Revolution to the Present* (Ithaca: Cornell University Press, 1971), p. 9.

47.   Reprinted in Davis, *op. cit.*, 1971, p. 77.

48.   A good discussion of Adams's anti-Semitism may be found in Barbara Miller Solomon, *Ancestors and Immigrants: A Changing New England Tradition* (Chicago: University of Chicago Press, 1956), pp. 32–42. Many of Adams's anti-Semitic utterances can be found in his own *Letters of Henry Adams, 1892–1918*, edited by Worthington Chauncy Ford (Boston: Houghton Mifflin, 1938).

49. Richard Ely, "Recent Phases of Socialism in the United States," (1884), reprinted as "The Identification of America's True Enemy" in Davis, *op. cit.*, 1971, p. 166.

50. Richard Hofstadter, *The Paranoid Style in American Politics and Other Essays* (New York: Knopf, 1965).

51. A frequently raised and widely accepted argument in American through the nineteenth century was that political and ecclesiastical tyranny are complementary systems and that both constitute grave dangers to liberty. The best, and probably best-known, explication of this thesis is John Adams, "Dissertation on the Canon and the Feudal Law," in *The Works of John Adams*, Vol. 3, edited by Charles Francis Adams (Boston: Charles C. Little and James Brown, 1851).

52. On nativist fears of a Catholic conspiracy to conquer America, see Billington, *op. cit.*; also Lyman Beecher, "A Plea for the West," (1835); and W. J. H. Traynor, "The Aims and Methods of the 'A. P. A.' " (1894). Relevant portions of the Beecher and Traynor works are reprinted in Davis, *op. cit.*, 1971, pp. 85–94 and 180–187, respectively.

53. Samuel F. B. Morse, *Foreign Conspiracy Against the Liberties of the United States*, 6th edition (New York, 1844); relevant portions are also reprinted in Davis, *op. cit.*, 1971, pp. 94–99. Billington, *op. cit.*, provides some discussion of the anti-Catholicism of both Beecher and Morse.

54. Michael F. Holt, "The Politics of Impatience: The Origins of Know Nothingism," *Journal of American History*, IX (September 1973), pp. 309–331.

55. Strong, *op. cit.*, p. 109.

56. Speech of Samuel W. Dexter, *Proceedings of the United States Anti-Masonic Convention*, reprinted in Davis, *op. cit.*, 1971, p. 80.

57. From the *Proceedings of the Antimasonic Republican Convention of the State of Maine, Held at Hallowell, July 3rd, and 4th 1883* (Hallowell, ME (1834); reprinted in Davis, *op. cit.*, 1971, p. 84.

58. Such a conspiracy was routinely charged in the pages of Ford's *Dearborn Independent*. See the reprints of relevant portions of articles from the *Independent* in Davis, *op. cit.*, 1971, p. 228–238, 239–240.

59. See John Higham, "American Anti-Semitism Historically Reconsidered," in Charles Herbert Stembler, *et al.* (eds.), *Jews in the Mind of America* (New York: Basic Books, 1966), pp. 237–258. Considering the virulent anti-Semitism of *Posse Comitas* and other contemporary versions of radical populism, the argument apparently still holds true.

60. See *Investigation of Un-American Activities and Propaganda. Report of the Special Committee on Un-American Activities...* January 3, 1939 (Washington, 1939); also Martin Dies, *The Trojan Horse in America* (New York: Dodd, Mead & Co., 1940). Relevant Portions of each are reprinted in Davis, *op. cit.*, 1971, pp. 279–282 and 282–284, respectively.

61. A. Mitchell Palmer, "The Case Against the 'Reds'," *Forum* (February 1920), pp. 173–176. Reprinted in Davis, *op. cit.*, 1971, pp. 226–227.

62. Good discussions of the Palmer raids can be found in Robert K. Murray, *Red Scare: A Study in National Hysteria, 1919–1920* (Minneapolis: University of Minnesota Press, 1955); and Robert D. Warth,

"The Palmer Raids," *South Atlantic Quarterly*, XLVIII (1949), pp. 1–23.

63. Morse, *op. cit.*, reprinted in Davis, *op. cit.*, 1971, p. 76.
64. *Address of the United States Anti-Masonic Convention* (1830), reprinted in Davis, *op. cit.*, 1971, p. 76.
65. Michael J. Schaak, *Anarchy and Anarchists: A History of the Red Terror and the Socialist Revolution in America and Europe* (Chicago, 1889). Relevant portions reprinted in Davis, *op. cit.*, 1971, pp. 176–180.
66. Davis, *op. cit.*, 1960 and 1963, makes much of the refusal of these groups to submit to public opinion in his essays on nativism.
67. So confident were Americans in the late eighteenth and early nineteenth centuries that truth would ultimately triumph in open, public discussion that, as Wood suggests, public opinion "soon came to dominate all of American intellectual life." Although Wood does not note the connection, as the "transcendent consequence of many utterances, none of which deliberately created it," public opinion in effect replaced God's word as the highest moral authority in the secular, democratic state. See Gordon S. Wood, "The Democratization of the Mind in the American Revolution," in Library of Congress Symposia on the American Revolution, *Leadership in the American Revolution* (Washington, D.C.: Library of Congress, 1974), pp. 63–88.
68. All of these examples are documented in Davis, *op. cit.*, 1960.
69. Davis, *op. cit.*, 1971, p. 84.
70. Gordon Clark, *Shylock: As Banker, Bondholder, Corruptionist, Conspirator* (Washington, 1894). Relevant portions are reprinted in Davis, *op. cit.*, 1971, p. 196.
71. Billington, *op. cit.*, provides a good account of such event.
72. Tocqueville, *op. cit.*, p. 237.

6 The Race Question and Liberalism: Casuistries in American Constitutional Law

Stanford M. Lyman

In 1989, a highly placed figure in the United States Department of State put forward the thesis that history (in the Hegelian sense of that term) had come to an end. To Francis Fukuyama, deputy director of the State Department's policy planning staff and a former analyst for the RAND Corporation, the tide of recent events – for example, the proclaimed end of the Cold War, a burgeoning economic union in Western Europe, the pending reunification of Germany and the latter's incorporation into NATO, the deconstruction of communist states in Eastern Europe, President Gorbachev's proposals in behalf of "glasnost" and "perestroika" in the Soviet Union, a potential collapse of the USSR's political economy, and the possibility that that state's republican structure would disintegrate – served as incontrovertible evidence of the "triumph of the West, of the Western idea." Fukuyama not only proclaimed Clio's imminent apotheosis, but also reinterpreted the Hegelian perspective on history to buttress his argument.[1] One part of that argument focused on the current conditions affecting the status and opportunities of blacks and other minorities in the United States and their relation to Fukuyama's general, and generally sanguine, thesis. It is this aspect – admittedly a minor part of his presentation but an important issue in its own right – that is the subject of the present discussion.

According to Fukuyama, "the century that began full of self-confidence in the ultimate triumph of Western liberal democracy seems at its close to be returning full circle to where it started: ... to an unbashed victory of economic and political liberalism."[2] Although Fukuyama readily concedes that this victory has not been accompanied by an equitable distribution of the material goods, social status, or political power among the several peoples making up the population of the United States, he remains generally sanguine about liberalism's beneficence. In particular, he admits that one minority group has been especially deprived: the African Americans. However, Fukuyama holds that this people suffers from an especially debilitating psychosocial heritage, and that that heritage derives from the ethos of a nonliberal, precapitalist era. Hence, he concludes, the plight of America's blacks is not chargeable either to liberalism's fundamental idea or to its present-day praxis. Whether the triumph of liberalism will eventually reward blacks is more or less a moot point for Fukuyama.

LIBERALISM: AS ECONOMY AND AS STATE FORMATION

"The state that emerges at the end of history," Fukuyama observes, "is liberal insofar as it recognizes and protects through a system of law man's universal right to freedom, and democratic insofar as it exists only with the consent of the governed."[3] Fukuyama derives both his interpretation of Hegelian historicism and his identification of liberal political economy as the ultimate form of the *polis* from the writings and life of the Russian-*émigré*-philosopher-turned-European-Economic-Community-bureaucrat, Alexandre Kojève (1902–68).[4] In a footnote to his essay, Fukuyama points out that Kojève at first had claimed that the "universal homogeneous state," that is, the liberal state formation that is supposed to emerge in Hegel's vision of history's cessation, had arisen in postwar Western Europe. But, as a dedicated American Hegelian, Fukuyama dismisses these countries as little more than "flabby, prosperous, self-satisfied, inward-looking, weak-willed states whose grandest project was nothing more heroic than the creation of the Common Market."[5] Fortunately, for Fukuyama's thesis, Kojève, in a later addendum to his study of Hegel, had "... identified the end of history with the postwar 'American way of life' toward which he thought the Soviet Union was moving as well."[6] In these pithy remarks are buried some of the pressing dilemmas and internal contradictions that accompany the alleged once and future triumph of liberalism in world history and in the United States.

Insofar as liberalism entails a concomitant economic system, that system is capitalism. In the Hegelian phenomenological tradition, Fukuyama notes, that system, like any other, is driven by ideas, or, to be more precise, by a single complex of ideas that has become so engrained as not only to undergird it, but also to make correlative and coordinate acts in support of it into unreflected-upon habits.[7] Other students of liberalism have made a similar argument. "Common to all contemporary classical liberals," writes the Oxford Fellow and Tutor in Politics at Jesus College, John Gray, is a vision of an ideal political economy: Its "goal [is] a form of limited government under the rule of law in which (aside from narrowly demarcated emergency provisions), the central economic powers – powers of taxation, spending and the issuance of money – are subject to rules no less stringent than those which protect personal liberties."[8] That goal, in turn, derives from liberalism's core idea, namely that "the individual is held to be the seat of moral worth."[9] However, it would seem that, if liberalism is to be fully secure in its triumph, the personal security and chances for advancement for each individual – irrespective of race, color, or previous condition of servitude – ought to be ensured. Failure in this aspect of its praxis would invite counter-ideological claims of conservatism or of socialism, liberalism's chief competitors, or of some other anti-individualist ideology (e.g., nationalism, chauvinism, irredentism, secessionism). These dissident ideologies might attract the allegiance – or arouse the passions – of the dissatisfied.

Fukuyama does not consider the potential attractiveness of conservatism, socialism, or racial nationalism for those who are currently consensually (or grudgingly) governed in accordance with his proclaimed liberalism triumphant. Indeed, insofar as non- or anti-liberal claimants couch their critiques of the new global *pax liberalis* in materialist terms, Fukuyama dismisses them out of hand: they are among those who fail "to understand that the roots of economic behavior lie in the realm of consciousness and culture... [and that failure, in turn,] leads to the common mistake of attributing material causes to phenomena that are essentially ideal in nature."[10] One need not quarrel with this phenomenological essentialism – (to which, incidentally, the present author subscribes) – to point out that there are structures of consciousness moving both the conservative and socialist alternatives to liberalism, and to take note of the fact that the other ideologies, for example, nationalism, racism, ethnochauvinism, that stand opposed to liberal capitalism's self-proclaimed triumph are rooted in what is probably the ultimate non-material secular idea – what Max Weber once referred to as the "mystic effects of a community of blood."[11] For more than three hundred years, black American intellectuals formulated alternative liberationist ideologies. These systems of thought and action fluctuated in popularity in direct relation to the degrees of felt hope (or futility) among the African American masses.

Although Fukuyama believes that the "two major challenges to liberalism" in the twentieth century have been fascism and communism, it is in fact the case that in the United States institutionalized racism has been far more pervasive than either of these essentially European ideologies. Moreover, racism, in both preachment and practice, opposes liberalism's promise of a universal individualism and an equal opportunity for all; indeed, it works to undermine the latter. Kojève, Fukuyama's mentor on the matter of the end of history, treated the American situation in a typically European – that is, class-oriented, rather than race-ridden – manner: "One can say," he wrote, "that, from a certain point of view, the United States has already attained the final stage of Marxist 'communism,' seeing that practically, all the members of a 'classless society' can from now on appropriate for themselves everything that seems good to them, without thereby working any more than their heart dictates."[12] Fukuyama shares much of Kojève's sanguine perception about America. He goes so far as to assert that "the class issue has actually been successfully resolved in the West."[13] Ultimately, he denies that the social and economic inequities that do continue to cause concern in the United States are fundamental challenges to either the liberal idea or to America's political economy. As Fukuyama sees the matter, "the root causes of economic inequality do not have to do with the underlying legal and social structure of our society, which remains fundamentally egalitarian and moderately redistributionist, so much as with the cultural and social characteristics of the groups that make it up, which are in turn, the historical legacy of pre-modern conditions." Although he does not tell us precisely what social and cultural characteristics are inimical to the achievement of equality, or how they have managed both to insinuate themselves into the hearts and minds of several generations of one group of Americans and to resist the liberal idea's tendency to overwhelm those counter-liberal elements that seek to halt its inevitable triumph, he does single out one racial group for notice in this regard: " ... black poverty in the United States is not the inherent product of liberalism, but is rather the 'legacy of slavery and racism' which persisted long after the formal abolition of slavery."[14]

Fukuyama's separation of the race question from both liberalism and the class struggle, his consignment of it to a resilient pre-modern heritage, and his inference that the legacy of slavery consists of certain dysfunctional social and cultural characteristics that cling to generation-after-generation of African Americans constitute a triple-line of defense against any challenge to his central claim: liberalism has triumphed over all its ideological opponents and that that triumph signals an end to history. Gertrude Himmelfarb, one of the critics of the Fukuyama thesis, took notice of this aspect of his argument, pointing out that even if the current forms of the race problem owe their origins to some ideational complex other than liberalism, they "continue to plague us and the solutions continue to evade us." Moreover, she goes on to observe that it is possible to argue that "black poverty, and the poverty of the underclass in general, is not the relic of an old problem but an entirely new problem . . ." Nevertheless, Himmelfarb observes, "it may be . . . subversive of liberal democracy; perhaps even more so because liberal democracy does not understand it, let alone know how to cope with it." And on this aspect of Fukuyama's argument, she concludes, "History has a habit of bequeathing to us disastrous legacies, bombs that can explode at any time and any place."[15]

However, valuable as it is, Himmelfarb's critique does not address certain larger aspects of Fukuyama's discussion of what once was called The Social Question. In this respect, it is worth observing that the race problem might indeed be related to the class struggle, but that relationship manifests itself in a form and moves according to a dynamic not imagined by conventional students of the subject. It was Friedrich Engels (1820–95) who observed in 1893 that no socialist revolution was likely to arise in America until and unless the race and nationality divisions within the working class could be overcome, permitting an interracial and inter-ethnic class consciousness to develop.[16] And, nearly fifty years later, it was the American socio- logist Robert E. Park (1864–1944) who argued that the class struggle in America would only begin after the race relations cycle – consecutive stages of which would occur as contact, competition, accommodation, and eventual assimilation – had completed itself.[17] However, as the researches of Herbert Hill and others have shown, racial and ethnic divisions were exacerbated and escalated by most of the elements of the labor movement. This resulted in the aggregate job eviction of blacks from their hard-won niches in the American occupational structure; their racially-based exclusion from craft and some industrial unions; their racial segregation within the few unions that would admit them. Taken as a whole, these events had the general effect of splitting off blacks, as well as Asians, Hispanics and Native Americans, from the supposedly emerging class-based interracial coalition.[18]

The claim from the Left that the class struggle would inevitably absorb and neutralize the racial conflict in America[19] has proved to be as evanescent as the assertion of nineteenth-century Liberals and their twentieth-century sociological epigoni that the introduction of a money economy would dissolve ethnic and racial sodalities in its rationalist-utilitarian flux.[20] America's often-proclaimed "exceptionalism" with respect to the Europe-originated class struggle might well have been purchased at the price of racial justice.

RACIAL CHARACTER AND AMERICAN SOCIAL STRUCTURE

Fukuyama's vague but powerful inference about how certain groups' dysfunctional social and cultural characteristics operate to interfere with liberalism's tendency to effect economic justice speaks to a one-sided analysis of the long-lasting vestiges of slavery and race discrimination. It suggests – or, to be fair, could be used to suggest – that the poverty so widespread in contemporary black America is a victim-precipitated phenomenon. Accordingly, the poverty found in today's American black communities could be explained by reference to a collective character defect that had insinuated itself within the *mentalité* of enslaved African Americans and been passed down through succeeding generations. This peculiar temperament, so it might be alleged, is antithetical to the individual effort required for success in a capitalist economy. Such a thesis has been enunciated by the neo-conservative black American economist, Thomas Sowell, who observes, "The slaves were kept dependent on the slave owners for rations of food or clothing and for the organization of their daily lives and living conditions... With many generations of discouragement of initiative and with little incentive to work any more than necessary to escape punishment, slaves developed foot-dragging, work-evading patterns that were to remain as a cultural legacy long after slavery itself disappeared." Sowell adds, "Duplicity and theft were also pervasive patterns among antebellum slaves, and these too remained long after slavery ended."[21] Presumably, indolence, deceitfulness, delinquency, and dependence are the character traits that have had a debilitating effect on black economic success.

A related point has been made more recently by an African American professor of English, Shelby Steele. Steele insists that the *angst* that he claims is so prevalent in the psyches of black

Americans is rooted in "an inferiority anxiety that makes the seizing of opportunity more risky for us, since setbacks and failures may seem to confirm inferiority."[22] Like Sowell – but without introducing the latter's implicit neo-Lamarckian argument in behalf of the intergenerational inheritance of an acquired character – Steele holds that the "most obvious and unarguable source" of the black's claim to their own innocence with respect to the racist crimes of America "is the victimization that blacks endured for centuries at the hands of a race that insisted on black inferiority as a means to its own innocence and power."[23] It is clear though unstated that Steele is referring to slavery when he speaks of victimization. However, like Fukuyama and Sowell, Steele associates slavery and its victimization of blacks with a pre-liberal political economy that quite properly could, ought to have been, and was challenged by the collective efforts of the advocates of liberalism and the Enlightenment. Moreover, he holds that in the current age of liberal democratic American capitalism, the politics of racially-based challenge and the encouragement of an active collective identity are no longer effective tools in the struggle to achieve ndividual mobility and social change. In their place, Steele, a true scion of Protestant Ethic liberalism, offers the strategy of bargaining and proposes a revival of individualistic self-assertion among African Americans.[24] "From this point on," he confidently asserts, "the race's advancement will come from the efforts of its individuals."[25]

There is, however, another legacy of the more than two-and-one-quarter centuries of African-American bondage, one that challenges Fukuyama's (and, even more, Sowell's and Steele's) sanguine image of liberal triumph and respecifies the purpose of egalitarian policy in a modern liberal capitalist regime. That legacy, it is argued, has been sedimented over many generations within the majority (i.e., white) element of the American population as racism. That legacy, moreover, was recognized by the leading members of both the Civil War and postwar congresses, who even before that bloody conflict had ended, sought to prevent racism from continuing to work its wicked will once institutionalized slavery had been abolished. Designated as the "badges," "indicia," and "incidents" of slavery,[26] this heritage of the era of bondage had been summed up by one dissenting Supreme Court justice – in the *Civil Rights Cases* [109 U.S. 3 (1883)] – as consisting in part in precisely the discriminatory practices that the Thirteenth Amendment to the United States Constitution had been devised to eradicate:

...I hold that since slavery...was the principal cause of the adoption of that amendment, and since it rested wholly upon the inferiority, as a race, of those held in bondage, their freedom necessarily involved immunity from, and protection against, all discrimination against them, because of their race, in respect of such civil rights as belong to freemen of other races.

Justice John M. Harlan went on to urge that in the Civil Rights Act of 1875 – which forbade racial segregation in transportation, inns, and theaters; required racial equality in the selection of juries; and directed enforcement of its provisions at the prohibited actions of both private individuals and corporations, (and which the majority of the Court had just declared to be an unconstitutional extension of the States' authority over a "private wrong") – the Congress had ordered "in effect, that since the nation has established universal freedom in this country, for all time, there shall be no discrimination, based merely upon race or color, in respect of the accommodations and advantages of public conveyances, inns, and places of public amusement." From Harlan's perspective – which appears to have been the point of view of both the post-1838 abolitionists as well as the more prominent framers of both the Civil War Amendments and subsequent supportive civil rights legislation[27] – the legacy of slavery consisted *not* (as Sowell, Steele, and, perhaps, Fukuyama would have it) in some characterological syndrome deposited in the hearts and minds of the Freedmen-and-women, but rather in the "burdens and disabilities" that a slavery-supportive racist ideology had inflicted and was still inflicting upon them. These burdens and difficulties, moreover, had not only not been removed by the Thirteenth Amendment's prohibition on slavery as an institution, but had been given nurturance by the newly established practices of racial segregation and color discrimination in public and business, as well as in private arenas of American life. "I am of the opinion," Harlan concluded, "that such discrimination practiced by corporations and individuals in the exercise of their public or quasi-public functions is a badge of servitude the imposition of which Congress may prevent, under its power, by appropriate legislation, to enforce the Thirteenth Amendment..."[28] Harlan's opinion was by way of a dissent from the Court's majority. Race discrimination by leave of law would continue for another seventy years in the United States.

In this brief discussion of the Harlan dissent in the *Civil Rights Cases* there are three points that serve to cast doubt upon Fukuyama's argument about the irrelevance of the race question for liberal capitalism's triumph. First, consistent with his Hegelian phenomenology, the legacy of slavery and racism to which Fukuyama refers all too obliquely might be reconceptualized as an engrained idea. Indeed, as Justice Harlan seemed to be predicting, it is the lingering badge of servitude that public law, corporate policy, labor union practices, and individual conduct in America would fasten on to generations of descendants of the slave population – as well as on to their racial surrogates, Asians, Hispanics, and Native Americans[29] – in the form of hundreds of discriminatory procedures and practices, overt and covert, and in accordance with an ideology that serves the interests of white supremacy. As such, and as an institutionalized and activated ideology, racism would curtail, and in fact has restricted the realization of the ideals of liberal capitalism, subverting (but not altogether obliterating) their universalist and egalitarian advancement.

Second, insofar as liberal capitalist ideology encourages support for a *laissez-faire* orientation toward rectifying economic or social inequities, Harlan's dissent in the *Civil Rights Cases* (as well as his ringing dissent in *Plessy v. Ferguson*, 163 U.S. 537 [1896]) offers a challenging corrective: Governmental intervention, in the form of civil rights statutes and concomitant legislation that will enforce the desired universal freedoms, would appear to be necessary in order that a democratic and egalitarian society might put its much-vaunted ideals into practice. Removing the badges of slavery would seem to require laws, programs, and public policies that secure freedom and equality for all those peoples who are still suffering under the yoke of this allegedly premodern and anti-liberal legacy. A truly civil society might require more not less governmental intervention in behalf of its least favored minorities.

Third, it is worth noting that even if one accepts Fukuyama's claim that a pre-modern or anti-liberal heritage from America's slave era affects contemporary black Americans' abilities to participate effectively, (i.e., successfully in a material sense) in a modern capitalist economy, there still remains the question whether the extant economic system of the United States is to be equated uncritically with productive efficiency, a positive work ethic, a democratic polity, and moral progress. From their statements on the matter alluded to in the previous discussion – and from Sowell's extensive writings on race and economics[30] – it would appear that Fukuyama, Steele, and Sowell subscribe to the functionalist thesis that links an undesirable political economy with an inefficient labor system and ties both to a degradation of human worth. Thus, Sowell makes much of the fact that the classical economists opposed slavery on both moral and economic grounds, noting that its most noticeable feature was the "absence of the incentives of self-interest by the worker."[31] Sowell insists that slavery was not only debilitating to the slave population's sense of individual self-worth but also conducive to the development of pro- fligate and unproductive habits, even when – especially when – mas- ters offered economic rewards that threatened to raise efficiency or productivity norms.[32] It is this claim – about the relationship of work norms to efficiency and morality – that links liberal capitalism to the unresolved race problem.

The claim that slavery was both morally reprehensible and econo- mically unprofitable is directly put forward by Sowell,[33] and it is implied in Fukuyama's attempt to detach the causes of black poverty from both the ideology and the operations of free market capitalism. However, the entire question of such a linkage has been reopened by the debate over whether and what kind of relationship exists between black personality, the slave heritage, various systems of political economy, individual incentive, and moral worth. The debate had begun earlier[34] but was enlivened and given even greater emphasis by the publication in 1974 of a study that threatened to undermine the established beliefs connecting slavery to inefficiency and to contem- porary black attitudes toward work. In *Time on the Cross*, their remarkable re-analysis of the economics of slave labor, Robert W. Fogel and Stanley L. Engerman sought to show that the efficient and productive efforts of the enslaved blacks have been obscured from the attention they deserve by a paternalistic but racist mythology that continues to stigmatize them to the present day:

> For they were held on the cross not just by the chains of slavery but also by the spikes of racism ... The spikes are fashioned of myths that turned diligent and efficient workers into lazy loafers and bunglers, ... that turned those who struggled for self-improvement in the only way they could into "Uncle Toms."[35]

The claim that there existed an African American equivalent of the Protestant work ethic among the slaves, an ethic that would resonate both with pre-capitalist bondage and with a liberal capitalist concep- tion of America's eventual abolition of enforced labor, is not without both conservative and liberal critics. Indeed, it has been widely chal- lenged: by advocates of the thesis that the South's form of black bondage was the centerpiece of a system of seigneurial socialism,[36] administered by a plantation magistracy and justified by a claim of warrantable obligation[37] owed by recalcitrant heathens to their masters;[38] by revisionist historian Kenneth M. Stampp's claim that the whip, rather than any internalized attitude (except, perhaps, that of fear and dependency) made up the more likely explanation of the slaves' expenditure of effort;[39] and by a multi-disciplinary critique of the methodology employed in Fogel's and Engerman's cliometric analysis.[40] Much of the conclusion on this issue depends on still unresolved debates over what legacy, if any, comes down to today's blacks as a heritage of master-slave relations; of what effects manumission policies and practices had on Afro-American mores; of the extent and kind of familism among the slaves and its later effects; of the extent and degree to which African and American sociocultural values, attitudes, and religious outlooks interpenetrated one another; and whether resistance orientations that developed among slaves affected their descendants and helped shape a unique and intergenerational African American personality and outlook.[41]

Of particular importance with regard to the latter point is Stanley Elkins' assertion that the "Sambo" characterology so commonly attributed to black slaves in the nineteenth century – an epithet that described slaves as typically lazy, shiftless, mischievous, and superstitious – was not a stereotype but an institutionally introduced collective character disorder of a kind similar to that induced among inmates of Nazi Germany's concentration camps.[42] Critics of Elkins' thesis, on the other hand, hold that slaves were neither efficient or good laborers nor victims of a personality disorder, but rather that their tomfoolery at work, their breakage and misuse of tools, their resistance to master-and-overseer authority, their runaways, and their outward appearances of abjection, sleepy-eyed indolence, superstitious fearfulness, as well as their more than two hundred armed revolts, constituted a calculated, multi-faceted, but less than perfectly coordinated campaign of opposition to the slave system.[43]

In replying to his host of critics, Fogel may not have satisfied all of their complaints, but for our purposes it is significant that he raised the question of functional linkage that has so long been taken for granted in western social science and which is central to both the substance and the epistemology of Sowell's, Steele's, and Fukuyama's arguments.[44]

It is as a part of the Occident's transvalued Protestant heritage, Fogel has recently observed, that a myth about slavery, ethics, personality, and political economy had emerged – first, to assuage the disappointment among certain overly sanguine abolitionists, and, later, to become sedimented in the latent morality underlying conventional theories of Western socio-economic development. Fogel writes: "The tenacity with which abolitionists clung to the contention that emancipation was bringing prosperity ... strongly suggests that they were swayed by a theory which told them that their expectation of prosperity had to be correct ..." According to this theory, or, as Fogel corrects himself, to the theological proposition that served as its *a priori* starting point, "... divine Providence rewarded virtue and punished evil." That proposition, he goes on to observe, is not only still prominent in the belief system of contemporary Protestant evangelicals, but also is more significantly employed in a secularized version by twentieth-century philosophers, historians, and social scientists. This "optimistic theory implies that immoral economic systems cannot be productive, for that would reward evil, and moral systems cannot be unproductive, for that would punish virtue." Hence, subscribers to either the religious or secular variants of this Protestant thesis must insist on both the inefficiency of slavery's system of labor and the unprofitability of a slavocratic economy. By the same token, the free-market political economy that emerged after slavery must be seen to be simultaneously productive, prosperous, and just, a sign that divine Providence, or its secular surrogate, the moral cunning of history, rewards the triumph of Good over Evil in human affairs.

A corollary of this myth requires that evidence that would contradict its promise of a providential outcome be explained as epiphenomenal, accidental, or that it be attributable to extra-systemic or extra-theoretical causes. In the years immediately following Emancipation and the abolition of slavery, Fogel asserts, the failure of prosperity to follow upon such good deeds evoked accounts blaming the Southern planter class, whose unreconstructed members, it was urged, were unable or unwilling to adjust to the emerging free-market economy. Later, when both economic success and social mobility continued to elude the Freedmen-and-women and their descendants, the causes of their plight were sought not in some basic defect in either the principles or actual operations of America's free-market capitalism but rather in a degradation of character, or will, or incentive, or sense of self-worth that was alleged to have undermined the black psyche. Conceived as a product of either an unfortunate legacy of slave mentality, or as a sign of constitutional inferiority, the low caste position of African Americans was regarded as an exception, and, in some cases, an obstacle to liberal free-market capitalism's march toward an ever-enlarging triumph over all other competing economic philosophies. From this perspective, it is not difficult to discern how Fukuyama's thesis, excepting black poverty from its potential of being charged against the liberal triumph, is but the latest variant of this species of argument.

Fogel holds that the "time has come to...cut the tie between economic success (or failure) and moral virtue (or evil)." Not only does he assert that a "quarter century of research on the economics of slavery...[demonstrates] that no such connection exists," but also he insists that the very idea that "systems that fail must be evil," while those that succeed must be virtuous must be set aside. In effect, in what might be seen as an American historian's introduction of the post-modern epistemology of deconstruction to that discipline, Fogel has veritably called for recognition of the separation of the Protestant ethic from the spirit of capitalism. "Slavery," he notes, "deserved to die despite its profitability and efficiency because it served an immoral end." Nevertheless, Fogel insists, it does not follow that "such technological advances [under free-market capitalism] as the blast furnace, electricity, and medical surgery...are intrinsically good...[E]ach has been used at various times for demonic ends." And, carrying Fogel's argument forward, we may observe – in criticism of Sowell, Steele, and Fukuyama – that the much-vaunted triumph of liberal capitalism does not carry with it any assurance of either continued prosperity or the inevitable furtherance of social justice. Indeed, the very fact that Fukuyama finds it necessary to blame black Americans for continuing to wear, however unwillingly, the badges of slavery indicates his own attempt to separate them and their problems from the liberal triumph.

AFFIRMATIVE ACTION: A MANDATE OF THE THIRTEENTH AMENDMENT

Whether valid or not, Fukuyama's assertion that the current socio-economic condition of blacks and other minorities is neither chargeable to nor any disconfirmation of the triumph of liberal capitalism in America does not disoblige American policymakers from their responsibility for ameliorating it. Indeed, as long ago as 1963, Seymour Martin Lipset urged,

> Unless whites are willing to take up their cause in order to force
> politicians, businessmen, labor organizations, and other relevant

groups to support the necessary measures, Negro inequality will remain a blot on the American claim to be democratic and will prevent foreigners from recognizing how real and significant is the national commitment to equalitarianism...[45]

Lipset attributed what he called "the low emphasis on achievement" in the measured accomplishments of African Americans to "their past, their weak family structure, and their segregated public schools, all adversely affect[ing] their capacity to gain from education."[46] To break what he called "this vicious cycle," Lipset called for a multi-faceted program that differed sharply from the *laissez-faire* attitude towards the problem evinced in more recent years by such critics as Sowell and Steele. As Lipset saw the matter, what was required was a policy that recognized the necessity of "treat[ing] the Negro *more than equally*... spend[ing] more money rather than equal amounts for Negro education... hav[ing] smaller classes with better teachers in predominantly Negro schools... enlarg[ing] the scope of counseling and recreation facilities available for Negro youth, and the like."[47] For far too long, Lipset asserted, "Americans have been under pressure either to deny the Negro's right to participate in the society, because he is an inferior, or to ignore his existence, to make him an 'invisible man.'"[48] Lipset abjured the notion of black inferiority and proposed making African Americans beneficiaries of a new and melioristic visibility.

Lipset seemed to be saying that the race-and-inequality question was sufficiently urgent to call for an unusual response – a concerted programmatic effort that would be so one-sided as to threaten the delicate balance of liberty and equality that had for so long prevailed in America's social institutions. That balance, he claimed, had been the basis for stability in the midst of the many social and economic changes that had taken place in the United States since the time of the American Revolution.[49] But, though he acknowledged the truth of Gunnar Myrdal's thesis that "even men who have strong prejudices against Negroes must assent publicly to their rights," Lipset insisted that the "pace is all too slow; the poison of anti-Negro prejudice is a part of American culture, and almost all white Americans have it, to a greater or lesser degree."[50] Undoing the process of dynamic equilibrium to resolve the inequities in American society seemed worth the risk. Indeed, Lipset then held to the position that assuring equal opportunity to blacks was both a "moral responsibility" of the white community and a matter that would require like-minded whites and blacks to use "[e]qualitarian values...as political weapons."[51] However, as he went on to observe, "The forces making for elitism, for inequality, will seek, often successfully, to strengthen themselves." Although not without hope for its survival, Lipset in 1963 warned that "The American experiment might fail," and that its "fostering [of] economic growth and democracy under the aegis of equalitarian values," would not be likely to hold "out hope for the rest of the world" if its "prosperity, freedom, and equality...[continued to exist] for white men only."[52]

Lipset's suggestion about treating blacks "more than equally" did not receive widespread support from other sociologists, nor did it resonate with an apparently growing public disapproval[53] that by 1991 had made "special treatment" and the fear of "quotas" in hiring a basis for both a conservative backlash and a race-baiting electoral weapon.[54] By 1979, Lipset had come to the conclusion that, while "White Americans look favorably upon 'compensatory action,' since compensation for past discrimination is consistent with the egalitarian creed and essentially makes the conditions of competition 'fairer' without violating the notion of a competitive system...most Americans, including many blacks, oppose the notion of 'preferential treatment,' since such treatment precisely violates the notion of open and fair individual competition."[55] In great part, however, comprehension of this issue, like so many others affecting a resolution of the race question in America, is clouded by the confusions entailed in what Lipset rightly terms "notions" about the actual meaning of the concept "equality" and about the judiciary's original understanding of the intent and appropriate policies designed to abolish all vestiges of slavery in America and assure to all persons under the jurisdiction of the United States the equal protections of the law. That confusion is so widespread and pervasive as to distort virtually all discussions of the further extension of civil rights and to render controversies over those programs designed to effect racial justice in education and in the job market for select minorities beyond possibility of resolution.

A first step toward overcoming this confusion, a proper analysis of the real issues in this matter, requires acceptance of the United States Supreme Court's long-recognized thesis that a legislature's imposition of burdens, requirements, or benefits on a particular group, or aggregate of persons or things, that is, the lawmakers' irrevocable duty to take notice of the different kinds and aspects of elements in the social order that require their legislative attention, does not of itself violate the Fourteenth Amendment's command to the states that they make no law denying to any person under their jurisdiction the equal protections of the law. Although the matter is not without numerous problems of interpretation – for which, incidentally, the holdings of the Supreme Court in the 125 years since the Amendment was adopted constitute a virtually untapped treasure trove of sociological data for analysis – the general principle is that a classification that is made in a law in order to accomplish a legitimate public purpose and that treats all persons similarly situtated with respect to that purpose in a like manner is, unless held to be otherwise unreasonable or for some other reason *ultra vires*, worthy of Constitutional respect and judicial approval.[56] Employing this principle as an intellectual resource and a methodological tool, it is possible not only to show that Lipset's proposed program is not a request to treat the Negro more than equally, but also to overcome most of the objections to current proposals seeking to implement affirmative action. Once they have become recognized as a legitimate means for accomplishing a goal of America's public philosophy, programs and policies of affirmative action could be recommended as one legitimate way to begin to obey the Thirteenth Amendment's command that America remove once and for all the ignominious badges of slavery that still stigmatize a portion of its people. Legitimation of such programs would go far to make Lipset's vision of America as the first nation to synthesize liberty and equality commensurate with Fukuyama's claim that Enlightenment liberalism has at last triumphed over all of its enemies.

In the past, selective legislation has not been held to be inconsistent with either the Fourteenth Amendment or the development of a civic-minded American industrial and corporate capitalism.[57] In this light, it should be recalled that Justice Oliver Wendell Holmes's oft-quoted dictum, namely, "The Fourteenth Amendment does not enact Mr. Herbert Spencer's Social Statics,"[58] was delivered in a rare dissent, one of only two cases out of 790 similar disputes adjudicated between 1889 and 1918, in which the Supreme Court's majority failed to uphold state-enacted regulatory statutes over particular kinds of businesses and various types of corporations.[59] In fact, recognition of much of the general principle we are here enunciating was made by the Court in 1884 in a case reviewing a San Francisco laundryman's challenge to the constitutionality of a municipal ordinance establishing a district within which laundries and wash-houses might be operated, requiring licensing after inspection of such places of business by public health authorities and fire-wardens, and setting the hours during which the washing and ironing of clothes would be prohibited. The Court first took notice of the city supervisors' claim that the ordinance in question had been enacted to protect against the outbreak of fire, but also considered the petitioner's assertion that his equal rights under the Constitution had been violated because no other type of business had been burdened by the law's hours of work requirements. On the latter point the Court observed:

> It may be a necessary measure of precaution in a city composed largely of wooden buildings like San Francisco, that occupations, in which fires are constantly required, should cease after certain hours at night until the following morning...

The Court went on to enunciate a more general principle under which it would declare that this regulation did not deprive the petitioner of his equal rights under the law:

> From the very necessities of society, legislation of a special character, having these objects in view, must often be had in certain districts, such as for draining marshes and irrigating arid plains. Special burdens are often necessary for general benefits – for supplying water, preventing fires, lighting districts, cleaning streets, opening parks, and many other objects. Regulations for these purposes may press with more or less weight upon one than upon another, but they are designed ... to promote ... the general good. Though in many respects special in their character, they do not furnish just ground of complaint if they operate alike upon all persons and property under the same circumstances and conditions.[60]

However, as Joseph Tussman and Jacobus tenBroek point out in their elaboration on the logic entailed in this thesis, the Court's reasoning here is incomplete; the test of a law's constitutionality with respect to equal protections requirements must turn on whether the classification made by the ordinance in question is one "which includes all persons who are similarly situated with respect to the purpose of the law."[61] A law's purpose, then, determines the classification to be made by it, that is, the particular variant of the public good to be accomplished by the law evokes, or, to be more exact, should evoke, a classification that will burden or benefit precisely that particular group or entity the regulation of whose conduct is related to the accomplishment of that good.

It is just this question, the one in which the demands for the equal protections of the law confront the necessity to determine the constitutionality of particularistic legislative classifications, that confounds the debate over affirmative action. Opponents of such programs decry the benefits that various affirmative action agreements would confer on African Americans, Asian Americans, Hispanic Americans, Native Americans, and women, treating these classifications in the same manner as late nineteenth-century progressive opponents of what was then called *laissez-faire* constitutionalism treated allegedly beneficial class legislation, that is, those laws and ordinances that supposedly gave undue support to the property rights and to the entrepreneurial classes at the expense of the working men and women and the poor. Calling programs that confer certain benefits on racial minorities and women instances of "racism in reverse," "reverse discrimination," or "affirmative discrimination," these critics seem to suggest that the very legislative act of singling out one group, or a cluster of groups, for special – and, in these instances, beneficial treatment – ought to be unconstitutional *ab initio*.[62] To this point, however, the Supreme Court has never assented. Indeed, it has often moved in quite a different direction. Justice Holmes's reasoning with respect to a lumber company's challenge to the state of South Dakota's anti-monopoly law, an ordinance that regulated the prices that might be fixed in the sale of commodities by a seller who operates in two places, but exempting one who sells in one establishment, goes far to establish the Constitutional right of a legislature to enact special legislation:

> The 14th Amendment does not prohibit legislation special in character ... If a class is deemed to present a conspicuous example of what the legislature seeks to prevent, the 14th amendment allows it to be dealt with, although otherwise and merely logically not distinguishable from others not embraced in the law.[63]

It could follow from an acceptance of this reasoning that if the economic, occupational and educational conditions affecting blacks, Asians, Hispanics, native Americans and women constitute a conspicuous example of what the legislature wishes to ameliorate in service to the general welfare of society, their receipt of special treatment would not of itself be fatal to a law's constitutionality or to the true understanding of equality.

However, in recognizing that the special class of entities singled out by a piece of legislation must be selected with an eye to accomplishing a legitimate public purpose, the Court has often warned against purposes unrelated to the public good and made clear its opposition to arbitrary, unreasonable, or capricious classifications. Classifications that impose a burden on racial minorities have been held to be especially suspect.[64] A fine example of such reasoning was presented in 1911, in an advisory opinion by the Supreme Judicial Court of Massachusetts, answering the legislature's query whether a statute proposed under the general police powers of the state to regulate health, morals, safety, and welfare, and "making it a criminal offense for any woman under the age of 21 years to enter a hotel or restaurant conducted by Chinese,... [etc.]" would be consistent with the equal protections clause of the Fourteenth Amendment. The Massachusetts justices pointed out that:

> The enactment of such legislation is not a proper exercise of the police power. It has no direct relation to the evil to be remedied. It forbids the entry of a young woman into the hotel or restaurant of a Chinese proprietor, even if it is a model of orderly and moral management, and it permits the entry of young women into a hotel or restaurant kept by an American, when it is known to be maintained in part for the promotion of immoral or criminal practices. The classification of hotels and restaurants into those that are open to young women and those that are closed to young women is not founded upon a difference that has any just or proper relation to the professed purpose of the classification... The fact that a man is white, or black, or yellow is not a just and constitutional ground for making certain conduct a crime in him, when it is treated as permissible and innocent in a person of a different color.[65]

With these principles of a public philosophy for equality in mind, let us examine the question of whether programs and plans, undertaken under state action, or by private corporations seeking to implement a civic interest – for example, agreements or contracts that provide for the awarding of contracts to minority entrepreneurs; that create set-aside seats in professional schools, postgraduate education, or job-training programs; that insure the employment of hitherto un- or under-represented elements in a particular labor force; that assure the entrance of hitherto disadvantaged members of the minority population into racially exclusive labor unions; or that guard against the inequities that unmodified seniority agreements ensure with respect to the laying off of newly-hired members of the minority labor force during a period of job retrenchment – are within the limits of the Fourteenth Amendment to the Constitution. Such programs as those just enumerated are not mere hypotheticals, but rather the reality of a variety of programs established in behalf of affirmative action and tested in the Supreme Court. Thus far, the Court's rulings on these matters have been inconclusive with respect to the general principles being questioned, on the one hand offering its belief in a vaguely defined idea of affirmative action as a policy, but, on the other, approving some and denying other of the various attempts by municipal authorities, state universities, business corporations, and minority public interest groups to implement particular forms of such a policy. What seems to be required is a firmer understanding of just what public purpose is being served by affirmative action programs and whether and to what extent the classifications of types of persons such programs make are reasonably related to that purpose.

It would not be inappropriate to justify affirmative action programs on the ground of fulfilling the mandate issued by the Congress that enacted the Thirteenth Amendment[66] and affirmed by Justice Harlan in his dissent in the *Civil Rights Cases*, namely, to remove the badges of slavery from all those to whom they are still affixed. The forms of race discrimination that derive their authority from the more than two centuries of involuntary servitude are the evil manifestation of such badges and are, hence, the proper objects of legislative attention with respect to effecting the public interest. Moreover, insofar as such legislation may be seen to be unwarranted interferences in free enterprise, namely, to restrict employers in the manner in which they use their property and laborers – and, thus, to be regarded as unwarranted interferences in the legitimate rights of entrepreneurs, employers, or other paragons of Enlightenment capitalism – it should be remembered that the Supreme Court long ago announced that

> Rights of property, like all other social and conventional rights, are subject to such reasonable limitations in their enjoyment as will prevent them from being injurious, and to such reasonable restraints and regulations established by law as the legislature, under the governing and controlling power vested in them by the Constitution, may think necessary and expedient.[67]

Moreover, because much affirmative action legislation affects the right of hitherto disadvantaged or deprived persons to be hired and promoted precisely because in the past their rights of this kind had been abridged on account of their race, color, creed, gender, or previous conditions of servitude, it is pertinent to take note of the fact that in 1880 a Federal District Court, in invalidating a California statute that prohibited the employment of any Chinese person in any corporation then existent or in future formed under the laws of that state, asserted:

> The right to labor is, of all others, after the right to live, the fundamental, inalienable right of man, wherever he may be permitted to be, of which he cannot be deprived, either under the guise of law or otherwise, except by usurpation and force.[68]

But, there is accumulating more and more evidence to the effect that it is precisely in the deprivation of the right to work – as well as in the ancillary and auxiliary right to an education[69] and to the opportunity to prepare oneself for the higher callings of expert jobs and professional careers[70] – that the post-Civil War local, state, and national governments engaged. After 1876, there was a retreat from the Reconstruction era's promise[71] to lift once and for all time the bar of race discrimination from all persons of color to whom it had and might in the future be applied. As a preeminent historian of that era, Kenneth Stampp has pointed out, after 1876, "The federal government had renounced responsibility for reconstruction, abandoned the Negro, and, in effect, invited southern white men to formulate their own program of political, social, and economic readjustment."[72]

That blacks – despite the post-Civil War granting of birthright citizenship to them if born in the United States and of the right to naturalization if not so born but of African nativity or African descent[73] – were still long denied most of the privileges and immunities that so many believed were attendant upon that citizenship is a matter of such well-known record that it need not detain us very long here.[74] The lasting import of the relevant section of Justice Taney's opinion in the *Dred Scott* case,[75] in the pithy summation of Professor Dudley O. McGovney, was that the slaves were not citizens at all and "that the free negroes were citizens, though without full rights."[76] In 1866, as if to reinforce *Dred Scott*, the Supreme Court observed that the conferral of citizenship on a person does not necessarily nor automatically confer upon him or her the full panoply of rights, privileges and immunities that some supposed are thereunto pertaining. "Citizenship," the Court announced, "has no necessary connection with the franchise of voting, eligibility to office, or indeed with any other rights, civil or political."[77]

For blacks, the era immediately following the Civil War seemed at first to portend the removal of all those burdens of life that had been their lot as slaves or free Negroes without full rights. But, as the historian John Hope Franklin summed up the matter, even "... the Reconstruction years were marked by half-hearted, light-hearted, inconclusive steps taken by the state and federal governments to introduce a semblance of racial equality in America. The feeble effort was an abject failure..." With the end of Reconstruction, "An uneasy peace settled over the South and North, as the old order of racial degradation, now buttressed by Supreme Court decisions and executive and legislative indifference and inactivity, continued to prevail."[78] Rather than being removed, the badges of slavery had been pinned ever more tightly on to the bodies of the Freedmen-and-women and their descendants, and, despite protests against them, would remain in place for nearly a century after Emancipation. Their newly-acquired citizenship was undermined by a veritable extension of the Taney doctrine of their status as less than equal citizens and by a growing use of color as a criterion of rights.

Citizenship, properly understood, should have entailed making the Freedmen-and-women and their descendants an equal part of the American national community. "Nationality," in turn, observed the legal scholar Dudley O. McGovney in 1911, "is the characteristic or status of a person by virtue of which he [or she] belongs to a particular state." McGovney went on to point out that the antonym of citizenship is "alienage," and that "Alienage is regarded as a disability, an incapacity."[79] Insofar as the state and federal laws, court decisions, and local ordinances disabused blacks of their civic and national rights, privileges, and immunities as citizens of the United States, while still recognizing them as *de jure* members of the body politic, they established them *de facto* in an oxymoronic status, namely, as, in effect, alien citizens. That status arose, in turn, from their having been reclassified in law as "colored persons." Nowhere was this ignominious status more fully realized than in the juridical support given to statutes establishing segregation and other limitations on civil rights for persons designated as persons of color.

In the majority decision delivered in *Plessy v. Ferguson* (1896), the Court had left the matter of determining what characteristics constituted the basis for a person's racial status up to the several states – the plaintiff Homer Adolphus Plessy having complained that Louisiana's railroad segregation statute had been inappropriately applied to him, a person of one-eighth Negro blood.[80] In 1910, after reviewing extensively the matter of race and color status in the law,[81] the District Court of Appeals of the District of Columbia, upheld a refusal by the superintendent of the Brookland School, a public school reserved for white pupils, to admit a young girl of one-sixteenth Negro blood, a girl who manifested no "ocular" sign of being black and who claimed to have always been treated and recognized as white by her neighbors and friends. The Court ruled that the popular meaning of the term "colored," as might be gleaned from consulting ordinary usages and dictionaries, must prevail in all such disputes over the matter, and that the term "as applied to persons or races is commonly understood to mean persons wholly or in part of negro blood or having any appreciable admixture thereof."[82]

But the Court went further in its quest to establish a permanent legal definition for the terms "Negro," "mulatto" and "colored," not only substituting a criterion of "blood" descent for one of visible epidermal pigmentation, but also insisting that the term "colored" was codeterminative with and limited to the term "Negro." In behalf of the latter thesis, Chief Justice Shapard quoted approvingly from the trial judge's opinion as to the meaning and scope of the term "colored":

> That the common use of the word throughout the United States is in nowise significant of mere complexion is quite definitely established by considering the universal habit of the people in their unalterable failure to apply it to the Indian, who is red, to the Mongolian, who is yellow, or to the Malay, who is brown; its application to one of these unfair complexions is not anytime to be heard; to those of negro blood alone it is ever found to be suited; and then, not depending for the propriety of its application upon a shade of particular blackness, but rather upon an admixture of a particular racial blood, the negro.[83]

What Justice Harlan had warned against in his dissents in the *Civil Rights Cases*, in *Plessy*, and, once again in 1908 in *Berea College v. Kentucky*[84] – that the command of the Thirteenth Amendment to protect the former slaves and their descendants from race discrimination, the badge of servitude, was being disobeyed and defied by acts of the legislatures, rulings of the lower courts, and by the majority votes of his brethren on the Supreme Court – seemed all too obvious.[85]

W. E. B. DuBois had predicted that the major problem of the twentieth century would be that of "the color line."[86] A few years later, Ray Stannard Baker traced out the contours of that color line as it meandered through the institutions of the United States.[87] In the midst of the Second World War, St Clair Drake and Horace Cayton followed that line as it had developed in the environs of Chicago.[88]

Later still, Herbert Blumer likened that demarcation to a bastion "like the Maginot Line," but one whose inner battlements would be more difficult to break than those of its military counterpart had proved to be.[89] A condition amounting to alienage – in McGovney's sense of the term – had become the law and praxis of the land as far as African Americans were concerned. So constrained was their situation that, in 1965 – eleven years after the Supreme Court had ruled that separate-but-equal school facilities were a violation of the Fourteenth Amendment – when he first took notice of their plight, Talcott Parsons sought to discover how "full citizenship for the Negro" might at last be effected.[90]

CITIZENSHIP, COLOR, AND EQUAL OPPORTUNITY

Contrary to the claims of either color-blind or class-oriented scholars, prejudices of race and culture have gone hand-in-hand with the development of America's modern industrial society. The light of Enlightenment Reason has not been so bright as to obliterate the less rational claims of "blood" and heritage, especially as they impinge on citizenship in the United States. The essentials of citizenship were denied to blacks for many years after their emancipation from slavery. Less obvious was how the establishment of a condition of permanent alienage for all those persons who were held to be neither "white" nor of "African nativity or descent" would bring together under a virtually common legal distinction persons whose ancestors had never been enslaved in America with those whose forebears had.

Chinese

That the alienating form of race discrimination that arose out of their historic condition as erstwhile enslaved persons would not be confined to the Freedmen-and-women and their descendants, or to the descendants of those Africans and African Americans who had always been free in America,[91] was, perhaps, first indicated in the vain attempt of an immigrant from China to become naturalized as a citizen of the United States in 1878. Nearly a half-century later, this extension was elaborated upon in the Supreme Court's sustaining of a Mississippi Court's ruling that the American-born citizen daughter of a Chinese alien was to be considered a "colored person" and, like Negroes, to be denied entrance to the public school set aside for white children in a county of that state.

In 1870, during the Congressional debate over revising the 1802 naturalization act that had limited United States citizenship to "Free white persons," Senator Charles Sumner had attempted to strike the word "white" from the new statute. He was unsuccessful. Opposition to his proposal turned on the assumption that if the term "white" were to be removed, the door would be open for Chinese immigrants to become citizens of the United States. The language of 16 Stat. 256, sec. 7 was changed to extend the right of naturalization to "aliens of African nativity and to persons of African descent," but the term "white" was retained to define all other eligibles.

Eight years later, Ah Yup, "a native and citizen of the empire of China, of the Mongolian race, presented a petition . . . praying that he be . . . admitted as a citizen of the United States." He was refused. The argument rejecting his petition was said to be consistent with anthropological science. According to the several admittedly disparate classifications of races that the Federal District Court was willing to accept – namely, that of Buffon as modified by Blumenbach, who claimed there were five of such; or that of Linnaeus, who allowed for the existence of four; or Cuvier, who only permitted three – only white persons belonged to the "Caucasian" or "European" race, while Chinese were of the "Mongolian" or "Asiatic" race. As neither "in popular language, in literature, nor in scientific nomenclature, do we ordinarily, if ever, find the words 'white person' used in a sense so comprehensive as to include an individual of the Mongolian race," and because it appeared to the Court that Congress had intended to exclude "Mongolians" from the right to naturalization, the Court concluded that "a native of China, of the Mongolian race, is not a white person within the meaning of the act of Congress."[92] This decision provided juridical legitimation to the burgeoning anti-Chinese movements in western America;[93] it also gave a judicial imprimatur to those municipal ordinances, state statutes, amendments to the California state constitution, and to earlier lower court decisions discriminating against Chinese. These decisions had already stripped California Chinese of the right to testify in court in cases involving white people,[94] at first expelled and then segregated Chinese children in the public schools,[95] limited their occupations,[96] and, with less success, attempted to inflict cruel and unusual punishments upon them.[97] In addition, anti-Chinese immigration legislation, not dissimilar from the pass laws that troubled the comings and goings of black slaves and the Freedmen-and-women subjected to the post-Emancipation "black codes,"[98] made Chinese aliens responsible to obtain and keep on their persons at all times a special certificate entitling them to enter, reside, and travel in the United States. Failure to have such a certificate would subject the person so found to deportation.[99] From 1882 to 1943 laborers and their wives and children from China were not only included in the category of those ineligible for naturalization,[100] but also were excluded from entry to the United States,[101] the prohibitions extending to their legitimate or illegitimate offspring, to persons only half-Chinese, and to Chinese aliens who had served in the United States armed forces.[102] As a result, the only other way by which persons of Chinese descent could acquire citizenship in the United States – birth on American soil – was narrowed considerably.[103]

As early as 1876 – that is, before passage of the Chinese Exclusion Act which, *inter alia* specifically denied citizenship to subjects of the Emperor of China – one Toy Long was dispossessed of his and his fellow Chinese workers' mining claim in Oregon in part because of a federal court's interpretation of his legal status as a "dreaded Chinaman."[104] Once denial of their right to naturalization had become part of the nation's law and of a revised treaty with China, Chinese who had somehow acquired United States citizenship in one of the several states discovered that their new status could be voided by a higher court; that their license to become an attorney-at-law could be withheld despite their qualification for it on the merits; that their US passport could be revoked; and that their re-entry to the United States could be denied after but a brief trip to their native land.[105] Years later, a federal district court ruled that not even the foreign-born though illegitimate son of a Chinese who was a lawful citizen of the United States could be admitted into the United States.[106] Until 1943, when a special act of Congress granted the subjects of America's ally in the war against Japan the right to become naturalized, Chinese aliens in the United States could not become United States citizens.[107]

Although the Court's opinion in *Wall v. Oyster* had stated that the term "colored" applied exclusively to Negroes, the noticeable presence of Chinese in the Southern states[108] – and the desire on the part of many Southern states to segregate the peoples of unknown racial origin from both whites and blacks[109] – prompted a reconsideration of the scope of that term. In 1925, the China-born mother of Martha Lum, "a minor of school age, of pure Chinese and Mongolian race, and...a native born citizen of the United States," filed a suit demanding that her daughter be admitted to Mississippi's Rosedale consolidated school, a public institution reserved for white children. Excluded from that school on the basis of her Chinese descent, Martha's mother's suit argued *inter alia* that since the term "colored" had been restricted to Negroes and to persons of some measure of Negro "blood," her American-born daughter could not be considered to be "colored" nor compelled to attend a school set aside for "colored" children. However, Mississippi's State Supreme Court, drawing upon an early California Supreme Court decision that barred black, mulatto, Indian, and Chinese testimony from admissibility in criminal trials,[110] as well as the decision in *Ah Yup* and in subsequent cases extending the denial of naturalization to immigrants from Japan[111] – and avoiding any mention of *Wall v. Oyster* – held "that the term 'colored persons' was not necessarily limited to negroes and those having an admixture of negro blood in their veins." The court went on to observe, that, because the people classified as "Mongolian" could not be included among those considered "white" but could, in accordance with Mississippi's miscegenation statute, maintain intimate social relations and intermarry with blacks, a person of Chinese descent would not be improperly treated when excluded from a white-only school and assigned to a school for "colored" children. As the court was careful to point out, "...the dominant purpose of...the Constitution of our state was to preserve the integrity and purity of the white race...[and] the segregation laws have been so shaped as to show by their terms that it was the white race that was intended to be separated from the other races."[112] Chinese had, in effect, been added to the peoples bearing the badges of a bygone slavery.[113]

Japanese

The denial of "white" status was extended to immigrants from Japan as well as from other parts of Asia and the Pacific islands. With that denial there ensued further restrictions – on their right to naturalization, to acquire land, to form corporations, to attend the school of one's choice, to marry across the color line, etc. These limitations on their life chances constituted a veritable consignment of them to the status then being visited upon the descendants of black slaves. The common feature defining their condition was "color," as that term was legally constructed by legislative enactments and court interpretations.

In 1891, the United States Supreme Court upheld the actions taken
to prevent the entry to the United States of Ms Nishimura Ekiu, a
young woman from Japan whose claim to be immigrating in order to
join her already domiciled husband was disbelieved. Ms Nishimura
was designated as a member of a class of persons ineligible to land
under an amendment to the immigration act – namely, "persons likely
to become a public charge" – but was not excluded on account of her
race or color.[114] Three years later, however, a federal district court
turned down Shebata Saito's application to become a United States
citizen on the ground that "The Japanese, like the Chinese, belong to
the Mongolian race... and that difference in color, conformation of
skull, structure and arrangement of hair, and the general contour of
the face are the marks which distinguish the various types." Unlike
later court decisions, this one held that "the color of the skin is
considered the most important criterion for the distinction of race."
In the *Saito* case, the Court distinguished human groups as either
"chocolate brown" (Australoid), "brown black" (Negroid), "yellow,"
(Mongoloid), "fair whites" (Xanthochroic), or "dark whites" (Mel-
anchroic). However, the court added that these differences "do not
exist in the case of each individual... but... are sufficiently distinct to
form the basis of well-recognized classification."[115] It was a classification, the court seemed to say, that could be used to distinguish those
ineligible to United States citizenship from those eligible.

After California and ten other states had passed laws prohibiting
aliens ineligible to citizenship in the United States from acquiring any
legal interest in agricultural land,[116] the question of how to determine
membership in the excluded and included categories would
become even more significant. With naturalization open only to free
white persons and persons of African descent or nativity, peoples
from Japan, Southeast Asia, South Asia, and Southwest Asia, as
well as from some other parts of the globe, became objects of juridical
scrutiny. A key statement on the matter was issued in a Supreme
Court decision of 1922, when the Court ruled that Takao Ozawa – a
lawfully admitted immigrant from Japan who, the Court readily conceded, had resided for two decades in the United States, graduated
from an American high school, attended the University of California,
been, together with his family, a regular churchgoer, and who regularly used the English language in his home as well as elsewhere – was
ineligible to be naturalized.[117] Ozawa's lawyers argued that the term
"white" should be read in the first instance solely to exclude Negroes
and Indians. But, regardless, they urged that Japanese be considered

"Caucasians," since there was ethnological evidence to indicate that they are descended from the Ainu[118] and thereby are racially distinguishable from the Chinese who are not.[119] The Court disagreed on every point, denying that the original intent of the first naturalization act had been to exclude only blacks and Native Americans; insisting "that the words 'white person' were meant to indicate only a person of what is popularly known as the Caucasian race"; disposing of Ozawa's claim to be "Caucasian" by a flat denial ("The appellant... is clearly of a race which is not Caucasion"); and introducing a new approach to determining the racial assignment of persons seeking naturalization in the United States:

> The effect of the conclusion that the words "white person" mean a Caucasian is not to establish a sharp line of demarcation between those who are entitled and those who are not entitled to naturalization, but rather a zone of more or less debatable ground outside of which, upon the one hand, are those clearly eligible, and, outside of which upon the other hand, are those clearly ineligible for citizenship. Individual cases falling within this zone must be determined as they arise from time to time by what this court has called, in another connection,... "the gradual process of judicial inclusion and exclusion."

When, in the *Dred Scott* case, Chief Justice Taney had excluded both free Negroes and black slaves from citizenship in the United States, he had made it clear that they had been excluded from "the people" that constituted the sovereign element in the republic.[120] Excluding those who were neither white nor of African nativity or descent – and forbidding them to intermarry with whites[121] – accomplished a similar objective. For example, Chinese and Japanese alien residents of California, and of the other states that imposed burdens on all those who were ineligible to naturalization, could not vote, serve on juries, acquire land, form corporations, or work at those professions that required United States citizenship as a prerequisite.[122] As a result, both peoples came to be confined to the residential areas and occupational niches that their alien status and the widespread color prejudice in America against Asiatics consigned them. Their children born on United States soil were United States citizens but all too often were made to bear the stigma attached to their racial ancestry and to their legally defined "color."[123] Japanese aliens did not receive the right to naturalization until 1952.[124]

Burmese, Koreans, Hawaiians

The "zone of more or less debatable ground" created by the Ozawa decision had, even before the Court's ruling, become a contested area on which peoples from East Asia, India, Southwest Asia, the Pacific islands, and certain elements of the population derived from lands south of the Rio Grande River would fight for decades for the right to become American citizens. Nothing reveals the embeddedness of race and color prejudice – as well as the triumph of ethnonational racism over Enlightenment liberal and meritocratic individualism – within the institutions of American peoplehood than the casuistries employed by the courts to deny various immigrant peoples the opportunities, privileges, and immunities that are a concomitant of United States citizenship.[125] Individuals representing at least sixteen different peoples repaired to the courts seeking naturalization by reason of their asserted membership in either the "white" race or, less often, as among those of "African nativity or African descent." Most would be disappointed in their quest.[126]

Among the peoples coming to the United States from parts of East Asia other than China or Japan, those from Burma[127] and Korea[128] – the latter applicant being a man who had been drafted into and served honorably in the United States army in 1918 – were also declared ineligible to naturalization on account of their membership in the "Mongolian," that is, non-white and non-African, race. And, as Messrs Kumagai, Bessho, Narasaki, and Toyota were each to discover, United States military service did not serve to lift the stigma of color from Japanese aliens either.[129] When in 1889, Kanaka Nian, an immigrant to the United States from the Kingdom of Hawaii, applied for naturalization after residing in the state of Utah for six years, his petition was rejected by that state's supreme court. As in *Ah Yup*, the court chose to review the findings of various scientific authorities on the classification of races – (i.e., Blumenbach, who, the Court said, had divided "the human family into five varieties, viz., the Caucasian, Mongolian, Ethiopian, Malay, and American"; Cuvier, as well as Jacquinot, who had "reduced the five classes of Blumenbach to three, viz., the Caucasian, Mongolian, and Ethiopian, treating the Malay and American as subdivisions of the Mongolian"; E. B. Tylor and Huxley, who had proposed a different division of humanity, namely, into "Australians, Negroes, Mongols, and Whites, dividing the whites into fair whites and the dark whites ... [and including among] the Mongols

...the Chinese, the Dyak Malays, and the Polynesians"; Van Rhyn, who, within the "Malayo-Polynesian Races and Languages, includes...the inhabitants of the Hawaiian islands"; Rev. J. F. Whitmee, who subdivided the "Polynesians into Nguto-Polynesians and Malayo-Polynesians, and among the latter places the Sandwich islanders"; and "the highest authorities...[who] class the Hawaiians among the Malay tribes") – and, without deciding definitively whether Mr Kanaka Nian or his countrymen were "Mongolians," "Mongols," "Polynesians," "Malayo-Polynesians" or merely among the peoples who made up the "Malay tribes," declared that since "No authority on such subjects classifies them with either the Caucasian or white races, or the Ethiopian or black races," neither he nor any other of "the Hawaiians" were entitled to citizenship in the United States.[130] Full and comprehensive citizenship was to be granted to those who could qualify as true members of what historian Alexander Saxton has recently designated as "the white republic."[131]

Armenians

If the courts of the United States were going to deny Burmese, Chinese, Japanese, Korean, and Hawaiian islanders the right to naturalization in the United States on account of the legal construction of their "color" status, there still remained the petitions for citizenship sent to them by the peoples of Southwest Asia, South-central Asia, Mexico, Puerto Rico, the Philippines, as well as those put forward by Amerindians and mixed bloods. In treating these, the courts further complicated the claims of law upon unfettered reason, unalloyed individualism, and true meritocracy. In what should have been taken as an instructive ruling of 1909, the Federal Circuit Court for the District of Massachusetts admitted four Armenians, Messrs Halladjian, Ekmakjian, Mouradian, and Bayentz, subjects of Ottoman Turkey, to citizenship in the United States over the objections of the United States attorney.[132] The latter had insisted that Armenians were not white and gone on to assert, "Without being able to define a white person, the average man in the street understands distinctly what it means, and would find no difficulty in assigning to the yellow race a Turk or Syrian with as much ease as he would bestow that designation on a Chinaman or a Korean."[133] However, indicating his keen distaste for the whole matter, Circuit

Judge Lowell would not accept the construction put by the US attorney on the terms "white," "European," or "race." In an exhaustive analysis of the etymology, ethnology, and history related to these terms, Judge Lowell found all of them to be ambiguous and unclear. With respect to the color term "white," the judge found it to have "been used in the federal and in the state statutes, in the publications of the United States, and in the classification of its inhabitants, to include all persons not otherwise classified; ... [and he took note of the fact that though] the word 'white' ... has been narrowed so as to exclude Chinese and Japanese in some instances, yet [it] still includes Armenians."[134]

However, even after this decision, not all would assent to the idea that Armenians were "white" and could, thence, be naturalized in the United States. In 1925, suit was brought in the District Court of Oregon to deny Cartozian, "a native of that part of the Turkish Empire known as Turkey in Asia, or Asia Minor, ... [a man] born in Sivas, which is located in Western Armenia, towards Anatolia, and ... of Armenian blood and race" the issuance of his certificate of naturalization in the United States.[135] Once again, the Oregon court examined the question of "whiteness" in American law. The court's decision reminded the US attorney that skin pigmentation could not be the definitive test of "color," and then undertook a summary of the ethnological evidence on Armenians, including in its hasty review, comments from Herodotus, Strabo, D. C. Brinton, H. F. B. Lynch, W. Z. Ripley, R. B. Dixon, A. C. Haddon, and the testimony presented in behalf of the petitioner by Franz Boas. The court also took note of the arguments set forth by the foreign secretary of the American Board of Foreign Missions, an already naturalized Armenian American attorney, an Armenian-born, Berlin-educated woman who had married an American citizen, and a sociologist who had studied intermarriage in New York City. All of these statements tended toward the court's conclusion that "Armenians in Asia Minor are of the Alpine stock, of European persuasion; ... that they are white persons, as commonly recognized in speech of common usage, and as popularly understood and interpreted by our forefathers, and by the community at large, ... and ... that they amalgamate readily with the white races, including the white people of the United States."[136] However, although Armenians had received the judiciary's imprimatur of "white," and thus been declared naturalizable, other groups would not be so fortunate.

Syrians

Syrians, also at that time subjects of Turkey, presented a more difficult challenge to the courts' construction of ethnoracial identity. In
1909, the federal district judge for the northern district of Georgia
allowed Costa George Najour – who hailed "from Mt. Lebanon, near
Beirut" and was "not particularly dark, and has none of the characteristics or appearance of the Mongolian race," and who had "the
appearance and characteristics of the Caucasian race" – to become a
citizen of the United States.[137] But, where other judges had occasionally acknowledged the ambiguities that arose when seeking to apply
the race-color classification system that had descended from Blumenbach and subsequent ethnologists, Judge Newman relied on a
"Quite... recent work... 'The World's People,' by Dr A. H. Keane"
to inform his decision that, following Keane, divided "the world's
people into four classes, the 'Negro or black, in the Sudan, South
Africa, and Oceania (Australasia); Mongol or yellow, in Central,
North, and East Asia; Amerinds (red or brown), in the New World;
and Caucasians (white and also dark), in North Africa, Europe,
Irania, India, Western Asia, and Polynesia.'" Because Keane, "unhe-
sitatingly places the Syrians in the Caucasian or white division,"
Judge Newman followed suit, only adding that the US attorney's
objection that Najour had been born "within the dominions of Turkey and was heretofore a subject of the Sultan of Turkey" could not
overcome the petitioner's claim to be white, lest "the extension of the
Turkish Empire over people unquestionably of the white race would
deprive them of the privilege of naturalization."[138]

One year later, one Mudarri (no first name is in the record), born in
Damascus, appeared before the same Massachusetts judge who had
admitted the petitioners in the Halladjian case to American citizenship. He too was granted citizenship, but Judge Lowell observed that

> Those who call themselves Syrians by race are probably of a blood
> more mixed than those who describe themselves as Armenians.
> However this may be, the older writers on ethnology are substan-
> tially agreed that Syrians are to be classed as of the Caucasian or
> white race. Modern writers on ethnology, who have departed from
> the ancient classification, are not agreed in substituting any
> other...[139]

In the face of these anomalies, Judge Lowell utilized the occasion of
Mudarri's case to challenge the basic racial dichotomy that excluded

"Mongolians" from citizenship and, in effect, he urged the federal government either to clarify or to abandon altogether the use of its constricted and confusing race and color classifications for naturalization:

> What may be called for want of a better name the Caucasian-Mongolian classification is not now held to be valid by any considerable body of ethnologists. To make naturalization depend upon this classification is to make an important result depend upon the application of an abandoned scientific theory, a course of proceeding which surely brings the law and its administration into disrepute... The court greatly hopes that an amendment of the statutes will make quite clear the meaning of the word "white"...[140]

In fact, however, abandonment of the color-race classification for naturalization would not occur until 1952.[141]

In the same year that Judge Lowell penned his critique of the terms of the naturalization statute, a federal district court in Oregon, while admitting a Syrian Maronite from the environs of Beirut to citizenship, found that the applicable "words 'free white persons' are devoid of ambiguity." Judge Wolverton saw no difficulty in rejecting the contention of the United States attorneys that those words should be defined to include "only those peoples of the white race who, at the time of the formation of the government, lived in Europe and were inured to European governmental institutions, or upon the American continent, and comprehended such only of the white races who, from tradition, teaching, and environment, would be predisposed toward our form of government, and thus readily assimilate with the people of the United States."[142] But, in a matter of three years, the issue was thrown open once more when in two cases involving Syrian petitioners before a federal district court in South Carolina, a judge denied their eligibility, ruling that the applicable definition of the words "free white persons" was that understanding which prevailed at the time of the adoption of the naturalization act of 1790, and that at that time they referred only to the peoples of Europe and their descendants considered to be white.[143]

In his rehearing of one of these matters involving Syrians, the *Dow* case, Judge Smith carried out one of the most elaborate disputations about the term "white persons": He inquired whether that term could refer to persons of the "Caucasian race" independent of their color; whether the term "Caucasian" included members of the "Semitic nation"; whether European Jews, having long been recognized as eligible for citizenship in the United States, were to be considerd "Semites" in the same sense as Syrians; and whether the history and position of Syrians, and especially "their connection through all time with the peoples to whom the Jewish and Christian peoples owe their religion, makes it inconceivable that the [naturalization] statute could have intended to exclude them."[144] To each of these queries, Judge Smith provided an answer that would lead him to exclude the Syrians from naturalization. Blumenbach's designation of the Caucasian race as encompassing the peoples of Europe, the Caucasus, Asia Minor, Western Asia (including Syria) and North Africa was held to be without either philological or ethnological foundation; the ethnolinguistic terms "Aryan" and "Indo-European" were not to be regarded as synonymous with "white persons" – lest the latter be forced to expel from their family the Magyars, the Finns, and the Turks, that is, speakers of Ugric and Turanian tongues, or the Basques, whose language was said to be unique unto itself; Syrians were not "Semites," but more likely the mixed-blood descendants of the ancient Hittites, "a Mongolic race," and, thus, "Asiatics in the sense that they are of Asian nativity and descent and are not Europeans"; European Jews are not "Semites" either, but "a professing Jew from Syria who was not of European nativity or descent would be as equally an Asiatic as the present [Syrian] applicant, and as such not within the terms of the statute"; a "dark complexioned present inhabitant of what formerly was ancient Phoenicia is not entitled to the inference that he must be of the race commonly known as the white race in 1790, merely because 2,000 years ago Judaea, a country whose inhabitants have since entirely changed, was the scene of the labor of one who proclaimed that He had come to save from spiritual destruction all mankind." In fine, Judge Smith declared that, "The broad fact remains that the European peoples taken as a whole are the fair skinned or light complexioned races of the world, and form the peoples generally referred to as 'white' and so classed since classification based on complexion was adopted."[145] Although Judge Smith was overruled – on the ground that the naturalization statute of 1873, revised in 1875, could not be interpreted in terms of the definitions understood in 1790 – the Circuit Court of Appeals declared Syrians among the group designated "white persons" because "the consensus of opinion at the time of the enactment of the statute now in force was that they were so closely related to their neighbors on the European side of the Mediterranean that they should be classed as white..."[146]

In addition, it is worth noting that Circuit Judge Woods complimen-
ted Judge Smith on his opinion in the matter, referring to it as
"supported with remarkable force and learning."[147]

Arabs

That a conflation of color, race, language, religion, and ethno-history
had come to confound the determination of what peoples might be
included within the classes eligible for naturalization is illustrated by
the outcomes and arguments in two cases before the district courts of
Massachusetts and Michigan in 1944. In the Massachusetts case,
petitioner Mohamed Mohriez, "an Arab born in Sanhy, Badan, Ara-
bia," a speaker of "Arabian [sic] as his native language" who had
arrived in the United States in 1921, sought naturalization in the
United States but was opposed by the local representative of the
Immigration and Naturalization Service (INS) on the ground that
he was not a "white person."[148] District Judge Schoonmaker rejected
the argument of the INS, pointing out that in accordance with previous court rulings and the Nationality Act of 1940,

> the question of whether one is a "free white person"...has
> now...to be settled "in accordance with the understanding of the
> common man" and turns on whether the petitioner is a member of
> one of the "races...inhabiting Europe or...living along the shores
> of the Mediterranean" or...perhaps, is a member of a race of
> "Asiatics whose long contiguity to European nations and assimila-
> tion with their culture has caused them to be thought of as of the
> same general characteristics."[149]

Mohriez should be placed with the population groups defined in the
latter two categories, according to Judge Schoonmaker. Philologi-
cally, and in common understanding, he asserted, "the Arab people
belong to that division of the white race speaking the Semitic languages...[so that both] the learned and the unlearned would compare the
Arabs with the Jews towards whose naturalization every American
Congress since the first has been avowedly sympathetic." Further, he
pointed to what "every schoolboy knows," namely, that "the Arabs
have at various times inhabited parts of Europe, lived along the
Mediterranean, been contiguous to European nations and been
assimilated culturally and otherwise, by them." Moreover, noting
the examples set by Avicenna and Averroes, as well as "the sciences
of algebra and medicine, the population and the architecture of Spain

and of Sicily, [and] the very words of the English language," Judge Schoonmaker urged how all of these "remind us as they would have reminded the Founding Fathers of the action and interaction of Arabic and non-Arabic elements of our culture," and he concluded "that even by the narrow criteria which were adopted in the opinions of Mr Justice Sutherland [in the *Ozawa* case and in *US v. Thind* discussed *infra*] the Arab passes muster as a white person."

Judge Schoonmaker added a dictum that persons lawfully admissible to the United States ought to be naturalizable, arguing that "It is contrary to our American creed to create a superior and inferior brand of permanent residents."[150] However, the fact was that such a hierarchy had already been created by the immigration and naturalization laws affecting persons deemed to be alien Asiatics – they could not be naturalized and, after 1923, could no longer be admitted to the United States, but their children born on American soil were United States citizens according to the principle of *jus soli*. It was this distinction that in some small measure had led Chief Justice Fuller together with Justice Harlan to dissent from the majority's ruling in *US v. Wong Kim Ark*, opposing a decision that granted automatic citizenship to American-born children of alien Chinese in part because it fostered just such a division within the Chinese population in America, but more because the two justices inferred that parents ineligible to United States citizenship would not be likely to bring up their children to be proper citizens of a country to which they themselves were permanently denied naturalization.[151] Judge Schoonmaker, who made no reference to *US v. Wong Kim Ark* in his decision in the *Mohriez* case, seemed to have its anomalies in mind when he concluded his *obiter dictum* in the latter proceeding by remarking favorably on the recent changes in the immigration and naturalization laws affecting Chinese, that is, the setting of a national quota of admissions and the granting to Chinese aliens of the right to apply for United States citizenship: " ... [W]e as a country have learned that policies of rigid exclusion are not only false to our professions of democratic liberalism but repugnant to our vital interests as a world power."[152]

However, if Judge Schoonmaker's liberal interpretation of the "white persons" phrase and his stated belief that "it is highly desirable that ... [the Nationality Act of 1940] should be interpreted so as to promote friendlier relations between the United States and other nations so as to fulfill the promise that we shall treat all men as created equal,"[153] seemed to indicate a fundamental change pending

in the outlook on race and color in citizenship matters, the decision of
Federal Judge Tuttle of the Eastern District Court of Michigan, in a
case decided in the same year involving the petition for naturalization
of a Yemeni Arab, illustrates how old, if confused, racialistic ideas
had remained as a thread running through the institutional fabric of
America. In the Michigan case, Mr Ahmed Hassan's petition for
naturalization was challenged, as in that of *Mohriez*, on the ground
that, as an Arab whose "skin was undisputedly dark brown in color"
and one who hailed from a region wherein "the extremely dark
complexion of petitioner's skin is typical of a majority of the
Arabians...which in fact is attributed to the intense heat and
the blazing sun of that area," he was not a "white person."[154] Judge
Tuttle fell back on earlier decisions to remind Mr Hassan that
although skin pigmentation was not to be regarded as decisive in
determining his legal status, "when an individual applying for citizenship has a skin of a different color than is usual for the members of
the group from which he claims to come, a strong burden of proof
then rests upon him to show by the usual measures of proving
genealogy that he is in fact a member of that group." Further,
Judge Tuttle also held to the earlier ruling, rejected in the final
proceeding of the *Dow* case, that the understanding of the lawmakers
and people of America in 1790 should prevail in determining the
definition and scope of the term "free white persons." In that regard,
he then found that "petitioner is an Arab and that Arabs are not
white persons within the meaning of the [Nationality] act."

Moreover, Judge Tuttle combined this restrictive understanding
with his view of how the religion and culture found among the
inhabitants of the Arabian peninsula would relate to that of Euro-
America: "Apart from the dark skin of the Arabs, it is well known
that they are a part of the Mohammedan world and that a wide gulf
separates their culture from that of the predominantly Christian peoples of Europe." Distinguishing the Hassan situation from that in the
Cartozian case, he noted that the latter involved Armenians, "a
Christian people living in an area close to the European border, who
have intermingled and intermarried with Europeans over a period of
centuries." Pointing to the evidence offered in *Cartozian* on the extent
of intermarriage among Armenian immigrants to America, Judge
Tuttle predicted that "It cannot be expected that as a class...[Arabs]
would readily intermarry with our population and be assimilated into
our civilization."[155] For doubtful cases, then, religious compatibility
and assimilation, the latter to be defined in accordance with a judge's

view of the likelihood and amount of amalgamation that would occur, would be crucial aspects of the test of whether an immigrant people were "white persons."[156]

East Indians

Armenians, Syrians, and Arabs were not the only peoples whose classification along the "white"/"Mongolian" dichotomy would become a matter of contradictory interpretations. Several representatives of the distinctive peoples of India who had migrated to and settled in various states of the United States also petitioned the courts for the right to become citizens. In some of these cases the matter was complicated by California's desire that no "Oriental" acquire agricultural land in the state[157] and by the American government's wish to offer no asylum to anti-colonial nationalists from India, who, it feared, might exploit their freedom and security in the first nation to throw off English colonial rule to mount a campaign to liberate what the British Empire considered the jewel in its imperial crown.[158] In the year 1909, in which *In Re Balsara*, an important case involving East Indians, was begun, only 337 "Asiatic" Indians were admitted to the United States, an enormous drop from the 1710 who had been admitted the previous year, or the 1782 who would be admitted in 1910. But the number excluded kept up a steady pace – 417 in 1907; 438 in 1908; 331 in 1909; 411 in 1910; 862 in 1911. The number deported – 9 in 1908; 1 in 1909; 4 in 1910; 36 in 1911; 20 in 1912; 32 in 1913 – speaks to a growing apprehension on the part of the American authorities.[159] In 1917, Congress enacted a new immigration law that prohibited the entry of laborers from any country behind the line of a newly demarcated "barred zone"; India was among the Asian countries behind that line.[160]

On May 28, 1909, Circuit Judge Lacombe of the Southern District of New York reluctantly conferred American citizenship on Bhicaji Franyi Balsara, a merchant from India, a Parsee who "appears to be a gentleman of high character and exceptional intelligence."[161] Judge Lacombe's reluctance stemmed from his belief that there "was much force in the argument that the Congress which framed the original act for naturalization of aliens... intended it to include only white persons belonging to those races whose emigrants had contributed to the building up on this continent of the community of people which declared itself a new nation...". and from his worry that if the phrase "free white persons" were to be broadened so as to include "all branches of the great race or family known to ethnologists as the Aryan, Indo-European, or Caucasian... it... [would] bring in, not only the Parsees,... which is probably the purest Aryan type, but also Afghans, Hindoos, Arabs, and Berbers."[162] Judge Lacombe granted Balsara's petition only on the publicly given assurance that the United States attorney would appeal his decision, and in the hope that the proceeding in a higher court would lead to "an authoritative interpretation" of the meaning of the terms indicating eligibility and ineligibility in the naturalization statute. The US attorney kept his promise, and the matter was carried to the Circuit Court of Appeals in 1910.

Both the District and Circuit Court decisions would exert a confusing hold on later cases. (Afghans presented a similar problem to the courts. A case involving one Abdullah Dolla – an Afghan born in Calcutta who had arrived in New York in 1894, resided in Savannah, Georgia, for twelve years, and had been awarded "white" status after a local court judge, noting Dolla's dark facial complexion and dark eyes, decided to examine the color of his skin under his shirt-covered arms and chest and determined that it was sufficiently fair to meet a "white" color standard – had been thrown out on appeal because of a technicality.[163] Eighteen years later, the petition of Feroz Din, described as a "typical Afghan and a native of Afghanistan" was rejected by the District Court of the Northern District of California on the grounds that he "is not a white person, nor of African nativity or descent," Judge Bourquin adding, "What ethnologists, anthropologists, and other so-called scientists may speculate and conjecture in respect to races and origins may interests the curious and convince the credulous, but is of no moment in arriving at the intent of Congress in the statute aforesaid."[164] In the *Balsara* case, the Circuit Court of Appeals decided the matter in behalf of the Parsee petitioner on five separate but not unrelated arguments. The court held that "The Parsees emigrated some 1,200 years ago from Persia into India and now live in the neighborhood of Bombay... [constituting] a settlement by themselves of intelligent and well-to-do persons, principally engaged in commerce, and are as distinct from the Hindus as are the English who dwell in India"; that a strict and literal construction of what the Congress of 1790 meant by the terms "free white persons" would require the court to exclude from citizenship Russians, Poles, Italians, Greeks and other Europeans who had not formed the basis of the original colonial populace; that Congress "probably had [had] principally in mind the exclusion of Africans, whether slave or free, and [Native American] Indians"; that those early "Congressmen certainly knew that there were white, yellow, black, red, and brown races"; and that, "Whether there is any pure white race and what peoples belong to it may involve nice discriminations,...for practical purposes there is no difficulty in saying that the Chinese, Japanese, and Malays and the American Indians do not belong to the white race...[while] in our opinion the Parsees do belong to the white race and the Circuit Court properly admitted Balsara to citizenship."[165]

However, neither the admission of Balsara to citizenship nor the distinction offered by the Circuit Court of Appeals to Parsees as opposed to Hindus secured for all time the naturalization of the former group. Twenty-nine years after Balsara had been granted his citizenship in the United States, the same Circuit Court of Appeals that had affirmed his naturalization rejected the petition of Rustom Dadabhoy Wadia, reversing the finding of the *Balsara* court and insisting that the understanding of the "common man," and the racial conceptions of the Congress of 1790 were to prevail in such matters.[166] Wadia had been born to Parsee parents in Bombay, India in 1899, emigrated to the United States in 1923, married Gladys Voorhees in 1928, and fathered two children with her. At the time of his application for citizenship he and his family were living on the Lower East Side of New York City; "his occupation was that of a life insurance agent and substitute teacher and in religion he was a follower of Zoroaster."

Judge Hand interpreted the *Balsara* decision to have held "that the words 'free white persons' conferred the privilege of naturalization upon members of the Caucasian race." Such a conferral could no longer be sustained, he ruled, because the United States Supreme Court had in 1923 denied the petition for citizenship of a Hindu while conceding that he was a "Caucasian."[167] The terms "free white persons" were to be interpreted as "common speech" and in accordance with the understandings of the "common man." So interpreted, Judge Hand went on, "A Parsee of a race which immigrated from Persia to India some 1,200 years ago, even though retaining, as is claimed, blood differing little, if any, from that of its original ancestors, can hardly be differentiated in the mind of the common man from that of the Hindus beside whom the Parsees have lived for 1,200 years." "Each stock is Caucasian," he admitted. "The language of each is of Aryan origin, but neither can properly be classed as 'white persons.'"

Judge Hand put a different construction on the historical understandings that should be accepted regarding the Congress of 1790.
Conceding that "at that time there was little or no thought of the
admission of immigrants who did not come from Great Britain,
Germany, Sweden, Norway, France or Holland," he slid over the
potentiality for limiting "free white persons" to emigrants from
those countries, adding, simply, "naturally, persons indigenous to
Spain, Italy, Russia and other European nations were regarded as
within the meaning of the words as soon as they sought to immi-
grate . . . " But, then, he quickly added, that this enlargement of the
white group had occurred "although some of their inhabitants were of
dark complexions and even in the case of certain Russians of a
Mongolian caste of countenance." Ultimately, admitting that "it is
not altogether safe to generalize," Judge Hand opined that "it may
fairly be said that members of races inhabiting Europe or living along
the shores of the Mediterranean are ordinarily to be classed as 'white
persons' [and that the] same thing may be true of some Asiatics whose
long contiguity to European nations and assimilation with their culture has caused them to be thought of as of the same general characteristics."[168] "Parsees" and "Hindus," however, were not to be
counted among those "Asiatics."

The citizenship of "Hindus" remained a matter of considerable
contention until 1946, when the bar to their immigration, naturalization, and right to acquire property, was lifted by Congressional passage of the Luce-Celler Bill.[169] Although a Washington court had
granted citizenship to Akhay Kumar Mozumdar in 1913[170] and a
California court had done the same to another East Indian in 1914
– and although by 1922 at least 69 East Indians had been admitted to
United States citizenship in 18 of the United States – the denial of
"white person" status to East Indian "Caucasians" in the case, *United
States v. Bhagat Singh Thind*, led to largely successful attempts to strip
those already naturalized of their citizenship and to enforce such
statutes as California's alien land law against them.[171] The *Thind*
case, following one year after that of *Ozawa*, provided the United
States Supreme Court with another opportunity to respond to the
requests of more than one federal district judge that it clarify the
meaning of such terms as "free white persons," "Caucasian," "Mongolian," and "Hindu" insofar as these words and phrases pertained to
the enforcement of the immigration and naturalization laws and the
rights obtaining to alien persons under the Constitution of the United
States.

In a 1917 decision, a district judge of the Federal Court of Eastern Pennsylvania had presented a remarkably ambivalent and confused tour through these terms before denying the petition for US citizenship of another "Hindu," Mr Sadar Bhagwag Singh, an "applicant [who] belongs to the race of people commonly known as Hindus,"[172] and one of the leaders of the anti-colonial Ghadar Party whom the US government had been seeking to deport.[173] Three years later, Judge Wolverton of the Federal District Court of Oregon granted the petition of Mr Bhagat Singh Thind, a "high caste Hindu born in Armitsar, Punjab, in the northwestern part of India," who had served six months in the United States army and been given an honorable discharge.[174] The district court judge passed lightly over Thind's possible involvement in the Ghadar movement and turned to questions of whether the Immigration Act of 1917, that is, the act creating a "barred zone," required either the deportation of East Indians who had entered the United States lawfully before its enactment or the denial of their right to naturalization. Judge Wolverton decided that it did not require either of these measures and went on to suggest that "it may well be that Congress designed thenceforth to exclude Hindus from entry into the United States, and still permit such as were domiciled here the privilege of being naturalized."[175] As to the government's assertion that Thind was ineligible because he was not a "white person," the judge declared, "I am not disposed to discuss the question ... [but] am content to rest my decision ... upon a line of cases of which In re Mohan Singh ... In re Halladjian ... and United States v. Balsara ... are illustrative." Other decisions contrary to these three, stated Judge Wolverton, "are not in line with the greater weight of authority."[176] The government immediately appealed this decision to the United States Supreme Court.

For the matter of race, color, and citizenship, the US Supreme Court's decision in the *Ozawa* and *Thind* cases – although riddled with contradictions – would prove definitive. In *Ozawa*, the Court had stated that the term "Caucasian" and the term "white persons" were synonymous, giving Thind and other East Indians the hope that, unlike Ozawa, their court-conceded identification as "Caucasians" would assure their right to naturalization. However, Justice Sutherland, who had only one year earlier written the *Ozawa* decision, did not agree. The "conclusion that the phrase 'white persons' and the word 'Caucasian' are synonymous does not end the matter," he began in his opinion in the *Thind* case. " 'Caucasian,' " he observed, "is a conventional word of much flexibility, ... and while it and the words 'white person' are treated as synonymous for the purposes of that [i.e., the *Ozawa*] case, they are not of identical meaning..." Although *Thind* and other "Hindus" had relied on their membership in the "Caucasian" race to secure their legal classification as "white persons," Justice Sutherland, pointing to the fact that the word "Caucasian" was not to be found in the naturalization statutes, and that "as used in the science of ethnology, the connotation of the word is by no means clear," declared that in matters affecting United States citizenship the popular as opposed to the scientific meaning of the fateful term was to be followed by the courts. That popular understanding of the term is "sufficiently [well-known] so as to enable us to say that its... application is of appreciably narrower scope" than that employed by the ethnologists. The term "white persons" imposed a racial test, the justice went on, "but the term 'race' is one which... must be applied to a group of living persons *now* possessing in common the requisite traits." In a burst of his own contribution to ethnological reasoning on the matter, Justice Sutherland set forth limits on the claims of common racial descent that a petitioner might make: "It may be true that the blond Scandinavian and the brown Hindu have a common ancestor in the dim reaches of antiquity," he allowed, "but the average man knows perfectly well that there are unmistakable and profound differences between them today; and it is not impossible, if that common ancestor could be materialized in the flesh, we should discover that he was himself sufficiently differentiated from both of his descendants to preclude his racial classification with either." Moreover, the understandings of the "common" or "average" man were imputed by Justice Sutherland to the legislators of the naturalization act of 1790, who were also said to subscribe to the "Adamite theory of creation – which gave a common ancestor to all mankind – ... [but, he added,] it is not at all probable that it was intended by the legislators of that day to submit the question of the application of the words 'white persons' to the mere test of an indefinitely remote common ancestry, without regard to the extent of the subsequent divergence of the various branches from such common ancestry or from one another." Noting that it might even be the case "that a given group cannot be properly assigned to any of the enumerated grand racial divisions," the justice held, together with his brethren on the Court, that "We are unable to agree with the district court, or with other lower Federal courts, in the conclusion that a native Hindu is eligible for naturalization." The words "white persons" were to be seen as "inclusive" rather than merely exclusive of Negroes and Amerindians, as Thind and his attorneys had contended, and its terms of inclusion were to be those of the original framers of the statute of 1790 – namely, peoples from "the British isles and northwestern Europe" to which were later added "immigrants from eastern, southern, and middle Europe, among them the Slavs and the dark-eyed, swarthy people of Alpine stock," because the latter groups had been "received as unquestionably akin to those already here, and readily amalgamated with them."[177]

Justice Sutherland's decision was to have proactive effects long after the date of its announcement, and it would modify America's relations with its allies during World War II. Two decades after the Thind decision, at a time when the United States was allied with the British Empire and others in a war against Germany, Japan and their other Axis allies, when Judge Haney, of the Ninth Circuit Court of Appeals, rejected Kharaiti Ram Samras's petition that his naturalization be granted – as well as his plea that the section restricting United States citizenship to free white persons and persons of African nativity and African descent be declared unconstitutional because, among other things, the statute was "manifestly and grossly unreasonable, irrational, illogical, arbitrary, capricious and [set into law a] discriminatory classification based on race or color"[178] – he felt constrained to follow the directives of the *Thind* decision, but he observed, pointedly, that the "power over naturalization is political," and that aliens had no Constitutional right to citizenship in the United States.[179]

Puerto Ricans and Filipinos

Not all persons subjected to naturalization proceedings by the United States were aliens in the legal sense of that term. Another category of non-citizens had been created by America's acquisition, as a spoil of the Spanish-American War, of territories once part of the Spanish seaborne empire. The anti-imperialist sociologist, William Graham Sumner, bitter over the American takeover of Cuba, Puerto Rico and the Philippines as part of the Treaty that settled that war, detailed a parade of horrors that connected the then current treatment of blacks to the likely outcome of the introduction of other non-whites into the racially prejudiced American body politic:

> ... Worse still, Americans cannot assure life, liberty, and the pursuit of happiness to negroes inside of the United States. When the [South Carolina] negro postmaster's house was set on fire ... and

not only he, but his wife and children, were murdered... and
when... this incident passed without legal investigation or punishment, it was a bad omen for the extension of liberty, etc., to Malays
and Tagals...[180]

In fact, full citizenship was not immediately extended to the non-
white former subjects of the king of Spain. Promising eventual independence to the Philippines, Congress enacted a law in 1916 that
enlarged the local powers of what Dudley O. McGovney called "this
inchoate independent nation" and three years later that entity enacted
its own exclusive naturalization law.[181] The matter of United States
citizenship for brown-skinned Filipinos and Puerto Ricans became
enormously complicated by the decades-long debate over whether
the non-racial citizenship provisions of the Fourteenth Amendment
were applicable to the Philippines or to Puerto Rico.[182] Professor
McGovney, perhaps the outstanding legal authority on the matter,
supposed that fear of the possible eligibility of the islands' Chinese
and Japanese residents to US citizenship had fueled the faction that
disputed the thesis that the entire Constitution followed the flag.[183] In
fact, however, the fears about Chinese immigrants would find their
own way into the law of the Philippines. In 1928, the Supreme Court
of the Philippines held that a Chinese born in China and domiciled in
the Philippines from 1881 to 1925, the date of his application for
citizenship, was ineligible to naturalization because of his race.[184]

However, the race and "color" of the "brown-skinned" Filipinos
and "dark-skinned" Puerto Ricans seemed to matter as much to the
Congress and the courts of the United States as that of the Chinese. In
a series of cases beginning in 1912, with two subsequent court proceedings in 1916, two in 1917, one in 1921, one in 1927, one in 1931,
and another in 1935, Filipinos sought, for the most part unsuccessfully, to change their status from that of non-citizen nationals to that
of citizens of the United States. In some of these cases, the petitioners
had served honorably in the United States military forces and hoped
to take advantage of an earlier law that permitted alien enlistees in the
United States navy or marine corps to apply for naturalization.
Puerto Ricans fared better in these cases than Filipinos, perhaps
because as persons of Spanish descent they were regarded as
"white," and if dark-skinned, as persons of "African" or mixed
African and white descent.[185] However, in many of these cases, the
Filipino petitioner was denied on the grounds of "color." Thus, in
1912, Eugenio Alverto, the grandson of a Spaniard and a "Philippino

woman," who had served seven years in the United States navy, was refused citizenship in the United States on the ground that he was not a "free white person," the latter category defined to embrace only "members of the white, or Caucasian race, as distinct from the black, red, yellow, and brown races."[186] Four years later, another US navy veteran, "one Lampitoe," described as "the son of a Filipino mother and a father whose mother was a Filipino and whose father was a full-blooded Spaniard, resident in Manila," was rejected on the same grounds as Alverto.[187] In the same year, and again in 1921, two more veterans of the US Navy were disallowed not on account of their race or color – for, in the first case, the district judge for Massachusetts interpreted the relevant section of the Naturalization Act of 1906 to have had no intended restriction with respect to Filipinos or Puerto Ricans – but on a non-racial technicality.[188] But, one year after the *Mallari* decision, a navy veteran and "Philippino," Penaro Rallos, was denied naturalization, the federal district judge for the eastern district of New York observing that were he to rule otherwise, it "would mean that Chinese, Japanese, and Malays could become [United States] citizens."[189] In 1921, however, a more thorough hearing was given to the legal status of Filipino veterans in the case of Engracio Bautista, "a Mestizo . . . born in the province of Bulacan on the Island of Luzon . . . on the 14th of March, 1888," for many years a resident of the United States, and a United States serviceman who was then serving his third four-year hitch in the navy. Referring to the debates over adoption of the Foraker Amendment to the naturalization act of 1906, Circuit Judge Morrow ruled that the act as amended intended "to admit to citizenship all persons, not citizens, who, owing 'permanent allegiance to the United States' and possessing the other qualifications provided by the statute, became residents of any state or organized territory of the United States . . . [and that this] was done by Congress with full knowledge that the Filipino belonged to the Malay or brown race."[190] However, the judge was quick to point out that Chinese, Japanese, and other aliens ineligible to citizenship in the United States, though residents in the Philippine Islands, were not in permanent allegiance to the Crown of Spain at the time of the Philippine cession and, hence, were still ineligible by the amended naturalization act of 1906.[191]

However, a decade later, and two years after a district court had granted citizenship to a Mr Javier, "a native-born Filipino . . . [who had not] served in the United States Navy, Marine Corps, or Naval Auxiliary Service," the Court of Appeals of the District of Columbia denaturalized him on the grounds that he "was not a free white person, nor a person of African nativity or descent," that he was not exempted from this prohibition on his naturalization by reason of military service, and that "his certificate was illegally obtained."[192] Even after 1929, when the provisions of the naturalization act covering the citizenship petitions of Filipinos and Puerto Ricans who had served in the military forces of the United States were broadened, US government attorneys sought – unsuccessfully, as it turned out – to prevent Filipino veterans from becoming United States citizens. In 1931, District Judge Byers rejected an attempt by the Department of Commerce to deny naturalization to Mariano Villamin Rena, a native-born Filipino who had served out honorably two enlistments in the US Navy, on the ground that he had not filed his application within six months of his last honorable discharge, a construction the Department put on a proviso of the amended statute.[193] But, the exemption of Filipino veterans of certain branches of the American armed forces from the "color" provisions of the naturalization acts was not extended to those Filipino non-citizen nationals who had not enlisted; hence, in 1935, the Ninth Circuit Court of Appeals found no difficulty in refusing the petition for naturalization of Roque Espiritu De La Ysla, "born in Manila on August 16, 1902, . . . of the Filipino race, . . . a citizen of the Philippine Islands . . . [who] has not served in the United States Navy or Marine Corps or the Naval Auxiliary Service," and who was neither a "free white person" nor a "person of African nativity or African descent."[194]

The anomalous citizenship status of Filipinos did not end until 1946 when Congress enacted special legislation making it possible for all Filipinos, regardless of race or color, to apply for United States citizenship.[195] On July 4, 1946, the Philippines became an independent republic, and emigration from the former US possession became subject to the various kinds of restrictions contained in the several immigration acts passed since that date.[196] In the final years of their status as non-citizen nationals, an unsuccessful attempt was made to enforce California's alien land law against them, the Supreme Court of California ruling that they were not "aliens" ineligible to citizenship in the United States, as had the Chinese been until 1943 and as would the Japanese be until 1952, but rather non-naturalized "nationals," who, therefore, could not be subjected to a law applying solely to a class of "aliens."[197] In the two years immediately preceding Philippine independence, Emory Bogardus, a sociologist who had devoted much of his life to measuring and working to reduce the "social distance" that separated one people of America from another, published an eloquent plea that Congress enact legislation granting Filipinos eligibility for United States citizenship.[198] Linking his exhortation to the events of the time, Bogardus asserted that the "proposed naturalization law would constitute another step toward changing the national policy of the United States from a provincial one to one consistent with the Four Freedoms and with the spirit of the Constitution of the United States."[199]

Aside from the various classes of "aliens" declared ineligible to citizenship in the United States and the non-citizen nationals also so declared, there remained two other categories: "Indians," that is, Amerinds or Native American aborigines, and non-citizen descendants of more than one "racial" or "color" stock. In treating these, again "color," culture, and conduct were intertwined to form a barrier against naturalization. That barrier gave the lie to the claim that "assimilation" or "assimilability" would provide a sure ticket of admissibility to American citizenship.[200] Emory Bogardus, an analyst as well as an advocate of assimilation, once pointed out that "Assimilation processes are easily halted and turned back upon themselves."[201] Definitive examples of Bogardus's thesis are to be found in the court struggles over the citizenship status of Native Americans and the restrictions on the naturalization of those of mixed Indian-white-African descent.[202] With respect to the former people, John Collier, who served as Commissioner of Indian Affairs from 1933 to 1945, observed, "The longest 'colonial' record of the modern world is that of the governments [of Europe and the Americas] toward their Red Indians."[203] "Red" men and women would test both the color and culture bars to full-fledged peoplehood in the United States.

The court proceeding that in its majority decision subverted the hope that Amerindian acquiescence to mainstream American folkways would be followed by the granting of full-fledged citizenship occurred in 1884.[204] John Elk, born a member of an Indian tribe inhabiting the central plains of the United States, had severed all relations with his tribe, and, according to his uncontradicted testimony, "fully and completely surrendered himself to the jurisdiction of the United States." Having moved into Omaha, Nebraska, acquired property in his own name, become a domiciled resident thereon, and become eligible to serve in the militia, Elk sought to vote in a municipal election in 1880. His application for registration as a voter was turned back on the grounds that he was an "Indian" and therefore neither a citizen, nor a person eligible to become a citizen of the

United States through his own efforts. Elk, however, claimed that his right to vote devolved from his United States citizenship, and that the latter, in turn, derived from that provision of the Fourteenth Amendment that declared that "all persons born or naturalized in the United States, and subject to the jurisdiction thereof, are citizens of the United States and of the state wherein they reside." The majority of the Supreme Court, speaking through Justice Gray, disagreed with his contention, however, holding that Elk's averments did not "allege that the United States [had] accepted his surrender [of tribal jurisdiction], or that he has ever been naturalized, or taxed, or in any way recognized or treated as a citizen by the state or by the United States." Justice Gray went on to insist that "The Indian tribes, being within the territorial limits of the United States, were not, strictly speaking, foreign states; but they were alien nations, distinct political communities, with whom the United States might... deal, as they thought fit, either through treaties... or through acts of congress." Moreover, he continued, echoing both the definitive Georgia cases, wherein Chief Justice John Marshall had decided the categorical identity and future status of the Amerinds,[205] and the *Dred Scott* decision, "The members of those tribes owed immediate allegiance to their several tribes and were not part of the people of the United States. They were in a dependent condition, a state of pupilage, resembling that of a ward to his guardian." Elk was informed that as such a "ward" he could not become a citizen of the United States merely by voluntarily placing himself outside the jurisdiction of his tribe and, equally voluntarily, defining his own status as that of a member of the people of the United States: "... an Indian cannot make himself a citizen of the United States without the consent and cooperation of the government."[206]

Although the Court did not bring up the matter of Elk's "color" as a bar to his becoming a registered voter, and although that issue had seemingly been settled in the *Dred Scott* case – wherein Chief Justice Taney had declared that Indians "may, without doubt, like the subjects of any other foreign government, be naturalized by the authority of Congress, and become citizens of a State, and of the United States; and if [such] an individual should leave his nation or tribe, and take up his abode among the white population, he would be entitled to all the rights and privileges which would belong to an emigrant from any other foreign people" – it would surface again when Indian emigrants from Canada and from the other Americas sought citizenship in the United States. For example, in 1900, a long-time Alaskan resident,

Samuel Burton, applied for United States citizenship.[207] Burton had been born in British Columbia. His application was denied on several grounds: that he was neither a free white person nor a person of African descent; that Indians in Alaska had according to the Territory's criminal code a special status akin to that of a "minor or intoxicated person"; and that Alaska's land laws treat Indians "as a race or peculiar people, and in no way [treat] them ... as persons having the rights of citizens of the United States."

The court conceded that "under some circumstances an Indian may acquire the rights of citizenship." But the circumstances of Burton's birth and color disqualified him. "By the act of February 8, 1887 ... an Indian born within the United States, to whom land has been allotted, and who has severed his tribal relations, and adopted the habits of civilized life, thereby becomes a citizen of the United States ..." However, the Court went on to observe, "This seems to be the only method provided by law whereby an Indian may become a citizen ... [for no other] provision has been made by Congress for the naturalization of Indians or other peoples of color or their descendants, except Africans." As for Mr Burton: "Mr Burton is an Indian ... If he was not born within the territorial limits of the United States, ... then there is no law of the United States, of which this court is advised, whereby he may be admitted to citizenship by the court." In effect, Burton and others like him had been assigned the same status as Chinese and Japanese aliens, namely, that of aliens ineligible to citizenship in the United States.

Although alien Indians seem to have remained ineligible to citizenship in the United States until race and color qualifications were dropped from the law,[208] Indian nationals received a blanket naturalization from the provisions of an act of Congress passed in 1924.[209] However, because this law had been enacted without any prior, accompanying, or subsequent treaty revisions, and because some states, notably Arizona, refused for many years to extend the vote to citizen Indians,[210] some tribes – especially those that felt deprived of a measure of their sovereignty by a section of the 1871 law stating that "no Indian nation or tribe within the territory of the United States shall be acknowledged or recognized as an independent nation, tribe, or power, with whom the United States may contract by treaty"[211] – refused to acknowledge it. The issue became important when the likelihood of an American involvement in the war against the Axis powers resulted in the passage of the Selective Service Act of 1940. The Native American responses to the military draft were many and varied. In one unsuccessful court proceeding, the mother of Warren Green, an Onandaga youth who was a member of the Six Nations Confederacy and a resident of Syracuse, New York, sought to have her son's induction into the armed services set aside on the grounds that he was not a United States citizen, the Iroquois having never been conquered or subjugated by the United States and his people, therefore, having never ceased to be a separate nation subject to the treaties between the United States and the Six Nations Confederacy of 1784, 1789, and 1794.[212] Other tribes resisted induction through selective service and insisted on their rights as separate nations to decide on a policy with respect to the Axis threat. In 1942 the Cheyenne Tribe of Oklahoma formally declared itself in a state of war with Germany, Japan and their allies;[213] "the Tunica, among other Louisiana Indians, objected to the military draft... claiming that only the tribe held sovereignty over its manpower and refusing to let Tunica youths be inducted into segregated units... [nevertheless,] virtually all the young men of that tribe went to war as volunteers";[214] the "Zunis of western New Mexico resisted by declaring all of their young men were priests and should receive religious deferments...[and as a result] only 213 of the populous Zuni were taken into military service";[215] after three largely unsuccessful attempts to enforce voluntary but universal registration for the draft among the Florida Seminoles, a special investigation by an army officer determined that they "possessed little knowledge of English and were somewhat unsanitary, and [that] it would not be worthwhile to use force against them...."[216]

Although a considerable number of Native Americans did serve in the armed forces during World War II, as well as in later American wars in Korea, Vietnam, and the Persian Gulf, the issue of their "color" and culture rankled. When, in the Second World War, they proved to be able and efficient soldiers, the *American Legion Magazine* treated their performance in commando fighting as natural: "Why not? his ancestors invented it...Some can smell a snake yards away and hear the faintest movement; all endure thirst and lack of food better than average."[217] When, on the other hand, those enlisting or drafted into army units in the South discovered that they would be classed as "colored" and placed in the same units as Afro-Americans, they resisted such designation, demanded to be treated as "whites," and, in some instances went to prison rather than accept what they considered to be an ignominious status.[218] Indians would also serve, the government seemed to be saying, but they would be made to stand

and wait for a long time before being granted the full measure of their citizenship and civil rights.

Mixed Bloods

Despite the claims put forward at least since the Reconstruction era ended,[219] and reiterated as recently as 1963 by Norman Podhoretz,[220] that racial intermarriage would eventually eliminate America's race problem by eliminating the separate races as distinctive units, neither the seventeenth and eighteenth-century American colonies,[221] nor the majority of states of the United States,[222] nor the courts[223] until the period 1948–67, when, one by one, the state laws forbidding miscegenation were declared unconstitutional,[224] would sanction such marriages.[225] Indeed, there has long been a hiatus in sociological thought separating those who regarded amalgamation as both the final solution to the race problem and the ultimate stage of assimilation[226] from those who perceived marriage across the color-culture line in American society as so anomalous that it required separate classification, as "intermarriage," and as a phenomenon that would have to be explained by special theories.[227] As for those who were American citizens by birth or naturalization, what little intermarriage that did take place – with the notable exception of American citizens of Chinese and Japanese descent in the third and fourth generations[228] – occurred across the line of nationality rather than color. Hence, black Americans find themselves still debating the worthwhileness of interracial marriage in terms not too different from those put forth by Edward Byron Reuter in 1931,[229] while one recent student of the subject projected whatever sanguine effects intermarriage might provide for resolving America's race problem into the next century.[230] Until 1952, however, for aliens of mixed racial or "color" stocks seeking naturalization in the United States, their parents' transgression against America's mores about miscegenation could and often did bring about a denial of admission to citizenship.

Mixed-blood aliens challenged the "color" test of the naturalization laws because of the latter's dependence on every individual's membership in but a single race.[231] Because, until 1952 – except for the provisions made in 1919 for those Native Americans and Filipinos who served in United States military services, for all Native Americans in 1924, for Chinese in 1943, and for Filipinos in 1946 – naturalization in the United States was limited to "free white persons" and "persons of African nativity and African descent," questions arose about the eligibility of those whose immediate forebears included white and "red" or "yellow" persons who had intermarried. Twenty-five years before the adoption of the Fourteenth Amendment, the Supreme Court of Ohio had ruled that a person of "more than one-half white blood" should be counted as "white" for purposes of racial assignment in a segregated public school system.[232] "Percentage" of "blood" would later become the basis for determining the eligibility of mixed-bloods for United States citizenship.

That the fundamental issues defining the race question in America determined both domestic regulations and naturalization laws is revealed in the first and most often cited court proceeding concerning a mixed-blood petitioner for United States citizenship. In 1880, the Circuit Court of the Oregon District passed judgment on the petition of Frank Camille, born in 1847 in Kamloops, British Columbia, to a "white Canadian" father and "an Indian woman," and a resident of Oregon since 1864.[233] District Justice Deady, noting that no less an authority than Chancellor Kent had expressed doubt about whether "the copper-colored natives of America, or the yellow or tawny races of the Asiatic... are 'white persons' within the purview of the law," and that the naturalization laws had not extended citizenship rights to the "copper-colored natives," stated that in the matter before the court the question was "what is the *status* in this respect of the petitioner, who is a person of one-half Indian blood?" Citing as authority the Ohio court's rulings in four earlier cases involving mixed-bloods, Deady ruled that "where the colored blood was equal to or preponderated over the white blood, the person was not white." Camille, hence, was not a white man, and his petition was rejected. But, to what race did he belong? Justice Deady's answer provides as precise a definition as the courts would offer of what later sociologists would call the racial hybrid, a "marginal man"[234]:

> As a matter of fact, he is as much an Indian as a white person, and might be classed with the one race as properly as the other. Strictly speaking, he belongs to neither.

And how did it come to pass that a man who is neither wholly Indian nor wholly white is by that fact also ineligible to citizenship in the United States? Justice Deady treats these matters in his summary of the legislative history of naturalization in the United States, an *obiter dictum* that related in less than approbative language how the Civil War Amendments extending citizenship to Negroes had been so worded that they implicitly denied naturalization to red and yellow persons and to all those who are not at least fifty-one percent white. In effect, his commentary illustrates how race prejudice, once the badge of slavery, has spread out from its original object to separate other non-whites from the white claimants to an exclusive status:

> From the first our naturalization laws only applied to the people who had settled the country – the Europeans or white race – and so they remained until 1870, ... when, under the pro-negro feeling, generated and inflamed by the war with the southern states, and its political consequences, congress was driven at once to the other extreme, and opened the door, not only to persons of African descent, but to all those of African nativity – thereby proffering the boon of American citizenship to the comparatively savage and strange inhabitants of the "dark continent," while withholding it from the intermediate and much-better-qualified red and yellow races.

> However, ... the negroes of Africa were not likely to emigrate to this country, and ... the provision concerning them was merely a harmless piece of legislative buncombe, while the Indian and the Chinaman were in our midst, and at our doors and only too willing to assume the mantle of American sovereignty ...

Indians, Asians, and mixed bloods were to be denied citizenship so that they could not share in the form of sovereignty that prevailed in a democratic republic, namely, that, as Chief Justice Taney had said in *Dred Scott*, vested that all important element of rule in "We the people."

Subsequent rulings followed the precedent set in the *Camille* case. That the matter of a "color" test would be put to persons of African nativity and African descent in terms of a preponderant percentage of the eligible "blood" was indicated in a Federal District court proceeding of 1938.[235] Bernedito Cruz, who testified that "My mother is half African and half Indian and my father is a full blooded Indian ... I believe my father's ancestors were all full blooded Indians," petitioned for United States citizenship as a person of African descent. The court rejected the petition, rephrasing the issue before it as an inquiry into "whether a person who is one-quarter Negro is of 'African descent'" within the meaning of the naturalization statute. In reaching his decision in this matter, District Judge Byers relied on an important dictum enunciated by Justice Cardozo in a 1933 case involving an alleged conspiracy to evade California's Alien Land Law. Citing the *Thind* case as precedent, Cardozo had observed that, "The privilege of naturalization is denied to all who are not white (unless the applicants are of African nativity or African descent); and men are not white if the strain of colored blood in them is a half or a quarter, or, not improbably, even less, the governing test always...being that of common understanding."[236] However, the *Cruz* case involved a claim of African descent, from a person of part Indian parentage, not one of membership in the exclusive white race. Indeed, that Cardozo was uneasy about the citizenship rights of persons of mixed eligible and ineligible blood is indicated in the same opinion in his footnote about the citizenship rights of part-Indian Mexicans:

> There is a strain of Indian blood in many of the inhabitants of Mexico as well as in the peoples of Central and South America... Whether persons of such descent may be naturalized in the United States is still an unsettled question.[237]

Judge Byers made no mention of Justice Cardozo's concern, referring instead to a 1909 law review article that had described the widely varying definitions of "Negro," "mulatto," and "person of color" in the several states and adding that "if this petitioner were of one-quarter white blood and three quarters Indian, he could not be admitted to citizenship." Byers then concluded that "in order for a petitioner to qualify [for naturalization] under the statute, his African descent must be shown to be at least an affirmative quantity, and not a neutral thing as in the case of the half blood, or a negative one as in the case of the quarter blood."[238] Hence, although some of the states classified a person as a "Negro" if he or she had but one-sixteenth Negro blood,[239] and a legislator of the state of Louisiana had in 1908 unsuccessfully attempted to extend the term to embrace a person of one thirty-second part-Negro blood,[240] for purposes of naturalization a person of mixed African and other non-white descent would have to have fifty-one or more percent of the former blood to qualify.

CONCLUSION

When Francis Fukuyama raised (if only briefly and in order to set the matter outside the purview of his analysis) the status of the race question in relation to the end of the Cold War, he was following in a little-explored tradition of discussion and policy on the matter. America's treatment of its racial minorities has been an element in the nation's foreign relations and in the maintenance of its image abroad as the first modern state society to throw off the yoke of European colonial domination. The basic problem has always been how the values enunciated in the Declaration of Independence might be squared with those practices of racial subordination permitted in the unamended version of the Constitution of 1787 – and how this resolution would be featured in America's picture of itself to other countries. Chattel slavery had been virtually confined to Africans and persons of African descent during the colonial era, but the "peculiar institution" continued until the Civil War ended it. However, the "badge of slavery" – race prejudice and discrimination – not only continued to be pressed on to African Americans after Emancipation, but also reached out from its original institutional base to engulf those persons of non-white color and non-Occidental culture who had come to the United States in search of political freedom, economic opportunity, and social advancement. Although the methods of total institutionalization – plantation slavery and government reservation – were not applied to Chinese, Japanese, Koreans, East Indians, and the peoples of Southwest Asia (as they had been to enslaved African-Americans and corralled Native Americans, respectively), other burdens, including the denial of naturalization; restrictions on jobs, occupations, union membership, and the professions; prohibitions on land ownership, corporation formation, licensing, and intermarriage; segregation and ghettoization; and the myriad of hurts that arise from racist slurs and the popular usage of ethnophaulisms – and, in the case of the Pacific coast Japanese Americans, wholesale incarceration during World War II – pinned that ignominious badge upon them as firmly as had the enslavement of blacks. America had – despite its protestations to the contrary – become a *herrenvolk* democracy and a white republic.[241]

The Second World War proved to be the first major challenge to America's domestic praxis of white supremacy. Such important social scientists as sociologist Robert Park (1864–1944)[242] and his anthropologist son-in-law, Robert Redfield (1897–1958)[243] pointed out the inconsistencies entailed in America's championing of freedom and equality abroad while enforcing white supremacy at home. At the end of the war, a research analyst for the Immigration and Naturalization Service pointed out on the basis of a careful analysis of the laws governing aliens in 35 nations that no country other than the United States utilized racial criteria for naturalization.[244] Moreover, this agent of the Justice Department took especial note of the fact that "The Nazi Nuremburg laws appear to be the only modern instance where a nation, other than the United States, has imposed a racial disqualification restricting eligibility for naturalization to members of designated racial groups."[245] Seven years later the color qualification for naturalization was eliminated from American naturalization law. Even more significant, perhaps, is the fact that desegregation and the extension of civil rights became not only the single most important domestic event in postwar America, but also an important feature of American international impression management during the entire era of the Cold War – the struggle against communism requiring the escutcheon of America to be cleansed of any racist blemishes.[246]

As the Cold War comes to an end, there appears to be less a rising of capitalist market economies or of newly invigorated Enlightenment than of angry ethnonationalism and parochial chauvinism. Marxism and Soviet communism seem in retrospect to have merely covered over the seething senses of ethnocentrism that had been so prominent before the first World War. In America, the toppling of the outer bastion of the white republic's institutionalized racism – legislatively established segregation, "Jim Crow" laws, and juridically enforced race discrimination – has made its second line of defense – the walls built against job opportunities and occupational advancement – both more visible and less vulnerable to assault.[247] Currently, the issue is popularly and politically defined in terms of "quotas" and the alleged need to resist "reverse discrimination." It should be seen in quite another way, in terms of the desire to enlarge upon a more humane enlightenment and a more comprehensive civil rights policy – in effect, to extend the principles of the Declaration of Independence to the performances required by the Constitution of the United States, and to remove from all who still wear them the badges of slavery.

One aspect of such an extension and elaboration would be a renewed understanding of the principle of equality as expressed through the Thirteenth and Fourteenth Amendments to the Constitution. Justice Thurgood Marshall recently remarked, "While the Union survived the civil war, the Constitution did not. In its place arose a new, more promising basis for justice and equality, the fourteenth amendment, ensuring protection of the life, liberty, and property of *all* persons against deprivations without due process, and guaranteeing equal protection of the laws."[248] Much of the present difficulty can be credited to the failure of so many to see that the protection of the life, liberty, and property of *all* persons sometimes required the enactment of laws that benefit *some* of those persons – namely, the minority whose rights have been violated, neglected, abrogated, or never before recognized.[249] Those who still bear the burden of the badge of slavery – and in this essay, I suggest that the evidence presented supports the claim of an aggregation of peoples that includes African Americans, Asian Americans, Hispanic Americans, and Native Americans and, though not discussed in this essay, women[250] – belong among the beneficiaries of laws, programs, and policies that seek to provide affirmative action in behalf of jobs, education, training, and professionalization. Such laws, programs, and policies are not rightly considered to be instances of reverse discrimination; rather, they apply precisely to those to whom they ought to apply and work in behalf of a legitimate public purpose – the mandate of the Thirteenth Amendment.

However, even if it should be agreed that the cluster of peoples designated *supra* are appropriately classified with respect to the fulfillment of the aims of the Civil War amendments, there still would remain the question of how to determine whether an individual, if challenged as to his or her ancestry, is in fact a member of the ethnoracial group that is benefitted. Here, the review of the naturalization cases discussed above provides a preview of what might occur and a warning about the difficulties yet to be overcome.

NOTES

The author would like to acknowledge the research assistance of Connie Tang.

1. Francis Fukuyama, "The End of History?" *The National Interest*, No. 16 (Summer, 1989), pp. 3–18.
2. *Ibid.*, p. 3.
3. Fukuyama, *op. cit.*, p. 5.
4. Alexandre Kojève, *Introduction to the Reading of Hegel: Lectures on the Phenomenology of Spirit*, ed. by Allan Bloom, trans. by James H. Nichols, Jr., (Ithaca: Cornell University Press, 1980).
5. Fukuyama, *op. cit.*, p. 5.
6. *Ibid.*, p. 5, n. 3. The addendum is to be found in a footnote added to the second edition published in France in 1947 and included in the English translation. See Kojève, *op. cit.*, pp. 159–162 n.
7. Fukuyama, *op. cit.*, pp. 6–7.
8. John Gray, *Liberalism*, (Minneapolis: University of Minnesota Press, 1986), p. 79.

9.   John A. Hall and G. John Ikenberry, *The State*, (Minneapolis: University of Minnesota Press, 1989), p. 3.
10.   Fukuyama, *op. cit.*, p. 7.
11.   Max Weber, "Structure of Power," *From Max Weber: Essays in Sociology*, trans. and ed. by H. H. Gerth and C. Wright Mills, (New York: Oxford University Press, 1946), p. 177.
12.   Kojève, *op. cit.*, p. 161 n.
13.   Fukuyama, *op. cit.*, p. 9.
14.   *Loc. cit.*
15.   Gertrude Himmelfarb, "Responses to Fukuyama," *The National Interest*, No. 16 (Summer, 1989), p. 26.
16.   Friedrich Engels to Friedrich A. Sorge, December 2, 1893, in Karl Marx and Friedrich Engels, *Basic Writings on Politics and Philosophy*, ed. by Lewis S. Feuer, (Garden City: Doubleday-Anchor, 1959), pp. 457–458.
17.   Robert E. Park, "The Nature of Race Relations," in *Race Relations and the Race Problem: A Definition and an Analysis*, ed. by Edgar T. Thompson, (Durham, N.C.: Duke University Press, 1939), p. 45.
18.   See Herbert Hill, *Black Labor and the American Legal System Race, Work, and the Law*, (Madison: University of Wisconsin Press, 1985). William B Gould, *Black Workers in White Unions: Job Discrimination in the United States*. (Ithaca: Cornell University Press, 1977); William H. Harris, *The Harder We Run: Black Workers Since the Civil War*, (New York: Oxford University Press, 1982); David Swinton, "Economic Status of Black Americans," in *The State of Black America*, 1989, ed. by Janet Dewart, (New York: National Urban League, 1989), pp. 9–40. For a discussion of occupational discrimination against Asians, see Herbert Hill, "Anti-Oriental Agitation and the Rise of Working-Class Racism," *Transaction: Social Science and Modern Society*, X:2 (January-February, 1973), pp. 43–54. For the situation affecting Asians, Hispanics, and Native Americans in the formative years of the United States, see Stanford M. Lyman, "The Significance of Asians in American Society," in *idem, The Asian in North America*, (Santa Barbara: ABC-Clio Press, 1977), pp. 25–38, esp. pp. 36–37, n. 88.
19.   See, e.g., Herbert Gutman, *Work, Culture and Society in Industrializing America*, (New York: Alfred A. Knopf, 1976), pp. 119–208; and Herbert Hill, "Myth-Making as Labor History: Herbert Gutman and the United Mine Workers of America," *International Journal of Politics, Culture and Society*, 11:2 (Winter, 1988), pp. 132–200, and his "Rejoinder to Symposium on 'Myth-Making as Labor History...," *Ibid.*, 11:4 (Summer, 1989), pp. 587–595.
20.   See Stanford M. Lyman, "Interactionism and the Study of Race Relations at the Macrosociological Level: The Contribution of Herbert Blumer," *Symbolic Interaction*, VII:I (Spring, 1984), pp. 107–120; reprinted in *idem, Civilization: Contents, Discontents, Malcontents, and Other Essays in Social Theory*, (Fayetteville: University of Arkansas Press, 1990), pp. 136–148.
21.   Thomas Sowell, *Ethnic America: A History*, (New York: Basic Books, Inc., 1981), p. 187.

22. Shelby Steele, *The Content of Our Character: A New Vision of Race in America*, (New York: St. Martin's Press, 1990), p. 170.

23. *Ibid.*, p. 14.

24. *Ibid.*, pp. 10–17.

25. *Ibid.*, p. 16.

26. See Jacobus ten Broek, "Thirteenth Amendment to the Constitution of the United States: Consummation to Abolition and Key to the Fourteenth Amendment," *California Law Review*, XXXIX (June, 1951), pp. 171–203.

27. See Jacobus tenBroek, *The Anti-Slavery Origins of the Fourteenth Amendment*, (Berkeley: University of California Press, 1951), esp. pp. 96–110.

28. Justice Harlan, dissent, in *Civil Rights Cases*, 109 U.S. 3 (1883).

29. See Stanford M. Lyman, "Asians, Blacks, Hispanics, Amerinds: Confronting Vestiges of Slavery," in *Rethinking Today's Minorities*, ed. by Vincent N. Parrillo, (New York: Greenwood Press, 1991), pp. 63–86.

30. See the following works of Thomas Sowell: *Black Education: Myths and Tragedies*, (New York: David McKay, 1972); *Race and Economics*, (New York: David McKay, 1975); "Three Black Histories," in *Essays and Data on American Ethnic Groups*, ed. by Thomas Sowell with the assistance of Lynn D. Collins, (Washington, D.C.: The Urban Institute, 1978), pp. 7–64; *Knowledge and Decisions*, (New York: Basic Books, 1980), *Pink and Brown People and Other Controversial Essays*, (Stanford: Hoover Institution Press, 1981), pp. 1–26, 65–67, 123–124; *Markets and Minorities*, (New York: Basic Books, 1981), esp. pp. 83–102; *The Economics and Politics of Race: An International Perspective*, (New York: William Morrow and Co., 1983), esp. pp. 15–20, 183–206, 243–258; *Civil Rights: Rhetoric or Reality?*, (New York: William Morrow and Co., 1984); *A Conflict of Visions: Ideological Origins of Political Struggles*, (New York: William Morrow and Co., 1987), esp. pp. 13–39, 67–140, 172–232; *Compassion Versus Guilt and Other Essays*, (New York: William Morrow and Co., 1987); *Preferential Policies: An International Perspective*, (New York: William Morrow and Co., 1990).

31. Thomas Sowell, *Classical Economics Reconsidered*. (Princeton: Princeton University Press, 1974), p. 13.

32. Thomas Sowell, *Markets and Minorities, op. cit.*, p. 90.

33. *Ibid.*, pp. 83–102; and Sowell, *Classical Economics Reconsidered, op. cit.*, p. 13.

34. See Alfred H. Conrad and John R. Meyer, "The Economics of Slavery in the Ante Bellum South," *Journal of Political Economy*. LXVI (April, 1958), pp. 95–122; and Harold D. Woodman. "The Profitability of Slavery: A Historical Perennial," *Journal of Southern History*, XXIX (August, 1963), pp. 303–325.

35. Robert William Fogel and Stanley L. Engerman, *Time on the Cross: The Economics of American Negro Slavery*, (Boston: Little, Brown and Co., 1974), pp. 263–264.

36. See Raimondo Luraghi, *The Rise and Fall of the Plantation South*, (New York: New Viewpoints – Franklin Watts, 1978).

37. See Henry Hughes, *A Treatise on Sociology, Theoretical and Practical*, (Philadelphia: Lippincott and Grambo, 1854; reprint, New York: Negro Universities Press, 1968). For a discussion of Hughes's thesis, See two essays by Stanford M. Lyman, "Henry Hughes and the Southern Foundations of American Sociology," in *Selected Writings of Henry Hughes: Antebellum Southerner, Slavocrat, Sociologist*, ed. by Stanford M. Lyman, (Jackson: University Press of Mississippi, 1985), pp. 1–72; and "System and Function in antebellum Southern Sociology," *International Journal of Politics, Culture, and Society*, II:1 (Fall, 1988), pp. 95–108. Reprinted in Stanford M. Lyman, *Civilization....op. cit.*, pp. 191–201. See also Arthur J. Vidich and Stanford M. Lyman, *American Sociology: Worldly Rejections of Religion and Their Directions*, (New Haven: Yale University Press, 1985), pp. 9–19.
38. "Long experience," complained John Waring (c. 1716–1794), one of the "Associates of Dr. Bray," a missionary society devoted to the often-resisted task of converting and educating African slaves in the American colonies, "shows that True Religion must make the Blacks as well as whites (notwithstanding some few exceptions) better Servants; and the former have as just a claim to the Knowledge of Christianity as the latter; & Wo be unto Them who wilfully keep 'em ignorant of it." John Waring to Robert Carter Nicholas, dated at London, May 25, 1769, in *Religious Philanthropy and Colonial Slavery: The American Correspondence of the Associates of Dr. Bray, 1717–1777*, ed. by John C. Van Horne, (Urbana: University of Illinois Press, 1985), p. 284.
39. Kenneth M. Stampp, *The Peculiar Institution: Slavery in the Antebellum South*, (New York: Alfred A. Knopf, 1963), pp. 140–191.
40. Herbert G. Gutman, *Slavery and the Numbers Game: A Critique of Time on the Cross*, (Urbana: University of Illinois Press, 1975).
41. See Paul A. David, *et al., Reckoning With Slavery*, (New York: Oxford University Press, 1976); Kenneth M. Stampp, "Time on the Cross: A Humanistic Perspective," *The Imperiled Union*, (New York: Oxford University Press, 1980), pp. 72–104; Donald Ratcliffe, "The *Das Kapital* of American Negro Slavery? Time on the Cross After Two Years," *The Durham University Journal*, LXIX (1976), pp. 103–130; and Peter Parish, *Slavery: History and Historians*, (New York: Harper and Row, 1989).
Still another point of view has been put forward by the anthropological historian Mechal Sobel. Attending to the rise of Afro-Baptist sectarianism and to the system of production and attitudes toward work that prevailed among eighteenth-century Virginia's African and Afro-American slaves, she points to the West African cultural orientation, a civilizational complex carried across the Atlantic by enslaved victims of the Middle Passage. As a way of life for blacks in bondage, it modified how and when work was performed, shaped their religious perspective as well as the architecture of newly constructed buildings, and, in general, diffused itself among white overseers and other whites, where, among other matters, it could resonate most comfortably with similar attitudes and orientations that had come across the Atlantic

with the Celts, a decidedly non-liberal populace from the hinterlands of the British Isles. See two works by Mechal Sobel, *Trabelin' On: The Slave Journey to an Afro-Baptist Faith*, (Princeton: Princeton University Press, 1988 [1979]); and *The World They Made Together: Black and White Values in Eighteenth-Century Virginia*, (Princeton: Princeton University Press, 1987). See also Grady McWhiney, *Cracker Culture: Celtic Ways in the Old South*, (Tuscaloosa: University of Alabama Press, 1988) and Grady McWhiney and Perry D. Jamieson, *Attack and Die: Civil War Military Tactics and the Southern Heritage*, (Tuscaloosa: University of Alabama Press, 1982), pp. 170–192; Michael Hechter, *Internal Colonialism: The Celtic Fringe in British National Development, 1536–1966*, (London: Routledge and Kegan Paul, 1975); David Hackett Fischer, *Albion's Seed: Four British Folk ways in America*, (New York: Oxford University Press, 1989); and two works by Bernard Bailyn, *The Peopling of British North America: An Introduction*. (New York: Alfred A. Knopf, 1986); and *Voyagers to the West: A Passage in the Peopling of America on the Eve of the Revolution*, (New York: Alfred A. Knopf, 1986).

42.   Stanley M. Elkins, *Slavery: A Problem in American Institutional and Intellectual Life*, 3rd edn., (Chicago: University of Chicago Press, 1976), pp. 81–139.

43.   See the essays by George M. Fredrickson, Sterling Stuckey, Roy Simon Bryce-Laporte, and Eugene Genovese in *The Debate Over Slavery: Stanley Elkins and His Critics*, ed. by Ann J. Lane, (Urbana: University of Illinois Press, 1971), pp. 223–324. See also Herbert G. Gutman, "Enslaved Afro-Americans and the 'Protestant' Work Ethic," *Power and Culture: Essays on the American Working Class*, ed. by Ira Berlin, (New York: Pantheon Books, 1987), pp. 298–325; and Kenneth M. Stampp, "Rebels and Sambos: The Search for the Negro's Personality in Slavery," *The Imperiled Union, op. cit.*, pp. 39–71; and Gerald Jaynes, "Plantation Factories and the Slave Work Ethic," in The *Slave's Narrative*, ed. by Charles T. Davis and Henry Louis Gates, Jr., (New York: Oxford University Press, 1985), pp. 98–112.

44.   The following – including the quotations – are from Robert William Fogel, *Without Consent or Contract: The Rise and Fall of American Slavery*, (New York: W. W. Norton, 1989), pp. 410–411.

45.   Seymour Martin Lipset, *The First New Nation: The United States in Historical and Comparative Perspective*, (New York: Basic Books, Inc., 1963), p. 333.

46.   *Ibid.*, p. 332.

47.   *Loc. cit.* Emphasis in original.

48.   *Ibid.*, p. 330.

49.   *Ibid.*, pp. 99–198.

50.   *Ibid.*, p. 330.

51.   *Ibid.*, pp. 332, 333.

52.   *Ibid.*, p. 343.

53.   Paul M. Sniderman and Michael Gray Hagen, *Race and Inequality: A Study in American Values*, (Chatham, N.J.: Chatham House Publications, 1985), pp. 79–118.

54. See Russell Nieli, ed., *Racial Preference and Racial Justice: The New Affirmative Action Controversy*, (Washington, D.C.: Ethics and Public Policy Center, 1991). See also the op-ed essay by United States Senator from Missouri, John C. Danforth, "Stop the Brawling About Quotas," *New York Times*, June 20, 1991, p. A13.

55. Seymour Martin Lipset, "Introduction to the Norton Edition," *The First New Nation: The United States in Historical and Comparative Perspective*, (New York: W. W. Norton, 1979), pp. xxiv–xxv. For a re-analysis and rejection of Lipset's findings about the content and distribution of black and white opinion on this issue, see Lee Sigelman and Susan Welch, *Black Americans' Views of Racial Inequality: The Dream Deferred*, (Cambridge: Cambridge University Press, 1991), pp. 132–139.

56. See Joseph Tussman and Jacobus tenBrock, "The Equal Protection of the Laws," *California Law Review*, XXXVII:3 (September, 1949), pp. 341–381.

57. For a thoughtful reconsideration of the Court's use of *laissez-faire* ideology in this era, see Michael Les Benedict, "Laissez-Faire and Liberty: A Re-Evaluation of the Meaning and Origins of Laissez-Faire Constitutionalism," *Law and History Review*, III:2 (Fall, 1985), pp. 293–331.

58. *Lochner v. New York*, 198 U.S. 45, 74 (1905).

59. Sheldon M. Novick, *Honorable Justice: The Life of Oliver Wendell Holmes*, (Boston: Little, Brown and Co., 1989), pp. 456–457 n. 29. See also David M. Currie, *The Constitution in the Supreme Court: The Second Century, 1888–1986*, (Chicago: University of Chicago Press, 1990), pp. 41–44. See, however, Yosal Rogat, "Mr. Justice Holmes: A Dissenting Opinion," *Stanford Law Review*, XV (March, 1963), pp. 254–308 for the view that Holmes was hardly the humanitarian that his admirers made him out to be and, on p. 308, that his opinions in cases on segregation in education and transportation, federal protection of political rights, rights arising under the Thirteenth Amendment, and the rights of those ordered to be sexually sterilized against their will, suggest "that the accepted image of Holmes as uniquely libertarian owes more to fantasies unloosed by the attractiveness of his personality than to the realities of his career."

60. *Barbier v. Connolly*, 113 U.S. 27, 30, 31 (1885).

61. Tussman and tenBroek, *op. cit.*, p. 346.

62. See, e.g. Nathan Glazer, *Affirmative Discrimination: Ethnic Inequality and Public Policy*, (New York: Basic Books, Inc., 1975); Terry Eastland and William J. Bennett, *Counting By Race: Equality from the Founding Fathers to Bakke and Weber*, (New York: Basic Books, Inc., 1979); Barry Gross, ed., *Reverse Discrimination*, (Buffalo: Prometheus Books, 1977).

63. *Central Lumber Co. v. South Dakota*, 226 U.S. 157, 158 (1912).

64. See the fine discussion of this issue in Judith A. Baer, *Equality Under the Constitution: Reclaiming the Fourteenth Amendment*, (Ithaca: Cornell University Press, 1983), pp. 28–30, 80, 112–130, 183–185, 196–204, 213–215, 231–232, 251.

65. *In re Opinion of the Justices*, 207 Mass. 601, 94 NE 558, 560 (1911).
66. See tenBroek, "Thirteenth Amendment to the Constitution of the United States," *op. cit.*, pp. 171–203.
67. *Commonwealth v. Alger*, 7 Cush. 84, quoted approvingly by Justice Brown in *Holden v. Hardy*, 169 U.S. 366, 392 (1898).
68. *In re Tiburcio Parrott*, 1 Fed. 481, 506 (1880).
69. See Carter Godwin Wilson, *The Mis-education of the Negro*, (Washington, D.C.: The Associated Publishers, Inc., 1933, 1969); Henry Allen Bullock, *A History of Negro Education in the South from 1619 to the Present*, (Cambridge: Harvard University Press, 1967), pp. 60–288; Horace Mann Bond, *Negro Education in Alabama: A Study in Cotton and Steel*, (New York: Atheneum, 1969 [1939]).
70. Cf. Robert A. Margo, *Race and Schooling in the South, 1880–1950: An Economic History*, (Chicago: University of Chicago Press, 1990), esp. pp. 129–133.
71. See Eric Foner, *Reconstruction: America's Unfinished Revolution, 1865–1877*, (New York: Harper and Row, 1988); and William Gillette, *Retreal From Reconstruction, 1869–1879*, (Baton Rouge: Louisiana State University Press, 1979).
72. Kenneth M. Stampp, *The Era of Reconstruction, 1865–1877*, (New York: Alfred A. Knopf, 1965), pp. 186–187.
73. James H. Kettner, *The Development of American Citizenship, 1608–1870*, (Chapel Hill: University of North Carolina Press, 1978), pp. 334–351.
74. For a spirited overview of the matter, see Lois B. Moreland, *White Racism and the Law*, (Columbus, Ohio; Charles E. Merrill Pub. Co., 1970).
75. *Dred Scott v. Sandford*, 19 How, 393 (1856).
76. Dudley O. McGovney, "American Citizenship," *Columbia Law Review*, XI:1 (January, 1911), p. 248.
77. *United States v. Rhodes*, abb. U.S. 28, Fed. Cas. No. 16, 151 (1866).
78. John Hope Franklin, *Racial Equality in America*, the 1976 Jefferson Lecture in the Humanities Presented by the National Endowment for the Humanities, (Chicago: University of Chicago Press, 1976), pp. 61–62.
79. Dudley O. McGovney, *op. cit.*, p. 231.
80. *Plessy v. Ferguson*, 163 U.S. 537 (1896).
81. See Gilbert Thomas Stephenson, *Race Distinctions in American Law*, (New York: Appleton-Century-Crofts, 1910; reprint, New York: AMS Press, 1969), pp. 12–25.
82. *Wall v. Oyster*, 36 App. D.C. 50, 31 LRA (n.s.) 180, 188 (1910).
83. *Ibid.*, p. 86.
84. *Berea College v. Kentucky*, 211 U.S. 45, 67–69 (1908).
85. See Edward F. Waite, "The Negro in the Supreme Court," *Minnesota Law Review*, XXX:4 (March, 1946), pp. 219–304.
86. W. E. B. DuBois, *The Souls of Black Folk*, (New York: Fawcett World Library, 1961 [1903]), p. 23.
87. Ray Stannard Baker, *Following the Color Line. American Negro Citizenship in the Progressive Era*, (New York: Harper Torchbooks, 1964 [1908]).

88. St. Clair Drake and Horace R. Cayton, *Black Metropolis A Study of Negro Life in a Northern City*, rev'd., enlarged edn., (New York: Harper Torchbooks, 1962 [1945]), I, pp. 99–173, 263–286.

89. Herbert Blumer, "The Future of the Color Line," in *The South in Continuity and Change*, ed. by John C. McKinney and Edgar T. Thompson, (Durham: Duke University Press, 1965), pp. 322–336.

90. Talcott Parsons, "Full Citizenship for the Negro American? A Sociological Problem," *Daedalus: Journal of the American Academy of Arts and Sciences*, XCIV:4 (Fall, 1965), pp. 1009–1054.

91. For an excellent discussion of slavery's role in fostering race and color prejudice, see George M. Fredrickson, *The Arrogance of Race: Historical Perspectives on Slavery, Racism, and Social Inequality*, (Middletown, Ct.: Wesleyan University Press, 1988), pp. 189–205.

92. *In re Ah Yup*, 1 Fed. Cas. 223 (Case No. 104), 223–224, (1878).

93. See Elmer C. Sandmeyer, *The Anti-Chinese Movement in California*, (Urbana: University of Illinois Press, 1939), pp. 40–108. For the Chinese struggle to desegregate the schools, see *Wong Him v. Callahan*, 119 Fed. Rep. 381 (1903) and the discussion in Charles Wollenberg, *All Deliberate Speed: Segregation and Exclusion in California Schools, 1855–1975*, (Berkeley: University of California Press, 1978), pp. 8–81. The most comprehensive analysis of the Chinese situation in American law is Hudson N. Janisch, *The Chinese, The Courts, and the Constitution: A Study of the Legal Issues Raised By Chinese Immigration to the United States, 1850–1902*. J.S.D. diss., University of Chicago, (March, 1971). See also four articles by Charles C. McClain: "The Chinese Struggle for Civil Rights in Nineteenth-Century America: The First Phase, 1850–1870," *California Law Review*, LXXII (1984), pp. 529–568; "The Chinese Struggle For Civil Rights in Nineteenth-Century America: The Unusual Case of *Baldwin v. Franks*," *Law and History Review*, III:2 (Fall, 1985), pp. 349–373; "Of Medicine, Race, and American Law: The Bubonic Plague Outbreak of 1900," *Law and Social Inquiry*, XIII:3 (Summer, 1988), pp. 447–513; "*In re Lee Sing*: The First Residential-Segregation Case," *Western Legal History*, III:2 (Summer-Fall, 1990), pp. 179–196. See also Sucheng Chan, ed., *Entry Denied: Exclusion and the Chinese Community in America, 1882–1943*, (Philadelphia: Temple University Press, 1991).

94. *People v. Hall*, 4 Cal. 399 (1854); and *People v. Brady*, 40 Cal. 198 (1870).

95. See Victor Low, *The Unimpressible Race: A Century of Educational Struggle By the Chinese in San Francisco*, (San Francisco: East-West Publishing Co., 1982); and Wollenberg, *op. cit.*, pp. 8–81.

96. Attempts to deny the Chinese the opportunity to operate laundries constituted one basis for numerous court cases in only some of which the Chinese were able to prevail. See, e.g., *In re Quong Woo*, 13 Fed. 229 (1882); *Soon Hing v. Crowley*, 7 Sawyer 526, 113 U.S. 703 (1885); *In re Tie Loy* (The Stockton Laundry Case), 26 Fed. 611 (1886); *State ex rel. Toi v. French*, 41 Pac. 1078 (1895); *State v. Camp Sing*, 18 Mont. 128 (1896); *In re Yot Sang*, 75 Fed. 983 (1896); *Quong Wing v. Kirkendoll*, 223 U.S. 350 (1912); In re Mark, 6 Cal. 2d (1936). One case, *Yick*

Wo v. Hopkins, 118 U.S. 356 (1886), provided the grounds for a fundamental interpretation of reasonable classification and permissible intent. See John Gioia, "A Social, Political and Legal Study of *Yick Wo v. Hopkins*," in *The Chinese American Experience: Papers from the Second National Conference on Chinese American Studies (1980)*, (San Francisco: Chinese Historical Society of the United States and the Chinese Cultural Foundation of San Francisco, 1980), pp. 211–220.

97. *Ho Ah Kow v. Nunan*, 12 Fed. Cas. 252 (Case No. 6, 546), (1879).
98. See Theodore B. Wilson, *The Black Codes of the South*, (University: University of Alabama Press, 1965).
99. *In re Ah Quan*, 21 Fed. 182 (1884); *Chae Chan Ping v. U.S.*, 130 U.S. 581 (1889); *Wan Shing v. U.S.*, 140 U.S. 424 (1890); *Fong Yue Ting v. U.S.*, 149 U.S. 698 (1893); *U.S. v. Mock Chew*, 54 Fed. 490, 7 U.S. App. 534, 4 C.C.A. 482 (1893); *Lem Moon Sing v. U.S.*, 158 U.S. 538 (1895); *Wong Wing et al. v. U.S.*, 163 U.S. 228 (1896); *In re Li Foon*, 80 Fed. 881, C.C.S.D., N.Y. (1897); *Ah How et al. v. U.S.*, 193 U.S. 65 (1904); *Ng Fung Ho et al. v. White*, 259 U.S. 276 (1921).
100. *In re Gee Hop*, 71 F. 274 (1895).
101. *Chae Chan Ping v. U.S.*, 130 U.S. 581 (1889). See Sucheng Chan, ed., *op. cit.*
102. On wives, see *In re Ah Moy* (Case of the Chinese Wife), 21 F. 785 (1884); *U.S. v. Chung Shee*, 71 F. 277 (1895); *U.S. v. Mrs. Gue Lim. et al.* 176 U.S. 459 (1900). On legitimate or illegitimate offspring whether wholly or part Chinese, see *In re Knight*, 171 F. 299 (1909); *Ex Parte Wong Foo*, 230 F. 534 (1916); *Quan Hing Sun et al. v. White*, 254 F. 402 (1918); *Palo v. Weedin*, 8 F. (2d) 607 (1925); *In re Fisher*, 21 F. (2d) 1007 (1927). On subjects of China who volunteered and were inducted into the American military, see *Petition of Dong Chong*, 287 F. 546 (1923).
103. Children born in the United States to alien Chinese parents were also challenged, unsuccessfully, with respect to their citizenship. *U.S. v. Wong Kim Ark*, 169 U.S. 649 (1898). See also Stanford M. Lyman, *Chinese Americans*, (New York: Random House, 1974), pp. 86–92, 105–115.
104. *Chapman et al. v. Toy Long*, 5 F. 497, 500 (Case No. 2, 611), 1876.
105. *In re Hong Yen Chang*, 84 Cal. 163, 24 Pac. 156 (1890); *In re Gee Hop*, 71 F. 274 (Case No. 11, 200) 1895.
106. *Louie Wah You v. Nagle*, 27 F. (2d) 573 (1928).
107. See *Patsone v. Pennsylvania*, 232 U.S. 138 (1913); and "An Act to Repeal the Chinese Exclusion Acts, To Establish Quotas, and for Other Purposes," United States Senate and House of Representatives, December 17, 1943, reprinted in William L. Tung, *The Chinese in America, 1820–1973*, (Dobbs Ferry, N.Y.: Oceana Publications, 1974), pp. 79–80; see also Sidney L. Weinstock and Edward D. Landels, "Right of Chinese Aliens to Take Title to Land," *Journal of the State Bar of California*, XIX:1 (Jan.-Feb., 1944), pp. 19–34.
108. Lucy M. Cohen, *Chinese in the Post-Civil War South: A People Without a History*, (Baton Rouge: Louisiana State University Press, 1984).

109. See *Tucker v. Blease et al.* 97 S.C. 303, 81 SE 668 (1914). See also Brewton Berry, *Almost White*, (New York: Macmillan, 1963) and Stanford M. Lyman, "The Spectrum of Color," *Social Research*, XXXI:3 (Autumn, 1964), pp. 364–373.
110. *People v. Hall*, 4 Cal. 399 (1854).
111. *Ozawa v. U.S.*, 260 U.S. 178 (1922) and *Yamashita v. Hinkle*, 260 U.S. 199 (1922).
112. *Rice et al. v. Gong Lum et al.*, 139 Miss. 760, 104 So. 105 (1925). The United States Supreme Court sustained this decision. *Gong Lum v. Rice*, 275 U.S. 78 (1927).
113. An interesting mitigation of their legal status took place in Arkansas in 1927 when the supreme court of that state granted an injunction against those seeking to halt the sale of land to a Chinese resident alien. The ground, however, was a unique section of the state constitution prohibiting legal distinctions between resident aliens and citizens with respect to the possession, enjoyment or descent of property. The court was careful to point out that, absent this provision, Arkansas's alien land law would have passed muster. *Applegate et al. v. Jung Luke et al.*, 173 Ark. 93, 291 SW 978 (1927). Recently a professor of law at the University of Hawaii has asserted that a form of race discrimination prevails with respect to certain vocal accents, especially those of Asian Americans and Pacific Islanders. See Mari J. Matsuda, "Voices of America: Accent, Antidiscrimination Law, and a Jurisprudence for the Last Reconstruction," *Yale Law Journal*, C:5 (March, 1991), pp. 1329–1407.
114. *Nishimura Ekiu v. U.S.*, 142 U.S. 651 (1891).
115. *In re Saito*, 62 Fed. 126, C.C., D. Mass. (1894).
116. Dudley O. McGovney, "The Anti-Japanese Land Laws of California and Ten Other States," *California Law Review*, XXXV (1947), pp. 7–60.
117. *Ozawa v. U.S.*, 260 U.S. 178 (1922). Quotations below are from this decision.
118. For revival of the thesis that some Japanese might be descended from the Ainu, see John Noble Wilford, "Samurai Roots Are in Dispute: Are They Japanese?," *San Francisco Chronicle*, undated clipping in possession of the author.
119. For the details of this matter which, while outside the scope of the present article, ought to be of great interest to students of anthropology, ethnology, and sociology, see "Ozawa Case," in The Consulate-General of Japan, comp., *Documental History of Law Cases Affecting Japanese in the United States, 1916–1924*, (San Francisco: Consulate-General of Japan, 1925; reprint, New York: Arno Press, 1978), I, pp. 1–121. For the background of the *Ozawa* case, see Yuji Ichioka, "The Early Japanese Quest for Citizenship: The Background of the 1922 Ozawa Case," *Amerasia Journal*, IV:2 (Fall, 1977), pp. 1–22. For a detailed discussion of court cases affecting alien Japanese in education, marriage, occupations, deportation, etc., see Frank F. Chuman, *The Bamboo People: The Law and the Japanese Americans*, (Del Mar, Calif.: Publisher's Inc., 1976), pp. 18–103.

120. *Dred Scott v. Sandford*, 19 Howard 393, 410–424 *et passum* (1857).
121. See Andrew D. Weinberger, "A Reappraisal of the Constitutionality of 'Miscegenation' Statutes," Appendix G. in Ashley Montagu, *Man's Most Dangerous Myth: The Fallacy of Race*, 4th edn. (Cleveland: Meridian Books, World Pub. Co., 1964), pp. 402–424.
122. *In re Takuji Yamashita*, 30 Wash. 234; 78 Pac. 482 (1902). See Milton R. Konvitz, *The Alien and Asiatic in American Law*, (Ithaca: Cornell University Press, 1946), pp. 22–32, 80–96, 148–211; and Dr. Moritoshi Fukuda, S.J.D., *Legal Problems of Japanese Americans: Their History and Development in the United States*, (Tokyo: Keio Tsushin Co., Ltd., 1980), pp. 3–214.
123. See, e.g., *Gordon Kiyoshi Hirabayashi v. U.S.*, 320 U.S. 81 (1943); *Fred Toyosaburo Korematsu v. U.S.*, 323 U.S. 214 (1944).
124. California's alien land law was finally declared unconstitutional, but it took two cases to invalidate all of its provisions. *Oyama v. California*, 332 U.S. 633 (1948), *Sei Fujii v. State*, 217 Pac. (2d) 481 (1950). California's statute forbidding the issuance of commercial fishing licenses was declared unconstitutional in 1948 *Takahashi v. Fish and Game Commission*, 334 U.S. 10 (1948).
125. On the privileges and immunities, See Dudley O. McGovney, "Privileges and Immunities Clause – Fourteenth Amendment," *Iowa Law Bulletin*, IV:4 (November, 1918), pp. 219–244. See also Judith N. Shklar, *American Citizenship: The Quest for Inclusion*, (Cambridge: Harvard University Press, 1991).
126. For critical discussions of the racial restrictions on naturalization in the United States, see Dudley O. McGovney, "Race Discrimination in Naturalization," *Iowa Law Bulletin*, VIII:3–4 (1923), pp. 129–161, 211–244; George W. Gold, "The Racial Prerequisite in the Naturalization Law," *Boston University Law Review*, XV (1935), pp. 462–506; Charles Gordon, "The Racial Barrier to American Citizenship," *University of Pennsylvania Law Review*, XCIII:3 (March, 1945), pp. 237–258.
127. *In re Po*, City Court of Albany – March, 1894, 28 N.Y. Supp. 383 (1894).
128. *Petition of Easurk Emsen Charr*, D.C., W.D., Mo. – 1921, 273 F. 107 (1921).
129. See *In re Buntaro Kumagai*, 163 Fed. 922, D.C., W.D., Wash., N.D. (1908); *Bessho v. U.S.*, 178 Fed. 245, 101 C.C.A. 605 (1910); *In re Zasuechi Narasaki*, 269 Fed. 643, D.C., S.D.N.Y. (1919); *Hidemitsu Toyota v. U.S.*, 268 U.S. 402 (1925).
130. *In re Kanaka Nian*, 6 Utah 259, 21 Pac. 993 (1889).
131. See Alexander Saxton, *The Rise and Fall of the White Republic: Class Politics and Mass Culture in Nineteenth-Century America*, (London: Verso, 1990).
132. *In re Halladjian, et al.*, 174 Fed. 834, C.C., Dist. Mass. (1909).
133. *In re Halladjian, et al.*, 174 Fed. 834, 838 (1909).
134. *In re Halladjian, et al.*, 174 Fed. 834, 845 (1909).
135. *United States v. Cartozian*, 6 F (2d) 919, D.C. Dist. Ore. (1925).
136. *U.S. v. Cartozian*, 6 F (2d) 919, 922 (1925).
137. *In re Najour*, 174 Fed. 735, C.C., N.D. Ga. (1909).

138.　*In re Najour*, 174 Fed. 735, 736; C.C., N.D. Ga. (1909).
139.　*In re Mudarri*, 17 Fed. 465, 466; C.C., D. Mass. (1910).
140.　*In re Mudarri*, 17 Fed. 465, 467; C.C., D. Mass. (1910).
141.　See David Carliner, *The Rights of Aliens: The Basic ACLU Guide to an Alien's Rights*, (New York: Avon Books, 1977), pp. 171–172.
142.　*In re Ellis*, 179 Fed. 1002; D.C., D. Ore, (1910).
143.　*Ex Parte Shahid*, 205 Fed. 812; D.C., E.D. So. Car. (1913); *Ex Parte Dow*, 211 Fed. 486; D.C., E.D. So. Car. (1914); *In re Dow*, 213 Fed. 355; D.C., E.D. So. Car. (1914); *Dow v. U.S., et al.*, 226 Fed. 145; C.C.A. – 4th Circ. (1915).
144.　*In re Dow*, 213 Fed. 355, 357; D.C., E.D. So. Car. (1914).
145.　*In re Dow*, 213 Fed. 355, 358–364; D.C., E.D. So. Car. (1914).
146.　*Dow v. United States, et al.*, C.C.A. – 4th Circ.; 226 Fed. 145, 148 (1915).
147.　*Dow v. United States, et al.*, C.C.A. – 4th Circ.; 226 Fed. 145 (1915).
148.　*Ex Parte Mohriez*, D.C., D. Mass.; 54 F. Supp. 941 (1944).
149.　*Ex Parte Mohriez*, D.C., D. Mass.; 54 F. Supp. 941, 942 (1944).
150.　*Ex Parte Mohriez*, D.C., D. Mass.; 54 F. Supp. 941, 942–3 (1944).
151.　*U.S. v. Wong Kim Ark*, 169 U.S. 649, 702–732 (1898).
152.　*Ex Parte Mohriez*, D.C., D. Mass.; 54 F. Supp. 941, 943 (1944).
153.　*Loc. cit.*
154.　*In re Ahmed Hassan*, D.C., E.D. Mich.; 48 F. Supp. 843 (1944).
155.　*In re Ahmed Hassan*, D.C., E.D. Mich.; 48 F. Supp. 843, 845–6 (1944).
156.　For an historical account of the Arabs in America, see Gregory Orfalea, *Before the Flames: A Quest for the History of Arab Americans*, (Austin: University of Texas Press, 1988). See also Earle H. Waugh, Baha Abu-Laban, and Regula B. Qureshi, eds., *The Muslim Community in North America*, (Edmonton, Alberta: University of Alberta Press, 1983).
157.　See Karen Leonard, "The Pahkar Singh Murder Case," *Amerasia Journal*, XI:1 (Spring, 1984), pp. 75–88.
158.　See Joan M. Jensen, *Passage from India: Asian Indian Immigrants in North America*, (New Haven: Yale University Press, 1988), pp. 246–269; and three works by Gary R. Hess, "The 'Hindu' in America: Immigration and Naturalization Policies and India, 1917–1946," *Pacific Historical Review*, XXXVIII (February, 1969), pp. 59–79; "The Forgotten Asian Americans: The East Indian Community in the United States," in *The Asian American: The Historical Experience*, ed. by Norris Hundley, Jr., (Santa Barbara: Cleo Books, 1976), pp. 157–179; *America Encounters India, 1941–1947*, (Baltimore: Johns Hopkins University Press, 1971). See also Ronald Takaki, *Strangers from a Different Shore: A History of Asian Americans*, (New York: Penguin Books, 1989), pp. 294–314. For the saga of one American-born radical who became intimately involved with the anti-colonial movement against British rule in India (and later went on to become an early supporter of the Peoples Republic of China), see Janice R. MacKinnon and Stephen R. MacKinnon, *Agnes Smedley: The Life and Times of an American Radical*, (Berkeley: University of California press, 1988), esp. pp. 69–133.

159. Joseph C. Misrow, *East Indian Immigration on the Pacific Coast*, (Stanford, Calif.: Stanford University, 1915; reprint, San Francisco: R and E Research Associates, 1971), p. 11. See also Jensen, *op. cit.*, pp. 226–245.
160. Takaki, *op. cit.*, pp. 297–298.
161. *In re Balsara*, C.C., S.D. N.Y.; 171 Fed. 294, 295 (1909).
162. *In re Balsara*, C.C., S.D. N.Y.; 171 Fed. 294, 295 (1909).
163. *U.S. v. Dolla*, 177 Fed. 101 (1910); Jensen, *op. cit.*, pp. 250–252.
164. *In re Feroz Din*, D.C., N.D. Calif. S.D.; 27 F. (2d) 568 (1928).
165. *United States v. Balsara*, C.C.A., 2d Circ.; 180 Fed. 694, 695–6 (1910).
166. *Wadia v. United States*, C.C.A., 2d Circ; 101 F. – (2d) 7 (1939).
167. *U.S. v. Bhagat Singh Thind*, 261 U.S. 204 (1923).
168. *Wadia v. United States*, C.C.A., 2d Circ; 101 F. (2d) 7, 8–9 (1939).
169. Arthur W. Helweg and Usha M. Helweg, *An Immigrant Success Story: East Indians in America*, (Philadelphia: University of Pennsylvania Press, 1990), pp. 55–56; Hess, *America Encounters India. 1941–1947, op. cit.*, pp. 150–151, 159–160.
170. *In re Akhay Kumar Mozumdar*, 207 Fed. 115 (1913).
171. Jensen, *op. cit.*, pp. 255–269. See, e.g., *United States v. Akhay Kumar Mozumdar*, 296 Fed. 173 (1923); *Akhay Kumar Mozumdar v. United States*, 299 Fed. 240 (1924); *U.S. v. Sakharam Ganesh Pandit and Mohan Singh*, D.D., S.D. Calif.; 297 F. 529 (1924). See also Takaki, *op. cit.*, pp. 294–314.
172. *In re Sadar Bhagwag Singh*, D.C., E.D. Penna.; 246 F. 496, 500 (1917).
173. Jensen, *op. cit.*, pp. 190, 210, 237, 242.
174. *In re Bhagat Singh Thind*, D.C., D. Ore.; 268 F. 683 (1920).
175. *In re Bhagat Singh Thind*, D.C., D. Ore.; 268 F. 683, 685 (1920).
176. *In re Bhagat Singh Thind*, D.C., D. Ore.; 268 F. 683, 684 (1920).
177. *United States v. Bhagat Singh Thind*, 261 U.S. 204, 204–15 (1923).
178. *Kharaiti Ram Samrao v. United States*, C.C.A., Ninth Circ., 12 F. (2d) 879, 880 (1942).
179. Even after East Indians became eligible for naturalization in 1946, the plight of East Indians or Pakistanis who hailed from some part of the British Commonwealth that had made citizenship for such persons difficult and who had entered the United States as students was extraordinarily difficult. For one instance – leading to an overthrow of the "Congressional veto" over deportation decisions – see *Immigration and Naturalization Service v. Jagdish Rai Chadha, et al.*, 462 U.S. 919 (1983); and Barbara Hinkson Craig. *Chadha: The Story of an Epic Constitutional Struggle*, (New York: Oxford University Press, 1988).
180. William Graham Sumner, "The Conquest of the United States By Spain," *Yale Law Journal*, VIII (1899); reprinted in *Essays of William Graham Sumner*, ed. by Albert Galloway Keller and Maurice R. Davie, (Hamden, Ct.: Archon Books, 1969), II, p. 300.
181. Dudley O. McGovney, "Our Non-Citizen Nationals, Who Are They?," *California Law Review*, XXII:6 (September, 1934), p. 606.
182. *Ibid.*, pp. 606–632.
183. *Ibid.*, pp. 608, 614.

184.   *Lucio v. Government of the Philippine Islands*, 51 Phil. Rep. 596 (1928);
       cited in McGovney, "Our Non-Citizen Nationals...," *op. cit.*, p. 608,
       n. 51.
185.   See *Gonzales v. Williams*, 192 U.S. 1 (1903); *In re Giralde*, D.C., D.
       Md.; 226 F. 826 (1915). For a comprehensive discussion of the debate
       over the status of Puerto Rico and the Puerto Ricans, see Benjamin
       Ringer, "*We the People" and Others: Duality and America's Treatment
       of its Racial Minorities*, (New York: Tavistock Publications, 1983),
       pp. 945–1097. See also Eric Williams, "Race Relations in Puerto Rico
       and the Virgin Islands," *Foreign Affairs*, XXIII (1945), pp. 308–317.
186.   *In re Alverto*, D.C., E.D. Penn; 198 Fed. 688, 699 (1912).
187.   *In re Lampitoe*, D.C., S.D. N.Y.: 232 Fed. 382 (1916).
188.   *In re Mallari*, D.C., D. Mass.; 239 Fed. 416 (1916); *In re Mascarenas*.
       D.C., S.D. Calif.; 271 Fed. 23 (1921).
189.   *In re Rallos*, D.C., E.D. N.Y.; 241 Fed. 686, 687 (1917).
190.   *In re Bautista*, D.C., N.D. Calif.; 245 Fed. 765, 769 (1917).
191.   *In re Bautista*, D.C., N.D. Calif.; 245 Fed. 765, 771 (1917).
192.   *United States v. Javier*, C.C.A., D.C.; 22 F. (2d) 879, 880 (1927).
193.   *In re Rena*, D.C., E.D. N.Y.; 50 F. (2d) 879, 880 (1927).
194.   *Roque Espiritu De La Ysla v. U.S.*, C.C.A., Ninth Circ.; 77 F. (2d) 988
       (1935).
195.   Tricia Knoll, *Becoming Americans: Asian Sojourners, Immigrants, and
       Refugees in the Western United States*, (Portland, Ore.: Coast to Coast
       Books, 1982), p. 113.
196.   *Ibid.*, p. 105.
197.   *Alfafara v. Fross*, 26 Cal. 2d 358 (1945).
198.   Emory S. Bogardus, "Citizenship for Filipinos," *Sociology and Social
       Research*, XXIX:I (September-October, 1944), pp. 51–54.
199.   *Ibid.*, pp. 53–54.
200.   For a good example of the thesis that full citizenship would be granted
       to the "Asiatic" immigrant who could assimilate – coupled with
       proposals that immigration restriction, rather than absolute exclusion,
       be substituted for the then operant American policy on the matter,
       and that eligibility for naturalization be based on "individual ability,
       achievement, worth, attitudes, [and] potentiality" – i.e., "The test
       resolves itself to one of constructive assimilative ability" – see
       Emory Bogardus, *Essentials of Americanization*, rev'd. edn., (Los
       Angeles: University of Southern California Press, 1920), p. 213.
201.   Emory Bogardus, *Immigration and Race Attitudes*, (Boston: D.C.
       Heath and Co., 1928), p. 9.
202.   Among studies of these mixed-bloods, see Brewton Berry, *Almost
       White: A Study of Certain Racial Hybrids in the Eastern United States
       op. cit.*: William Loren Katz, *Black Indians: A Hidden Heritage*, (New
       York: Atheneum, 1986), and Jack D. Forbes, *Black Africans and
       Native Americans: Color. Race and Caste in the Evolution of Red-
       Black Peoples*, (New York. Basil Blackwell, 1988).
203.   John Collier, "United States Indian Administration as a Laboratory
       of Ethnic Relations," *Social Research: An International Quarterly of
       Political and Social Science*, XII:3 (September, 1945), p. 265.

204. *Elk v. Wilkins*, 112 U.S. 94 (1884).
205. *Cherokee Nation v. Georgia*, 30 U.S. (5 Pet.) 1 (1831); *Worcester v. Georgia*, 31 U.S. (6 Pet.) 515 (1832). For the effects of these decisions on the Cherokees, see William L. Anderson, ed., *Cherokee Removal: Before and After*, (Athens: University of Georgia press, 1991).
206. *Elk v. Wilkins*, 112 U.S. 94, 109 (1884), quoting *U.S. v. Osborne*, 6 Sawy. 406, 409 (1880).
207. *In re Burton*, 1 Alaska 111 (1900).
208. "Indians not born in the United States and not entitled to the special privileges growing out of service in the war ... are ineligible for citizenship." *Morrison, et al. v. People of State of California*, 291 U.S. 82, 96 n. 5 (1933).
209. Konvitz, *op. cit.*, pp. 113–114.
210. See Daniel McCool, "Indian Voting," in *American Indian Policy in the Twentieth Century*, ed. by Vine Deloria, Jr., (Norman: University of Oklahoma Press, 1985), pp. 105–134, esp. pp. 106–114.
211. Rev. St. U.S. sec. 2079 (1871). Quoted in *In re Burton*, 1 Alaska 111, 113 (1900).
212. *Ex Parte Green*, 123 F. (2d) 862 (1941). For the particulars of this and related cases, see Alison R. Bernstein, *American Indians and World War II. Toward a New Era in Indian Affairs*, (Norman: University of Oklahoma Press, 1991), pp. 22–39.
213. Harry A. Kersey, *The Florida Seminoles and the New Deal, 1933–1942*, (Boca Raton, Fla.: Florida Atlantic University Press, 1989), p. 156.
214. Fred B. Kniffen, Hiram F. Gregory, and George A. Stokes, *The Historic Indian Tribes of Louisiana: From 1542 to the Present*, (Baton Rouge: Louisiana University Press, 1987), p. 296.
215. Kersey, *op. cit.*, p. 155.
216. *Ibid.*, p. 159.
217. Donald Culross Peattie, "Lo Takes the Warpath," *American Legion Magazine*, (July, 1943), p. 30. Quoted in Bernstein, *op. cit.*, p. 45.
218. *Branham v. Langley, et al.*, 139 F. (2d) 115 (1943). See the discussion in Bernstein, *op. cit.*, pp. 41–42, 187 n. 7.
219. See Joseph LeConte, *The Race Problem in the South*. (New York: D. Appleton and Co., 1892; reprint, Miami: Mnemosyne Pub. Inc., 1969), pp. 367–375.
220. Norman Podhoretz, "My Negro Problem – and Ours," *Commentary*, XXXV (February, 1963), pp. 93–101; reprinted in *Racial and Ethnic Relations: Selected Readings*, ed. by Bernard E. Segal, (New York: Thomas Y. Crowell Co., 1966), pp. 239–250. Recently, a sociologist examined the ambiguities, difficulties, legal issues, and international implications of the "one-drop" rule designating descendants of Negroes of any degree as "blacks." See F. James Davis, *Who is Black?: One Nation's Definition*, (University Park: Pennsylvania State University Press, 1991).
221. Ernest Porterfield, *Black and White Mixed Marriages: An Ethnographic Study of Black-White Families*, (Chicago: Nelson-Hall, 1978), pp. 9–12. See also Edward Byron Reuter, *The Mulatto in the United States – Including a Study of the Role of Mixed-Blood Races Throughout*

the World, (New York: Negro Universities Press, 1969 [1918]), pp. 105–182.

222. Weinberger, *op. cit.*, pp. 402–424.

223. See, e.g., *Scott v. Georgia*, 39 Ga. 321 (1869); *Doc. Lonas v. The State*, 50 Tenn. (3 Heisko) 287 (1871); *Pace v. Alabama*, 106 U.S. 583 (1883); *State v. Tutty*, 41 F. 753 (1890); *Dodson v. State*, 61 Ark. 57, 31 S.W. 977 (1895); *In re Paquet's Estate*, 101 Ore. 393, 200 p. 911 (1921); *Kirby v. Kirby*, 24 Ariz. 9, 206 P. 405 (1922); *Eggers, et al. v. Olson, et al.*, 104 Okla. 297, 231 p. 483 (1924); *Roldan v. Los Angeles County, et al.*, 29 Cal. App. 267, 18 P. (2d) 706 (1935); *In re Monk's Estate*, 48 Cal. App. 2d 603, 120 p. (2d) 167 (1941); *In re Stark's Estate*, 48 Cal. App. 2d 209, 119 P. (2d) 961 (1942); *Jackson, et al. v. City and County of Denver*, 109 Colo. 196, 124 p. (2d) 240 (1942).

224. *Perez v. Sharp*, 32 Cal. 2d 711; 196 P. (2d) 17 (1948); *Loving v. Virginia*, 388 U.S. 1 (1967).

225. See Robert J. Sickels, *Race, Marriage, and the Law*, (Albuquerque: University of New Mexico Press, 1972); and Paul R. Spickard, *Mixed Blood: Intermarriage and Ethnic Identity in Twentieth-Century America*, (Madison: University of Wisconsin Press, 1989).

226. See the discussion in Milton M. Gordon, *Assimilation in American Life: The Role of Race, Religion, and National Origins*, (New York: Oxford University Press, 1964), pp. 61–131.

227. E.g., Robert K. Merton, "Intermarriage and the Social Structure," *Psychiatry*, IV (August, 1941), pp. 361–374; and Kingsley Davis, "Intermarriage in Caste Societies," *American Anthropologist*, XLIII (July-September, 1941), pp. 376–395.

228. Spickard, *op. cit.*, pp. 23–158.

229. Cf. Edward Byron Reuter, *Race Mixture: Studies in Intermarriage and Miscegenation*, (New York: Negro Universities Press, 1969 [1931] with Cloyte M. Larsson, ed., *Marriage Across the Color Line*, (New York: Lancer Books, 1965) and with Spickard, *op. cit.*, pp. 233–342, and Porterfield, *op. cit.*, pp. 59–172.

230. Joel Williamson, *New People: Miscegenation and Mulattoes in the United States*, (New York: The Free Press, 1980), esp. pp. 187–195.

231. See Dudley O. McGovney, "Naturalization of the Mixed Blood – A Dictum," *California Law Review*, XXII:4 (May, 1934), pp. 376–391.

232. *Thomas Lane v. Matthias W. Baker, Gideon Spahr, and John Ginn*, 12 Ohio 237 (1843).

233. *In re Camille*, C.C., D. Ore.; 6 F. 256 (1880).

234. See Everett Stonequist, *The Marginal Man: A Study in Personality and Culture Conflict*, (New York: Russell and Russell, Inc., 1961 [1937]), pp. 10–53.

235. *In re Cruz*, 23 F. Supp. 774 (1938).

236. *Morrison, et al. v. People of State of California*, 291 U.S. 82, 86 (1933).

237. *Morrison, et al. v. People of State of California*, 291 U.S. 82, 96 n. 5 (1933).

238. *In re Cruz*, 23 F. Supp. 774, 775 (1938). An interesting problem in American law and international relations would have arisen had the illegitimate Eskimo-white and Eskimo-Afroamerican offspring of

Commander Robert E. Peary and Matthew A. Henson, respectively, petitioned for citizenship in the United States before 1952. Although both Kali Peary and Anaukaq Henson might have claimed *jus soli* citizenship because each had been born in 1906 aboard an American ship, the *USS Roosevelt*, during the Peary-Henson expedition to the North Pole, it is possible that their petitions would have been challenged. Such a challenge might have argued that Eskimos were "Mongolians," and that, in accordance with the decisions in *Camille* and *Cruz*, Kali's "white blood" and Anaukaq's "African blood" were each one percentage point short of the eligibility criterion. As it happened, Kali and Anaukaq were not discovered until 1986, when S. Allen Counter, a member of the Explorers Club and a professor of neuroscience at Harvard came upon them in Greenland and introduced them to their white and Afroamerican families in the United States. See S. Allen Counter, *North Pole Legacy: Black, White and Eskimo*, (Amherst: University of Massachusetts Press, 1991).

239. Weinberger, *op. cit.*
240. *State v. Treadaway*, 126 La. 500 (1910). – See Virginia R. Dominguez, *White By Definition: Social Classification in Creole Louisiana*, (New Brunswick, N.J.: Rutgers University Press, 1986), pp. 30–35.
241. For the concept *Herrenvolk democracy*, see Pierre van den Berghe, *Race and Racism: A Comparative Perspective*, (New York: John Wiley and Sons, Inc., 1967), pp. 18, 29, 77, 88, 101, 109, 126, 147. See also Stanford M. Lyman, "The Significance of Asians in American Society," *The Asian in North America, op. cit.*, pp. 25–38.
242. Robert E. Park, "Racial Ideologies," in *American Society in Wartime*, ed. by William Fielding Ogburn, (Chicago: University of Chicago Press, 1943; reprint, New York: DaCapo Press, 1972), pp. 165–184.
243. Robert Redfield, "The Japanese-Americans," in Ogburn, ed., *op. cit.*, pp. 143–164.
244. Charles Gordon, "The Racial Barrier to American Citizenship," *op. cit.*, pp. 250–251.
245. *Ibid.*, p. 251.
246. For a comprehensive description and analysis, see Mary L. Dudziak, "Desegregation as a Cold War Imperative," *Stanford Law Review*, XLI (1988–89), pp. 61–120.
247. For this military imagery of the race problem in America, see Herbert Blumer, "The Future of the Color Line," *op. cit.*, pp. 322–336.
248. Thurgood Marshall, "Reflections on the Bicentennial of the United States Constitution," *Harvard Law Review*, CI:I (November, 1987), p. 4.
249. Recently one state governor and a President of the United States seemed to recognize this point. Governor Jim Edgar of Illinois ordered that state's Department of Human Rights to add Asian Americans and Native Americans to all affirmative action plans field by agencies under its jurisdiction. "Illinois Governor Orders Affirmative Action Goals," *The Pacific Citizen*, CXIII:1 (July 5–12, 1991), p. 1. On November 3, 1990, President George Bush signed the Seneca Nation Settlement Act, providing $35,000,000 in compensation to the Native Americans of southwestern New York for the failure of the United

States to fulfill its responsibilities under 19th Century leasing arrangements. See Laurence M. Hauptman, "Compensatory Justice: The Seneca Nation Settlement Act," *National Forum: The Phi Kappa Phi Journal*, LXXI:2 (Spring, 1991), pp. 31–33.

250.   The status of women has often been compared to that of slaves. This was the case in the writings of America's first sociologist [See Stanford M. Lyman, "Henry Hughes and the Southern Foundations of American Sociology," *op. cit.*, pp. 40–44], and in the perspective on America's race problem provided by Gunnar Myrdal. [See Gunnar Myrdal, with the assistance of Richard Sterner and Arnold Rose, "A Parallel to the Negro Problem," appendix 5 in *idem. An American Dilemma: The Negro Problem and Modern Democracy*, (New York: Harper and Brothers, 1944), pp. 1073–1078. See also Leslie Friedman Goldstein, *The Constitutional Rights of Women: Cases in Law and Social Change*, rev'd. edn., (Madison: University of Wisconsin Press, 1988; and Dorothy McBride Stetson, *Women's Rights in the U.S.A.: Policy Debates and Gender Roles*, (Pacific Grove, Calif.: Brooks/Cole Publishing Co., 1991), esp. pp. 14–41].

7 The New American Pluralism: Racial and Ethnic Sodalities and Their Sociological Implications
Michael W. Hughey and Arthur J. Vidich

I

Historically in American society, ethnicity was something to be overcome. America's dominant Anglo-Protestant groups expected the immigrant to "melt" or, more accurately, to assimilate to their norms, values and cultural styles. This metamorphosis was encouraged not only by routine discrimination against those whose accents, names, or styles of dress revealed the taint of another heritage, but sometimes also by more forceful pressures, such as the many Americanization movements of the late 19th and early 20th centuries and the anti-hyphen and prepardness movements associated with World War I. However, such pressures were seldom needed to spur most immigrants toward assimilation and, indeed, they were usually nurtured much more by the insecurities of America's dominant groups than by the recalcitrance of its ethnic minorities. This is not to suggest, of course, that the various ethnic and racial peoples in America were possessed of some uniform orientation toward assimilation. To the contrary, some groups, such as the Amish or the French Canadians in Maine, offered considerable resistance. Despite such exceptions, however, the great majority of ethnic groups and individuals either actively sought their own assimilation or simply drifted toward it by more or less unconsciously discarding features of their own ethno-racial heritage while adopting the orientations of the dominant group. For the most part, immigrants to America wanted – and continue to want – nothing more than to gain acceptance in their new country.

The terms and conditions of that acceptance, however, have under-gone significant changes during this century. Up to and even during the era of the New Deal, assimilation, or "Anglo-conformity," was the condition for what immigrants hoped would be full scale entry into the mainstream of American life and its social, political and economic institutions. This was so despite the fact that some national political leaders, such as Roosevelt, recognized and courted as voting blocs the ethnic enclaves in all the northeastern industrial cities. In the midst of the Great Depression, when many ethnics discovered that they would not realize the American dream, Roosevelt's political recognition of them softened the impact of their economic failure. In this sense, Roosevelt began to slightly mitigate the requirements of the older ideology of assimilation and unwittingly signaled at least some recognition of the idea of pluralism.

It was not until World War II, however, that the ideal of a plur-alistic society gained widespread acceptance, even though some groups, particularly Jewish intellectuals,[1] had been promoting it since World War I out of fear of losing their distinctive religious and cultural identity. From the perspective of ethnic groups, the idea of pluralism essentially granted cultural autonomy in return for patriotism, wartime solidarity, and loyalty to Americanism. Many ethnic youth proved their loyalty by their deaths or willingness to die for America in the war. This ultimate sacrifice provided their entire ethnic group with evidence of their Americanization. From the perspective of the dominant white Protestant groups, pluralism represented a necessary compromise – and perhaps even a deliberate military policy – to achieve a wartime consensus in a multi-ethnic society.

In the post-World War II Cold War period, dominant groups continued to accept internal cultural pluralism as a way of presenting a politically and economically unified front against the threat posed by international communism, which then was thought to be a greater evil than that of foreigners within the social order. Although the term "assimilation" was abandoned, it continued to be expressed in a muted and limited form as pro-Americanism and anti-communism: for minorities and ethnics, the stridency of their anti-communism was taken as a measure of their pro-Americanism. That this compromise was accepted on all sides can be seen in the fact that only since the war has there been a formal public acceptance of ethnic names, in the minimal sense of a willingness to learn how to pronounce them and of their non-stereotypical appearance in popular cultural settings.

Perhaps more importantly, in the post-war years members of ethnic groups have increasingly participated in nearly all previously White Anglo-Saxon Protestant (WASP) dominated institutions, such as the State Department, the higher reaches of the military, Wall Street law firms, investment banking firms, and boards of directors of cultural institutions such as universities, art museums, and scientific organizations. Real and symbolic participation by pre-World War II immigrant groups in the great American crusade against totalitarianism amounted to a ticket of admission into the dominant society. Immigrants who had arrived before the Immigration Restriction laws of 1924 could now consider themselves as "true" Americans, and as having been accepted as such, regardless of any lingering reservations about them that might have been held by segments of the older WASP community.

World War II represents a turning point in the history of American ethnic group relations. It is also a watershed that separates pre-war and post-war immigrant groups, whose experiences in and assumptions and expectations about life in the United States are quite different. Pre-war immigrants were expected to conform to the dominant culture, and most did so willingly in return for what they saw as the privilege of becoming an American. The movement of most pre-war ethnic groups toward assimilation was evident even in the ethnic ghetto communities that existed in many American cities. Despite exceptions, the ethnic ghettos did not generally represent organized resistance to assimilation, but rather served as zones of transition where immigrant groups could live in the relative comfort of ethnic familiarity even as they – or their children – eased toward a more complete integration into the dominant American culture. Most post-war immigrants have also continued to strive to assimilate at most levels, but, in contrast to earlier immigrant groups who lived under an assimilationist ideology, they have had the option of preserving and cultivating their ethnic heritage while still being able to claim acceptance as Americans.[2] This option, which has enabled both their integration into all levels of American life and its institutions and their now-conscious efforts to preserve some dimensions of their ethnicity, presents post-war ethnics with all sorts of social and cultural possibilities and ambiguities. The pre-war immigrants are now in the third, fourth and fifth generations. Post-war immigrants are in the first and second generations, but in many cases they are layered on top of earlier arriving waves of the same ethnic group, resulting in contemporary ethnic communities of considerable social and cultural complexity.

Regardless of assimilationist or pluralist ideologies, the very circumstances of American life have usually mitigated against the retention of ethnic loyalties and identities. For example, the American liberal tradition, with its cultural and political focus on the individual rather than the group, has worked over time to erode primary identifications with ethnicity and its symbols. In addition, the economic independence and mobility provided by a job, as well as by the financial and emotional supports furnished by welfare agencies and settlement houses, also often proved liberating for the children and wives of Old World patriarchs, thus eroding traditional authority and undermining a primary institutional support and focus for ethnic identity. In broader terms, the promise of America was itself the greatest solvent of ethnicities. To the disadvantaged masses of Europe, South America and Asia, America has represented economic opportunity and personal and political freedom. From their perspective, an old world ethnicity stood in the way of their acceptance as full-fledged Americans. Acceptance was precisely what they desired, and most were willing to cast aside their ethnic heritage to attain it.

And yet, despite the many pressures and incentives in American society that have tended to erode ethnic loyalties and identities, not only have some groups successfully resisted assimilation, but they have maintained an almost undiluted ethnicity as the basis of their community life. The Hassidic Jews of Brooklyn, for example, while accommodating to their urban American context, have not only resolutely maintained many of the Eastern European cultural styles, standards, symbols, and practices that make them a distinctive ethnic group, but have deepened their cultural independence by universalizing it among Jewry in Israel and throughout the world. Their ability to do so has undoubtedly been aided by the fact that they share very specific values, beliefs, customs, and ritual practices which give concrete substance to their ethnic and religious self-awareness and communal identity. Their self-confidence in their way of life is also reinforced by their linkage to an international network of other Hassidim who adhere to the same values and practices: they can be anywhere in the world and yet remain the same, and their sameness is not specifically American. Brooklyn's Hassidim manage to preserve their ethnic distinctiveness by separating their sources of income – e.g., business outlets, including retail computer outlets on 47th Street – from their community life, enabling them to protect their community and its religious distinctiveness from the intrusions of the values of all other groups, including those of earlier generations of German and Eastern European Jews. The Hassidim represent an extreme case, comparable in part only to the Hutterites, Amish, Mennonites, the Chinese residents of America's older China-towns, and many Native American tribal groups. These examples indicate that resistance to assimilation has not only been possible, but that it has been the preferred choice for some groups who, as a result, offer themselves as examples of what it means to live in the United States without accepting and adapting to its dominant values, standards, and cultural styles.

A similar resistance to the assimilative pressures of the broader culture cannot often be claimed by most other ethnic groups, whose members usually lack an ideological, religious, or ritual focus for their ethnicity. To the extent that the Hassidim and other groups preserved their ethnicity and community, or even tried to, they have been exceptions to the usual rule, which required that groups gradually "become" Americans by conforming to the patterns and styles of the dominant culture.

II

In American society today, however, ethnicity has re-emerged as a central aspect of peoples' identities and as a common focus for community life. Ironically, its re-emergence has in many ways resulted from some of the same social and cultural pressures toward individuation that contributed to its erosion in the first place. America is a nation of immigrants who were uprooted from family and friends and stripped of traditional sources of support and status. They came to a land of strangers where they too would have become strangers had they not sought out their ethnic likenesses. Thrown onto their own resources and impressed with the value of self-reliance and personal initiative in the struggle to make it and get ahead, they sought and found their psychological props in the ethnic community. Given these circumstances, it is to be expected that America's immigrants have always tended to associate with others from their country of origin, frequently in ghetto-like enclaves in big cities, mining regions, rural farming areas, and small towns. Wherever they settled, they established their own newspapers, churches, fraternal orders, bakeries, butcheries, and other businesses and networks for enhancing their chances to attain a piece of the American dream.

However, their pursuit of the American dream of a middle class way of life often carried with it an unspecified and unanticipated price. As immigrants attained upward mobility they often experienced physical mobility as well. Even the successful post-war ethnics for whom cultural pluralism was a socially acceptable alternative usually chose to dispense with most remnants of their ethnic heritage, and so moved from the urban ethnic community to antiseptic middle class suburbs. Upon "arriving" as middle class Americans, they began to move from house to house – perceiving their "home" mainly as real estate, as an object of speculation in value – often without ever developing a strong attachment to any particular street or neighborhood. Among the professional middle classes, friendship itself is often merely a matter of convenience or, at worst, is reduced to a network of contacts useful to one's career, and is therefore lacking in genuine sentiment and loyalty. Americans have few roots, and those they put down are often shallow and temporary.

American rootlessness is further reinforced by broader, more abstract circumstances, in particular by the rationalized organization of modern life. Individuals often come to feel personally isolated and lonely in the midst of an urbanized, bureaucratized society, in which the bulk of their social relations are reduced to rational agreements, self-interested involvements, and contractual associations. Ultimately, such limited forms of sociability are experienced as meaningless and personally unfulfilling, leaving a void of soulless emptiness and ennui.

American society does not offer a viable substitute for the personal loyalties and attachments or the social supports for personal identity which were once furnished by the ethnicity the immigrants shed for the sake of becoming Americans. There are few easy points of identification with American culture apart from its abstract political symbolism (e.g., the flag, the Pledge of Allegiance, etc.) and military prowess (expressed in victories over foreign countries and in the prestige value of military dominance). Indeed, historically it has been far more difficult to define what America *is* than to define what it is *not*. Nativists proclaiming a hatred of the foreigners in their midst have repeatedly emerged in American history to decry the "un-Americanism" of one or another group or creed, and in doing so have proclaimed themselves as "true" Americans without being able to adequately articulate its meaning. Americanism has never lent itself to specific definition because, in part, the country has always been composed of a vast mix of ethnic immigrants and their cultures. This mix of cultures would appear to offer a better definition of Americanism than the symbols and chauvinisms embraced by nativists. At least in part because of its inability to offer a well defined American cultural style and identity to ethnic arrivals, WASP culture and its dominant political leadership was eventually moved to an acceptance of the ideology of pluralism.

Since WASP leaders no longer insisted upon their assimilation, and since America could not offer them a coherent cultural identity to replace the ethnic identity they had largely abandoned, many groups and individuals began to rediscover and resurrect ethnicity as a a central component of their personal identity and ways of life. As a result, in contemporary American society the most primitive biological form of identification – that of descent – has been reasserted as a major basis for organizing the lives of virtually all immigrant groups, regardless of how many generations they have resided in the United States. Jews were the first group to actively promote the idea of pluralism in order to retain the cultural and intellectual traditions associated with religion and to free themselves from the missionary efforts of others. The kind of cultural pluralism advocated by Jewish leaders was made acceptable by the Constitutional separation of church and state and by the fact that it was not inconsistent with a determination of social and occupational mobility based on merit. This formula allowed the Jews to essentially have it both ways, that is, to enjoy both cultural autonomy and political and economic integration. Under the new system of ethno-racial dispensation, however, claims need not be made on the basis of merit, but can be made on the basis of descent alone. For the first time in America, social, political, legal and cultural recognition is now given to many groups on the basis of their descent, marking a major change in the traditional American ideology of individualism and open mobility based on merit.

These legally and/or socially recognized ethno-racial groupings appear to be like vastly enlarged clans, recognizable by the totemic markings of their names. But the intense bonds and loyalties that made the clan a powerful and historically persistent form of social organization appear here as a gossamer web. Indeed, like the concept of "Americanism," the enlarged clan – contemporary ethno-racial identity – lacks specific content, and is often most easily defined in terms of what it is not. For example, despite efforts in the 1960s to provide substantive content for the idea of "negritude" or "soul," the importance of "blackness" as an identifier lies mainly in its ability to evoke a broad identity and loyalty that categorically includes all blacks in relation to whites or excludes all whites in relation to blacks. Similarly, Italian-Americans may have lost virtually all cultural connections to the old country, and in fact may carry in mummified form cultural traits that no longer exist in Italy, but a sense of ethnic identity and boundaries persist based largely on last names, knowledge of a few Italian words, the visibility of some successful group members, and perhaps a return to a putative Italian cuisine.

This hardly suggests the sort of primordial attachments that are usually associated with traditional ethnic communities. And indeed, something has clearly been lost as immigrant groups now in their third and fourth generations seek to resurrect the ethnicity that their parents or grandparents had largely abandoned as they assimilated into the American mainstream. What the new ethnic communities have gained in breadth as enlarged clans, they seem to have lost in intensity. The new attachments to ethnicity often find no deeper or less trivial expression than attendance at annual ethnic festivals, summer vacations to the "motherland," or slogans and national flags printed on T-shirts. Frequently, revived ethnic identities seem to provide little more than a means of self-location, or even self-advertisement, in a society in which individualism means everything but the individual counts for little. Yet, even in its current diluted form, ethnicity is resurgent at least partly because it provides new, if limited and inherently exclusive, feelings of attachment that can provide a basis for both personal identity and communal solidarity.

For the newer ethnic immigrants from the Caribbean, Asia, South America, and Africa, a different psychological orientation applies. They have arrived at a time when pluralism and multiculturalism prevail as strong ideological currents, if not as dominant cultural ideals. As a result, they can openly and immediately begin to assert their claims for political and economic resources based on ethno-racial identity as well as on merit. At times, the stridency of their claims has encouraged blacks as well as the older ethnic groups to emulate the new styles and strategies of multiculturalism that are currently in the process of being invented.

Thus, ethno-racial identity or, more broadly, extended clan-based loyalty, has emerged as a matter of great significance for virtually all immigrant groups, regardless of how long they have resided in America. For those whose ancestors underwent assimilation, a rediscovered ethnicity offers an available foundation for community and identity that can be asserted against the impersonality, isolation, and meaninglessness of life in the cultural lacuna of modern, industrial, bureaucratic society. It also provides a rallying point for those others who in recent times have made a virtue out of publicly declaring and adhering to the symbols of their ethnicity, whether it be for political and economic or purely personal reasons. Clearly, race and ethnicity are resurgent in the contemporary United States as meaningful categories for the organization of personal and social life.

III

The ethnic confrontation with the American social, cultural, and political context has yielded all sorts of extraordinarily complex reactions by and transmutations of ethnic identities and sodalities, which have found concrete expression in the diverse and creative ways ethnic groups have coped with their ethnicity. The range of ways in which ethnic groups have coped with and given creative expression to their ethnicity appears much greater than existing theories of ethnicity allow. In fact, theoretical systemization may be defied by the tremendous diversity of ethnic responses, which appear to be as great as the range of ethnic cultures represented in the United States. By shifting our perspective to a focus on ethnic culture itself, and away from its assimilative potentials, we gain an alternative way of examining ethnic communities in the United States.

The ethnic community refers to a much broader social organization than can be contained by the physical borders of Little Italys, Irans, Cubas, Saigons, Chinatowns and other urban ethnic enclaves. The spatial location of a group does not define the group's psychological boundaries, which often includes members who have returned to the old country, moved elsewhere in the United States, or, with the passage of time, are remembered as heroes of past generations. The ethnic community does not exist in a fixed location but rather, one could say, as a form of consciousness, as a widely variable set of loyalties and personal identifications.

Regardless of their time and place of arrival, all ethnic groups confront a social, cultural and political order that contrasts with that of their country of origin. Once in the United States, the burden of adaptation is placed on the immigrant. How different individuals and segments of a group have adapted and/or resisted adaptation has often been decisive in determining the kinds of ethnic communities they created.

Some groups, for example, have attempted to resist the assimilationist pressures of American society to maintain a sense of community and identity that is grounded in their ethnic heritage. To offer an unusual historical example, a political community of German immigrants in the mid-19th century turned the requirement of Anglo-conformity on its head. Thoroughly convinced of the superiority of their native German culture, they set about the task of shaping the American culture to their own understanding of what it should become. These émigrés "expanded the idea of assimilation to include its reverse, the molding of the culture they sought to make their own."[3] Although it managed to retain many of its own cultural institutions, forms of entertainment, and dominance of cities like Milwaukee, Kohler, Wisconsin, and Hershey, Pennsylvania, this German political community did eventually find its acceptance in the United States. But its early expressions of resistance left an indelible mark on the host culture. Its efforts to transform America according to its own ideals and cultural values, especially in the areas of race relations and immigration policy, effectively contributed to the "Anglo-Saxonization" of American society, thus deepening a development that already had strong indigenous roots and making its own unique contribution to American cultural life.

The orientation of pre-World War II ethnic intellectuals was generally to promote the assimilability or accomplished assimilation of their group.[4] Today, however, at a time when ethnicity has been "recovered" as a self-conscious possession, the tendency is for intellectuals to claim limited assimilation and a preserved ethnicity on behalf of their group. In this vein, Salvatore Primeggia and Joseph A. Varacalli have suggested that an authentic ethnic identity and community has survived among Brooklyn Italians in post-war American culture.[5] Italian-Americans have found middle ground between the choices of complete assimilation on the one hand and devotion to a mummified replica of the ethnic heritage on the other. Instead of a wholesale adaptation to the urban American culture, they have "authentically adapted their ethnicity to fit the ever-evolving social contexts in which they find themselves," including the assimilation of newer Italian immigrants into existing Little Italys in America's major cities. Assimilating only into the "outer American culture" they are able to maintain "a vital sense of their Italianicity." According to Primeggia and Varacalli, the Italian community in Brooklyn continues to be grounded in this fundamental sense of "Italianicity" as it is expressed in and nurtured by strong familial, neighborhood, and religious ties. And, they suggest, while Italian ethnicity is today more self-conscious and voluntary than in the past, it is no less authentic as a result.

Yet, even when ethnicity does survive to form the basis for new community formations, it does not necessarily do so as a totality, as the complete bundle of surviving cultural ideals, values, practices, and understandings. Once ethnicity has become a self-conscious possession, its symbols and images can be readily adapted to serve more strategic purposes. For example, a very narrow and specialized form of ethnic community, one devoted essentially to fun and recreation, can be found in lounges throughout Brooklyn.[6] Each evening in the lounge, the Irish and Italian working and lower middle classes cast aside the dullness of their everyday lives and enter into a carefully constructed and well-managed communal fantasy. In the community of the lounge, each participant borrows selectively from favorable ethnic stereotypes to create a persona that can be strategically presented in pursuit of "personal expressiveness, self enhancement, and exotic experience." Such personae include "the 'tough guys' and 'wise guys' and 'tigresses' of the Italians" and "the plain, adventurous, hard drinking good old boys of the Irish." Ethnicity, in these communities, is not the wellspring of community solidarity, as it was in the more traditional ethnic community. Rather, it is but a cultural resource from which bits and pieces can be selectively borrowed to patch together both a temporary personal identity and, in collusion with others, a constructed community of compensatory dreams, expressed in the quintessential American institution of the working class lounge.

A limited escape from the organization of modern industrial life can also be provided by a very different kind of community formation. "Staged symbolic communities" – recreated or "performed" and sanitized reconstructions of past real or generic organic communities such as those at Williamsburg in Virginia and Old Sturbridge Village in Massachusetts, Shaker and Amana villages, and the Navajo village in Taos, New Mexico – express the nostalgia of contemporary urbanites for the kind of traditional communities that are no longer possible within the context of modern industrial society.[7] Each staged community is ethnically homogeneous and, in its presentation, is sanitized to reflect "an idealized representation of social harmony." At a time when ethnicity has been resurrected as a source of group pride, staged symbolic communities offer an opportunity to put on display the favorable features of a given ethnic heritage. This may be especially important for America's historically dominant ethnic groups, the Anglo-Protestants, since, at a time when ethnicity counts, they generally have none to count on. Staged symbolic communities at least provide them with an opportunity to implicitly claim an ethnic heritage of their own and to present images of Americanism as it may have once existed. Staged communities appear to be an effort on the part of both Native Americans and Anglo-Protestants to lay a claim to a history of their own, and to market it with pride in a segment of the tourist industry that is devoted to ethnic images. For ethnic visitors to these staged communities, they offer a glimpse of America's past before either they or their ancestors arrived, a view into a society that no longer exists except as a nostalgic recreation of a lost past. The life portrayed in such recreations is in some ways reminiscent of the ethnic Americans' village and peasant ancestry in the old country prior to the industrial revolution, and thus can serve to bolster the nostalgia of virtually all contemporary urban ethnic groups. For Anglo-Protestants, the staged communities also represent a last gasp of a once dominant but now declining stratum as it attempts to uphold a pristine image of the earlier way of life of its ancestors.

Once it is detached from lived experience, ethnicity provides a vast reservoir of cultural styles, symbols and images that are available for selective retrieval by any groups or individuals for their own needs and purposes. In this sense it becomes possible for ethnic images and symbols that enjoy high status in American culture to become the objects of consumption by groups who have no historical connection with them. For example, Washington, Connecticut was historically dominated by an upper crust Yankee stratum dedicated to the DAR, gentlemens' clubs, *The Social Register*, golf, and other symbols of high status WASP ethnicity.[8] Since 1980, however, Washington has witnessed a significant infusion of upper middle class professionals from New York City, including a high proportion of Jews, who have purchased weekened homes in the town. The "Weekenders" are attracted to the images of WASP gentility, colonial New England, traditional community ties, stone chimneys, and such antiquity as exists in America. However, for them these images do not express deeply felt commitments but rather are items of personal consumption which are "played at" as features of their chosen lifestyles. As such, the Weekenders display few inhibitions about mixing them with other features of their upscale ways of life which they import into the town, such as chic shops, gourmet foods, recreational styles, etc. As an ironic result, the Weekenders violate the traditional ethnic imagery that attracted them to Washington in the first place, and they cause significant dislocations and adjustments to the traditional class and social organization of the community. Such confrontations between competing life styles indicate that the newcomers into the old established community are no longer willing to accommodate to it, but instead have the self-confidence to impose its way of life on others,

which further weakens the self-assurance of native residents and pro-
vokes their resentment. To the extent that the newcomers become
dominant in the town, they develop a new hybrid of a traditional
American style of life.

In their efforts to nourish group pride, ethnic groups are not limited
to adopting or presenting sanitized images of past ethnic communities.
It is also possible to self-consciously adapt the meaning of contemporary ethnic identities and communities in order to make them as
favorable as possible, whether for reasons of group psychology or
public display. For example, the most decisive and defining event for
the contemporary Iranian-American community was the Iranian hostage crisis in 1979. As a result of that event, Iranians in the United
States suffered a common plight as victims of public opinion. Their
shared defensiveness reinforced their ethnic self-awareness, which was
expressed, for example, not only in a renewed interest in Farsi but also
in a strengthening of their social organizations and of the bonds on
which the community was based. Their ethnic self-consciousness was
elevated, then, even as they continued to undergo and strive toward
assimilation into the American mainstream. Rejecting both the contemporary Iranian regime and feeling somewhat superior to the shal-
lowness of American bourgeois culture (the result of their own very
strong literary and cultural heritage), they sought cultural distance
from both by emphasizing features of their ethnic heritage that are
derived from ancient Persia. The resulting symbolism and imagery on
which their sense of ethnic identity and community rests is therefore
"neither American nor strictly Iranian." Rather, it is a consciously
reconstructed ethnic identity that is nourished and disseminated
through a combination of old practices, new technologies, and a
deepening awareness that the Iranian community is nationwide in its
composition and organized to respond with a unified voice to American policy toward Iran.[9]

By contrast, contemporary pan-Hispanic ethnicity and community
were not merely adapted from older ethnic images, but literally created from scratch through the self-conscious efforts of Hispanic group
leaders. According to Patricia Kolb,[10] in the post-Civil Rights era
assimilation is no longer a desirable road toward upward mobility
for many immigrant groups. Rather, ethnic, racial, and gender identities have emerged as bases for making legitimate claims for social,
political, and economic resources, at least if these groups are
sufficiently politically organized to claim them. Initially, pan-Hispanic
unity was discouraged by the differential federal treatment of various

Hispanic national groups and by their differing times and places of arrival. However, recognizing the potential advantages of pan-Hispanic unity, leaders of various Hispanic nationalities began to encourage group cooperation and to define common interests and a common identity. For example, recognizing that a combined Hispanic identification could create greater political clout and enable stronger claims for federal benefits, leaders of Hispanic nationalities worked with federal agencies to list "Hispanic ancestry" on the 1980 census, and then worked together to ensure that as many such persons as possible were included in the final census count. In effect, the census created a pan-Hispanic ethnicity as a bureaucratic category. Efforts to gain support for bilingual instruction in New York City public schools provided another focus for developing a pan-Hispanic identity and unity around a common set of concerns. And New York City's Hispanic Parade supplied an opportunity both for behind-the-scenes cooperation among the Hispanic nationalities and a forum for publicly proclaiming and celebrating a unified Hispanic ethnic identity. In her examination of these developments, Kolb points to the specific political and legal steps and processes by which a pan-Hispanic ethnicity and community was socially constructed.

Black Americans who descended from the slave population also faced the problem of constructing an ethno-racial identity. In doing so, however, they have also had to deal with a unique dilemma that makes them a special case in American history: they have had to construct a collective identity while at the same time taking pride in and deriving esteem from it. Whereas other peoples such as the Chinese, Germans, Irish and almost all others could look to established cultural and national identities and histories, and whereas even the Hispanics can take pride in their separate national traditions, black Americans have been cut off from any real cultural identifications. Even if some African "survivals" do exist in America,[11] they have not been sufficient to form the basis of a collective ethno-racial identity. As a result, the generations of African Americans have sought to uncover or manufacture a usable past for themselves. In attempting to construct a genuinely *common* heritage, however, black Americans have had to claim that the many black ethnic groups that exist in Africa, and which form their ancestry, share a common culture. The most recent scholarly expressions of this claim can be found in Martin Bernal's controversial work, *Black Athena*, which purports to show that much of the civilization of ancient Greece was derived from that of black, Egyptian Africa. Similarly, other African

American scholars such as Molefi Asante have proclaimed the reality of "Afrocentricity," that is, that there is a single "African Cultural System" that binds all peoples of African descent to a common "emotional, cultural, psychological connection...that spans the ocean."[12] A non-intellectual and less specific – but more effective – expression of the same claim is contained in Jesse Jackson's widely accepted declaration that black Americans should henceforth be referred to as "African Americans" instead of "blacks." The very term invokes a common land of origins, implies the same kind of common ethnic heritage shared by other "hyphenated" American groups, and at least attempts to confirm an identity capable of engendering group esteem.

It is perhaps ironic that many contemporary American blacks now emphasize the group's uniform identity and common cultural heritage, particularly in light of the fact that the white imagination has often viewed blacks precisely in such terms, that is, as a monolithic group perceived strictly in terms of its common racial characteristics irrespective of any internal social, cultural, and class-based distinctions. In fact, of course, the American black community consists of a multiplicity of cultures and class divisions, which are often more important than its common racial identity in shaping individual interests, identifications, and loyalties. For example, as the black middle class has continued to grow,[13] its sources of personal identity and esteem are increasingly derived from professional associations and job demands, resulting in a gradual erosion of its racial identification with the urban black "underclass."[14] In a pattern that parallels the history of white ethnic groups, the satisfactions of upward mobility take precedence over ethno-racial solidarity. The black community in America is further divided into numerous ethnic and national groupings, many of which have few points of identification with the American blacks who descended from the original slave population. The social organization of these as well as of white ethnic communities are given internal complexity by further divisions that are based on class, ethnic, political, and cultural factors, and on the relationships that different groups within the immigrant communities have with the country of origin.

For example, in the Haitian community in New York the cultural styles and traditional status structure of Haiti continue to exert a decisive influence over the community's social organization even as segments of that community enter into the occupational, educational, class, and status structures of the United States.[15] Different groups and classes within the Haitian community adapt differently to American conditions, and press their claims for status and social recognition based on whichever criteria – Haitian or American – are most supportive of an individual's self-esteem. Although this creates opportunities for strong internal divisions and conflicts to emerge, Haitians tend to resist deeper assimilation and maintain a distinctive ethnic community based, among other things, on their strong sense of nationalism and ethnic pride, on their earlier opposition to the Duvalier regime, and on their more recent support of the now-deposed Aristide. In the Haitian case, almost all political issues are transnational, as has been made abundantly clear by the American government's policies regarding the problem of Haitian refugees.

The social organization of the Grenadian community in Brooklyn is determined primarily by the distinctive reactions of various segments of that community to the American social context.[16] The degree to which Grenadians either resist or embrace assimilation into the American culture and its stratification system depends mainly upon their traditional status in Grenada. The American context offers new opportunities for the lower classes and status groups of Grenada, and creates resentment and status defensiveness among those whose traditional economic and social standing was high. The resulting tensions between claimants for social esteem according to the criteria of different stratification systems adds considerable complexity to the social organization of the ethnic community. These complexities are further amplified by the retention of traditional Grenadian social distinctions – such as the importance attributed to family name and skin color – and by the infusion of political immigrants following the 1979 revolution.

The complex social organization of the Hungarian community in New Brunswick is characterized by several layers of social, economic, and political distinctions.[17] These layers are based on: three major waves of immigrants who arrived at different times with different motivations for immigrating; the Old World backgrounds they brought with them; their degree of economic and cultural assimilation into the American context; the varying orientations and expectations of the generations that succeeded each wave of immigration; new occupational statuses, the effects of which tend to be mitigated by the retention of traditional status distinctions; and the opportunities and conflicts introduced by each new phase of geopolitical developments, which have included the initial post-war Soviet-American alliance, the Cold War, detente, and the recent collapse of the Soviet empire. These many differences are overlaid by widespread, unifying sentiments, such as the preference for the Hungarian language and the conscious cultivation of national sentiments and cultural images and symbols. Hungarians in America also share an identification with what was once a great empire in Central Europe. Although that empire is long since defeated, it represents a moment of collective historical greatness that is capable of fostering personal pride and a sense of cultural superiority among its descendants. The self-confidence borne of this identification with past glory has enabled generations of Hungarians in America to resist many of the pressures and persuasions of assimilation and to preserve much of their ethnic identity.

As the Haitian, Granadian, and Hungarian examples indicate, the ongoing redefinitions of ethnic identities and reconstructions of ethnic communities are affected by various internal characteristics of these communities. An adequate description and analysis of any ethnic community would have to take into consideration such factors as the following:

- The degree to which the class and status structures of the country of origin continue to be recognized within the immigrant community, and how this recognition is reconciled with the entry of at least some members of the ethnic community into the occupational and class structure of the United States.
- The degree to which different groups within the ethnic community assimilate to mainstream American cultural forms, and on what bases other members resist assimilation.
- Time of arrival, which takes into account the fact that different generations arrive with different expectations and experiences, all of which may be expressed in the internal life of the ethnic community. The expectations of generations whose entire lives have been spent in the United States adds a further dimension of complexity.
- American foreign policy toward the country of origin, which may cause splits and political conflicts within the ethnic group based on such factors as attitudes toward communism and whether individuals immigrated for political or economic reasons.
- Political developments within the country of origin, which may intensify or depress feelings of nationalism, provide the community with new waves of immigrants, and give rise to internal political conflicts.

- Varying degrees of commitment to maintaining the national tradition, disagreements over which aspects of the ethnic heritage should be maintained (e.g., religion, language, music, etc.), and how it should be maintained (e.g., festivals, culture centers, autonomous schools, etc.) can lead to significant internal conflict and reorganization.
- The extent to which different members of the ethnic community seek recognition and status within the group and on its terms, or in the terms of the larger society or some segment of it.

The changing composition and organization of ethnic communities in the United States can be further affected by broader considerations. The level of performance of the American economy at the time of their arrival, for example, will determine the range and types of opportunities available to the members of a group, and perhaps limit their ability to find economic niches for themselves. A poor economy may also lead to conflict with nativist segments of the larger population who may resent having to compete with ethnic arrivals for jobs. Also, the political relationship between the United States and their country of origin affects not only the internal structure of the group, but the status of the group itself within American society. The ethnic group can lose status, and even become the target of suspicion and discrimination, if the United States goes to war with its homeland or is in diplomatic conflict with it.

These and other factors are given concrete expression in the social organization of ethnic communities in metropolitan regions throughout the country. In various combinations, they account for the extraordinary richness and complexity of contemporary ethnic community structures and point to the instability of the political and social psychology of all ethnic communities. To the extent that the United States is composed of its ethnic communities, the multiple and unsynchronized hybridization of American culture is in a continuous process of formation and transformation.

IV

Collectively, the issues raised here point to some of the most important sociological issues relating to ethnicity and ethnic communities in America. They suggest a deeper ethnic politicization of the society, a re-ordering of the foundations of group formations and personal identities, and, potentially, a redefinition of the foundations of American culture and civil society.

Politically, ethno-racial (and gender[18]) identities have been elevated into a recognized and, to some degree, an institutionalized basis for making claims to economic and political resources. Some ethnic and racial groups have already established themselves as political constituencies in the hopes of advancing further claims and/or preserving gains already made. Others may follow their example, making it more likely that race and ethnicity will be the overt basis of political appeals by candidates for office. The politicization of ethnicity also makes possible new combinations of ethnically and racially based political alliances, as the example of Jesse Jackson's Rainbow Coalition indicates. All of this makes the problem of making political appeals infinitely more complicated than it was for Roosevelt in the 1930s, when the ethnic players were fewer in number. Today, an appeal to one ethnic group may be taken as an insult to another, thus opening up a quagmire of risks for America's new class of political campaign consultants and managers, and possibly offering job opportunities to a new cadre of ethnic political consultants. Regardless of how one might assess such developments, to the extent that ethno-racial groups and group alliances replace the individual as the primary unit of political action, political liberalism is further undermined as the foundation of American democracy.

The new ethnicity has also fostered a new public moralism of sorts within the political culture. With the decline of the Anglo-Protestant stratum and the demise of its assimilationist expectations, all ethno-racial identities are proclaimed as equally positive values, as self-consciously embraced, cherished possessions. No distinctions of value or worth are to be drawn among them, and everyone is expected to approach group differences with an ecumenical attitude, to not only tolerate but celebrate our ethno-racial diversity in all its multitudinous expressions. At the level of public political discourse, this means that no overt critical or pejorative references to any ethno-racial identities are allowable, and any public figure who makes insensitive remarks, even if unintended, is quickly called to task by the aggrieved group. However, this new linguistic moralism often reflects merely a public and not always a private morality since members of various groups continue to hold stereotypic images of and biases toward one another. Therefore, ethnic and racial prejudices can still be exploited in politically strategic ways, but, in keeping with the new public moralism, all efforts to do so must be couched in coded terms. For example, the Willie Horton ads used so successfully by George Bush in the 1988 Presidential campaign accused Michael Dukakis of being "soft on crime" but were obviously designed to arouse and exploit white fears of black men. Some of the same "law and order" rhetoric has recently been used to refer to racial issues in the wake of the 1992 Los Angeles riots, although in much more muted terms. The political careers of Geraldine Ferraro and Mario Cuomo have both occasionally been beset by whispering campaigns charging that they have Mafia connections. During the 1988 election, Michael Dukakis's Greek heritage was subtly exploited to question his patriotism, especially regarding his refusal as governor of Massachusetts to sign a law requiring the recitation of the Pledge of Allegiance in public schools. As these and other examples indicate, the new ethno-racial moralism has been joined by a new dimension of hypocrisy as features of the political culture.

As ethno-racial identities have come to be embraced as positive cultural values in and of themselves, some of those who have recently and self-consciously recovered their ethnic roots have expressed heated indignation at the earlier expectation that they discard those roots in favor of Anglo-Protestant cultural orientations. In their view, the ideology of assimilation, as it was put into practice by the dominant groups, constituted a form of personal and group repression. As a result, some embraced their recovered ethnic identity with a sense of victimization and resentment. Theirs is an ethnicity that combines belligerent pride and angry defensiveness. This form of ethno-racial self-awareness has perhaps found its fullest expression on university campuses in the form of "multiculturalism," which expresses rage at WASP "hegemony" and the assimilation ideal at a time when assimilation is no longer a cultural norm and its WASP carriers are in decline. As an ideological orientation, multiculturalism seems to assume that the cultural and intellectual products of Third World ethnic and racial groups have been denied proper recognition by the political, economic, and intellectual dominance of white men. As a result, multiculturalists – who have recently played a major role in reshaping university curricula – tend to celebrate the cultural and intellectual contributions of non-white and non-European persons while denigrating those of Dead White European Males in general and Anglo-Saxon-Protestant males in particular. Since universities are among the most important and influential agents of cultural socialization in American society, the institutionalization of multiculturalism on campus has potentially far-reaching implications for the direction and content of American culture.

Socially, if the ethnic resurgence continues, it is possible to imagine the traditional network of American voluntary associations, as described by Tocqueville, giving way to new group formations based on ethnic loyalties. If current trends continue, one can even envision the "Balkanization" of American civil society into fixed ethno-racial divisions. One would also expect the development of stronger inter-linkages between local ethnic groups and their overseas brethren, possibly leading to commercial ties and transcontinental cultural groupings. Conceivably, such bonds could create the possibility for much greater foreign involvement in the development of American economic and political policy, perhaps even in the form of strong foreign government lobbies such as those already established by Israel and Japan.

Even if an American "Balkanization" did occur, however, the United States would likely not experience the scale and intensity of the violent ethnic conflicts that now plague Europe. This is mainly because ethnic groups in America have no fixed spatial locations; there are no connections between ethnic nationalism and defined territories. The reservations of Native Americans provide a partial exception to this, but Native Americans are a small population who are internally divided by older tribal loyalties and whose legal status is ambiguous. Other efforts at group separatism – by blacks, for example – resulted in failure. In many large cities, some ethnic groups regard their own neighborhoods as their "turf," which has occasionally led to small, sporadic conflicts with members of other groups, but the boundaries of these neighborhoods are somewhat fluid and subject to change as a result of demographic movement, urban renewal, zoning changes, and so forth. And in any event, ethnic conflict between rival neighborhoods would be local by definition and therefore small scale by the standards currently being set in Europe. America would probably also be spared an equivalent to Europe's ethnic conflicts precisely because the real hostility of ethnic nationalism is expressed in wars over territory in Europe, where the issues of contention have longer standing, the battle lines are more clearly drawn, and the hatreds and prejudices are more immediate and better nourished. For example, some fighting has recently been reported between Serbs and Croats in the United States, but this represents a pale and perhaps half-hearted reflection of the bloody civil war that has left much of what was once Yugoslavia in ruins. Such fighting in the United States is restrained by the fact that it comes under the jurisdiction of a police force that is not ethnically aligned and whose purpose in such disputes is to preserve the social peace. Because ethno-racial communities in the United States are not territorially defined, antagonisms between groups tend to find expression in political and legal arenas rather than on the battlefield.

At a personal level, ethnic images, styles and symbols now provide a broad pool of cultural resources which can be tapped for the construction and organization of personal identities. In developing one's own identity and way of life, one can choose ethnic styles and images either from among ethnicities or from among the styles and images of different ethnicities. This obviously suggests a fundamental shift both in the meaning of ethnicity and in the organization of personal identities.

These processes are, of course, in the throes of continuous change. At this point, to predict their outcome would stand no greater chance of success than those who, in an earlier era, predicted that all ethnicities would "melt" into a uniform American character. It is not possible to determine whether ethnicity will yet cease to matter, or whether these new forms, versions and styles of ethnicity and ethnic organization will come to be stabilized into new American traditions, cultural patterns, and social structures. In either case, the contemporary era appears destined to establish a new foundation for the civic and political order of American society.

NOTES

1. Horace Kallen's work on the idea on cultural pluralism was particularly influential. See his *Culture and Democracy in the United States* (New York: Arno Press and the *New York Times*, 1970).
2. This is evident in the contemporary Little Italys, Chinatowns, and other survivals of what were once ethnic ghetto areas. No longer the urban eyesores of a previous era, today these communities are often self-consciously preserved as the objects of pride and booster-like acclaim and as prime tourist attractions in their metropolitan regions. The former ghetto has "arrived" along with the immigrant groups who gave them their ethnic character.
3. Mary E. McMorrow, "An Ideological Immigrant Community: Assimilating Americans to the Germans of 1846." McMorrow's essay appears in Michael W. Hughey and Arthur J. Vidich, *The Ethnic Quest for*

Community: Searching for Roots in the Lonely Crowd (Greenwich: JAI Press, 1993). This and the other illustrations cited in this essay are taken from this volume and are used here to develop a conception of ethnicity in the United States that takes into account the ethnic cultures of origin, different times of arrival for and within various groups, and differences in "starting points" for various groups both in terms of their own social psychology at the time of arrival and in terms of social, political, and economic developments in the United States. This essay is an expanded version of our introduction to that volume.

4. The intellectual participants in this tradition have been referred to as "filiopietistic historians." For a discussion of much of their work, see Edward N. Saveth, *American Historians and European Immigrants, 1875–1925* (New York: Russel & Russel, 1965).

5. Salvatore Primeggia and Joseph A. Varacalli, "Community and Identity in Italian-American Life," in Hughey and Vidich, *op. cit.*

6. Karl Kavadlo, "World Rejecting Hedonism of the Working Classes: Irish and Italians in Queens and Brooklyn," in Hughey and Vidich, *ibid.*

7. Diane Barthel, "Back to Utopia: Staged Symbolic Communities," in Hughey and Vidich, *ibid.* Also see Barthel, "Nostalgia for America's Village Past," *The International Journal of Politics. Culture, and Society*, Volume 4, Number 1 (Fall 1990); pp. 79–93.

8. Roberta Satow, "Strangers in Paradise: Class, Status and Ethnicity in a Connecticut Town," in Hughey and Vidich, *ibid.*

9. Mahmoud Ansari, "The Making of the Iranian Community in America," in Hughey and Vidich, *ibid.*

10. Patricia Kolb, "The Development of the Pan-Hispanic Community in the United States," in Hughey and Vidich, *ibid.*

11. This, of course, is the well known thesis of Melville J. Herskovitz, *Myth of the Negro Past* (New York: Harper, 1941).

12. Molefi Asante, *Afrocentricity* (Trenton, NJ: African World Press, 1988). The quote is taken from Arthur Schlesinger, Jr., *The Disuniting of America: Reflections on a Multicultural Society.* (Whittle Direct Books, 1991), p. 32.

13. In 1985, Bart Landry estimated that 27% of black workers were employed in middle class occupations, as opposed to only 10% at roughly the middle of the century. See Landry, *The New Black Middle Class.* (Berkeley: University of California Press, 1987).

14. Arthur S. Evans, Jr. examines the emergence and implications of this expanding class-based division within the black community in "The Black Middle Class," *The International Journal of Politics, Culture, and Society*, Vol. 6, No. 2.

15. Yolaine Armand, "Ethnic Identity of the Haitian Community," in Hughey and Vidich, *op. cit.*

16. Robert E. Millette, "Grenadians in Brooklyn: Social Ranking and Adaptation," in Hughey and Vidich, *ibid.*

17. Tamas Tamas "Class, Status, and Politics in an American-Hungarian Community," in Hughey and Vidich, *ibid.*

18.   Gender, as well as age, sexual preference, disability or handicapped
       status, etc. all cut across ethno-racial lines and thus provide individuals
       with two or more sets of group identifications that can furnish bases for
       the formation of personal identity. Which group loyalties become the
       chief basis of identification for an individual and, perhaps, the primary
       source of personal identity, depends upon a number of factors, includ-
       ing the following:

- the personal interests that are foremost in the life of an individual
  at any given time;
- the social group from which the individual can claim the greatest
  social and self-esteem, or which can provide the most meaningful
  or favorable connections between personal identity and broader
  political, social, and cultural issues and developments;
- the social group that offers the greatest victimization status, which
  could provide both psychological self-justification for personal
  failures and misfortunes as well as legal protections and preferences to redress group victimization.

In cases of multiple group loyalties, personal identity can rest on
shifting foundations, with no single group identification emerging as
primary. In this case, the hierarchy of personal importance of group
loyalties can shift according to external political, social, and cultural
events that affect them. It is also possible for a single group loyalty and
source of personal identity to become primary (e.g., black rather than
female). And, of course, an individual may not strongly identify with
any of the social groups in which he/she could claim membership.
Whichever outcome results in any given case is an empirical question
that will be decided on the basis of the unique background of individual experiences and predispositions.

8 Contesting the Meaning of Race in the Post-Civil Rights Period

Howard Winant

There were two senior proms in May 1991 at the Brother Rice High School, a Catholic college preparatory academy in Chicago – an official one that was virtually all white and, for the first time, an alternative, all-black prom.

Popular music, in this instance, provided the rallying point for racial consciousness and self-segregation. The trouble began when a white prom committee announced that the playlist for the music to be featured at the prom would be based on the input of all the members of the senior class. Each student would list his or her three favorite songs, and the top vote getters would be played. While this procedure was ostensibly democratic, African-American students (who constituted 12 percent of the student body) complained that their preferences would be effectively shut out in a system of majority rule – tracks by Public Enemy would be overwhelmed by those of Guns N' Roses.

But parity was not the only issue. One African-American senior noted that even if they got half the requests, he and his friends would still be unhappy since "we would have sat down during their songs and they would have sat down during ours." So the African-American students organized their own prom against the wishes of school administrators, who disavowed the prom and barred the use of the Brother Rice name. The principal of the school, Brother Michael Segvich, said, "There is only one prom this year at Brother Rice. [The black prom] is something we don't want. I think it has to do with racism" (Wilkerson 1991).

Ah yes, but "racism" on whose part? The controversy over two proms raises a host of questions regarding the relationship of majority and minority cultures, fairness and representation, and (in the immortal words of soul singer Aretha Franklin) "who's zoomin' who." In essence, issues that debate the very meaning of racial integration and equality in American life.

While educational institutions have been formally integrated for decades, we are nonetheless witnessing a growing "balkanization" among students of different racial backgrounds, and a parallel increase in racial conflict and tension. Such difficulties are by no means confined to the schools. The workplace, neighborhoods, the health care industry, the media, and political parties are equally sites of conflicts regarding issues of racial organization and composition. Despite legal guarantees of equality and access, race continues to be a fundamental organizing principle of individual identity and collective action. The "continuing significance of race" results in part from the *contested meaning* of race – and of terms like "equality," "difference," and "racism" – in the post-civil rights period.

More than twenty-five years since the passage of key pieces of federal legislation outlawing racial discrimination in jobs, public accommodations, immigration policy, and voting rights, we remain consumed by political and cultural attempts to define and redefine the meaning of race for institutional life and individual identity. Discrimination's scope and meaning are still debated, legislated, and litigated. "Self-segregation" in daily practice and institutional life is both denounced and defended. While an overwhelming majority of whites favors egalitarian principles, according to survey data, only a minority supports state attempts to ensure equality (Schuman et al. 1985).

Despite the civil rights movement's profound impact on racial attitudes and institutional arrangements, in the post-civil rights period the issue of race remains more controversial than ever. Why is this so? I would argue that specific patterns of *racialization* that create new racial subjects and significantly transform existing ones have emerged. Far from declining in significance, the racial dimensions of political and social life have expanded.

RACIALIZATION

Over the past several decades, we have witnessed attempts from across the political spectrum to define the appropriate meaning of race in institutional life and to establish coherent racial identities based on that meaning.[1] In my view, such objectives were, and continue to be, unattainable. This is because race, a pre-eminently social construct, is inherently subject to contestation; its meaning is intrinsically unstable.

From a *racial formation* perspective (Omi and Winant 1986), race is understood as a fluid, unstable, and "decentered" complex of social meanings constantly being transformed by political conflict. Race both shapes the individual psyche and "colors" relationships among individuals on the one hand, and furnishes an irreducible component of collective identities and social structures on the other.

Employing this approach, I argue that it is necessary to interpret the meaning of race not in terms of definitions, but in terms of racial formation processes. Chief among these processes is the construction of racial identity and meaning that I call racialization.

The concept of racialization signifies the extension of racial meaning to a previously racially unclassified relationship, social practice, or group.[2] A historical example would be the consolidation of the racial category of *black* in the United States from Africans whose specific identity was Mande, Akan, Ovimbundu, or Ibo, among others. Parallel to this, as Winthrop Jordan (1977 [1968]) observes, was the evolution of the term *white* as a crucial form of self-identity for Europeans, who had earlier thought of themselves under such categories as *Christian, English,* and *free.*

As Lieberson and Waters (1988) note, racial/ethnic groups should not be viewed as static categories, but "as products of labeling and identification processes that change and evolve over time." They suggest "a continuous process of combining and recombining" in which "groups appear and disappear" (252). In line with this approach, I utilize the concept of racialization to argue that race and racial meanings have been significantly transformed by the civil rights movement. In its wake, North Americans have witnessed state and policy reforms (such as affirmative action), demographic changes (influenced in large part by the "liberalization" of immigration policy), and dramatic shifts in sociocultural understandings of race and racism.

In the post-civil rights period, new forms and expressions of racialization have unfolded. These include the emergence and consolidation of new racial categories, the appearance of differences and divisions within previously well defined racial groups, and the phenomenon of groups confronting previously unexamined questions regarding their racial identity and status. In the sections that follow, I examine in turn three key examples of these tendencies: the development of new racial subjects as a result of panethnic consciousness; the increasing significance of class for African-Americans; and the crisis of white identity.

PANETHNICITY AND THE DEVELOPMENT OF NEW RACIAL SUBJECTS

In the post-civil rights period, groups whose previous national or ethnic identities were quite distinct have become consolidated into a single racial category.

Prior to the late 1960s, for example, there were no "Asian Americans." In the wake of the civil rights movement, distinct Asian ethnic groups, primarily Chinese, Japanese, Filipino, and Korean Americans, began to frame and assert their common identity as Asian Americans. This political label reflected the similarity of treatment that these groups historically encountered at the hands of state institutions and the dominant culture at large. Different Asian ethnic groups had been subject to exclusionary immigration laws, restrictive naturalization laws, labor market segregation, and patterns of ghettoization by a polity and culture that treated all Asians as alike.

The *racialization* of Asian Americans involved muting the profound cultural and linguistic differences, and minimizing the significant historical antagonisms, that had existed among the distinct nationalities and ethnic groups of Asian origin. In spite of enormous diversity, Asian American activists found this new political label a crucial rallying point for raising political consciousness about the problems of Asian ethnic communities and for asserting demands on state institutions.

The racialization of Asian ethnic groups was paralleled by the racialization of other groups, notably Latinos and Native Americans. Such panethnic activism was inspired by the civil rights movement and anticolonial nationalist movements in Asia, Africa, and Latin America. Somewhat ironically, the very movements that sought an end to racial discrimination at home and colonial rule abroad also fostered an increased political awareness among formerly fragmented ethnic groups that they constituted a larger, racially defined entity.

David Lopez and Yen Espiritu (1990) define panethnicity as "the development of bridging organizations and solidarities among subgroups of ethnic collectivities that are often seen as homogeneous by outsiders" (198). Such a development, they claim, is a crucial feature of ethnic change – "supplanting both assimilation and ethnic particularism as the direction of change for racial/ethnic minorities" (198). Lopez and Espiritu suggest that panethnic formations are not merely "alliances of convenience" but are shaped by an ensemble of cultural factors such as common language and religion, and by structural factors such as race, class, generation, and geographical concentration. They do conclude, however, that a specific concept of race is fundamental   to   the   construction   of   panethnicity,   since "those...groups that, from an outsider's point of view, are most racially homogeneous are also the groups with the greatest panethnic development" (219–20).

The rise of panethnicity is a process of racialization that is driven by a dynamic relationship between the specific group being racialized and the state. The elites representing such groups find it advantageous to make political demands by using the numbers and resources that panethnic formations can mobilize. The state, in turn, can more easily manage claims by recognizing and responding to large blocs as opposed to dealing with the specific claims of a plethora of ethnically defined interest groups. Conflicts often occur over the precise definition and boundaries of various racially defined groups and their adequate representation in census counts, reapportionment debates, and group-specific social programs (scholarships, bilingual education, etc.).

Panethnic consciousness and organization are, to a large extent, contextually and strategically determined. There are times when it is advantageous to be in a panethnic bloc, and times when it is desirable to mobilize along particular ethnic lines. Therefore, *inclusionary* and *exclusionary* politics are involved in panethnicity, as racial and ethnic boundaries and definitions are contested.

Two examples illustrate the situational nature of this dynamic. In an attempt to boost their political clout and benefits from land trust arrangements, native Hawaiians voted four to one in January 1990 to expand the definition of their people to anyone with a drop of Hawaiian "blood." Previously, only those with at least 50 percent Hawaiian "blood" were eligible for certain benefits (Essoyan 1990). By contrast, in June 1991 in San Francisco, Chinese American architects and engineers protested the inclusion of Asian Indians under the city's minority business enterprise law. Citing a Supreme Court ruling that requires cities to define narrowly which groups had suffered discrimination in order to justify specific affirmative action programs, Chinese Americans contended that Asian Indians should not be considered "Asian" (Chung 1991). At stake were obvious economic benefits accruing to designated "minority" businesses.

The post-civil rights period has witnessed the rise of panethnicity as a phenomenon of racialization. Groups that were previously self-defined in terms of specific ethnic background, and that were marginalized by the seemingly more central dynamic of black/white relations, began to confront their own racial identity and status in a political environment of heightened racial consciousness and mobilization.

Panethnicity will continue to be an enduring feature of political life as we enter the next century. The dramatically changing demographic landscape, the transformation of global, regional, and sectoral economies, and the contested nature of political power all conspire to insure a role for panethnic identity, consciousness, and political organization in the foreseeable future.

THE INCREASING SIGNIFICANCE OF CLASS

According to law professor Roy Brooks, "Deep class stratification within African-American society is without a doubt the most significant development in the 'American dilemma' since the civil rights movement of the 1960s" (Brooks 1990: xi). Few analysts today would take issue with him. When William Julius Wilson argued in 1978, however, that the contemporary life chances of individual African-Americans "have more to do with their economic class position than with their day-to-day encounters with whites" (1980: 1), he created a storm of debate about the relative importance of race and class in American life.

Since then, many scholars have emphasized the primacy of nonracial factors, particularly class variables, in shaping African-American life chances in the post-civil rights period. Thomas Sowell (1983), for example, asserts that differences in racial/ethnic group economic performance are solely a function of the group's human capital, and not a function of society-wide discrimination. Wilson himself, in *The Truly Disadvantaged* (1987), argues that the impersonal forces of the market economy explain more about the current impoverishment of the inner city African-American poor than analyses relying on notions of racial discrimination. While he does not dismiss the effects of historical racial discrimination, he concludes that capital is "colorblind," and that the large-scale demographic, economic, and political changes that have negatively affected the ghetto have little to do with race.

Stressing the role of class in shaping the African-American experience is nothing new. As pioneering studies by Du Bois (1967 [1899]) and Frazier (1957) have demonstrated, class antagonisms within the

African-American community have a venerable history. Socioeconomic homogeneity has never existed in any racially defined community. So are class divisions any more significant today than they were in the past?

I think the answer is yes. Previous conflicts between the "black bourgeoisie" and the "black masses" took place in a context of nearly complete segregation. However much these two sectors of the community viewed each other with suspicion and mistrust, they were forced to live together, and frequently to ally against the system of white supremacy. But the civil rights movement created a new context for racialization. With the passage of civil rights reforms, patterns of racial segregation in a range of institutional arenas were severely challenged.

Thus, twenty-five years after the enactment of major civil rights reforms, the African-American community is both the beneficiary and the victim of its own success. A community once knitted together by survival imperatives in a segregated society and bound up by internal "thick" relationships of intracommunal labor, commerce, residence, and religion has now been divided, and this division has occurred primarily along *class* lines.

African-Americans who could take advantage of the slow but real lowering of racial barriers in education, employment, and housing have been able to achieve an unprecedented degree of upward mobility since the late 1960s (Freeman 1976). This does not mean that they are shielded from discriminatory acts or that they have abandoned their identification as "black." But it does mean that they are living in a far more integrated world and that racial identity and racism no longer determine their fates or futures as inexorably as before (Landry 1987). At the same time, capital flight and fiscal crisis have further impoverished low-skilled and undereducated African-Americans, leading to the much-publicized dilemma of the "under-class," or "ghetto poor" (Wilson 1991).

The result of these transformations, therefore, is the *differential racialization* of African-Americans along the lines of class. Such differentiation has important consequences for individual identity, collective consciousness, and political organization. For the African-American middle class, for example, it generates profound ambivalence about racial identity. As Dr Alvin Poussaint notes:

There's a lot of pressure on the black middle class to stay black.... It's kind of a contradiction. Your kids are living in an integrated community, and you want them to feel part of the community, participating equally in it. Then you feel very ambivalent about it psychologically, when they do. (Garreau 1987)

Nor are middle-class African-Americans shielded from discriminatory treatment by virtue of their class position. In a study of anti-black discrimination in public places, Joe R. Feagin found that African-American shoppers were subject to excessive surveillance and frequently received curt and discourteous services from clerks: "No matter how affluent and influential, a black person cannot escape the stigma of being black, even while relaxing or shopping" (Feagin 1991: 107; see also Williams 1991).

Poussaint and Feagin suggest that racial identity is still conflictual, and racial discrimination is still problematic, for all strata of the African-American community. Such analyses also reveal, however, that the effects of these conflicts and problems vary widely by class. The middle-class ambivalence about racial identity described by Poussaint contrasts sharply with the bitter frustration and pervasive violence through which impoverished ghetto youth experience their blackness (Eric B. and Rakim 1990). The sites and types of discriminatory acts, and the range of available responses to them, obviously differ by class. Yet in other instances, the malevolent attention that police devote to African-Americans reveals a frightening uniformity across all classes; such is the judgment of the Christopher Commission report on the Los Angeles Police Department (Dunne 1991).

The "increasing significance of class" does not, therefore, suggest a "declining significance of race." In the wake of civil rights reforms, distinct paths of opportunity created a modicum of upward mobility for the African-American middle class, but did little or nothing to improve conditions for the ghetto poor. Despite this dramatic transformation, African-Americans remain a pre-eminently racialized group in politics, cultural representation, and social life. They are not, however, racialized in a uniform and homogeneous manner.

Such a perspective is important since much of the race versus class debate suffers from the imposition of rigid categories and analyses that tend to degenerate into dogmatic assertions of the primacy of one category over the other. Wouldn't a more fruitful mode of inquiry seek to account for the impact of class transformation within a social order still highly structured by race? We need a way, in other words, to grasp the increasing significance of class for African-Americans and other racially defined groups that does not deny the centrality of race in the formation of identity and everyday experience.

THE CRISIS OF THE WHITE IDENTITY

It is an unremarkable observation that we are increasingly becoming a multiracial society. The dramatic increase in "minority" populations in the United States renders much of the very language of race relations obsolete and incongruous. By 2003, whites are expected make up less than 50 per cent of the population of California, for example, and the demographics of the workplace and the campus are changing faster than those of the general state population (Institute for the Study of Social Change 1990).

The prospect that whites may not constitute a clear majority nor exercise unquestioned racial domination in various institutional settings has led to a *crisis of white identity*. As previous assumptions erode, white identity loses its transparency, the easy elision with "racelessness" that has accompanied racial dominance since the end of the Reconstruction period in 1877. Today the very meaning of "whiteness" has become a matter of anxiety and concern. In this respect, whites have been racialized in the post-civil rights era.[3]

During the 1970s, as the influence of the civil rights movement waned, there was a backlash against the institutionalization of civil rights reforms and to the political realignments set in motion in the 1960s. Resistance to affirmative action programs grew among whites who felt that it was they, and not racially defined minorities, who were discriminated against by state policies ostensibly designed to promote racial equality in the schools, the workplace, and other institutional settings. As one respondent noted in *The Report on Democratic Defection*, the "average American white guy" gets a "raw deal" from the government because "Blacks get advantages, Hispanics get advantages, Orientals get advantages. Everybody but the white male race gets advantages now" (Greenberg 1985: 70). The idea that white racial identification could be a *handicap* is unprecedented. In the aftermath of the civil rights era, though, the nature of whiteness has become more controversial than at any time in this century.

One response to the civil rights challenge was to assert the primacy of ethnicity over race. In this account, there was no such thing as a homogeneous white majority. Many whites were really minorities in their own right, "unmeltable" ethnic minorities (Novak 1972). More recent research, however, suggests that most whites do not experience their ethnicity as a definitive aspect of their social identity. They perceive it dimly and irregularly, picking and choosing among its varied strands to exercise, as Mary Waters (1990) suggests, an "ethnic option." The specifically ethnic components of white identity are fast receding with each generation's additional remove from the old country. Unable to speak the language of their immigrant forebears, uncommitted to ethnic endogamy, and often unaware of their ancestors' traditions (if in fact they can still identify their ancestors as, say, Polish or Scots, rather than a combination of four or five European – and non-European! – groups), whites undergo a racializing panethnicity as "Euro-Americans" (Alba 1990).

The "twilight of white ethnicity" in a racially defined, and increasingly polarized, environment means that white racial identity will grow in salience. The racialization process for whites is very evident on university campuses, as white students encounter a heightened awareness of race that calls their own identity into question. Students quoted in a recent study on racial diversity (Institute for the Study of Social Change 1990) conducted at the University of California at Berkeley illustrate the new conflictual nature of white identity:

> Many whites don't feel like they have an ethnic identity at all and I pretty much feel that way too. It's not something that bothers me tremendously but I think that maybe I could be missing something that other people have, that I am not experiencing. (52)

> Being white means that you're less likely to get financial aid.... It means that there are all sorts of tutoring groups and special programs that you can't get into, because you're not a minority. (50)

> If you want to go with the stereotypes, Asians are the smart people, the Blacks are great athletes, what is white? We're just here. We're the oppressors of the nation. (52)

Here we see many of the themes and dilemmas of white identity in the post-civil rights period: the anomic absence of a clear culture and identity, the perceived disadvantages of being white with respect to the distribution of resources, and the stigma experienced in thinking of one's group – even somewhat facetiously – as the "oppressors of the nation."

How will white identity be interpreted at the turn of the twenty-first century? What political and ideological elements will be involved in the refashioning of whiteness? Already, far right political actors such

as David Duke actively seek to organize whites to defend their supposedly threatened racial privileges, all in the name of equality. Such
racist populism is not all that distinct from the demagogic use of the
code word *quotas* by Jesse Helms and George Bush to attract white
votes.

On the other hand, white resentments cannot be wholly dismissed;
they are not solely the result of racist demagogy or a last-gasp attempt
to retain some vestige of racial privilege. Such sentiments also express
loyalty to an idealized and seemingly threatened civic culture in which
individual equality was enshrined as a core democratic principle. That
culture was never guaranteed to most whites, much less to nonwhites,
but it was certainly espoused, across the political and cultural spectrum, as a central ideal. At present it seems to many Americans to be
a receding ideal, obscured by hypocrisy and greed. The future avoid-
ance of racial polarization will depend on resuscitating and rearticulating that vision, combining it with a heightened awareness of race to
demand greater social justice for all.

Whites have not been immune to the process of racialization. Racial
mobilization in the post-civil rights era has not been limited to "people of color," and whites have had to consider the racial implications
of an order that formally disavows "white privilege." The changing
demographic scene, global economic competition, and the perception
that America has fallen from grace have provoked a profound crisis of
white identity. What direction this takes politically depends to a great
extent on the way racial difference and social inequality are interpreted in the years ahead. There are many sources of "common
ground" – to use Jesse Jackson's phrase – across the lines of race.
Those lines are increasingly porous and flexible, but they are not
about to disappear. On the other hand, the racial right has proved
adept at drawing political capital from its exploitation of white fears,
and these cannot be expected to diminish dramatically in the years
ahead. The politics of whiteness, in short, remains unresolved.

CONCLUSION: THE CHALLENGES TO RACIAL "COMMON SENSE"

The civil rights movement challenged long-standing racial understandings and oppressive racial practices, ushering in a period of desegregation efforts, equal opportunity mandates, and other state reforms.
Various forms of racial discrimination – in the labor market, in

housing, in public accommodations, and in marriage laws – were overthrown in this process. But, despite these tremendous accomplishments, patterns of institutional discrimination proved to be quite obstinate, and the precise meaning of race, in politics and law as well as in everyday life, remained undefined. The ambiguity of race in the post-civil rights period has now reached the point where any hint of *race consciousness* is viewed suspiciously as an expression of *racism*.[4]

Ironically, the present situation is a legacy of the civil rights movement. While the movement cannot be seen as a homogeneous or monolithic entity, it contained from its very inception an irresoluble dilemma regarding racial consciousness and identity and their meaning for social and political life. On the one hand, the movement sought an end to racial inequality by advancing a vision of an integrated, "color-blind" society. On the other, it simultaneously sought to increase the level of racial identification among African-Americans and other people of color. This contradictory stance was structured not only by movement ideology and strategy, but also by its conflictual and accommodative relationship to the state.

Different currents within the civil rights movement sought to synthesize the two movement objectives, arguing that integration and the politics of racial difference could coexist. All such attempts – ranging from cultural pluralism through neo-Marxism to various forms of nationalism – were ultimately unsuccessful. The two horns of the movement dilemma apparently could not be articulated in a single comprehensive political and cultural outlook.

As a result, the issues of racial equality and identity were later vulnerable to *re*articulation from political projects on the right (Omi and Winant 1987). These have ranged from "white racial nationalism" (Walters 1987) to neoconservative critiques of affirmative action and other "color-conscious" remedies. Despite their clear ability to mobilize sectors of the white electorate, the arguments of the right have been no more successful than those of the left in establishing a new understanding of the relationship between racial equality and racial identity. The right's failure to resolve the dilemma has led to continuing controversies surrounding the role race plays, or should play, in various institutional arenas and in US society as a whole.

Neither the civil rights movement nor the racial reaction, therefore, have been able to advance and consolidate a new racial *common sense* – a general conception of the role of race, if any, in a good and just society. But both political forces have succeeded in weakening or even demolishing the system of racial categories, meanings, and institutions that they opposed. The repressive racial order of legally sanctioned segregation has been overthrown, but no clear and consensual racial order has been consolidated in its place.

The paradoxical result of all this has been that, far from decreasing, the significance of race in American life has expanded, and the racial dimensions of politics and culture have proliferated. The process of *racialization* continues apace. New racial identities and meanings continue to be created as a result of panethnic linkages. Differentiation within racially identified communities continues as a result of the partial but significant reforms wrought by the civil rights movement. And to the extent that the "complexion" of US society changes and widespread shifts in patterns of racial inequality and the rules of racial difference actually occur, whites too experience the contradictions and conflicts of racial identification.

Debates about the meaning of racial equality, the nature of racial identity, and the role of the state with respect to race will deepen and intensify in the immediate future. From the senior prom in Chicago to the disputed nomination of Clarence Thomas to the Supreme Court, racialization continues.

NOTES

1. Indeed, the very meaning of political labels such as conservative, liberal, and radical has been transformed by ongoing debates about race, including those on affirmative action, social welfare policy, and immigration reform.
2. In a similar vein, Stephen Small (1991: 4) has elaborated what he calls the *racialization problematic* as "a paradigm within which different theories can be advanced for the description and explanation of the creation and maintenance of 'racialised' group boundaries in different socio-historical contexts."
3. Interestingly enough, one of the earliest applications of the "panethnic" framework applied the term to whites. See Erickson 1975.
4. Mounting evidence in the field of medicine, for example, suggests that race and ethnicity can and should be factors in the diagnosis and treatment of specific illnesses. Some medical researchers and practitioners, however, fear that such "race consciousness" could result in a return to racist, eugenic notions. See Leary 1990.

210 *Resurgent Tribalisms*

REFERENCES

Alba, Richard D., *Ethnic Identity: The Transformation of White America* (New Haven, Conn.: Yale University Press, 1990).

Brooks, Roy L., *Rethinking America's Race Problem* (Berkeley: University of California Press, 1990).

Chung, L.A., "S.F. Includes Asian Indians in Minority Law," *San Francisco Chronicle*, June 25, 1991.

Du Bois, *The Philadelphia Negro: A Social Study* (New York: Schocken, 1967 [1899]).

Dunne, John Gregory, "Law and Disorder in Los Angeles" (two parts), *New York Review of Books*, October 10 and 24, 1991.

Eric B. and Rakim, "The Ghetto," on idem, *Let the Riot Hit 'Em* (MCA Records, 1990).

Erickson, Frederick, "Gatekeeping and the Melting Pot: Interaction in Counseling Encounters," *Harvard Educational Review* 45 (1975).

Essoyan, susan, "Native Hawaiians Vote for Clout," *San Francisco Chronicle*, January 31, 1990.

Feagin, Joe R., "The Continuing Significance of Race: Antiblack Discrimination in Public Places," *American Sociological Review* 56 (1991): 101–17.

Frazier, E. Franklin, *Black Bourgeoisie: The Rise of a New Middle Class in the United States* (New York: Free Press, 1957).

Freeman, Richard, *The Black Elite: The New Market for Highly Educated Black Americans* (New York: McGraw-Hill, 1976).

Garreau, Joel, "Competing Bonds of Race and Class," *Washington Post*, November 30, 1987.

Greenberg, Stanley B., *Report on Democratic Defection*, prepared for the Michigan House Democratic Campaign Committee (Washington, D.C.: Analysis Group, 1985).

Institute for the Study of Social Change, *The Diversity Project: An Interim Report to the Chancellor* (Berkeley: University of California Press, 1990).

Jordon, Winthrop, *White Over Black: American Attitudes Toward the Negro, 1550–1812* (New York: Norton, 1977 [1968]).

Landry, Bart, *The New Black Middle Class* (Berkeley: University of California Press, 1987).

Leary, Warren E., "Uneasy Doctors Add Race-Consciousness to Diagnostic Tools," *New York Times*, September 25, 1990.

Lieberson, Stanley and Mary C. Waters, *From Many Strands: Ethnic and Racial Groups in Contemporary America* (New York: Russel Sage Foundation, 1988).

Lopez, David and Yen Espiritu, "Panethnicity in the United States: A Theoretical Framework," *Ethnic and Racial Studies* 13 (1990): 198–225.

Novak, Michael, *The Rise of the Unmeltable Ethnics* (New York: Macmillan, 1972).

Omi, Michael and Howard Winant, "Race and the Right: The Politics of Reaction," in John H. Stanfield II, ed., *Research in Social Policy: Historical and Contemporary Perspectives*, vol. 1 (Greenwich, Conn.: JAI Press, 1987)

Omi, Michael and Howard Winant, *Racial Formation in the United States: From the 1960s to the 1980s* (New York: Routledge, 1986).

Schuman, Howard, et al, *Racial Attitudes in America: Trends and Interpretations* (Cambridge: Harvard University Press, 1985).

Small, Stephen, " 'Racialised Relations' in Britain: An Introspective and International Perspective," unpublished paper, 1991.

Sowell, Thomas, *The Economics and Politics of Race: An International Perspective* (New York: Quill, 1983).

Walters, Ronald, "White Racial Nationalism in the United States," *Without Prejudice I* 1 (Fall 1987).

Wilkerson, Isabel, "Separate Senior Proms Reveal an Unspanned Racial Divide," *New York Times*, May 5, 1991.

Williams, Lena, "When Blacks Shop, Bias Often Accompanies Sale," *New York Times*, April 30, 1991.

Wilson, William Julius, "Studying Inner-City Social Dislocations," *American Sociological Review* 56, no. 1 (1991): 1–14.

Wilson, William Julius, *The Truly Disadvantaged: The Inner City, the Underclass, and Public Policy* (Chicago: University of Chicago Press, 1987).

Wilson, William Julius, *The Declining Significance of Race: Blacks and Changing American Institutions*, 2nd ed. (Chicago: University of Chicago Press, 1980).

9 Multiculturalism and Universalism: A History and Critique
John Higham

People, I just want to say, you know, can we all get along? Can we get along? Can we stop making it, making it horrible for the older people and the kids? . . . We'll, we'll get our justice. . . . We all can get along. I mean, we're all stuck here for a while. Let's try to work it out. Let's try to beat it. Let's try to work it out.

– Statement by Rodney G. King May 1, 1992,
urging an end to the riots provoked in Los Angeles by
a court's exoneration of his tormenters.
(*New York Times*, May 2, 1992)

I

Two distinct demands for greater equality run through the history of the Western world in the twentieth century. One opposes discrimination against people on grounds of race, ethnicity, gender, or physical condition. These inescapably given traits are commonly understood as personal, as internal, as part of the very substance of who we are. To use them as devices or reasons for subordinating outgroups affronts our sense of equal justice. Recognition of a moral equivalence of endowment is therefore a fundamental objective in modern society.

A second egalitarian force pushes against the disadvantages of external condition, the burdens of class. Here the distribution of tangible resources – a nexus of property, skill, and political power – constitutes a more generalized structure of inequality. To reduce such external disadvantages, people of all kinds demand equality of opportunity; some claim equality of condition as well. My interest is in the pursuit of equality along the first path, that is, between groups defined by their cultural or biological inheritances. But the second path also runs through this story. Our current preoccupation with an egalitarian understanding of collective endowments too often lacks a full historical context, in which struggles to equalize society-wide relations between classes play a significant part.

212

Rising and falling, entwining and separating, these two great modern movements against unacceptable inequities have always interacted. Occasionally, the discontents of underprivileged races or ethnic groups converge with those of underprivileged classes. When that occurs, as in the United States in the 1930s, equality makes a mighty leap forward. Only infrequently, however, can such a coalition of the disinherited come together, much less prevail. Class typically cuts across ethnicity and gender, since endowment groups generally occupy more than one class level. Altogether, inequalities lace modern society in so many cross-cutting directions that movements to level one citadel of privilege usually reinforce others, intentionally or unwittingly.

When distinct ethnic segments join forces, either with one another or with a discontented class, their alliance requires a guiding ideology to define a common plight and inspire hopes of a common redemption. The United States has had such a belief system from its beginnings as a nation; during the first half of the twentieth century egalitarian movements drew on it more freely and comprehensively than at any time before or since. Channeled by this deeply rooted ideology, the outcries of excluded races and ethnic groups flowed together and mingled simultaneously with the energies of class protest.[1]

At the time of its greatest power, Gunnar Myrdal labelled this familiar bundle of beliefs "The American Creed."[2] Today many scornfully call it "American exceptionalism."[3] I shall try to avoid both the piety and the scorn by resorting to a neutral oxymoron. Let us name our egalitarian ideology "American universalism." Molded by the Enlightenment and forged in the Revolution. American universalism has been simultaneously a civic credo, a social vision, and a definition of nationhood.

As a civic credo, it is universal in grounding public life and institutions not on an exclusive heritage but on natural rights – that is, on rational principles, supposedly valid everywhere, that grant all citizens equality in public life and encourage all residents to claim a common citizenship. These principles not only legitimize American governments but should also ultimately spread around the world and win universal approval by protecting everyone's basic rights. American universalists expected, in the words of Thomas Jefferson, that "a just and solid republican government maintained here...will be a standing monument & example for...a great portion of the globe."[4] The civic credo was exceptionalist in what it stood for, but universal in what it could become.

At this level, as an official proclamation of human rights, American universalism remains sturdy and intact. As a social vision, it endures but has lost its early buoyancy. Originally, it was a message of hope, holding out to individuals a promise of overcoming all social barriers external to the self. It celebrated the mobility, renewal, and self-transformation that the pioneer, the immigrant, and the self-made man symbolized; its special animus was against the privileges of entrenched social classes. Classes, in this parochially universalist view, were unnatural: the artificial creation of bad laws in a corrupt Old World. Any tendency to import them here, and thus to harden existing lines of privilege, must be opposed. In conservative times, Americans liked to boast of their nation's exemption from the sharp class divisions of Europe. In times of stress and challenge, however, class conflict exploded in the form of broadly popular uprisings against privileged minorities. In short, American universalism either denied that class inequalities had taken root in America or struggled to drive them out.

Inequalities of endowment presented a knottier conceptual problem. Unlike class, distinctions in endowment were generally seen to have a certain fixity in nature. These supposedly "natural" inequalities authorized the "herrenvolk" definitions of American nationality that developed in the nineteenth century.[5] Nevertheless, a universalist point of view lived on. It insisted that the task of nation-building was to be as inclusive and as egalitarian as possible.

We come to the crux of American universalism in recognizing that it embodied an invigorating paradox. Supposedly universal rights had become institutionally and socially operative through the collective efforts of people who used them to create a bounded community of their own to the disadvantage of others. What was theoretically and potentially universal was soon understood, therefore, as the sacred possession – the very lynchpin of identity – of a peculiar people. The Americans stand out, said James Fenimore Cooper, for having "dared the war of their independence in the maintenance of a perfectly abstract principle, for no one pretends that the taxation of England was oppressive in fact." More loftily still, Henry James the elder contrasted the insularity of the English with the unbounded identity of Americans: "We are no mere civil polity. We are at bottom nothing more than a broad human society or brotherhood, of which every man is in full membership by right of manhood alone."[6]

Such expansive affirmations, ritualized on every Fourth of July, provided the connective tissue that was vital for a new nation with a loose-knit social fabric, an extraordinarily decentralized political system, and a highly rhetorical religion. At the same time, the celebration of human rights as the distinguishing feature of a singular nation – however fallacious that may appear in retrospect – gave an impetus to wider humane concerns. In the early republic, sympathy for the suffering of humanity everywhere was readily experienced as a natural extension of patriotic feelings. Nationalism and a proto-universalism fertilized one another, their symbiosis represented in the classical goddess of Liberty whom Congress in 1792 designated as the obligatory female symbol complementing the masculine eagle on all American coins.[7]

The coupling, in many national icons, of a distinctively American bird of prey with a transnational symbol of freedom cannot be fully understood as a smokescreen or a delusion. It reflects the inescapable locatedness of any universalistic perspective. More specifically, it displays the enduring tension, in what I have called American universalism, between closure and openness, between separateness and inclusion.[8] From the time of the American Revolution onward, a principal way of managing this tension has been to extend the circle of those who are acknowledged as makers of an American nationality and to project each incremental addition as a promise of still wider inclusiveness.

Tom Paine took an early step by arguing in 1776 that Americans owed the cosmopolitan breadth of their social sympathies to the freedom-loving refugees who had flocked to the new world "from *every part* of Europe," not just from "the narrow limits" of little England. By the middle of the nineteenth century, the idea was widespread that a mixed population is more vigorous, and more variously endowed, than any single ethnic strain. Immigrant groups, especially the Germans, eagerly adopted the claim that they were making important contributions to an American character.[9] Often these hyphenates constructed an ethnic identity and a new American identity concurrently. Generation after generation, they came from more and more homelands, and their infusion into the host society gave increasing substance and visibility to its cosmopolitan bent. Admittedly, European ethnic groups generally shrank from drawing interracial implications from their own ongoing assimilation; but African Americans and radical Republican intellectuals took the idea of fusion all the way. "My idea of American nationality," declared Wendell Phillips in a great Lyceum lecture, makes it the last best growth of the thoughtful mind of the century, treading underfoot sex and race, caste and condition, and collecting on the broad bosom of what deserves the name of an empire, under the shelter of noble, just, and equal laws, all races, all customs, all religions, all languages, all literature, and all ideas.[10]

To be sure, a defensive, ethnically based national consciousness, gathering strength in the mid-nineteenth century and after, persistently obstructed the advance of American universalism.[11] Even now, a presumption that white males of European descent should remain the solid core of American society is weakening only haltingly. Yet the pursuit of equality quickened greatly in the twentieth century. For a while, it reached across the gulf between excluded races and a largely white working class.

By the opening of the new century, unanticipated dangers to equal rights were becoming too visible and menacing to ignore. The self-segregation of middle and upper classes in exclusive neighborhoods, suburban enclaves, country clubs, and automobiles accompanied the elaboration of corporate bureaucracies and the concentration of an industrial work force in factory-dominated districts. Although the anger and bewilderment of native white Americans at the hardening of social categories released a storm of racism, the revitalizing movement that called itself "Progressive" simultaneously produced a new egalitarianism. The agencies of revitalization were numerous and powerful. They included the Democratic party, industrial and interracial labor unions, churches infused with a social gospel and an ecumenical spirit, universities and public schools, and a multiethnic popular culture industry.

The revival of American universalism between the 1910s and the 1950s was fired also by a new intellectual class, which significantly modernized the terms of the national ideology. These modernizers introduced a more realistic, critical, and historically contextualized understanding of human rights and social processes. They also identified personally with, and in many cases emerged from, ethnic groups which had never before had such influential and creative spokespersons. John Dewey, Jane Addams, W. E. B. DuBois, and Thorstein Veblen variously exemplify the new intellectual class. In making American universalism more truly cosmopolitan and more responsive to the aspirations of ethnic minorities and underprivileged classes, they infused into the promise of America a concrete sense of the common good. This social-democratic perspective virtually took possession of the social sciences and of the literary intelligentsia between the two world wars.[12]

By the early 1960s, the renewal of American democracy had made impressive headway. European and Asian immigrant groups had emerged from the shadow of racism. The urban working class, moving to the suburbs, was blurring distinctions between itself and an amorphous middle class. The desegregation of public space and the integration of public schools and the political process were progressing with surprising speed. Among young people, appreciation of African-American culture was no longer condescending, but was hearty and widespread. In important ways, however, the movement was running out of steam.

One ominous sign was Martin Luther King, Jr.'s failure in 1966 and 1967 to turn his civil rights crusade into a broader class coalition. King realized that without a common front of underprivileged people – white and black – committed to a broad redistribution of wealth, the problems of northern ghettoes would remain intractable. At first he won some union support; then riots intruded. King's assassination soon followed.[13]

Indeed, this last dream of Martin Luther King, Jr., so deeply imbued with American universalism, was already foreclosed. A new style of black leadership, speaking the language of racial power rather than the ideal of universal rights, was on the march. In truth, the era had already passed when claims for racial and for class equality could buttress one another. In the late 1950s, labor unions, having lost their militancy, entered a long decline that continues to this day. A sad observer, looking back across his lifetime, recently remarked: "The hopes of the Thirties, the complacencies of the Fifties, and the slumbers of the Seventies are gone past recall for industrial labor. Nothing remains but the breaking of hearts."[14]

Meanwhile, suburbanization and economic advancement were draining from white ethnics the class resentments that the Democratic party had mobilized. In Washington, policy debates narrowed from broadly social issues to fiscal policies and interest-group politics.[15] Altogether, the alarm that had awakened Americans in the first half of the twentieth century – the danger of impending entrapment in an increasingly stratified society – gave way among the majority of whites to a consumer-oriented spirit of expansiveness and self-indulgence.

The people who were being left farthest behind were not an entire social class but were the poorly organized segments of certain endowment groups, notably lower-class blacks, middle-class women, and

uncared-for children. This was the context in which an outpouring of
rage in black America, in the 1960s, sent shudders of guilt and anxiety
through the affluent classes of white America, and the mixture of rage
and guilt sparked an educational reform movement. The reformers
proposed to make education more accessible and supportive to minorities by infusing both the curriculum and the entire educational
environment with recognition and respect for "ethnic diversity." The
schools could thereby nourish ethnic pride and, at the same time,
assuage a fearsome anger. At first, in the 1970s, the reform movement
was known as multiethnic education, or occasionally as multicultural
education.[16] (Only recently has the latter name gained a provocative
notoriety.) Regardless of nomenclature, however, for the last fifteen
years the multicultural movement has tried to carry forward the great
campaigns of the mid-twentieth century against racial and ethnic
inequalities without reviving the wider outcry of that earlier era
against class inequalities.

To sum up the breadth that the project gradually attained, multiculturalism fosters cultures of endowment while drawing a veil over
the cultures of class. The new curricula have made a fetish of
"diversity." Only an occasional rhetorical flourish, however, hints
that different social classes – with all their complications of region
and religion – have had subcultures just as distinct from one another
(and just as overlapping) as those of racial or ethnic groups.[17]

Officially, invocations of class are obligatory in defining programs
and objectives, since the academic leaders of the multicultural movement cluster on the Left. Thus Paul Lauter, an influential proponent
of overhauling the teaching of American Studies, notes that a

> loosely constituted "Left" comprised of feminists, black scholars,
> gay and lesbian academics, educational progressives, and cultural
> radicals, wishes to reconstitute curricula around the central percep-
> tion of difference – especially of race, gender, class, and sexual
> orientation – and to open colleges to more democratic decision-
> making.[18]

In 1988, the American Studies Association took up the cry. For the
first time the association chose "Cultures of Gender, Race, Ethnicity,
and Class" as the theme of its annual meeting. Since then, American
studies programs around the country have increasingly redesigned
themselves as multicultural alliances, "worshipping" – in the words
of one enthusiastic participant – "the 'holy trinity' of race, class and
gender."[19]

In practice, however, class is among the absentees from the celebration of diversity. Multiculturalists care little more about class as a fully elaborated identity – bearing its own meanings, associations, and vulnerabilities – than they do about differences between religions, regions, and nations. Fresh scholarship on the structure and mentality of all of these groups continues to instruct us but owes little or nothing to multicultural auspices.[20] To its academic apostles, multiculturalism signifies a preoccupation with race and gender – a preoccupation that allows just a whiff of class consciousness to sharpen the pungent odor of subjugation and resistance.

How shall we construe this extraordinary dissociation in American academic culture between two great structures of inequality, which (in the same academic culture) are generally assumed to reinforce one other? Is the deflection of attention from broad disadvantages of class to specific disabilities of endowment simply an expediential mimicry of practical politics? Is the academic Left simply acknowledging that supporters of "endowment" issues – such as racism, sexism, abortion, gay rights, defense of Israel, and protection of the environment – have won significant victories in recent years, while class-oriented demands have only stiffened resistance to change?[21]

Or is this shift in national priorities from class to endowment, and the accompanying response of multiculturalists, explicable from a larger perspective as a reversion to a traditional politics of race? After a period when class and race were seen as jointly responsible for violating the "American Dream," an older diversionary pattern – going back to the country's earliest experience – has reappeared. Again, as in the eighteenth and nineteenth centuries, racial antipathies submerge and suppress class identities. The troubling contradiction between the ideal of a classless society and the realities of racial enslavement and degradation has long tempted Americans to use race as an antidote to class divisions. Mostly this practice has meant diverting onto endowment groups an anger aroused by class injustice. Now, in a variant of that pattern, multiculturalism cultivates the anger of unequal endowment groups as an alternative to class consciousness. Class has ceased to excite us, but the politics of race live on. In David Brion Davis's words: "We seem ... to have entered another period when race has preempted class."[22]

If multicultural education unwittingly defeats its own egalitarian purpose by absolutizing racial differences while obscuring the broader inequalities of class, some changes in its instructional aims would seem to be in order. Young Americans need to learn what

anthropologists have known all along: that race and ethnicity do not
always confer desirable identities, nor are these identities unalterable,
uncontested, or monolithic. They are surprisingly fluid, at least in
America. In changing circumstances, individuals continually
reinvent their ethnic identities. They renegotiate the loyalties they
must choose among, or alter the dimensions of a predominant identity
that begins to pinch.[23] An effective civic education should widen
instead of narrowing the options that people can entertain. It must
not allow race and ethnicity to seem intractable or class to remain
invisible.

II

The contrast between the boundless diversity that multiculturalism
appears to espouse and the focused agenda it actually pursues is
only one of the confusions that have made it a subject of angry
controversy. On other problems of civic education, which have nothing directly to do with the issue of class, multiculturalism offers very
unclear guidance. To understand why this is so, we will need to
explore its teachings and its recent history more closely.

The truth is that, for two decades, multiculturalism has remained a
stubbornly practical enterprise, justified by immediate demands rather
than long-range goals: a movement without an overall theory. Understandably, the multicultural strategies of academic intellectuals and
educators began as *ad hoc* responses to the outcries of minorities in a
crisis situation. The schools were failing; the streets were burning.
Something had to be done for ghetto children – something to raise
their self-esteem and engage their energy and attention. Still, it is
troubling that twenty years after those convulsive beginnings, multiculturalism has suddenly become a policy issue in America's colleges,
universities, and secondary schools without yet proposing a vision of
the kind of society it wants. In view of the indistinctness of multicultural goals, it is hardly surprising that no independent assessment
of what it is accomplishing has yet appeared.

Sorting out the confusions that have sprung up in the absence of a
multicultural theory of society takes us back to the intellectual origins
of the movement. The seeds of the present disarray were sown in the
intellectual ferment of the early twentieth century, above all in the
haunting, ambiguous visions of a more inclusive America that era has
left us. Those rival visions, so innocent and far away, will lead

circuitously to the angry disputes that have exploded throughout the educational system in the last few years.

The great reconstruction of American universalism in the Progressive era produced the first systematic studies of ethnic processes and the first college courses on race relations. As never before, the actual diversity in the American population was documented and dissected.[24] Nevertheless, most of the revisionists clung to a traditional reliance on assimilation as the path to equality. They believed that the cauldron of the modern city, aided by intermarriage, would gradually meld the country's various ancestral strains into a single people. In the spirit of Robert E. Park, the outstanding pioneer of race relations research, they foresaw an irreversible (if sometimes painful) process of assimilation. But a daring handful of social prophets went further. These cultural pluralists, as they were soon called, declared that ethnic minorities in the United States were proving so tenacious of their own identities that no distinctively American culture existed or could be expected. Not an ultimate homogeneity, said Randolph Bourne, but a mutually invigorating, egalitarian pluralism is the incomparable distinction of America, "the first international nation ... the world-federation in miniature."[25]

The new perspective was an intellectually intriguing deviation from the mainstream of liberal thought. As a philosophy of minority rights, it conceived of America as a federation of minorities, in which one (the Anglo-Saxon ruling class) had usurped hegemony.[26] The predominant version of American universalism, on the other hand, remained distrustful of the danger that accentuation of group differences posed to equal rights. Most universalists were concerned less with the cohesiveness of groups than with the freedom of individuals to move beyond their origins and make themselves over. Until the 1960s, however, the disagreement was of little consequence. Pluralists and assimilationists alike looked forward to a great community, both national and transnational, in which law and voluntary cooperation could increasingly soften group differences.[27]

Then, suddenly, accommodation and inclusiveness lost credibility. In a revolution of rising expectations amid a disintegrating national consensus, Black Power introduced themes of anger, enmity, and intimidation toward whites. Other minorities soon moved in the same direction. For them, too, conflict became an imperative. Thus a harsher form of pluralism emerged in the 1970s to demand that the schools recognize the power of ethnic and racial minorities, not just the value of their cultures. The term "cultural pluralism" acquired an ever-wider popularity, while its meaning for society as a whole became more difficult to define. Some radical multiculturalists still invoke cultural pluralism as their founding principle, but their indignant opponents often describe multiculturalism as an abandonment and betrayal of pluralism, and middle-of-the-road educators represent pluralism as a strain within multiculturalism, balanced by assimilation.[28] Lurking in this verbal confusion is a good deal of the old commitment to universal principles, to a common culture, and to a long-term process of acculturation. But those ideas all seem somehow on the defensive. What had happened?

Essentially, universalism had largely lost its link to any great community, especially to the American nation. In earlier times, Americans had felt connected to one another through the ideological origins that enabled their country more than any other to unite heterogeneous peoples. On that common ground, down to the 1950s, both cultural pluralists and assimilationists stood. Both planted themselves on what they regarded as the "American Idea." Their confidence in the possibility of building "a house for all peoples" was reinforced, moreover, by a belief in progress as the overall course of modern history.

The loosening of this sturdy civil culture did not begin in the 1960s. After the nationalistic excesses of World War I and the technological impersonality of postwar society, patriotism and urban boosterism never fully regained their earlier adhesive power. By the 1940s, the acids of modernity were also corroding popular faith in social or moral progress. Not until the upheavals of the 1960s, however, did the tendency of cultural pluralists to emphasize the separateness of ethnic cultures in this country take on a darker, anti-American meaning. Now any claim for centeredness, any affirmation of a unifying national culture, became *ipso facto* oppressive. By the early 1970s, popular television serials displayed a society without shared ideals or respected institutions.[29] All in all, a cynical state of mind made it difficult to discuss, and impossible to clarify, common loyalties and responsibilities within a population as diverse as that of the United States.[30]

Nevertheless, the sense of crisis that launched the present era in ethnic studies eased. From the early 1970s through most of the 1980s, polemical posturing subsided. The rhetoric of black nationalism collapsed,[31] while cumulative improvements in race relations – often modest but sometimes dramatic – went steadily forward. Moderate black politicians increasingly won elections, not just because they were moderates but also because young white voters gave them record levels of support. With little complaint, whites also accepted new voting-rights legislation designed to create safe electoral districts for minority candidates. Intermarriage rates rose because opposition to intermarriage on the part of whites gradually weakened. The black middle class, expanding and prospering, gained sometimes grudging but substantial respect. Overall, through the recession of the 1970s and onward to the most recent statistics, racial differences in education and median household income have persistently diminished.[32]

The scale of these changes went largely unnoticed. Most whites grew weary of racial issues in the 1970s, while a continuing bitterness and fear of the future kept many blacks edgy and defensive. Neither side could fully appreciate that a great, incomplete, but irreversible social transformation was under way. In the midst of large, continuing disparities of income and education, deep and persisting segregation, and the degradation of urban ghettoes, many blacks and whites were learning that accommodation is a beneficial, reciprocal process.

Alan Peshkin has recently reported in depth on a multiethnic public high school in California, in which teachers give no special attention to ethnicity and hold all students to a common standard. Without rejecting their own identities, the students interact positively and unselfconsciously across ethnic lines. Although such a school is unusual today, it exemplifies the possibility of a more egalitarian future.[33] Some recent polling data have sent a similar signal. A cross section of adults was asked in 1990 which ethnic groups in America should have more power. Forty-seven percent of the respondents said blacks should have more power; 46 percent said Hispanic Americans; 6 percent said whites.[34]

This is the puzzling context in which a new eruption of ethnic tensions has shaken us. It began around 1986 in universities, secondary schools, and fear-ridden urban neighborhoods. The street incidents were deadly criminal encounters between black and nonblack individuals. Self-anointed black spokesmen inflamed the incidents into dramatic protests against an allegedly oppressive and conspiratorial power structure. The fuel for these often self-destructive but intimidating protests came from the angry misery of ghetto dwellers who found themselves more and more trapped and abandoned as middle-class black neighbors fled to safer areas.[35]

About the same time, similar themes of outrage, isolation, and demagoguery were played out on college campuses without the personal violence. Here the provocation was verbal harassment by white students, many of whom had grown up in escapist suburbs with no knowledge or appreciation of the civil rights movement. Crass racial humor in student newspapers and in fraternity high jinks, along with worse slurs in anonymous graffiti, were shocking to faculty and administrators. To black and Hispanic students, who often felt out of place even in polite campus settings, these incidents were searing. Minority students responded by demanding more university support for their own campus centers and organizations. That, in turn, resulted in a sharper splintering of the student body into separate racial blocs.[36]

Another strategy, pushed especially by multicultural activists in the faculty, requires every student to take a course in ethnic studies. Such courses, it was hoped, would teach the delights of diversity and puncture provincial stereotypes. (They would also most certainly create new faculty positions for minority teachers.) Again, anxious authorities rushed to oblige. The requirement is now common in the larger universities.[37]

These new demands and confrontations are the setting in which multiculturalism has become a buzzword, a crusade, and a gigantic mystification. Some teachers, equating multiculturalism with global inclusiveness, point out that social studies curricula have developed strongly in that direction since the 1960s. Leading the way, the state of California adopted in 1987 a new curriculum that provides a working balance between American and world history. Diane Ravitch, a co-author of the curriculum, says that "the United States has a common culture that is multicultural." In her view, radical multiculturalists have pushed a sound principle to a pernicious extreme. They have turned the pluralist impulse into a virulently explicit assault on the European heritage that undergirds American education.[38]

The critics of the California plan, however, see it as just another instrument of cultural imperialism. America has no common history. To escape intellectual oppression, every race has to center its children in its own distinctive culture and its own proud history. From the critics' perspective, pluralism merely "disguises the perpetuation of exclusion." Mainstream pluralists such as Ravitch are purveying a "white self-esteem curriculum" that kills the mind and spirit of non-white children.[39]

In this polarization between a rebellious sense of exclusion and an inclusiveness built on European foundations, the two versions of multiculturalism are locked in defensive suspicion of one another. Between them, left-of-center academics have tried to stake out a middle ground. "I am baffled why we cannot be students of Western

culture and of multiculturalism at the same time," Catharine R.
Stimpson declared in her presidential address to the Modern
Languages Association. "Surely some Western texts," she continued,
"are also multicultural."[40] Unfortunately, her phrasing betrays a
widespread presupposition that what is multicultural stands outside
of a common arena. Typically, it has to do with marginal groups and
oppositional attitudes, not with a standard human condition.

Conceivably, the concept of multiculturalism can find a center of
gravity in a centerless space where outsiders resist and simultaneously
enrich an overall national culture. As it stands, however, the multicultural idea is shaped by its explosive emergence from clashing
ethnocentric demands and antagonisms. Afrocentric, Eurocentric,
phallocentric, and so on. Among alienated, postmodern intellectuals,
this oppositional thrust has released a rejuvenating rhetoric. By the
late 1980s, the older language of cultural pluralism, from which
multiculturalism stems, sounded too soft and tame to articulate a
radical critique of America.

Yet an easing of current ethnic hostilities will not by itself resolve
the problems of multiculturalism. As the legatee of cultural pluralism,
it will still contain the limitations, and reflect the incompleteness, that
the pluralist perspective has never lost. America is more than a
federation of minorities. It encompasses many millions who will
never conceive of themselves in those terms. Americans are a people,
molded by processes of assimilation. An adequate theory of American
culture will have to address the reality of assimilation as well as the
persistence of differences.[41]

III

In brief, the present disarray in multicultural education leads us back
before the angry disputes of the 1990s, and also before the immediate
sources of those disputes in the cultural divisions of the 1960s.
Imbedded in cultural pluralism from its beginnings are underlying
dilemmas with which a constructive educational policy will have to
deal. There are no easy answers for these dilemmas, but teachers and
scholars who aspire to be in some sense multiculturally responsible
can find guidance from them.

One dilemma is methodological. It concerns how teachers and
scholars structure their work in the most general sense. Should we
analyze problems or hold celebrations? Since few will admit to being

unabashedly celebratory, the right answer might seem clear-cut, at least for high school and college classes. At mature levels, education tackles problems. But appreciation and advocacy (to substitute less inflammatory words in place of celebration) are unavoidable in any institutionally established study of the sponsor's culture and heritage. How is it possible for any program created in the interest of a particular constituency *not* to be a vehicle of sympathy and support, unless that consituency becomes alienated from itself?[42] Moreover, this practical reality is by no means deplorable. People who are conscious of unequal antecedents need to feel some collective affirmation of their rightful membership in a heterogeneous community. At the same time, scholars betray their professional code if they fail to maintain a critical distance from subjects who engage their own personal loyalties. Appreciation is merely provincial if not grounded in knowledge and values that bring into judgment a range of humanity far wider than the people who are immediately at issue.

Of course every inquiry in the humanities must wrestle with the dilemma of celebration versus analysis. But multicultural studies pose it in a particularly acute way because they compel scholars to problematize overlapping and conflicting identities. However much one may wish to represent sympathetically more than a single ethnic or sexual identity, empathy tends to slide from the "multi" to the "mono," from diversity to specialty. Logically, all the cultures in a multicultural situation deserve what each desires alone.

In this connection, we need more awareness of how rapidly fashions in the distribution of empathy can change and of how vulnerable to the careless winds of history our own passionate sympathies may become. Forty years ago, when historians and literary critics were still largely untouched by cultural pluralism, the paramount object of appreciation in American studies was what is now called "mainstream" culture, and the icon of celebration was the famous American melting pot. History textbooks took note of ethnic problems, but viewed them in the light of specific stereotypes and disadvantages of particular groups. There was a Negro problem, an Indian problem, and an immigration problem and each inflected inequalities that the melting pot could ultimately dissolve. Then, in the 1960s, the relation between problems and celebrations turned upside down. The ethnic groups now got the celebrations; the melting pot became the problem.[43]

Today, the distribution of empathy is shifting again. Some European ethnic groups, such as Jews and Italians, are losing the benefit of being considered minorities. Not long ago, an ethnic scholar who was widely influential in the 1970s and early 1980s is said to have remarked, "I feel as if I have been abolished." In a good many ethnic studies programs the multicultural faculty seems to exclude professors who are identified in any way with European antecedents. Ethnicity is equated with race, and all whites are lumped together.[44] Recently, for example, a stalwart scholar of European descent, long established in comparative ethnic studies, was forced out of a state-wide conference he had organized. The steering committee insisted that only "people of color" qualified as ethnic.[45]

Less striking but surely unsettling to multiculturalists is the emergence of a scholarly literature that applies sympathetic ethnic perspectives to numerous subgroups within the old-stock white population or even to the larger (but always conflicted) experience of becoming American. The New England Puritans now stand forth as paradigmatic exemplars of the anguish of emigration and of the immigrant's struggle for cultural survival.[46] One new monograph, published within the last year, brings out a hitherto neglected civic consciousness among rank-and-file members of the Ku Klux Klan of the 1920s. Another illuminates a special sense of identity among the Civil War veterans who formed the Grand Army of the Republic.[47] On a popular level, but supported by heavy academic credentials, Ken Burns's powerful television series, *The Civil War*, has taught contemporary audiences a lesson in grief for the hundreds of thousands of young men who suffered and died in that terrible struggle.[48] These extensions of scholarly empathy to people who lived within the dominant American culture would not have been possible a decade ago. They suggest that without a universal standard the reservoirs of academic empathy can flow in unforeseeable directions that may leave some minorities more vulnerable than ever.

The dilemmas of empathy – who deserves it and how much should they have – are at least familiar. Other underlying dilemmas, springing from the special aims of multicultural studies, may be more damaging because they are systematically ignored. Multiculturalists, in fact, have nothing to say about goals as we usually understand that term. Instead, they dwell on needs: the needs of victims for greater self-esteem, more ethnic recognition, compensatory assistance, and role models of their own kind. Needs are subjective and difficult to measure. To question them is to challenge the complainant's inner strength. Goals are public and therefore more open to challenge and to critical assessment. Needs are a present hunger, not a direction.

Goals imply change over time and the importance of purpose in shaping growth. Shifting from needs to goals brings us up against policy dilemmas, that multiculturalism has been unwilling to address. Here are some of those unspoken dilemmas.

Arousal or Restraint?

Should scholarship and teaching arouse or subdue ethnicity as a social force? If we wish to strengthen feelings of attachment, loyalty, and pride in one's own group (or in a particular group we happen to favor), we do so to enhance the power of that group in dealing with others. At the same time, we want to build self-esteem in members of the group who have been damaged by its poor reputation. Whether inner confidence – rather than aggressive egotism – can be produced by school lessons that teach the good news about one's own group and the bad news about others seems highly doubtful.[49] In today's world, ego strength means incorporating contrarities within the self. There is little doubt, of course, that a *group* is strengthened politically by teachings that mobilize it for encounters with opponents. The problem is that ethnic mobilization rapidly spreads to other groups, creating situations full of danger for all of them.

Shall we then seek to subdue ethnicity, either by harnessing it to other social forces or by tempering its impact? The goal of harnessing ethnicity is mostly pursued by scholars on the Left, for whom ethnic and other cultural discontents offer a substitute for class as a basis for building coalitions to challenge capitalist society. Recently, for example, a radical faction in Brookline, Massachusetts, temporarily succeeded in revamping the high school curriculum along supposedly multicultural lines. In reality, it was a Third Word curriculum in anti-colonialism. European history disappeared from the required sequence. The breakup of the Soviet Union went unmentioned, and a new required course, "World in Crisis," focused on Northern Ireland, Vietnam, and Israel.[50]

A better way to subdue ethnicity is to temper the presentation of group differences and conflicts by rendering the experience of minorities and majorities as a scene of lights and shadows, of satisfactions as well as failures, all the while questioning the sharpness of the social boundaries separating groups from one another. This can have a wide appeal. It does not, however, produce a deep and burning commitment. It cannot satisfy the core constituencies for ethnic studies, those who want affirmations of their importance and autonomy. Anyone who seeks to temper the claims of ethnic groups is therefore easily charged with rationalizing a conservative complacency. So the dilemma between arousal and containment remains.

Convergence or Divergence?

Should multicultural studies anticipate or seek a future of greater or reduced separateness and autonomy between ethnic groups? Should they promote convergence or divergence in group identities? In spite of all the slogans about diversity, this fundamental question is never posed in the present controversy or in the scholarship accompanying it.

In pursuit of an answer I have studied the "platforms" that candidates for office in the American Studies Association write for the guidance of those who must elect them. Last year, the twelve candidates who ran for the top offices sounded very much alike in their ardent espousal of diversity. Eight of them explicitly championed multiculturalism. Another urged an examination of "our culture not as a totality but...as a structure of diversity," while another denounced any "kind of...homogenizing, consensual 'we.'" The eleventh spoke ambiguously of mapping "the interface of class, race, gender, and aesthetics," but failed to be elected. That left only one candidate to strike a genuinely different note. Recommending a "continuing internationalization of American Studies" and a "more *integrated* understanding of the culture of the United States," he, too, was defeated. In this massive multicultural unanimity, however, I could find no clue to whether the future leaders of the ASA want to foster greater diversity or simply bring out what they fervently believe is already there.[51]

This is curious, since the whole multicultural movement – if my account of it is correct – stems from the long striving in America for greater equality. On the surface, one would think that the goal of equality would not be well served by highlighting or increasing differences among people. At least, we are entitled to some explanation of how an emphasis on differences of endowment will advance equality. To my knowledge none has been suggested by our multiculturalists. Between divergence and convergence they leave us guessing.[52]

Preserving or Creating?

A third dilemma that multiculturalists steadfastly ignore acutely betrays the absence of any long-term historical perspective from pluralist thought since the 1960s. In championing group identities, should ethnic studies be prospective or retrospective? Should they look to the past to save what is being lost, or to the future to gain something new? How can these two desirable goals be reconciled or accommodated?

Within individual minority groups, these questions arise obsessively. Every group has its fundamentalists who jealously guard the ancient ways; its reformers, ready to adopt new ways; and its equivocal mainstream. The balance between them varies from group to group and shifts as the specific history and dynamics of each group changes. Fundamentally, ethnicity is a conservative force. It stresses continuity, survival, and the links between generations. At certain historical junctures, however, it has a revolutionary potential. Briefly, that was the case with Black Nationalism at the end of the 1960s. Today revolutionary nationalists are little heard from, but the differences between racialist conservatives and flexible reformers are great. While Afrocentric fundamentalists reinvent an ancient racial heritage, reformers argue "that race and history and metaphysics do not enforce an identity; that we [blacks] can choose within broad limits ... what it will mean to be African in the coming years."[53]

An unequivocal concern with building new identities is clearly uppermost among other dissident minorities who associate themselves with multiculturalism. Feminists, for example, are not looking for roots. They may search the past for clues to women's underrecognized potentialities, but their object is to reshape the traditional woman. The issue of preserving, as opposed to creating, identities arises in such different ways in the circumstances of individual groups that no truly multicultural agenda can address it.

All three of these unexamined dilemmas have a common source. Multiculturalism is silent on problems of arousal, divergence, and direction because, like so much else in American life today, it lacks a vision of what it wants the country to become. For young people in search of some common purpose beyond the confines of their own endowment, multiculturalism offers no nourishing center or beckoning horizon.

Nevertheless, an indispensable heritage of equality lives on amid the contradictions of the multicultural movement. Although truncated and fragmented, this heritage awaits a wider understanding and employment. If multiculturalism can shake off a fixation on diversity, autonomy, and otherness, the vision that American universalism sustained and enlarged through two centuries can be renewed. It

can teach us that we are all multicultural and increasingly transnational – that minority and majority cultures alike are becoming more
and more interconnected, interpenetrative, and even indistinguishable.
To adopt the fashionable language of multiculturalism, we are all
"others" to others. But otherness is only relatively so, and diminishes
as the bounds of "our" own identities expand, overlap, and combine.
On that basis, Rodney King's distraught appeal to the "consensual
'we'" whom multiculturalists scorn might be heard. We can work it
out. Unless we have grown too cynical or self-enclosed, an American
universalism can be rebuilt.

NOTES

1. John Higham. "From Process to Structure: Formulations of American
    Immigration History," in *American Immigrants and Their Generations:
    Studies and Commentaries on the Hansen Thesis after Fifty Years*, ed.
    Peter Kivisso and Dag Blanck (Urbana: University of Illinois Press,
    1990), 18–41.
2. Gunnar Myrdal, *An American Dilemma: The Negro Problem and Modern
    Democracy* (New York: Harper Collins 1944), 8–27. See also Walter A.
    Jackson. *Gunnar Myrdal and: Harper Collins America's Conscience:
    Social Engineering and Racial Liberalism, 1938–1987* (Chapel Hill,
    N.C.:University of North Carolina Press 1990).
3. Dorothy Ross, *The Origins of American Social Science* (Cambridge:
    Cambridge University Press, 1991).
4. Quoted in Robert W. Tucker and David C. Hendrickson, *Empire of
    Liberty: The Statecraft of Thomas Jefferson* (New York, Oxford Uni-
    versity Press, 1990), 83.
5. Rogers M. Smith. "The American Creed and American Identity: The
    Limits of Liberal Citizenship in the United States." *Western Political
    Quarterly* 41 (June 1988), 225–51.
6. James Fenimore Cooper. *Notions of the Americans*. 2 vols. (Philadelphia:
    Carey, Lea and Carey, 1828), 1: 239; Henry James, *The Social Signific-
    ance of Our Institutions* (Boston: Ticknor and Fields, 1861), 28.
7. John Higham, "Indian Princess and Roman Goddess: The First Female
    Symbols of America," *Proceedings of the American Antiquarian Society*
    100 (1990): part 1, 63–67; Gordon S. Wood, *The Radicalism of the
    American Revolution* (New York: Alfred A. Knopf, 1992), 222–23.
8. I share much common ground with David A. Hollinger's important art-
    icle. "Postethnic America," *Contention* 2 (Fall 1992): 79–96. His definitions
    of universalism and cosmopolitanism, however, seem too restrictive and
    too precisely differentiated to designate, as I wish to do, substantial bodies

of social thought. I have not, for example, run into any universalists, with the possible exception of Henry David Thoreau, "for whom the [human] species as a whole can be community enough" (84).

9. Thomas Paine, "Common Sense" (1776), in *American Issues*, ed. Willard Thorp, Merle Curti, and Carlos Baker (Philadelphia: Lippincott, 1955), 1: 83–84; *Speeches, Correspondence, and Political Papers of Carl Schurz*, ed. Frederic Bancroft (New York: G. P. Putnam's Sons, 1913), 1: 48–59, 71–72; Richard Conant Harper, *The Course of the Melting Pot Idea to 1910* (New York: Ayer Company Publishers, 1980), 118–23, 132–48, 176–86. See also: Kathleen Neils Conzen, "German-Americans and the Invention of Ethnicity," in *America and the Germans: An Assessment of a Three-Hundred-Year History*, ed. Frank Trommler and Joseph McVeigh (Philadelphia University of Pennsylvania Press, 1985), 1: 131–47; Kathleen Neils Conzen et al., "The Invention of Ethnicity: A Perspective from the U.S.A.," *Journal of American Ethnic History* 12 (Fall 1992): 3–41.

10. Wendell Phillips, "Idols" (1859), in *Speeches, Lectures, and Letters* (Boston: Lee and Shepard, 1900), 1: 243. See also. "The United States of the United Races," *National Era* 7 (Sept. 15, 1853): 146; John Todd. "The Future of the Pacific Slope and the Chinese Question," *Home Missionary* 42 (Mar. 1970): 253–59; David Herbert Donald, *Charles Sumner and the Rights of Man* (New York: Knopf, 1970), 422; Waldo E. Martin, Jr., *The Mind of Frederick Douglass* (Chapel Hill, N.C.: University of North Carolina Press, 1984), 197–224; Charles Shanabruch, *Chicago's Catholics: The Evolution of an American Identity* (Notre Dame: University of Notre Dame Press, 1981), 76.

11. See David A. Gerber's finely grained account of a growing ethnicization of native-born Americans in *The Making of an American Pluralism: Buffalo, New York, 1825–60* (Urbana, Ill.: University of Illinois Press, 1989), 96–109.

12. David A. Hollinger, "Ethnic Diversity, Cosmopolitanism, and the Emergence of the American Liberal Intelligentsia," in *In the American Province: Studies in the History and Historiography of Ideas* (Bloomington, Ind.: Indiana University Press, 1985), 56–73; Ross, *Origins*. 143–71, 195–216, 303–19, James T. Kloppenberg, *Uncertain Victory: Social Democracy and Progressivism in European and American Thought, 1870–1920* (New York: Oxford University Press, 1986). The accompanying expansion of women's rights and women's issues must not be forgotten. I am concentrating, however, on relations between class and ethnicity because those seem to me to have produced the problematic structure of multiculturalism, within which academic feminism has located itself.

13. Jack M. Bloom, *Class, Race, and the Civil Rights Movement* (Bloomington, Ind.: Indiana University Press, 1987), 204–13.

14. Murray Kempton, "Brother, Can You Spare a Dime?" *New York Review of Books*, (23 Apr. 1992), 55.

15. Ira Katznelson, "Was the Great Society a Lost Opportunity?" in *The Rise and Fall of the New Deal Order*, ed. Steve Fraser and Gary Gerstle (Princeton: Books on Demand, 1989), 185–211.

16. Nathan Glazer cites both usages in a perceptive article, "The Problem of Ethnic Studies" (1977), reprinted in his *Ethnic Dilemmas, 1964–1982* (Cambridge, Mass.: Harward University Press, 1983), 107. The principal handbook for teachers was James A. Banks, *Multiethnic Education: Theory and Practice* (Boston: Allyn and Bacon, 1981), and he retained that title in a second edition in 1988. The new works that Banks edited in the late 1980s, however, were *Multicultural Education in Western Societies* (New York: Greenwood Publishing Group, 1986) and *Multicultural Education: Issues and Perspectives* (Boston: Allyn and Bacon, 1989).

17. The recent Banks-edited text for teachers devotes a chapter to social class, but treats it only as an obstacle to multiculturalism, not as a subject for classroom discussion. See *Multicultural Education: Issues and Perspectives*, 67–86.

18. Paul Lauter, *Canons and Contexts* (New York: Oxford University Press, 1991), ix.

19. James A. Miller, "American Studies at Trinity College," *American Studies Association Newsletter* 14 (Dec. 1991): 7. See also Jane De Hart. "Report on the Program for the 1988 Convention." *American Studies Association Newsletter* 12 (Mar. 1989): 1, which raises but then allays concerns about "this celebration of multicultural diversity." For a semi-official account of "the speed with which we have discovered diversity of race, class, gender, and ethnicity," see Linda Kerber. "Diversity and the Transformation of American Studies." *American Quarterly* 41 (Sept. 1989): 415–31.

20. Stuart M. Blumin, *The Emergence of the Middle Class: Social Experience in the American City, 1760–1900* (Cambridge: Cambridge University Press, 1989); Olivier Zunz, *Making America Corporate, 1870–1920* (Chicago: University of Chicago Press, 1990); Michael Denning, *Mechanic Accents: Dime Novels and Working-Class Culture in America* (New York: Routledge, Chapman and Hall, 1987).

21. "Democratic Platform Shows Shift in Party's Roots," *New York Times*, 14 July 1992.

22. David Brion Davis, "The American Dilemma," *New York Review of Books*, 16 July 1992, 13–17.

23. Jonathan Okamura, "Situational Ethnicity," *Ethnic and Racial Studies* 4 (Oct. 1981): 452–65; William L. Yancey et al., "Emergent Ethnicity: A Review and Reformulation," *American Sociological Review* 41 (June 1976): 391–403.

24. Compare Stow Persons, *Ethnic Studies at Chicago, 1905–45* (Urbana, Ill.: University of Illinois Press, 1987) with R. Fred Wacker's more sympathetic assessment in *Ethnicity, Pluralism, and Race: Race Relations Theory in America Before Myrdal* (Westport, Conn.: Greenwood Reblishing Group, 1983).

25. Randolph Bourne, "Trans-National America," in *The Radical Will: Selected Writings*, ed. Olaf Hansen (New York: Urizen Books, 1977), 248–64. The assimilationist position is best represented in Robert E. Park, *Race and Culture*, vol. 1, *The Collected Papers of Robert E. Park*, ed. Everett C. Hughes et al. (Glencoe, Ill: Free Press, 1950). See, in

234   *Resurgent Tribalisms*

general: John Higham, "Ethnic Pluralism in Modern American Thought," in *Send These to Me: Immigrants in Urban America*. rev. ed. (Baltimore: Johns Hopkins University Press, 1984), 198–232; Philip Gleason, "American Identity and Americanization." in *Harvard Encyclopedia of American Ethnic Groups*, ed. Stephan Thernstrom (Cambridge, Mass.: Harvard University Press, 1980), 31–58, and especially Philip Gleason, *Speaking of Diversity Language and Ethnicity in Twentieth-Century America* (Baltimore: Johns Hopkins University Press, 1992).

26. Hollinger's *In the American Province*, 56–65, contrasts Bourne's "cosmopolitanism" with the "cultural pluralism" of his immediate antecedent. Horace Kallen. In my terms both were pluralists. To the key question. "Where are authentic cultures located?" both men gave in effect the same fateful answer. "Only in minorities." Bourne's minorities included a "young intelligentsia," with whom he identified himself. But the masses of Americans who had lost their Old World ties were only "half-breeds...without a spiritual country, cultural outlaws, without taste, without standards but those of the mob...They become the flotsam and jetsam of American life, the downward undertow of our civilization...which we see in our slovenly towns, our vapid moving pictures, our popular novels, and in the vacuous faces of the crowds on the city street." Bourne, *The Radical Will*, 254–55.

27. See, for example, J. Christopher Eisele, "John Dewey and the Immigrants," *Journal of Education Quarterly* 15 (Spring 1975): 67–85.

28. Diane Ravitch, "Multiculturalism: E. Pluribus Plures," *American Scholar* 59 (Summer 1990): 337–54; Molefi Kete Asante, "Multiculturalism: An Exchange." *American Scholar* (Spring 1991): 271; Robert Fullinwider. "Multicultural Education." *University of Maryland Institute for Philosophy & Public Policy* (Winter 1991): 12–14. See also Banks's manual for teachers, *Multiethnic Education: Theory and Practice*, 2d ed. (Boston: Allyn and Bacon, 1988), 115–25.

29. James B. Gilbert, "Popular Culture," *American Quarterly* 35 (Spring/ Summer, 1983): 141–54. See also the polling data in Louis Harris, *The Anguish of Change* (New York: W. W. Norton and Co., 1973).

30. Mary Ann Glendon, *Rights Talk: The Impoverishment of Political Discourse* (New York: Free Press, 1991); Jeffrey C. Goldfarb, *The Cynical Society: The Culture of Politics and the Politics of Culture in American Life* (Chicago: University of Chicago Press, 1991).

31. Compare two columns by Chuck Stone in the Detroit *Free Press*: the first a militant appeal. "Black Nationhood Antidote to Gangs," 25 Sept. 1972; the second a complacent and apolitical article, "Black Crime Syndicates Grow Across Nation," 21 June 1973.

32. Paul Ruffins, "Interracial Coalitions," *The Atlantic* 265 (June 1990): 28–34. See also *New York Times*, 2 Dec. 1991, on intermarriage, and 24 July 1992, on black-white income gap; Lawrence H. Fuchs, *The American Kaleidoscope: Race, Ethnicity, and the Civic Culture* (Hanover, N. H.: University Press of New England, 1990), 190–205, 425–30, 482–84; Reynolds Farley, "Trends in Racial Inequalities: Have the Gains of the 1960s Disappeared in the 1970s?" *American Sociological Review* 40 (Apr. 1977): 189–208; Charlotte Steeh and Howard Schuman.

"Young White Adults: Did Racial Attitudes Change in the 1980s?" *American Journal of Sociology* 98 (Sept. 1992): 340–67.

33. Alan Peshkin, *The Color of Strangers The Color of Friends: The Play of Ethnicity in School and Community* (Chicago: University of Chicago Press, 1991). On other well-integrated school districts, in places where low-income minorities have not been highly ghettoized and public schools link city and suburb, see David Rusk, "America's Urban Apartheid," *New York Times*, 21 May 1992. More generally, on convergence between blacks and whites, see Bob Blauner, *Black Lives, White Lives: Three Decades of Race Relations in America* (Berkeley: University of California Press, 1989), 163–71, 332; Andrew Hacker, "The Myths of Racial Division," *New Republic* 206 (23 Mar. 1992): 21–25; and the powerful, broadly based argument of Fuchs's *American Kaleidoscope*.

34. *New York Times*, 8 Jan. 1992.

35. *New York Times*, 2 Jan. 1987, 16 Mar. 1987, 29 Mar. 1987. In New York city the first of the dramatically inflamed confrontations over crime occurred in December 1986, when a pack of white youths in Howard Beach chased three black men, one of whom was killed by a passing car. In May of that year a more deliberately murderous assault by whites had taken place in Coney Island without receiving any special notice. The Howard Beach incident, however, released a paroxysm of televised rage. Jim Sleeper, *The Closest of Strangers: Liberalism and the Politics of Race in New York* (New York: W. W. Norton and Co., 1990), 138–40, 183–88; *New York Times*, 20 Dec. 1992.

36. Jon Wiener, *Professors, Politics and Pop* (London: Verso, 1991), 136–51: *New York Times*, 3 Oct. 1990, 18 May 1991. On 23 Dec. 1986 the *Times* published a perceptive editorial linking, but not explaining, the resurgence of racism on campuses and on city streets.

37. *New York Times*, 28 Oct. 1991: Dinesh D'Souza, *Illiberal Education: The Politics of Race and Sex on Campus* (New York: Free Press, 1991), 59–93.

38. *New York Times*, 22 June 1991; Ravitch, "Multiculturalism," 339 and "A Culture in Common," *Educational Leadership* (Dec. 1991–Jan. 1992): 8–11; Robert K. Landers, "Conflict over Multicultural Education." *Editorial Research Reports* (Congressional Quarterly, 1990): 681–95. See also Robert J. Cottroll, "America the Multicultural," *American Educator* (Winter 1990): 18–21, 38.

39. David A. Kirp, "Textbooks and Tribalism in California," *The Public Interest* 104 (Summer 1991): 20–36; Washington *Times*, 13 Nov. 1990; Abdul R. JanMohamed and David Lloyd, eds., *The Nature and Context of Minority Discourse* (New York: Oxford University Press, 1990), 8; Molefi Kente Asante, "Afrocentric Curriculum," *Educational Leadership* (Dec. 1991–Jan. 1992): 28–31.

40. "Presidential Address 1990: On Differences," *PMLA* 106 (May 1991): 404.

41. I have discussed this central issue more fully in *Send These to Me*, x–xiii, 198–248.

Resurgent Tribalisms

42. For a related point, stressing the needs of black educators, see Nathan Glazer, "In Defense of Multiculturalism." *The New Republic* 205 (2 Sept. 1991): 18–22.

43. Frances Fitzgerald, *America Revised: History Schoolbooks in the Twentieth Century* (Boston: Little, Brown, 1979), 80–105; Eva Moskowitz, "Lessons in Achievement in American History High School Textbooks of the 1950s and 1970s," *Pennsylvania Magazine of History and Biography* 112 (Apr. 1988): 268–69.

44. Elliott Robert Barkan, "Strategies for Multicultural Teaching: The Quest for Social Justness and a Multicentric Perspective," in *Changing College Classrooms: The Challenge of Educating Students for the 21st Century*, ed. Diane F. Halpern (San Francisco, forthcoming). This racial dualism may be partly understandable as an expression of a Hispanic tendency in the American West to label all whites as Anglos, but it does suppress a vital span of the nation's diversity.

45. Personal communication.

46. Andrew Delbanco, *The Puritan Ordeal* (Cambridge, Mass.: Harvard University Press, 1989). On subgroups see David Hackett Fischer, *Albion's Seed: Four British Folkways in America* (New York: Oxford University Press, 1989).

47. Leonard J. Moore, *Citizen Klansmen: The Ku Klux Klan in Indiana, 1921–1928* (Chapel Hill, N. C.: University of North Carolina Press, 1991): Stuart C. McConnell, *Glorious Contentment: The Grand Army of the Republic, 1865–1900* (Chapel Hill, N.C.: University of North Carolina Press, 1992).

48. Kenneth Lauren Burns, *The Civil War*, P.B.S. Home Video (Beverley Hills, 1990). The series incorporated a dignified black perspective, but left it quite muted. What viewers overwhelmingly experience is the death of white men.

49. Kirp, "Textbooks and Tribalism," 33–35 and Robert Fullinwider, "Multicultural Education," *University of Chicago Legal Forum* (1991) 88–91, review several sociological studies that have failed to find any relationship between low self-esteem among black youth and "any problematic behavior" such as teen pregnancy or drug use.

50. Sandra Stotsky, "Multicultural Education in the Brookline Public Schools: The Deconstruction of an Academic Curriculum." *Network News & Views* (June 1991) included in *Multicultural Education: A Compilation of the Literature*, ed. Ruth McGrath (Office of Multicultural Education, Pittsburgh Public Schools, 1992).

51. *American Studies Association Newsletter* 15 (Feb. 1992): 1–8. Election results were reported in the *American Studies Association Newsletter* (May 1992): 1.

52. David Hollinger has brought to my attention a partial exception: Iris Marion Young, *Justice and the Politics of Difference* (Princeton: Princeton University Press, 1990), an argument for strengthening divergence institutionally, which captures the spirit of multiculturalism without ever invoking the name.

53. Kwame Anthony Appiah, *In My Father's House: Africa in the Philosophy of Culture* (New York: Oxford University Press, 1992), 176–77.

10 Constructing Ethnicity: Creating and Recreating Ethnic Identity and Culture*

Joane Nagel

INTRODUCTION

Contrary to expectations implicit in the image of the "melting pot" that ethnic distinctions could be eliminated in US society, the resurgence of ethnic nationalism in the United States and around the world has prompted social scientists to rethink models of ethnicity rooted in assumptions about the inevitability of assimilation.[1] Instead, the resiliency of cultural, linguistic, and religious differences among populations has led to a search for a more accurate, less evolutionary means of understanding not only the resurgence of ancient differences among peoples, but also the actual emergence of historically new ethnic groups.[2] The result has been the development of a model of ethnicity that stresses the fluid, situational, volitional, and dynamic character of ethnic identification, organization, and action – a model that emphasizes the socially "constructed" aspects of ethnicity, that is, the ways in which ethnic boundaries, identities, and cultures, are negotiated, defined, and produced through social interaction inside and outside ethnic communities.[3]

According to this constructionist view, the origin, content, and form of ethnicity reflect the creative choices of individuals and groups as they define themselves and others in ethnic ways. Through the actions and designations of ethnic groups, their antagonists, political authorities, and economic interest groups, ethnic boundaries are erected dividing some populations and unifying others (see Barth 1969; Moerman 1965, 1974). Ethnicity is constructed out of the material of language, religion, culture, appearance, ancestry, or regionality. The location and meaning of particular ethnic boundaries are continuously negotiated, revised, and revitalized, both by ethnic group members themselves as well as by outside observers.

237

To assert that ethnicity is socially constructed is not to deny the historical basis of ethnic conflict and mobilization.[4] However, a constructionist view of ethnicity poses questions where an historical view begs them. For instance, to argue that the Arab-Israeli conflict is simply historical antagonism, built on centuries of distrust and contention, asserts a certain truth, but it answers no questions about regional or historical variations in the bases or extent of the conflict, or about the processes through which it might be ameliorated. In fact, scholars have asserted that both Israeli and Palestinian ethnic identities are themselves fairly recent constructions, arising out of the geopolitics of World War II and the Cold War, and researchers have documented the various competing meanings of the Arab-Israeli conflict in American political culture.[5]

Similarly, to view black-white antagonism in contemporary American society simply as based in history – albeit a powerful and divisive history – is to overlook the contemporary demographic, political, social, and economic processes that prop up this ethnic boundary, reconstructing it, and producing tension along its borders and within the two bounded ethnic groups.[6] For instance, Lemann's (1991) study of the post-World War II demographic shift of African Americans from rural to urban areas and from the South to the North reveals a reconfiguration of the black-white ethnic boundary in northern and southern cities. This migration magnified urban ethnic segregation, stratified black society, increased interethnic tensions, promoted ethnic movements among both blacks and whites, and produced a black urban underclass. All of these changes reflect the dynamic, constructed character of black ethnicity in US society.[7]

Since ethnicity is not simply an historical legacy of migration or conquest, but is constantly undergoing redefinition and reconstruction, our understanding of such ethnic processes as ethnic conflict, mobilization, resurgence, and change might profit from a reconsideration of some of the core concepts we use to think about ethnicity. This paper examines two of the basic building blocks of ethnicity: identity and culture. Identity and culture are fundamental to the central projects of ethnicity: the construction of boundaries and the production of meaning. In this paper, I attempt to answer several questions about the construction of identity and culture: What are the processes by which ethnic identity is created or destroyed, strengthened or weakened? To what extent is ethnic identity the result of internal processes, and to what extent is ethnicity externally defined and motivated? What are the processes that motivate ethnic boundary

Ethnicity created thru' interactions b/n groups — cf Epstein an idon.

Nagel *Constructing Ethnicity* 239

construction? What is the relationship between culture and ethnic identity? How is culture formed and transformed? What social purposes are served by the construction of culture? Rather than casting identity and culture as prior, fixed aspects of ethnic organization, here they are analyzed as emergent, problematic features of ethnicity. By specifying several mechanisms by which groups reinvent themselves – who they are and what their ethnicity means – I hope to clarify and organize the growing literature documenting the shifting, volitional, situational nature of ethnicity. Next I examine the construction of ethnic identity, followed by a discussion of the construction of culture.

CONSTRUCTING ETHNIC IDENTITY

Ethnic identity is most closely associated with the issue of boundaries. Ethnic boundaries determine who is a member and who is not and designate which ethnic categories are available for individual identification at a particular time and place. Debates over the placement of ethnic boundaries and the social worth of ethnic groups are central mechanisms in ethnic construction. Ethnicity is created and recreated as various groups and interests put forth competing visions of the ethnic composition of society and argue over which rewards or sanctions should be attached to which ethnicities.

Recent research has pointed to an interesting ethnic paradox in the United States. Despite many indications of weakening ethnic boundaries in the white American population (due to intermarriage, language loss, religious conversion or declining participation), a number of studies have shown a maintenance or increase in ethnic identification among whites (Alba 1990; Waters 1990; Kivisto 1989; Bakalian 1993; Kelly 1993, 1994). This contradictory dualism is partly due to what Gans terms "symbolic ethnicity," which is "characterized by a nostalgic allegiance to the culture of the immigrant generation, or that of the old country; a love for and pride in a tradition that can be felt without having to be incorporated in everyday behavior" (1979: 205). Bakalian (1991) provides the example of Armenian-Americans:

For American-born generations, Armenian identity is a preference and Armenianness is a *state of mind* .... One can say he or she is an Armenian without speaking Armenian, marrying an Armenian, doing business with Armenians, belonging to an Armenian church,

joining Armenian voluntary associations, or participating in the
events and activities sponsored by such organizations

(Bakalian 1991: 13).

This simultaneous decrease and increase in ethnicity raises the interesting question: How can people behave in ways which disregard
ethnic boundaries while at the same time claim an ethnic identity?
The answer is found by examining ethnic construction processes – in
particular, the ways in which individuals and groups create and recre-
ate their personal and collective histories, the membership boundaries
of their group, and the content and meaning of their ethnicity.

Negotiating Ethnic Boundaries

While ethnicity is commonly viewed as biological in the United States
(with its history of an obdurate ethnic boundary based on color),
research has shown people's conception of themselves along ethnic
lines, especially their ethnic identity, to be situational and changeable
(see especially Waters 1990, Chapter Two). Barth (1969) first convin-
cingly articulated the notion of ethnicity as mutable, arguing that
ethnicity is the product of social ascriptions, a kind of labeling process
engaged in by oneself and others. According to this perspective, one's
ethnic identity is a composite of the view one has of oneself as well as
the views held by others about one's ethnic identity. As the individual
(or group) moves through daily life, ethnicity can change according to
variations in the situations and audiences encountered.

   Ethnic identity, then, is the result of a dialectical process involving
internal and external opinions and processes, as well as the individual's self-identification and outsiders' ethnic designations – that
is, what *you* think your ethnicity is, versus what *they* think your
ethnicity is. Since ethnicity changes situationally, the individual carries
a portfolio of ethnic identities that are more or less salient in various
situations and vis-à-vis various audiences. As audiences change, the
socially-defined array of ethnic choices open to the individual
changes. This produces a "layering" (McBeth 1989) of ethnic identities which combines with the ascriptive character of ethnicity to reveal
the negotiated, problematic nature of ethnic identity. Ethnic boundaries, and thus identities, are constructed by both the individual and
group as well as by outside agents and organizations.

   Examples can be found in patterns of ethnic identification in many
US ethnic communities.[8] For instance, Cornell (1988) and McBeth

Ethnicity is situational — not segmentary [handwritten annotation] *knowledge* *

(1989) discuss various levels of identity available to Native Americans: *subtribal* (clan, lineage, traditional), *tribal* (ethnographic or linguistic, reservation-based, official), *regional* (Oklahoma, California, Alaska, Plains), *supra-tribal* or *pan-Indian* (Native American, Indian, American Indian). Which of these identities a native individual employs in social interaction depends partly on where and with whom the interaction occurs. Thus, an American Indian might be a "mixed-blood" on the reservation, from "Pine Ridge" when speaking to someone from another reservation, a "Sioux" or "Lakota" when responding to the US census, and "Native American" when interacting with non-Indians.

Pedraza (1992), Padilla (1985, 1986), and Gimenez, Lopez, and Munoz (1992) note a similar layering of Latino or Hispanic ethnic identity, again reflecting both internal and external defining processes. An individual of Cuban ancestry may be a Latino vis-à-vis non-Spanish-speaking ethnic groups, a Cuban-American vis-à-vis other Spanish-speaking groups, a Marielito vis-à-vis other Cubans, and white vis-à-vis African Americans.[9] The chosen ethnic identity is determined by the individual's perception of its meaning to different audiences, its salience in different social contexts, and its utility in different settings. For instance, intra-Cuban distinctions of class and immigration cohort may not be widely understood outside of the Cuban community since a Marielito is a "Cuban" or "Hispanic" to most Anglo-Americans. To a Cuban, however, immigration cohorts represent important political "vintages," distinguishing those whose lives have been shaped by decades of Cuban revolutionary social changes from those whose life experiences have been as exiles in the United States. Others' lack of appreciation for such ethnic differences tends to make certain ethnic identity choices useless and socially meaningless except in very specific situations. It underlines the importance of external validation of individual or group ethnic boundaries.

Espiritu (1992) also observes a layering of Asian-American identity. While the larger "Asian" pan-ethnic identity represents one level of identification, especially vis-à-vis non-Asians, national origin (e.g., Japanese, Chinese, Vietnamese) remains an important basis of identification and organization both vis-à-vis other Asians as well as in the larger society. Like Padilla (1985, 1986), Espiritu finds that individuals choose from an array of pan-ethnic and nationality-based identities, depending on the perceived strategic utility and symbolic appropriateness of the identities in different settings and audiences. She notes the larger Asian-American pan-ethnic boundary is often the basis for identification where large group size is perceived as an

* *But what makes some [vary] to others? See 243/12.* [handwritten annotation]

advantage in acquiring resources or political power. However she also observes that Asian-American pan-ethnicity tends to be transient, often giving way to smaller, culturally distinct nationality-based Asian ethnicities.

Waters (1991) describes similar situational levels of ethnic identification among African Americans. She reports that dark-skinned Caribbean immigrants acknowledge and emphasize color and ancestry similarities with African Americans at some times; at other times Caribbeans culturally distinguish themselves from native-born blacks. Keith and Herring (1991) discuss the skin tone distinctions that exist among African Americans, with the advantages and higher social status that accrue to those who are lighter skinned. This color consciousness appears to be embraced by blacks as well as whites, and thus demarcates an internal as well as external ethnic boundary.

White Americans also make ethnic distinctions in various settings, vis-à-vis various audiences. They sometimes emphasize one of their several European ancestries (Waters 1990: Alba 1990); they sometimes invoke Native American lineage (Beale 1957; Quinn 1990); they sometimes identify themselves as "white," or simply assert an "American" identity (Lieberson 1985). The calculations involved in white ethnic choices appear different from those of other ethnic groups, since resources targeted for minority populations are generally not available to whites, and may not directly motivate individuals to specify an ethnicity based on European ancestry or "white"-ness. In these cases, white ethnicity can take the form of a "reverse discrimination" countermovement or "backlash" against the perceived advantages of non-whites (Burstein 1991). In other cases, white ethnicity is more symbolic (Gans 1979), representing less a rational choice based on material interests than a personal option exercised for social, emotional, or spiritual reasons (Waters 1990; Fischer 1986).

External Forces Shaping Ethnic Boundaries

The notion that ethnicity is simply a personal choice runs the risk of emphasizing agency at the expense of structure. In fact, ethnic identity is *both* optional and mandatory, as individual choices are circumscribed by the ethnic categories available at a particular time and place. That is, while an individual can choose from among a set of ethnic identities, that set is generally limited to socially and politically defined ethnic categories with varying degrees of stigma or advantage attached to them. In some cases, the array of available ethnicities can be quite restricted and constraining.

For instance, white Americans have considerable latitude in choosing ethnic identities based on ancestry. Since many whites have mixed ancestries, they have the choice to select from among multiple ancestries, or to ignore ancestry in favor of an "American" or "unhyphenated white" ethnic identity (Lieberson 1985). Americans of African ancestry, on the other hand, are confronted with essentially one ethnic option – black. And while blacks may make intra-racial distinctions based on ancestry or skin tone, the power of race as a socially defining status in US society makes these internal differences rather unimportant in interracial settings in comparison to the fundamental black/white color boundary.[10]

The differences between the ethnic options available to blacks and whites in the United States reveal the limits of individual choice and underline the importance of external ascriptions in restricting available ethnicities. Thus, the extent to which ethnicity can be freely constructed by individuals or groups is quite narrow when compulsory ethnic categories are imposed by others. Such limits on ethnic identification can be official or unofficial. In either case, externally enforced ethnic boundaries can be powerful determinants of both the content and meaning of particular ethnicities. For instance, Feagin's (1991, 1992) research on the day-to-day racism experienced by middle-class black Americans demonstrates the potency of *informal* social ascription. Despite the economic success of middle-class African Americans, their reports of hostility, suspicion, and humiliation in public and private interactions with non-blacks illustrate the power of informal meanings and stereotypes to shape interethnic relations (see also Whitaker 1993).

If informal ethnic meanings and transactions can shape the everyday experiences of minority groups, formal ethnic labels and policies are even more powerful sources of identity and social experience. Official ethnic categories and meanings are generally political. As the state has become the dominant institution in society, political policies regulating ethnicity increasingly shape ethnic boundaries and influence patterns of ethnic identification. There are several ways that ethnicity is "politically constructed," that is, the ways in which ethnic boundaries, identities, cultures, are negotiated, defined, and produced by political policies and institutions (J. Nagel 1986): by immigration policies, by ethnically-linked resource policies, and by political access that is structured along ethnic lines.

Immigration and the production of ethnic diversity
Governments routinely reshape their internal ethnic maps by their
immigration policies. Immigration is a major engine of new ethnic
group production as today's immigrant groups become tomorrow's
ethnic groups (Hein 1994). Around the world, immigrant populations
congregate in both urban and rural communities to form ethnic
enclaves and neighborhoods, to fill labor market niches, sometimes
providing needed labor, sometimes competing with native-born
workers, to specialize in particular commodity markets, and as "mid-
dlemen."[11] Whether by accident or design, whether motivated by
economics, politics, or kinship, immigrant groups are inevitably
woven into the fabric of ethnic diversity in most of the world's states.
    It is also through immigration that both domestic and foreign
policies can reshape ethnic boundaries. The growing ethnic diversity
and conflict in France and Britain are direct legacies of both their
successes and failures at colonial empire – building. In many other
European states, such as Sweden and Germany, economic rather than
political policies, in particular the importation of guest workers to fill
labor shortages, encouraged immigration. The result has been the
creation of permanent ethnic minority populations. In the United
States, various Cold War policies and conflicts (e.g., in Southeast
Asia and Central America) resulted in immigration flows that make
Asians and Latin Americans the two fastest growing minority populations in the United States (US Census 1991). Political policies
designed to house, employ, or otherwise regulate or assist immigrant
populations can influence the composition, location, and class position of these new ethnic subpopulations.[12] Thus the politics of immigration are an important mechanism in the political construction of
ethnicity.

Resource competition and ethnic group formation
Immigration is not the only area in which politics and ethnicity are
interwoven. Official ethnic categories are routinely used by governments worldwide in census-taking (Horowitz 1985), and acknowledg-
ment of the ethnic composition of populations is a regular feature of
national constitutions (Maarseveen and van der Tang 1978; Rhoodie
1983). Such designations can serve to reinforce or reconstruct ethnic
boundaries by providing incentives for ethnic group formation and
mobilization or by designating particular ethnic subpopulations
as targets for special treatment. The political recognition of a particular ethnic group can not only reshape the designated group's

Anti-Arab-Amer feeling/actions - US
~ so, why = this are H/9/01 attacks.

Nagel *Constructing Ethnicity* 245

self-awareness and organization, but can also increase identification
and mobilization among ethnic groups not officially recognized, and
thus promote new ethnic group formation. This is especially likely
when official designations are thought to advantage or disadvantage a
group in some way.

For instance, in India, the provision of constitutionally guaranteed
parliamentary representation and civil service posts for members
of the "Scheduled Castes" or "Untouchables" contributed to the
emergence of collective identity and the political mobilization of
Untouchables from different language and regional backgrounds;
one result was the formation of an Untouchable political party, the
Republican Party (Nayar 1966; Rudolph and Rudolph 1967). This
affirmative action program produced a backlash and a Hindu revival
movement, mainly among upper caste Indians who judged Untouchables to have unfair political and economic advantages (Desai 1992).
Such backlashes are common around the world. In Malaysia,
constitutional provisions granting political advantages to majority
Malays prompted numerous protests from non-Malays – mainly Chinese and Indians (Means 1976). In many of the new republics of the
former Soviet Union, nationalist mobilizations are built as much on a
backlash against Russia and local Russians (who comprise a significant part of the population in most republics) than on a strong historic
pattern of national identity.[13] In the United States, white ethnic self-
awareness was heightened as desegregation and affirmative action
programs got under way in the 1960s and 1970s. The result was a
white anti-busing movement, and a "legal countermobilization" and
cultural backlash against affirmative action (Rubin 1972; Burstein
1991; Faludi 1991). American Indians have also been the targets of
white backlashes, mainly against treaty-protected hunting and fishing
rights in the Pacific Northwest and the northern Great Lakes region
(Adams and La Course 1977; Wright 1977; Kuhlmann forthcoming).

Official ethnic categories and policies can also strengthen ethnic
boundaries by serving as the basis for discrimination and repression,
and thus reconstruct the meaning of particular ethnicities. Petonito
(1991a, 1991b) outlines the construction of both "loyal American"
and "disloyal Japanese" ethnic boundaries during World War II, a
process which led to the internment of thousands of Japanese-
Americans. Similarly, violence directed toward Iranians and Middle
Easterners in the United States increased when American embassy
staff were taken hostage during the Iranian revolution in 1980 and
attacks against Iraqis and Arab-Americans escalated during the 1991

Gulf War (Applebome 1991). In the former case, official actions of the Carter administration, such as requiring Iranian nationals in the United States to report for photographing and fingerprinting, contributed to an elevation of ethnic awareness and tended to legitimate the harassment of Iranians. In the latter case, official US military hostilities against Iraq "spread" into US domestic politics, prompting attacks on Arab and Iraqi "targets" living in the United States.

Political policies and designations have enormous power to shape patterns of ethnic identification when politically controlled resources are distributed along ethnic lines. Roosens (1989) attempts to trace the rise of ethnicity and ethnic movements in the contemporary United States. He argues that the mobilization of ethnic groups in the United States has paralleled the development of the US welfare state and its racial policies:

> There were few advantages in the United States ... of the 1930s to define oneself visibly as a member of the Sicilian or Polish immigrant community. When one considers the current North American situation, however, one concludes that ethnic groups emerged so strongly because ethnicity brought people strategic advantages
> (Roosens 1989: 14).

Padilla's (1985, 1986) description of the emergence of a Latino ethnicity among Mexicans and Puerto Ricans in Chicago in response to city programs focused on Hispanics, is consistent with Roosens's analysis. Another example is Espiritu's (1992) account of the emergence of Asian-American ethnic identity as a strategy to counter official policies thought to disadvantage smaller Asian nationality groups. Similarly, the white backlashes described above represent one response to exclusion from what are seen as ethnically-designated rights and resources.

The observation that ethnic boundaries shift, shaping and reshaping ethnic groups according to strategic calculations of interest, and that ethnicity and ethnic conflict arise out of resource competition, represent major themes in the study of ethnicity (see Banton 1983). Barth and his associates (1969) link ethnic boundaries to resource niches. Where separate niches are exploited by separate ethnic groups (e.g., herders versus horticulturalists), ethnic tranquility prevails; however, niche competition (e.g., for land or water) results in ethnic boundary instability due to conflict or displacement (see also Despres 1975). Examining labor markets, Bonacich (1972) and Olzak (1989, 1992) have shown how informal job competition among different ethnic groups can heighten ethnic antagonism and conflict, strengthening ethnic boundaries as ethnicity comes to be viewed as crucial to employment and economic success. Hannan argues that the pursuit of economic and political advantage underlies the shift in ethnic boundaries upward from smaller to larger identities in modern states.[14] Thus, in electoral systems, larger ethnic groups mean larger voting blocs; in industrial economies regulated by the political sector, and in welfare states, larger ethnic constituencies translate into greater influence (see also Lauwagie 1979 and B. Nagel 1986).

This research paints a picture of ethnicity as a rational choice (Hechter 1987a). According to this view, the construction of ethnic boundaries (group formation) or the adoption or presentation of a particular ethnic identity (individual ethnic identification), can be seen as part of a strategy to gain personal or collective political or economic advantage.[15] For instance, Katz (1976) reports the creation of racially restrictive craft unions by white settlers in South Africa in order to gain an edge in labor market competition and create class distance from competing black laborers. Such competitive strategies not only provide ethnic advantages, they stimulate ethnic identity and group formation. An example is "whiteness" which Roediger (1991: 13–14) argues emerged as an American ethnicity due to the efforts of working class (especially Irish) whites who sought to distance themselves and their labor from blacks and blackness; by distinguishing their "free labor" from "slave labor," they redefined their work from "white slavery" to "free labor."

Political access and ethnic group formation
The organization of political access along ethnic lines can also promote ethnic identification and ethnic political mobilization. As Brass notes, "the state...is not simply an arena or an instrument of a particular class or ethnic group...the state is itself the greatest prize and resource, over which groups engage in a continuing struggle" (1985: 29). Much ethnic conflict around the world arises out of competition among ethnic contenders to control territories and central governments. The civil war in the former republic of Yugoslavia is a clear example of ethnic political competition (Hodson, Sekulic, and Massey (1994)).[16] The long-standing grievances of the various warring linguistic and religious groups there did not erupt into combat until the Soviet Union lifted the threat of intervention in the late 1980s and opened the door to the possibility of ethno-political competition. The result was an armed scramble for territory based on

a fear of domination or exclusion by larger, more powerful ethnic groups.

In the United States, the construction of ethnic identity in response to ethnic rules for political access can be seen in the national debate over affirmative action, in the composition of judicial (judges, juries) and policy-making bodies (committees, boards), and in the enforcement of laws designed to end discrimination or protect minorities (see Gamson and Modigliani 1987). For example, the redistricting of US congressional districts based on the 1990 census led to ethnic mobilization and litigation as African-American and Latino communities, among others, sought improved representation in the federal government (Feeney 1992). Similarly, concern based on the importance of ethnic population size for representation and resource allocation led Asian Americans to demand that the Census Bureau designate nine, Asian nationality groups as separate "races" in the 1980 and 1990 census (Espiritu 1992; Lee 1993).[17]

Ethnic Authenticity and Ethnic Fraud

Politically-regulated ethnic resource distribution and political access have led to much discussion about just what constitutes legitimate membership in an ethnic group, and about which individuals and groups qualify as disadvantaged minorities. For instance, Hein (1991: 1) outlines the debate concerning the extent to which Asian immigrants to the United States should be seen to be ethnic "minorities" with an "historical pattern of discrimination," and thus eligible for affirmative action remedies. In universities, concerned with admissions practices, financial aid allocation, and non-discriminatory employment and representation, the question of which ethnic groups fulfill affirmative action goals is often answered by committees charged with defining who is and is not an official minority group (see Simmons 1982).

Discussions about group eligibility are often translated into controversies surrounding individual need, individual ethnicity, and ethnic proof. The multi-ethnic ancestry of many Americans combines with ethnically-designated resources to make choosing an ethnicity sometimes a financial decision. In some instances, individuals respond to shifting ethnic incentive structures (Friedman and McAdam 1987, 1992) by asserting minority status or even changing their ethnicity. Ethnic switching (Barth 1969) to gain advantage can be contentious when resources are limited. In many cases, particularly those involving individuals of mixed ancestry; the designation of a resource-endowed ethnicity for public or official purposes can elicit suspicion and challenge. For instance, Snipp (1993) reports concern among Native American educators about "ethnic fraud" in the allocation of jobs and resources designated for American Indian students; this concern was reflected in the inclusion of ethnic fraud among the topics of discussion at a recent national conference on minority education.[18]

Indeed, questions of who is Indian or Latino or black[19] are often raised and often are difficult to resolve one way or the other. Even when ancestry can be proven, questions can arise about the cultural depth of the individual's ethnicity (Was he or she raised on a reservation or in the city? Does he or she speak Spanish?), or the individual's social class (Was he or she raised in the inner city or in the suburbs?). Solutions to questions of authenticity are often controversial and difficult to enforce. For instance, the federal government has attempted to set the standards of ethnic proof in the case of American Indian art. The Indian Arts and Crafts Act of 1990 requires that in order for artwork to be labeled as "Indian produced," the producer must be "certified as an Indian artisan by a [federally recognized] Indian tribe" (United States Congress 1990: 4663). By this legal definition, artists of Indian ancestry cannot produce Indian art unless they are enrolled in or certified by officially recognized tribes. The act has thus led a number of Indian artists to seek official tribal status (some have refused to do this) and has also served to exclude some recognized American Indian artists from galleries, museums, and exhibits (Jaimes 1992; *Kansas City Star* 1991).[20] Similar local restrictions on who can sell Indian art and where it can be sold have caused bitter divisions among American Indians and other minority communities in the Southwest (Evans-Pritchard 1987).[21]

In sum, the construction of ethnic boundaries through individual identification, ethnic group formation, informal ascriptions, and official ethnic policies illustrates the ways in which particular ethnic identities are created, emphasized, chosen, or discarded in societies. As the result of processes of negotiation and designation, ethnic boundaries wax and wane. Individual ethnic identification is strongly limited and influenced by external forces that shape the options, feasibility, and attractiveness of various ethnicities.

As we have seen above, research speaks fairly clearly and articulately about how ethnic boundaries are erected and torn down, and the incentives or disincentives for pursuing particular ethnic options. However, the literature is less articulate about the *meaning* of ethnicity

to individuals and groups, about the forces that shape and influence
the contents of that ethnicity, and about the purposes ethnic meanings
serve. This requires a discussion of the construction of culture.

Culture and history are the substance of ethnicity. They are also the
basic materials used to construct ethnic meaning. Culture and history
are often interwined in cultural construction activities. Both are part
of the "toolkit" – as Swidler (1986) called it – used to create the
meaning and interpretative systems seen to be unique to particular
ethnic groups (see Tonkin, McDonald, and Chapman 1989). Culture
is most closely associated with the issue of meaning. Culture dictates
the appropriate and inappropriate content of a particular ethnicity
and designates the language, religion, belief system, art, music, dress,
traditions, and lifeways that constitute an authentic ethnicity. While
the construction of ethnic boundaries is very much a saga of structure
and external forces shaping ethnic options, the construction of culture
is more a tale of human agency and internal group processes of
cultural preservation, renewal, and innovation. The next section
explores the ways in which ethnic communities use culture and history
to create common meanings, to build solidarity, and to launch social
movements.

CONSTRUCTING CULTURE

In his now classic treatise on ethnicity, Fredrik Barth (1969) challenged anthropology to move away from its preoccupation with the
content of culture, toward a more ecological and structural analysis of
ethnicity:

> ...ethnic categories provide an organizational *vessel* that may be
> given varying amounts and forms of content in different socio-
> cultural systems...The critical focus of investigation from this
> point of view becomes the ethnic *boundary* that defines the group,
> not the cultural stuff that it encloses
>   (Barth 1969: 14–15 [emphasis mine]).

Barth's quarrel was not with the analysis of culture, per se, but with
its primacy in anthropological thinking. In fact, by modernizing
Barth's "vessel" imagery, we have a useful device for examining the
construction of ethnic culture: the shopping cart. We can think of
ethnic boundary construction as determining the *shape* of the shopping cart (size, number of wheels, composition, etc.); ethnic culture,

then, is composed of the things we put into the cart – art, music, dress, religion, norms, beliefs, symbols, myths, customs. It is important that we discard the notion that culture is simply an historical legacy; culture is *not* a shopping cart that comes to us already loaded with a set of historical cultural goods. Rather we construct culture by picking and choosing items from the shelves of the past and the present. As Barth reminds us:

> ...when one traces the history of an ethnic group through time, one is *not* simultaneously...tracing the history of "a culture": the elements of the present culture of that group have not sprung from the particular set that constituted the group's culture at a previous time' (Barth 1969: 38).

In other words, cultures change; they are borrowed, blended, rediscovered, and reinterpreted. My use of the shopping cart metaphor extends Swidler's (1986) cultural toolkit imagery. Swidler argues that we use the cultural tools in the toolkit in our everyday social labors; I argue that we not only use the tools in the toolkit, but that we also determine its contents – keeping some tools already in the kit, discarding others, adding new ones. However, if culture is best understood as more than mere remnants of the past, then how did it get to its present state – how did the cart get filled, and why? What does culture do?

Culture is constructed in much the same way as ethnic boundaries are built, by the actions of individuals and groups and their interactions with the larger society. Ethnic boundaries function to determine identity options, membership composition and size, and form of ethnic organization. Boundaries answer the question: Who are we? Culture provides the content and meaning of ethnicity; it animates and authenticates ethnic boundaries by providing a history, ideology, symbolic universe, and system of meaning. Culture answers the question: What are we? It is through the construction of culture that ethnic groups fill Barth's vessel – by reinventing the past and inventing the present.

CULTURAL CONSTRUCTION TECHNIQUES

Groups construct their cultures in many ways which involve mainly the *reconstruction* of historical culture, and the *construction* of new culture. Cultural reconstruction techniques include revivals and restorations of historical cultural practices and institutions; new cultural constructions include revisions of current culture and innovations – the creation of new cultural forms. Cultural construction and reconstruction are ongoing group tasks in which new and renovated cultural symbols, activities, and materials are continually being added to and removed from existing cultural repertoires.[22]

Cultural revivals and restorations occur when lost or forgotten cultural forms or practices are excavated and reintroduced, or when lapsed or occasional cultural forms or practices are refurbished and reintegrated into contemporary culture. For example, for many, immigrant and indigenous ethnic groups' native languages have fallen into disuse. Efforts to revitalize language and increase usage are often major cultural reconstruction projects. In Spain, both in Catalonia and the Basque region, declining use of the native tongues (Catalan and Euskera, respectively) due to immigration and/or Castilian Spanish domination, has spurred language education programs and linguistic renewal projects (Johnston 1991; Sullivan 1988). In the United States, the threatened loss of many Native American languages has produced similar language documentation and education programs, as well as the creation of cultural centers, tribal museums, and educational programs to preserve and revive tribal cultural traditions. Study and instruction in cultural history is often a central part of cultural reconstruction.

Cultural revisions and innovations occur when current cultural elements are changed or when new cultural forms or practices are created. As part of US authorities' various historical efforts to destroy Native American cultures by annihilation or assimilation, many Indian communities and groups used cultural revision and innovation to insulate cultural practices when they were outlawed by authorities. Champagne (1989, 1990) reports that the Alaska Tlingits revised traditional potlatch practices, incorporating them into Russian Orthodox or Protestant ceremonies to conceal the forbidden exchanges. Prucha (1984) reports a form of cultural innovation to protect the use of peyote in American Indian religious rites. The creation of the Native American Church imbedded peyote use in a syncretic, new Indian–Christian religious institution, thus protecting practitioners under the First Amendment of the US constitution. Such cultural camouflage in the form of religious syncretism is reported in many societies, particularly those penetrated by missionaries operating under governmental auspices.[23]

These various cultural construction techniques, and others that will be described below, serve two important collective ends which will be the focus of the remainder of this paper. They aid in the construction of community and they serve as mechanisms of collective mobilization. Cultural constructions assist in the construction of community when they act to define the boundaries of collective identity, establish membership criteria, generate a shared symbolic vocabulary, and define a common purpose. Cultural constructions promote collective mobilization when they serve as a basis for group solidarity, combine into symbolic systems for defining grievances and setting agendas for collective action, and provide a blueprint or repertoire of tactics.

The Cultural Construction of Community

In *Imagined Communities*, Benedict Anderson argues that there is no more evocative a symbol of modern nationalism than the tomb of the unknown soldier. The illustrative power of this icon lies in the fact that such tombs "are either deliberately empty or no one knows who lies inside them" (Anderson 1991:9) – thus, they are open to interpretation and waiting to be filled. The construction of culture supplies the contents for ethnic and national symbolic repositories. Hobsbawm (1983) refers to this symbolic work as "the invention of tradition" – that is, the construction or reconstruction of rituals, practices, beliefs, customs, and other cultural apparatus. According to Hobsbawm, invented traditions serve three related purposes: (a) to establish or symbolize social cohesion or group membership, (b) to establish or legitimize institutions, status, and authority relations, or (c) to socialize or inculcate beliefs, values, or behaviors (1983:9). By this analysis the invention of tradition is very much akin to what Cohen (1985) calls "the symbolic construction of community."

The construction of history and culture is a major task facing all ethnic groups, particularly those that are newly forming or resurgent. In constructing culture, the past is a resource used by groups in the collective quest for meaning and community (Cohen 1985: 99). Trevor-Roper provides an example of the construction of a national culture:

Today, whenever Scotchmen gather to celebrate their national identity, they assert it openly by certain distinctive national apparatus. They wear the kilt, woven in a tartan whose colour and pattern indicates their "clan"; and if they indulge in music, their

Isn't this as much pol as symc? See A. Cohen's work.

instrument is the bagpipe. This apparatus, to which they ascribe
great antiquity, is in fact largely modern.... Indeed the whole concept of a distinct Highland culture and tradition is a retrospective
invention. Before the later years of the seventeenth century, the
Highlanders of Scotland did not form a distinct people. They were
simply the overflow of Ireland   (Trevor-Roper 1983:15).

Other scholars concur with Trevor-Roper's assertions about the constructed character of Scottish identity and culture (Chapman 1979;
Prebble 1963). However, the fictive aspects of Scottish ethnicity in no
way lessen the reality of Scottish nationalism in Great Britain, particularly during its heydey during the 1970s and early 1980s. During
that time, Scottish and Welsh nationalism combined with the escalating violence in Northern Ireland to represent a major political and
economic threat to the integrity of the United Kingdom.[24] Indeed,
despite its invented origins, Scottish nationalism contributed to a
major devolution of political authority to the British Celtic states
(Mercer 1978; Davies 1989; Harvie 1977).

For newly forming ethnic and national groups, the construction of
community solidarity and shared meanings out of real or putative
common history and ancestry involves both cultural constructions
and reconstructions. Smith refers to ethnic and national groups'
"deep nostalgia for the past" that results in efforts to uncover or, if
necessary, invent an earlier, ethnic "golden age" (1986:174). For
instance, Karner (1991) describes the reconstruction of Finnish cultural history (folklore, music, songs) by Swedish-speaking Finnish
intellectuals during the mobilization for Finnish independence. Similarly, Kelly (1993) discusses the efforts of Lithuanian-Americans to
learn the Lithuanian language and to reproduce Lithuanian foods,
songs, dances, and customs illustrating the process whereby people
transform a common ancestry (whether by birth or by marriage) into
a common ethnicity.[25] And in their homeland, Lithuanians themselves
are embarked on a journey of national reconstruction, as decades of
Russian influence are swept away in an effort to uncover real and
historical Lithuanianness.

The importance of cultural construction for purposes of community
building is not limited to the creation of national unity. Cultural
construction is especially important to panethnic groups, as they are
often composed of subgroups with histories of conflict and animosity.
For instance, Padilla (1985) discusses the challenges facing Mexican-
Americans and Puerto Ricans in Chicago as they attempt to construct

Kwanzaa festival

both Latino organizations and an identity underpinned by the assertion of common interests and shared culture – a commonality that is sometimes problematic. Espiritu (1992) also documents the tensions surrounding nationality and cultural differences in the evolution of an Asian-American pan-ethnicity.

One strategy used by polyethnic groups to overcome such differences and build a more unified pan-ethnic community is to blend together cultural material from many component group traditions. About half of the American Indian population lives in urban areas (US Census Bureau 1989). Urban Indians have borrowed from various tribal cultures as well as from non-Indian urban culture to construct supratribal or "Indian" cultural forms such as the powwow, the Indian Center, Indian Christian churches, Indian bowling leagues and softball teams, and Indian popular music groups. In the urban setting, tribal differences and tensions can be submerged in these pan-Indian organizations and activities.[26]

Building a cultural basis for new ethnic and national communities is not the only goal prompting cultural reconstruction. Cultural construction is also a method for revitalizing ethnic boundaries and redefining the meaning of ethnicity in existing ethnic populations. The Christmas season celebration of Kwanzaa by African Americans is an example of the dynamic, creative nature of ethnic culture, and reveals the role scholars play in cultural construction. Created in the 1960s by Professor Maulana Karenga, Kwanzaa is a seven-day cultural holiday which combines African and African-American traditions (Copage 1991).[27] The reconstruction and study of cultural history is also a crucial part of the community construction process and again shows the importance of academic actors and institutions in cultural renewal. Examples can be found in the recent emergence of various ethnic studies programs (e.g., Latino, American Indian, African-American, Asian Studies) established in colleges and universities around the United States during the past three decades (Deloria 1986). Such programs are reflective of a renewed and legitimated interest in ethnicity and cultural diversity. These programs, as well as classes in oral history and ethnic culture, serve as important resources in cultural revivals and restorations.[28]

Cultural Construction and Ethnic Mobilization

Cultural construction can also be placed in the service of ethnic mobilization. Cultural renewal and transformation are important

Ethnicity as basis for social mvts

aspects of ethnic movements. Cultural claims, icons, and imagery are used by activists in the mobilization process; cultural symbols and meanings are also produced and transformed as ethnic movements emerge and grow. While there is a large literature on the structural determinants of ethnic mobilization,[29] recent social movement research reflects increased interest in the nature of social movement culture and the interplay between culture and mobilization (see Morris and Mueller 1992). An examination of this literature offers insight into the relationship between culture and ethnic mobilization.

For instance, Snow and his associates argue that social movement organizers and activists use existing culture (rhetorical devices and various techniques of "frame alignment") to make movement goals and tactics seem reasonable, just, and feasible to participants, constituencies, and political officials (Snow et al. 1986; Snow and Benford 1988, 1992). For example, nuclear disarmament movement leaders responded to questions about the hopelessness of opposing a military-industrial complex bent on the production of nuclear weapons by drawing a parallel between the elimination of nuclear weapons and the abolition of slavery – namely, the success of abolitionism was achieved despite an equally daunting opposition (Snow et al. 1986). Thus, by drawing on available cultural themes, the discourse surrounding movement objectives and activism is more likely to recruit members, gain political currency, and achieve movement goals.

Gamson and his associates document the ideational shifts and strategies used by movements, policymakers, and opposition groups to shape debates, define issues, and to paint the most compelling portrait of each side's claims and objectives (Gamson 1988, 1992; Gamson and Modigliani 1987; Gamson and Lasch 1983). For instance, Gamson and Modigliani (1987) argue that the changing culture of affirmative action results from a struggle over the definition of equality, justice, and fairness, as various political actors frame the issues in competing ways, e.g., affirmative action as "remedial action" versus "reverse discrimination." The rhetorics, counter-rhetorics, and rhetorical shifts characterized in this research are common to all social movements, including ethnic movements. They reflect the use of cultural material and representations in a symbolic struggle over rights, resources, and the hearts and minds of constituents, neutral observers, and opponents alike.

The work of Snow and Gamson illustrates the use of existing culture by movement organizers and activists, and shows several forms of cultural reconstruction, where cultural symbols and themes are borrowed and sometimes repackaged to serve movement ends. There is another way in which cultural construction occurs in movements – where protest is a crucible of culture. For instance, Fantasia (1988) describes a "culture of solidarity" that arises out of activism. Cultures of solidarity refer to the emergence of a collective consciousness and shared meanings that result from engaging in collective action. Ethnic movements often challenge negative hegemonic ethnic images and institutions by redefining the meaning of ethnicity in appealing ways or by using cultural symbols to effectively dramatize grievances and demands.

Examples of the construction and reconstruction of history and culture in order to redefine the meaning of ethnicity can be found in the activities of many of the ethnic groups that mobilized during the civil rights era of the 1960s and 1970s in the United States. During these years, a renewed interest in African culture and history and the development of a culture of black pride – "Black is Beautiful" – accompanied African-American protest actions during the civil rights movement. The creation of new symbolic forms and the abandonment of old, discredited symbols and rhetoric reflected the efforts of African Americans to create internal solidarity and to challenge the prevailing negative definitions of black American ethnicity. For instance, the evolution of racial nomenclature for African American can be excavated by a retrospective examination of the names of organizations associated with or representing the interests of black Americans: the National Association for the Advancement of Colored People, the United Negro College Fund, the Black Panther Party, and the National Council of African-American Men, Inc. The fluidity of names for other American ethnic groups reflects similar shifts in constructed ethnic definitions and revised meanings associated with evolving collective identities: from Indians to American Indians to Native Americans; from Spanish-Surnamed to Hispanics to Latinos.[30] Such changes in ethnic nomenclature were an important part of the discourse of civil rights protest, as were changes in dress, new symbolic themes in art, literature, and music, and counterhegemonic challenges to prevailing standards of ethnic demeanor and interracial relations.[31]

The expropriation and subversion of negative hegemonic ethnic definitions and institutions is an important way that culture is used in ethnic mobilization around the world. British conceptions of "tribe" and "tribal" shaped many of their colonial policies, such as geographic administrative boundaries, education policies, and hiring practices. These tribal constructions were reshaped by Africans into the anti-colonial ethnic politics of a number of African states (Melson and Wolpe 1971; Young 1976). For instance, Wallerstein (1960) and Iliffe (1979) document the mobilization of various "tribal" unions and associations into nationalist movements for independence in many African countries. In India, similar subversion of colonial cultural constructions designed to facilitate British domination occurred. Cohn (1983) argues that the pomp and ceremony of the British Imperial Assemblage and the Imperial Durbars in nineteenth century India were expropriated by Indian elites, who indigenized and institutionalized this invented tradition, incorporating it into the symbolism and idiom of an independent Indian politics.[32]

This "turning on its head" of cultural symbols and institutions can be seen in the ways ethnic activists use culture in their protest strategies. The tactics used in ethnic movements rely on the presentation, and sometimes the reconstruction, of cultural symbols to demonstrate ethnic unity, to dramatize injustice, or to animate grievances or movement objectives. For instance, Zulaika (1988), Sullivan (1988), and Clark (1984) report the use of various cultural symbols and conventions by Basque nationalist groups, noting, for instance, the central symbols importance of demands for Basque language rights, although fewer than half of the Basque population speaks the Basque language. The Red Power movement for American Indian rights during the 1960s and 1970s drew its membership from mainly urban Indians from a variety of tribal backgrounds. The movement created a unified pan-Indian cultural front by borrowing cultural forms from many native communities (e.g., the teepee, eagle feathers, the war dance, the drum). Red Power repertoires of contention – as Tilly (1986) called them – also employed a rhetorical and dramaturgical cultural style that reflected movement leaders' sensitivity to the place of the American Indian in American popular culture and history. The American Indian Movement (AIM) was especially skilled in the use of such symbolic dramaturgy, as illustrated in the following description of an AIM-sponsored counter-ceremony in 1976:

> *Custer Battlefield, Mont.* Today, on the wind-buffeted hill... where George Armstrong Custer made his last stand, about 150 Indians from various tribes danced joyously around the monument to the Seventh Cavalry dead. Meanwhile, at the official National Parks Service ceremony about 100 yards away, an Army band played.... Just as the ceremony got underway, a caravan of Sioux, Cheyenne,

and other Indians led by Russell Means, the American Indian Movement leader, strode to the speakers' platform to the pounding of a drum. Oscar Bear Runner, like Mr. Means, a veteran of the 1973 takeover of Wounded Knee, carried a sacred peace pipe
(Lichtenstein 1976:II-1).

The above example shows the interplay between pre-existing cultural forms and the new uses to which they are put in ethnic movements. What we see is the National Parks Service's efforts to commemorate the "official story" (Scott 1990), and the American Indian Movement's challenge to this hegemonic interpretation of history. Both groups employed the symbolic paraphernalia available to them, drawn from similar strands of American history and culture, but used in opposing ways. By recasting the material of the past in innovative ways, in the service of new political agendas, ethnic movements reforge their own culture and history and reinvent themselves.

CONCLUSION

At the beginning of this paper I posed a number of questions about ethnic boundaries and meaning, inquiring into the forces shaping ethnic identity and ethnic group formation, and the uses of history and culture by ethnic groups and movements. My answers have emphasized the interplay between ethnic group actions and the larger social structures with which they interact. Just as ethnic identity results both from the choices of individuals and from the ascriptions of others, ethnic boundaries and meaning are also constructed from within and from without, propped up by internal and external pressures. For ethnic groups, questions of history, membership, and culture are the problematics solved by the construction process. Whether ethnic divisions are built upon visible biological differences among populations or rest upon invisible cultural and ideational distinctions, the boundaries around and the meanings attached to ethnic groups reflect pure social constructions.

Yet questions remain. What is driving groups to construct and reconstruct ethnic identity and culture? What is it about ethnicity that seems to appeal to individuals on so fundamental a level? From what social and psychological domains does the impulse toward ethnic identification originate? Why is ethnicity such a durable basis for group organization around the world? If ethnicity is in part a *[handwritten: Rather long list of qu's — has JN really got to (sat) heart of the matter?]*

political construction, why do the goals of some ethnic activists favor equal rights, while others demand autonomy or independence? Other questions remain about the social meaning of ethnicity. How are particular meanings (values, stereotypes, beliefs) attached to different ethnic groups, and by whom? What are the implications of these different meanings for conceptions of social justice, intergroup relations, political policy? Concomitantly, how does ethnic stratification (material and ideational) arise? Can constructionist explanations of ethnicity account for persistent prejudice and discrimination, particularly where race or color are involved? To the extent that the constructionist model emphasizes change, how should we understand intractable racial and ethnic antagonism and stratification?

These questions comprise not only an agenda for future research, they are also warnings. While ethnic boundaries and the meanings attributed to them can be shown to be socially constructed, they must not, therefore, be underestimated as social forces. In fact, the constructionist model constitutes an argument for the durability, indeed the inevitability, of ethnicity in modern societies. As such, it represents a challenge to simple historical, biological, or cultural determinist models of human diversity.

[handwritten: Ethnicities will persist]

NOTES

*I wish to thank Richard Alba, Stephen Cornell, Jim Holstein, Carol A. B. Warren, and Norman Yetman for their helpful comments on an earlier version of this paper.

1. The failure of the American melting pot is a qualified one. As Alba and Logan (1991) point out, some groups, particularly whites, have "melted" quite well. Despite the maintenance of a kind of social or symbolic ethnicity among white groups, white ethnicity does not generally involve high levels of ethnic exclusiveness or ethnic group affiliation.

2. An ethnic group can be seen as "new" or "emergent" when ethnic identification, organization, and collective action is constructed around previously nonexistent identities, such as "Latino" or "Asian-American." An ethnic group can be seen as "resurgent" when ethnic identification, organization, or collective action is constructed around formerly quiescent historical identities, such as "Basque" or "Serbian" (see Yancey, Erickson, and Juliani 1976).

3. See Berger and Luckmann (1967) and Spector and Kitsuse (1977) for discussions of the social constructionist model: see Holstein and Miller (1993) for an assessment of the current state of social constructionism.

4. I define ethnic mobilization as the organization of groups along ethnic lines for collective action.

5. See Gerner (1991); Plascov (1981); Gamson (1982). Layne (1989) also describes the construction of a Jordanian national identity in the decades following World War I, and especially during King Hussein's rule beginning in 1953.

6. The use of the term "ethnic group" rather than "race" or "racial group" to describe African Americans is not intended to discount the unique importance of color or race as a basis for discrimination and disadvantage in US society (and elsewhere). However, the arguments about ethnicity I put forth here are meant to apply to all racial and ethnic groups, whether distinguished by color, language, religion, or national ancestry.

7. See Wilson (1987); Burstein (1991); James (1989); Massey (1985); Massey and Denton (1993); Morris (1984).

8. The examples here are drawn from American groups, but the layering of identity is not unique to the United States. Similar levels of ethnic identification have been observed around the world. See Horowitz (1985), Young (1976), and Enloe (1973) for other examples.

9. The racial self-definition of the Hispanics represents an interesting example of the negotiated and constructed character of ethnicity. In 1980 and 1990, nearly half of respondents who identified themselves as "Hispanic" on an ancestry item, reported their race as "other," i.e. they did not choose any of the more than a dozen "races" offered in the Census or Current Population Survey questionnaires (e.g., black, white, American Indian, Japanese, Chinese, Filipino, Vietnamese, etc.) The Census Bureau recoded most of them as "white" (US Bureau of the Census 1980, 1990).

10. Despite the practice of "hypodescent" (Harris 1964) or the "one drop rule" in the classification of African Americans as "black," Davis (1991) shows that throughout US history, there has been considerable controversy and reconstruction of the. *meaning* and *boundaries* associated with blackness.

11. See Cohen (1974); Bonacich (1972, 1973); Fernandez-Kelly (1987); Light and Bonacich (1988); Portes and Rumbaut (1990); Sassen (1988, 1991).

12. See Yetman (1983, 1991); Pedraza-Balley (1985); Horowitz (1985); Light and Bonacich (1988); Whorton (1994).

13. This is more the case in the southern republics, such as Tadzhikistan or Uzbekistan, than in formerly independent republics such as in the Baltics – Latvia, Estonia, Lithuania – where national identities are more historically firmly fixed (see Allworth 1989).

14. Examples are from the town-based Oyo or Ilorin to Yoruba linguistic, regional identity in Nigeria (Laltin 1985); from various regional or linguistic Untouchable groups into an organized national party in India (Nayar 1966): from Chicano or Puerto Rican to Latino or from

Cherokee or Apache to Native American in the United States (Padilla 1986; Cornell 1988).
15. See also Hechter (1987b, 1992); Hechter and Friedman (1984); Hechter, Friedman, and Appelbaum (1982); Banton, 1995.
16. The distinction between "ethnic" and "national" groups is the subject of much definition and debate in the social sciences. I use the terms synonymously, thus "ethnic" group includes religious, linguistic, cultural, and regional groups with claims to political rights, sovereignty, or autonomy. See Connor (1991), Hobsbawm (1990), Smith (1986), and Gellner (1983, 1987) for discussions of nationalism, ethno-nationalism, and ethnicity.
17. On the 1990 census form there were actually 10 Asian nationality groups designated as separate races. They were: Asian Indian, Chinese, Filipino, Guamanian, Hawaiian, Japanese, Korean, Samoan, Vietnamese, and Other Asian or Pacific Islander. Asian American groups were concerned that if the term "Asian" were used in the census race item (Item number 4: "What is this person's race"), that many Asian Americans would not mark the choice, and the result would be an undercount of the Asian-American population (Espiritu 1992).
18. In an October, 1993 conference sponsored by the American Council on Education in Houston (American Council on Education 1993), Jim Larimore (Assistant Dean and Director of the American Indian Program at Stanford University) and Rick Waters (Assistant Director of Admissions at University of Colorado, Boulder) presented a session. "American Indians Speak Out Against Ethnic Fraud in College Admissions." The session was designed to "identify the problem and its impact on the American Indian community ... [and to] discuss effective institutional practices for documenting and monitoring tribal affiliations" (Larimore and Waters 1993).
19. An example is when individuals who are not of African-American ancestry, such as dark-skinned Asians or native-born Africans, are counted as "black" or "minority" for such purposes as demonstrating compliance with affirmative action hiring goals.
20. The entire Indian art authentication process has been criticized as having as its primary purpose, a way of guaranteeing the value of art for mainly non-Indian art owners and purchasers. My thanks to C. Matthew Snipp for bringing this to my attention.
21. The importance and meaning of official recognition as a basis for individual ethnicity, ethnic group formation, and ethnic mobilization is by no means unique to Native Americans or to the United States. Where a particular ethnicity is especially stigmatizing, ethnic conversions (or "passing") often occur. For example, Schermerhorn (1978) reports a common form of ethnic switching in India – religious conversion, when Hindu Untouchables convert to Islam in order to escape untouchability. Also in India, the British colonial preference for Sikh military recruits, led to many Sikh conversions in order to qualify (Nayar 1966). Lelyveld (1985) discusses the phenomenon of individuals officially changing their race under South African apartheid regulations (see also Adam and Moodley 1993). Official recognition or resources

tied to particular ethnic groups can prompt not only individual, but also ethnic group formation and mobilization as well. Burstein (1991) documents a white ethnic legal counter-assault against the perceived ethnic advantages of American minority populations. In Canada, the passage of policies favoring the use of the French language in Quebec during the 1970s and 1980s led to ethnic organizational formation and protests among non-French-speaking Canadian ethnic groups, such as those of Italian and Portuguese descent, who feared disadvantage or exclusion under the new language policies (Murray 1977; Lupul 1983).

22. For a detailed discussion of cultural construction, see Nagel (1994).

23. For example, see Whiteman (1985); Salamone (1985); Sanneh (1989); and Taber (1991).

24. Given the location of Britain's North Sea oil holdings off Scotland's coast.

25. An interesting aspect of Lithuanian-American ethnic renewal is what Kelly calls the "ethnic pilgrimage" where Lithuanian-American visit Lithuania to learn firsthand about their ethnic roots and to partricipate in building the new independent state and nation (Kelly 1994).

26. See Hertzberg (1971); Welbel-Orlando (1991); Steele (1975); Whitehorse (1988); Clark (1988).

27. Tanzanian-born Maulana Karenga is professor and chair of Black Studies at the University of California at Long Beach.

28. The use of historical or anthropological research by ethnic groups engaged in reconstruction projects has its pitfalls. These center on the accuracy and objectivity of such academic work. Recent research "deconstructing" historical and contemporary ethnographies (Wagner 1975; Clifford 1988; Clifford and Marcus 1986; Geertz 1988) has been aimed at revealing the voices and viewpoints of researchers imbedded in "objective" reports of their subjects' social and cultural organization.

29. See Enloe (1973); Hechter (1975); Young (1976); Nagel and Olzak (1982); Brass (1985); Horowitz (1985); Olzak (1992); A. Smith (1992).

30. See Martin (1991), Stein (1989), and T. Smith (1992) for a discussion of shifting nomenclature among African Americans. My thanks to Norm Yetman for raising the issue of evolving nomenclature.

31. See Cleaver (1968); Carmichael and Hamilton (1967); Willhelm (1970); Lister (1968).

32. A less liberating but common cultural construction technique used in ethnic mobilization is the demonization or villification of opposition ethnic groups in civil wars, pogroms, and genocides (e.g., against Armenlans in World War I Turkey, against Jews in World War II Germany, against Muslims in post-Soviet Yugoslavia).

REFERENCES

Adam, Heribert, and Kogila Moodley 1993 *The Opening of the Apartheld Mind: Options for the New South Africa.* Berkeley: University of California Press.

Adams, June, and Richard La Course 1977 "Backlash barrage erupts across U.S." *Yakima Nation Review*, July 18:12.

Alba, Richard D. 1990 *Ethnic Identity: The Transformation of White America*. New Haven: Yale University Press.

Alba, Richard D., and John R. Logan 1991 "Variations on two themes: Racial and ethnic patterns in the attainment of suburban residence." *Demography* 28:431–453.

Allworth, Edward 1989 *Central Asia: 120 Years of Russian Rule*. Durham, NC: Duke University Press.

American Council on Education 1993 "Educating One-Third of a Nation IV: Making our reality match our rhetoric." Washington, D.C.: American Council on Education.

Anderson, Benedict 1991 *Imagined Communities: Reflections on the Origin and Spread of Nationalism*. London: Verso.

Applebome, Peter 1991 "Arab-Americans fear a land war's backlash." *New York Times*, February 20:A1.

Bakalian, Anny 1991 "From being to feeling Armenian: Assimilation and identity among Armenian-Americans." Paper presented at the annual meeting of the American Sociological Association, Cincinnati.

—— 1993 *Armenian-Americans: From Being to Feeling Armenian*. New Brunswick, NJ: Transaction Books.

Banton, Michael 1983 *Ethnic and Racial Competition*. Cambridge: Cambridge University Press.

—— 1995 "Rational choice theories." *American Behavioral Scientist* 38: 478–

Barth, Fredrik 1969 *Ethnic Groups and Boundaries*. Boston: Little, Brown.

Beale, Calvin 1957 "American tri-racial isolates: Their status and pertinence to genetic research." *Eugenics Quarterly* 4:187–196.

Berger, Peter L., and Thomas Luckmann 1967 *The Construction of Reality: A Treatise on the Sociology of Knowledge*. Garden City, NJ: Anchor Books.

Bonacich, Edna 1972 "A theory of ethnic antagonism: The split labor market." *American Sociological Review* 37:547–559.

—— 1973 "A theory of middleman minorities," *American Sociological Review* 38:583–594.

Brass, Paul 1985 "Ethnic groups and the state." In *Ethnic Groups and the State*, ed. P. Brass, 1–56. London: Croome-Helm.

Burstein, Paul 1991 "'Reverse discrimination' cases in the federal courts: Legal mobilization by a countermovement." *Sociological Quarterly* 32:511–528.

Carmichael, Stokely, and Charles Hamilton 1967 *Black Power: The Politics of Liberation in America*. New York: Vintage.

Champagne, Duane 1989 American Indian Societies – Strategies and Conditions of Political and Cultural Survival, CS Report 32. Cambridge: Cultural Survival, Inc.

—— 1990 "Culture, differentiation, and environment: Social change in Tlingit society." In *Differentiation Theory and Social Change*, eds. J. Alexander and P. Colomy, 88–118. New York: Columbia University Press.

Chapman, Malcolm 1979 *The Gaelic Vision in Scottish Culture*. London: Croome-Helm.

Clark, Blue 1988 "Bury my heart in smog: Urban Indians." In *The American Indian Experience. A Profile: 1524 to the Present,* ed. P. Weeks, 278–291. Arlington Heights, Ill.: Forum Press, Inc.

Clark, Robert 1984 *The Basque Insurgents: ETA, 1952–1980.* Madison: University of Wisconsin Press.

Cleaver, Eldridge 1968 *Soul on Ice.* New York: McGraw-Hill.

Clifford, James 1988 *The Predicament of Culture: Twentieth Century Ethnography, Literature, and Art.* Cambridge: Harvard University Press.

Clifford, James, and George Marcus, eds. 1986 *Writing Culture: The Poetics and Politics of Ethnography.* Berkeley: University of California Press.

Cohen, Abner 1974 *Urban Ethnicity.* New York: Harper and Row.

Cohen, Anthony P. 1985 *The Symbolic Construction of Community.* New York: Tavistock.

Cohn, Bernard S. 1983 "Representing authority in Victorian India." In *The Invention of Tradition,* eds. E. Hobsbawm and T. Ranger, 165–210. Cambridge: Cambridge University Press.

Connor, Walker 1991 "When is a nation?" *Ethnic and Racial Studies* 13:92–103.

Copage, Eric V. 1991 "The seven days of Kwanzaa." *New York Times,* December 1:18.

Cornell, Stephen 1988 *The Return of the Native: American Indian Political Resurgence.* New York: Oxford University Press.

Davies, Charlotte 1989 *Welsh Nationalism in the Twentieth Century: The Ethnic Option and the Modern State.* New York: Praeger.

Davis, James 1991 *Who is Black? One Nation's Definition.* University Park: Pennsylvania State University.

Deloria, Vine, Jr. 1986 "Indian studies – the orphan of academia." *The Wicazo Sa Review* 2:1–7.

Desai, Manisha 1992 "The demise of secularism and the rise of majority communalism in India." Paper presented at the annual meeting of the Midwest Sociological Society, Kansas City.

Despres, Leo 1975 "Toward a theory of ethnic phenomena." In *Ethnicity and Resource Competition,* ed. L. Despres, 186–297. The Hague: Mouton.

Enloe, Cynthia 1973 *Ethnic Conflict and Political Development.* Boston: Little, Brown.

Espiritu, Yen 1992 *Asian American Panethnicity: Bridging Institutions and Identities.* Philladelphia: Temple University Press.

Evans-Pritchard, Deirdre 1987 "The Portal case: Authenticity, tourism, traditions, and the law." *Journal of American Folklore* 100:287–296.

Faludi, Susan 1991 *Backlash: The Undeclared War Against American Women.* New York: Crown.

Fantasia, Rick 1988 *Cultures of Solidarity.* Berkeley: University of California Press.

Feagin, Joe R. 1991 "The continuing significance of race: Antiblack discrimination in public places." *American Sociological Review* 56:101–116.

—— 1992 "The continuing significance of racism: Discrimination against black students at white colleges." *Journal of Black Studies* 22:546–578.

Feeney, Patrick G. 1992. "The 1990 census and the politics of apportionment." *Footnotes.* Washington, D.C.: American Sociological Association (March): 5–6.

Fernandez-Kelly, Maria Patricia 1987 "Economic restructuring in the United States: The case of Hispanic women in the garment and electronics industries in southern California." Paper presented at the annual meeting of the American Sociological Association, Chicago.

Fischer, Michael M.J. 1986 "Ethnicity and the post-modern arts of memory." In *Writing Culture: The Poetics and Politics of Ethnography*, eds. J. Clifford and G. Marcus, 194–233. Berkeley: University of California Press.

Friedman, Debra, and Doug McAdam 1987 "Collective Identity as a selective incentive." Paper presented at the annual meeting of the American Sociological Association.

—— 1992 "Collective identity and action: Networks, cholces, and the life of a social movement." In *Frontiers in Social Movement Theory*, eds. A.D. Morris and C.M. Mueller, 156–173. New Haven: Yale University Press.

Gamson, William 1982 "The political culture of the Arab-Israeli conflict." *Conflict Management and Peace Sciences* 5:79–93.

—— 1988 "Political discourse and collective action." In *International Social Movements Research*, eds. B. Klandermans, B. Kriesi, and S. Tarrow. Greenwich, Conn.: JAI Press.

—— 1992 "The social psychology of collective action." In *Frontiers in Social Movement Theory*, eds. A.D. Morris and C.M. Mueller, 53–76. New Haven: Yale University Press.

Gamson, William, and Kathryn E. Lasch 1983 "The political culture of welfare policy." In *Evaluating the Welfare State: Social and Political Perspectives*, eds. S.E. Spiro and E. Yuchtman-Yaar, 397–415. New York: Academic Press.

Gamson, William, and Andre Modigliani 1987 "The changing culture of affirmative action." In *Research in Political Sociology*, ed. R.G. Braungart. Greenwich, Conn.: JAI Press.

Gans, Herbert 1979 "Symbolic ethnicity: The future of ethnic groups and cultures in America." *Ethnic and Racial Studies* 2:1–20.

Geertz, Clifford 1988 *Works and Lives: The Anthropologist as Author*. Palo Alto: Stanford University Press.

Gellner, Ernest 1983 *Nations and Nationalism*. London: Basil Blackwell.

—— 1987 *Culture, Identity, and Politics*. Cambridge: Cambridge University Press.

Gerner, Deborah J. 1991 *One Land, Two Peoples: The Conflict over Palestine*. Boulder, Colo.: Westview.

Girnenez, Marta E., Fred A. Lopez, and Carlos Munoz, Jr. 1992 *The Politics of Ethnic Construction: Hispanic, Chicano, Latino?* Beverly Hills: Sage Publications.

Harris, Marvin 1964 *Patterns of Race in the Americas*. New York: Norton.

Harvie, Christopher 1977 *Scotland and Nationalism*. London: Allen and Unwin.

Hechter, Michael 1975 *Internal Colonialism*. Berkeley: University of California Press.

—— 1987a *Principles of Group Solidarity*. Berkeley: University of California Press.

—— 1987b "Nationalism as group solidarity." *Ethnic and Racial Studies* 10:415–426.

—— 1992 "The dynamics of secession." *Acta Sociologica* 35:267–283.

Hechter, Michael, and Debra Friedman 1984 "Does rational choice theory suffice? Response to Adam." *International Migration Review* 18:381–388.

Hechter, Michael, Debra Friedman, and Malka Appelbaum 1982 "A theory of ethnic collective action." *International Migration Review* 16:412–434.

Hein, Jeremy 1991 "Do 'new immigrants' become 'new minorities?:' The meaning of ethnic minority for Indochinese refugees in the United States." *Sociological Perspectives* 31:61–77.

—— 1994 "From migrant to minority." *Sociological Inquiry* 64.

Hertzberg, Hazel 1971 *The Search for an American Identity: Modern Pan-Indian Movements*. Syracuse: Syracuse University Press.

Hobsbawm, Eric 1983 "Introduction: Inventing traditions." In *The Invention of Tradition*. eds. E. Hobsbawm and T. Ranger, 1–14. Cambridge: Cambridge University Press.

—— 1990 *Nations and Nationalism Since 1780*. London: Cambridge University Press.

Hodson, Randy, Dusko Sekulic, and Garth Massey 1994 "National tolerance in 1994, the Formen: 1534–59. Yugoslavia." *American Journal of Sociology* 99

Holsteln, James A., and Gale Miller, eds. 1993 *Perspectives on Social Problems: Reconsidering Social Constructionism (Volume 5)*. New York: Aldine.

Horowitz, Donald 1985 *Ethnic Groups in Conflict*. Berkeley: University of California Press.

Iliffe, John 1979 *A Modern History of Tanganyika*. Cambridge: Cambridge University Press.

Jaimes, M. Annette 1992 "Federal Indian identification policy: A usurpation of indigenous sovereignty in North America." In *The State of Native America: Genocide, Colonization, and Resistance*, ed. M.A. Jaimes, 123–128. Boston: South End Press.

James, David R. 1989 "City limits on racial equality: The effects of city-suburb boundaries on public-school desegregation, 1968–1976." *American Sociological Review* 54: 963–985.

Johnston, Hank 1991 *Tales of Nationalism: Catalonia: 1939–1979*. New Brunswick: Rutgers University Press.

Kansas City Star 1991 "Indian art protection law may end up hurting the artists." August 4:1–5.

Karner, Tracy X. 1991 "Ideology and nationalism: The Finnish move to independence, 1809–1918." *Ethnic and Racial Studies* 14:152–70.

Katz, Elaine N. 1976 *A Trade Union Aristocracy. African Studies Institute Communication*, No. 3. Johannesburg: University of the Witwatersrand.

Keith, Verna M., and Cedric Herring 1991 "Skin tone and stratification in the black community." *American Journal of Sociology* 97:760–778.

Kelly, Mary 1993 "Lithuanian-Americans in the United States and Lithuania." *Sociologija Lietuvoje: Praeitis ir Dabartis* (Kaunas Technological University, Lithuania) 3:158–159.

—— 1994 "Ethnic pilgrimages: People of Lithuanian descent in Lithuania." Paper presented at the annual meeting of the Midwest Sociological Society, St. Louis.

Kivisto, Peter, ed. 1989 *The Ethnic Enigma: The Salience of Ethnicity for European-Origin Groups.* Philadelphia: The Balch Institute Press.

Kuhlmann, Annette "Steelheads and walleyes: Changes in political culture in and around Indian country and the fishing rights struggle in the Pacific Northwest and the Great Lakes." In *Research in Human Capital and Development.* eds. C. Ward and C.M. Snipp. Greenwich, Conn.: JAI Press.

Laitin, David D. 1985 "Hegemony and religious conflict: British imperial control and political cleavages in Yorubaland." In *Bringing the State Back In*, eds. P.B. Evans, D. Rueschemeyer, and T. Skocpol, 285–312. Cambridge: Cambridge University Press.

Larimore, Jim, and Rick Waters 1993 "American Indians speak out against ethnic fraud in college admissions." Paper presented at a conference sponsored by the American Council on Education: "Educating One-Third of a Nation IV: Making Our Reality Match our Rhetoric," Houston.

Lauwagie, Beverly 1979 "Ethnic boundaries in modern states: Romano Lavo-Lill revisited." *American Journal of Sociology* 87:23–47.

Layne, Linda L. 1989 "The dialogics of tribal self-representation in Jordan." *American Ethnologist* 16:24–39.

Lee, Sharon M. 1993 "Racial classification in the U.S. census: 1890–1990." *Ethnic and Racial Studies* 17:75–94.

Lelyveld, Joseph 1985 *Move Your Shadow: South Africa, Black and White.* New York: Penguin.

Lemann, Nicholas 1991 *The Promised Land: The Great Black Migration and How it Changed America.* New York: A.A. Knopf.

Lichtenstein, Grace 1976 "Custer's defeat commemorated by entreaties of peace." *New York Times*, June 25:II–1.

Lieberson, Stanley 1985 "Unhyphenated whites in the United States." *Ethnic and Racial Studies* 8:159–180.

Light, Ivan, and Edna Bonackh 1988 *Immigrant Entrepreneurs: Koreans in Los Angeles, 1965–1982.* Berkeley: University of California Press.

Lister, Julius 1968 *Look Out Whitey! Black Power's Gon' Get Your Mama.* New York: The Dial Press. Inc.

Lupul, M.R. 1983 "Multiculturalism and Canada's white ethnics." *Multiculturalism* 6:14–18.

Maarseveen, Henc T., and Ger van der Tang 1978 *Written Constitutions: A Computerized Comparative Study.* Dobbs Ferry, NY: Oceana Publications.

Martin, Ben L. 1991 "From Negro to black to African American: The power of names and naming." *Political Science Quarterly* 106:83–105.

Massey, Douglas S. 1985 "Ethnic residential segregation: A theoretical synthesis and empirical review." *Sociology and Social Research* 69:315–350.

Massey, Douglas S., and Nancy Denton 1993 *American Apartheid.* Chicago: University of Chicago Press.

McBeth, Sally 1989 "Layered identity systems in western Oklahoma Indian communities." Paper presented at the annual meeting of the American Anthropological Association.

Means, Gordon P. 1976 *Malaysian Politics.* London: Hodder and Stoughton.

Melson, Robert, and Howard Wolpe, eds. 1971 *Nigeria: Modernization and the Politics of Communalism.* East Lansing: Michigan State University Press.

Mercer, John 1978 *Scotland: The Devolution of Power*. London: Calder.

Moerman, Michael 1965 "Ethnic identification in a complex civilization: Who are the Lue?" *American Anthropologist* 76:1215–1230.

—— 1974 "Accomplishing ethnicity." In *Ethnomethodology*, ed. R. Turner, 54–68. New York: Penguin Education.

Morris, Aldon 1984 *The Origins of the Civil Rights Movement*. New York: The Free Press.

Morris, Aldon D., and Carol M. Mueller, eds. 1992 *Frontiers in Social Movement Theory*. New Haven: Yale University Press.

Murray, Janice 1977 *Canadian Cultural Nationalism*. New York: New York University Press.

Nagel, Beverly 1986 "Gypsies in the United States and Great Britain: Ethnic boundaries and political mobilization." In *Competitive Ethnic Relations*, eds. S. Olzak and J. Nagel, 69–90. New York: Academic Press.

Nagel, Joane 1986 "The political construction of ethnicity." In *Competitive Ethnic Relations*, eds. S. Olzak and J. Nagel, 93–112. New York: Academic Press.

—— 1994 *American Indian Ethnic Renewal: Red Power and the Resurgence of Identity and Culture*. New York: Oxford University Press.

Nagel, Joane, and Susan Olzak 1982 "Ethnic mobilization in new and old states: An extension of the competition model." *Social Problems* 30: 127–143.

Nayar, Baldev Raj 1966 *Politics in the Punjab*. New Haven: Yale University Press.

Olzak, Susan 1989 "Labor unrest, immigration, and ethnic conflict in urban America, 1880–1914." *American Journal of Sociology*, 94:1303–1333.

—— 1992 *The Dynamics of Ethnic Competition and Conflict*. Stanford: Stanford University Press.

Padilla, Felix 1985 *Latino Ethnic Consciousness: The Case of Mexican Americans and Puerto Ricans in Chicago*. Notre Dame: University of Notre Dame Press.

—— 1986 "Latino ethnicity in the city of Chicago." In *Competitive Ethnic Relations*, eds. S. Olzak and J. Nagel, 153–171. New York: Academic Press.

Pedraza, Silvia 1992 "Ethnic identity: Developing a Hispanic-American identity." Paper presented at the 5th Congreso Internacional sobre las Culturas Hispanas de los Estados Unidos, Madrid. Spain.

Pedraza-Bailey, Silvia 1985 *Political and Economic Migration in America: Cubans and Mexicans*. Austin: University of Texas Press.

Petonito, Gina 1991a "Constructing 'Americans:' 'Becoming American,' 'loyalty' and Japanese internment during World War II." In *Perspectives on Social Problems*, eds. G. Miller and J. Holstein. Greenwich, Conn.: JAI Press.

—— 1991b "Racial discourse, claims making and Japanese internment during World War II." Paper presented at the annual meeting of the American Sociological Association. Cincinnati.

Plascov, Avi 1981 *The Palestinian Refugees in Jordon, 1948–1957*. London: Frank Cass.

Portes, Alejandro, and Reuben Rumbaut 1990 *Immigrant America: A Portrait*. Berkeley: University of California Press.

Prebble, John 1963 *The Highland Clearances*. London: Secker and Warburg.
Prucha, Francis P. 1984 *The Great Father. The United States Government and the American Indians*. Lincoln: University of Nebraska Press.
Quinn, William W., Jr. 1990 "The southeast syndrome: Notes on Indian descendant recruitment organizations and their perceptions of Native American culture." *American Indian Quarterly* 14:147–154.
Rhoodie, Eschel 1983 *Discrimination in the Constitutions of the World*. Atlanta: Orbis.
Roediger, David R. 1991 *The Wages of Whiteness: Race and the Making of the American Working Class*. London: Verso.
Roosens, Eugeen E. 1989 *Creating Ethnicity: The Process of Ethnogenesis*. Newbury Park: Sage Publications.
Rubin, Lillian B. 1972 *Busing and Backlash: White Against White in a California School District*. Berkeley: University of California Press.
Rudolph, Lloyd, and Susanne Rudolph 1967 *The Modernity of Tradition: Political Development in India*. Chicago: University of Chicago Press.
Salamone, Frank A., ed. 1985 *Missionaries and Anthropologists, Part II*. Athens, Ga.: University of Georgia, Department of Anthropology.
Sanneh, Lamin 1989 *Translating the Message: The Missionary Impact on Culture*. New York: Orbis Books.
Sassen, Saskia 1988 *The Mobility of Labor and Capital*. New York: Cambridge University Press.
——1991 *The Global City*. NJ: Princeton University Press.
Schermerhorn, R.A. 1978 *Ethnic Plurality in India*. Tucson: University of Arizona Press.
Scott, James C. 1990 *Domination and the Arts of Resistance: Hidden Transcripts*. New Haven: Yale University Press.
Simmons, Ron 1982 *Affirmative Action: Conflict and Change in Higher Education After Bakke*. Cambridge, Mass.: Schenkman.
Smith, Anthony D. 1986 *The Ethnic Origins of Nations*. New York: B. Blackwell.
——1992 *Ethnicity and Nationalism*. Leiden: E.J. Brill.
Smith, Tom W. 1992 "Changing racial labels: From colored to Negro to black to African American." Chicago: University of Chicago, General Social Survey Topical Report No. 22.
Snipp, C. Matthew 1993 "Some observations about racial boundaries and the experiences of American Indians." Paper presented at the University of Washington, Seattle, April.
Snow, D.A., E.B. Rochford, Jr., S.K. Worden, and R.D. Benford 1986 "Frame alignment processes, micromobilization, and movement participation." *American Sociological Review* 51:464–481.
Snow, D.A. and Robert D. Benford 1988 "Ideology, frame resonance, and participant mobilization." In *International Social Movements Research*, eds. B. Klandermans, B. Kriesi, and S. Tarrów, 197–217. Greenwich, Conn.: JAI Press.
——1992. "Master frames and cycles of protest." In *Frontiers in Social Movement Theory*, eds. A.D. Morris and C.M. Mueller, 133–155. New Haven: Yale University Press.

Spector, Malcolm, and John I. Kitsuse 1977 *Constructing Social Problems.* New York: Aldine.
Steele, C. Hoy 1975 "Urban Indian identity in Kansas: Some implications for research." In *The New Ethnicity: Perspectives from Ethnology,* ed. J.W. Bennett, 167–178. St. Paul: West Publishing Company.
Stein, Judith 1989 "Defining the race, 1890–1930." In *The Invention of Ethnicity,* ed. W. Sollors, 77–104. New York: Oxford University Press.
Sullivan, John 1988 *ETA and Basque Nationalism: The Fight for Euskadi, 1890–1986.* New York: Routledge.
Swidler, Ann 1986 "Culture as action: Symbols and strategies." *American Sociological Review* 51:273–286.
Taber, Charles R. 1991 *The World is Too Much with Us: "Culture" in Modern Protestant Missions.* Macon, Ca.: Mercer University Press.
Tilly, Charles 1986 *The Contentious French.* Cambridge: Harvard University Press.
Tonkin, Elizabeth, Maryon McDonald, and Malcolm Chapman, eds. 1989 *History and Ethnicity.* New York: Routledge.
Trevor-Roper, Hugh 1983 "The invention of tradition: The highland tradition of Scotland." In *The Invention of Tradition,* eds. E. Hobsbawm and T. Ranger, 15–42. Cambridge: Cambridge University Press.
U.S. Bureau of the Census 1980 U.S. Census of Population and Housing Public Use Microdata Sample (PUMS) file (1% sample).
—— 1989 Census of Population, Subject Reports, Characteristics of American Indians by Tribes and Selected Areas, 1980, Vol 2, Sections 1 and 2. Washington, D.C.: Government Printing Office.
—— 1990 1990 March Current Population Survey (CPS) file.
—— 1991 "Census Bureau completes distribution of 1990 redistricting tabulations to states." Census Bureau Press Release CB91-100, Monday, March 11.
United States Congress 1990 United States Statutes at Large, 101st Congress, 2nd Session. Volume 104, Part 6:4662–4665. Washington, D.C.: U.S. Government Printing Office.
Wagner, Roy 1975 *The Invention of Culture.* Chicago: University of Chicago Press.
Wallerstein, Immanuel 1960 "Ethnicity and national integration." *Cahiers d'Etudes Africaines* 3:129–138.
Waters, Mary 1990 *Ethnic Options: Choosing Identities in America.* Berkeley: University of California Press.
—— 1991 "The intersection of race and ethnicity: Generational changes among Caribbean immigrants to the United States." Paper presented at the annual meeting of the American Sociological Association, Cincinnati.
Welbel-Oriando, Joan 1991 *Indian Country, L.A.* Champaign: University of Illinois Press.
Whitaker, Mark 1993 "White and black lies." *Newsweek* (November 15): 52–63.
Whitehorse, David 1988 *Pow-wow: The Contemporary Pan-Indian Celebration.* San Diego: San Diego State University, Publications in American Indian Studies, No. 5.

Whiteman, Darrell L, ed. 1985 *Missionaries and Anthropologists, Part L.* Athens, Ga.: University of Georgia, Department of Anthropology.

Whorton, Brad 1994 "The transformation of American refugee policy in the 1970s and 1960s." Paper presented at the annual meeting of the Midwest Sociological Society, St. Louis.

Willhelm, Sidney 1970 *Who Needs the Negro?* Cambridge, Mass.: Schenkman.

Wilson, William J. 1987 *The Truly Disadvantaged: The Inner City, the Underclass, and Public Policy.* Chicago: University of Chicago Press.

Wright, Carole 1977 "What people have formed backlash groups?" *Yakima Nation Review*, July 18:10.

Yancey, William L., Eugene P. Ericksen, and R. Juliani 1976 "Emergent ethnicity: A review and reformulation." *American Sociological Review* 41:391–402.

Yetman, Norman R. 1983 "The 'new immigrant wave': Migration pressures and the American presence." Paper presented at the annual meeting of the American Studies Association, Philadelphia.

—— 1991 "Race and ethnicity in 1980s America." In *Majority and Minority: The Dynamics of Race and Ethnicity in American Life.*, ed. N. Yetman, 379–401. Boston: Allyn and Bacon.

Young, Crawford 1976 *The Politics of Cultural Pluralism.* Madison: University of Wisconsin Press.

Zulaika, Joseba 1988 *Basque Violence: Metaphor and Sacrament.* Reno: University of Nevada Press.

11 The Costs of a Costless Community

Mary C. Waters

What does claiming an ethnic label mean for a white middle-class American? Census data and my interviews suggest that ethnicity is increasingly a personal choice of whether to be ethnic at all, and, for an increasing majority of people, of which ethnicity to be. An ethnic identity is something that does not affect much in everyday life. It does not, for the most part, limit choice of marriage partner (except in almost all cases to exclude non-whites). It does not determine where you will live, who your friends will be, what job you will have, or whether you will be subject to discrimination. It matters only in voluntary ways – in celebrating holidays with a special twist, cooking a special ethnic meal (or at least calling a meal by a special ethnic name), remembering a special phrase or two in a foreign language. However, in spite of all the ways in which it does not matter, people cling tenaciously to their ethnic identities: they value having an ethnicity and make sure their children know "where they come from."

I suggest two reasons for the curious paradox posed by symbolic ethnicity. First, I believe it stems from two contradictory desires in the American character: a quest for community on the one hand and a desire for individuality on the other. Second, symbolic ethnicity persists because of its ideological "fit" with racist beliefs.

AMERICAN VALUES AND SYMBOLIC ETHNICITY

Analysts of American culture have long noticed the fundamental tension between the high values Americans place on both individuality and conformity. Writing over a hundred years ago on the American psyche and character, Alexis de Tocqueville developed a theme that has been a recurrent observation of all students of the nature of American character – the tension between the conflicting values of individualism and conformity, or between self-reliance and cooperation. In fact, Tocqueville coined the term *individualism* to describe the

273

particular way in which people in America "turned in on themselves" all of their feelings and beliefs:

> Individualism is a calm and considered feeling which disposes each citizen to isolate himself from the mass of his fellows and withdraw into the circle of family and friends; with this little society formed to his task, he gladly leaves the greater society to look after itself.
>   (Tocqueville [1835–39] 1969, 506)

Tocqueville noticed that while individualism led people to find their own beliefs within themselves, this isolation was at the same time compatible with conformity, because people are constantly looking for affirmation of those beliefs in the people around them. Contrasting democratic societies with aristocratic ones, Tocqueville argues that while "knowing your place" in an aristocratic society binds individuals to their ancestors and descendants, the peculiar effect of democracy is to isolate individuals from one another and from the generations that precede and follow them:

> As social equality spreads there are more and more people who, though neither rich or powerful enough to have much hold over others, have gained or kept enough wealth and enough understanding to look after their own needs. Such folk owe no man anything and hardly expect anything from anybody. They form the habit of thinking of themselves in isolation and imagine that their whole destiny is in their own hands.
>
> Thus not only does democracy make men forget their ancestors, but also clouds their view of their descendants and isolates them from their contemporaries. Each man is forever thrown back on himself alone, and there is danger that he may be shut up in the solitude of his own heart.   (Tocqueville [1835–39] 1969, 508)

Tocqueville saw the uniquely American proclivity for joining voluntary groups – associations of all different kinds – as a necessary moderating influence on this individualism. By participation in these small groups – local government and communities – Americans would find the sense of connection to others that would inoculate them from the dangers of despotism. Without these communities, the danger of a mass society of isolated individuals is that they are easy prey to despots taking advantage of a democratic system.

Since Tocqueville first noticed this tension between individualism and conformity, it has been a central theme in discussions of the nature of American culture and character. Rupert Wilkinson, in

The Pursuit of American Character (1988), a review of writing on American character between 1940 and 1980, argues that the dual attraction of Americans to individualism and community is the overriding theme of all accounts of American character in this period. He argues that the course from the 1940s to the 1980s was full circle, starting with a renewed interest in Tocqueville's concern with individualism, proceeding through a period of concern with social pressure and conformity in books like David Riesman's *The Lonely Crowd* and William H. Whyte's *The Organization Man*, and then returning to a concern with unstable, isolating egoism in Christopher Lasch's *The Culture of Narcissism* and Robert Bellah et al.'s *Habits of the Heart*. Describing the situation in the 1980s and the most recent books examining the elusive "American character," Wilkinson focuses on the concern of these authors with the conflict "between modern American culture and deep yearnings for community," and a renewed stress on the problems caused for people by social atomism, rather than conformity.[1]

Wilkinson asks the interesting question of whether this shift reflects merely a change in writers' sensibilities or an actual change in American behavior and values. He suggests that the massive suburbanization that has occurred since the 1940s may have led to this move on the part of most Americans away from extensive involvement in community:

> Suburbia itself may have become less communal...[one] sees a mass of over-equipped houses and yards which have become small, private islands. Front porch society, where everyone met everyone, has been closed down by domestic technology: the automobile, electronic entertainment, and air conditioning. Families either vanish indoors (or into their backyards) or whisk themselves away on wheels. (Wilkinson 1988, 43)

The people I have studied are the families that live in these suburbs and live these lives, and it is possible that the isolation described here is in part responsible for the expressed wishes of some of my respondents for more "community." Symbolic ethnicity fulfills this particularly American need to be "from somewhere." Having an ethnic identity is something that makes you both special and simultaneously part of a community. It is something that comes to you involuntarily through heredity, and at the same time it is a personal choice. And it allows you to express your individuality in a way that does not make you stand out as in any way different from all kinds of other people. In short, symbolic ethnic identity is the answer to a dilemma that has deep roots in American culture.

THE ELEMENT OF CHOICE

Symbolic ethnicity was appealing to my respondents for another reason as well – the element of choice involved. In a contemporary study of the strategies of successful advertising campaigns devised by Madison Avenue firms, William O. Beeman describes how clever advertisers devise ad campaigns that appeal simultaneously to the opposite values of individuality and conformity. He adds another important theme, freedom of choice. Freedom of choice, writes Beeman, quoting the advertisers, "comes close to being sacred for Americans." People must be persuaded that they are meeting contradictory goals in selecting the advertiser's product: making a choice that shows their individuality while at the same time giving them membership in a group – the group of people who have made the same choice. He writes:

> In the United States, through exercise of individual choice, people not only demonstrate their uniqueness, they also recognize and actualize their integration with others. They do this by making, acknowledging, and perpetuating social ties based solely on the affinity that arises through making the same choices.
>
> (Beeman 1986, 59)

Of course, it is the job of the advertiser to convince people that purchasing a product makes them part of a group. The group of people one feels a part of may not exist in any real sense as a group, existing only within the framework of the advertisement itself: "By buying a Pepsi you take place in an exchange, not only of money, but of yourself as a Pepsi person. You have become special, yet one of a clan: however, you do not meet those others, except *in* the advertisement" (Williamson 1978, 53).

Beeman claims that advertisers who create successful campaigns based on combining these American values have a very persuasive and attractive package prepared for the target audience. In fact, he describes it as a surefire recipe for success:

> These double messages are remarkable in that they tell consumers they can achieve contradictory but laudable goals merely by

exercising choice on a microcosmic level. Every time we choose one brand of liquid detergent or motor oil over another, we are subtly being told both: "you are unique and special" and "you are in the company of the millions of others who choose this." This is the opposite of a no-win situation. It is an always-win situation in cognitive terms, and it is as powerful as it is subtle.

(Beeman 1986, 64)

Symbolic ethnicity embodies a great deal of choice. Even among those who have a homogeneous background and do not need to choose an ancestry to identify with, it is clear that people do choose to keep an ethnic identity. And until recently many social scientists who have attempted to understand this persistence of ethnic identity have looked at the nature of the particular ethnic groups – extolling the virtue of particular strands of the ethnic culture worth preserving. Yet if one looks at ethnicity almost as though it were a product one would purchase in the marketplace – Stein and Hill's "dime store" ethnics – one can see that symbolic ethnic identity is an attractive product.

The choice to have a symbolic ethnicity . . . is an attractive and widespread one despite its lack of demonstrable content, because having a symbolic ethnicity combines individuality with feelings both of community and of conformity through an exercise of personal choice. These themes recur throughout my interviews.

Part of the reason that ethnicity is so appealing to people is evident in the reasons people give to the question of *why* they "like being ethnic." Being ethnic makes them feel unique and special and not just "vanilla," as one respondent put it. They are not like everyone else. At the same time, being ethnic gives them a sense of belonging to a collectivity. It is the best of all worlds: they can claim to be unique and special while simultaneously finding the community and conformity with others that they also crave. But that "community" is of a type that will not interfere with a person's individuality. The closest this type of ethnic identity brings a person to "group activity" is something like a Saint Patrick's Day parade. It is not as if these people belong to ethnic voluntary organizations or gather as a group in churches or neighborhood or union halls. They work and reside within the mainstream of American middle-class life, yet they retain the interesting benefits – the "specialness" of ethnic allegiance.

An exaggerated way of examining the reasons behind these choices is through a question I asked that freed respondents from any constraint based on the belief that ethnicity is inherited. I asked people,

"If you could be a member of any ethnic group you wanted, which one would you choose?" It is clear from the answers that having an ethnic identity gives people a feeling of "specialness" and fulfills a longing for community. Liz Field articulates this "hunger for ethnicity":

> I would like to be a member of a group that is living a culture, like on an American Indian reservation, or a gypsy encampment... or an Italian neighborhood. Where there is some meat to the culture. Mine was very wishy-washy. There was not much to make it strong and appealing. It was just supposed to be this thin little rod in the back of my spine. Scotch Irish. It was thin. It was diluted. I would like to be in a rich cultural society. I don't know which one it would be. Whichever one is the richest... Where they have a tight familial structure of aunts and uncles and cousins. And they all know their second cousins intimately and they are all involved in each other's lives. Which didn't happen to me. Although cousins lived nearby, we weren't tight. We didn't know if they were in town. We were just not as aware of them as I think other ethnic groups are, the ones that are rich and the ones that are tight. It could be Alaskan Eskimo. I mean, I am on my own here. I don't have that many friends. I do my work. I play my instrument. I travel a lot. But I don't have a big cultural... People who have stayed where they grew up have a larger cultural... Well, I don't even have it at home, where my mother lives. It has just not been there for me, ever. The kind of thing where you know everybody and you know all the back roads. There is a richness there. Maybe that is what draws me to some rich, thick, culture. [Laughs.] But flexible too, open to new ideas.   [Laughs again.]

What Liz Field ironically adds at the end of her description of the "thick culture" she craves shows that even those who hunger for a romanticized version of an all-encompassing ethnic community realize that they only want the positive aspects of that community. Liz wants the warmth of a close community without the restrictions that she admits usually accompany such a community. But while Liz fantasizes that the warmth and familial ties missing from her own life would be present if she were American Indian or a gypsy, in fact, the situation she describes is precisely what a symbolic ethnic identity gives to middle-class Americans – a sense of rich culture through a community with no cost to the other contradictory values we also crave: individuality, flexibility, and openness to new ideas.

In fact the very idea that Americans have of "community" is very much tied up in their minds with ethnicity. Ethnicity is sometimes defined as family writ large. The image that people conjure up of "community" is in part one based on common origins and interests. The concrete nature of those images in America is likely to be something like a small town or an ethnic ghetto, while in many other parts of the world this sense of peoplehood or community might be realized through nationalist feelings. The idea of being "American" does not give people a sense of one large family, the way that being French does for people in France. In America, rather than conjuring up an image of nationhood to meet this desire, ethnic images are called forth.

The immensely popular book *Habits of the Heart* exemplifies the invocation of ethnicity as an example of community. The authors diagnose the problems with Americans as stemming from a lack of community – a community that people really want, but lack even a language to talk about, because it challenges the independence they have traditionally valued. Bellah et al. mourn the passing of the strong ethnic ties that vanish as Americans move into the middle class. They cite in contrast "ethnic and racial communities, each with its own story and its own heroes and heroines" as examples of "genuine communities" of memory (p. 153). The optimal solution for Bellah et al. would be if people belonged to a community of memory – a community people do not "choose," but are born into, where people inherit a commitment to traditional ties.[2]

The "thick culture" and tradition that Liz Field described is in Americans' minds associated with strong ethnic groups. But Liz has recognized the crucial point that precisely what we crave about community and tradition is also tied to things we don't crave – conformity, lack of change, and rigidity. The maintenance of boundaries around a community involves costs to the individuals inside as well as providing the benefits of nurturance and security. Community seen one way is warm and nurturing; seen another, it is stifling and constricting.

This is the essential contradiction in American culture between individuality and community. Thus Liz Field's ironic comment that she wanted a thick culture that was also flexible and open to new ideas indicates the fact that she is very American. She wants both. And I think this is the best way to understand the symbolic ethnicity I have described – it gives middle-class Americans at least the appearance of both: conformity with individuality; community with social change.

And as an added bonus – which almost ensures its appeal to Americans – the element of choice is also there. Ethnicity has a built-in sense of appeal for Americans that should make Coke and Pepsi envious. Madison Avenue could not have conspired to make a better and more appealing product. This partly explains the patterns in the choices people make about their ethnic identities. When given a choice, whites will choose the most "ethnic" of the ancestries in their backgrounds.

Over and over again people told me that they liked keeping an ethnic identity because it gave them a sense of who they were, where they had come from, and, as one respondent said, made them "more interesting." And the more unusual your ancestry sounds, the more "interesting" you are. Cindy Betz:

> I work in an office and a lot of people in there always talk about their background. It's weird because it is a big office and people are of all different backgrounds. People are this or that. It is interesting I think to find out. Especially when it is something that you don't hear a lot about. Something that is not common like Lithuania or something. That's the good part about being Czech. People think it is something different.

Joe Bajko felt that being Lithuanian made him feel special:

> It's nice to feel that you are one of a thousand. You are not exactly in a big crowd. In fact, rarely do you find any Lithuanians around. It's nice to feel that you are in an elite group. Like in grade school, when everyone would brag, like saying, "I'm Italian," I would say, "I'm Lithuanian."

Those who don't have a strong ethnic identity or who don't have an ancestry in their past that makes them feel special or interesting feel as though they should at least hold on to what they do have. Ted Jackson:

> It gives you something to identify with. Lets you know where you are coming from. Something to hold on to. It is something that no one can take away from you. Something that is all yours ... When everyone else has something. And if you are not Italian, or whatever, and you don't have these strong ethnic identities or just things that come with it – all these celebrations and activities and all that ... if you don't have that and everyone else is going here and going there ... it makes you feel kind of left out. Yeah, I really do think you have to have something.

Again and again the same message comes through. You have to have something you can identify with. If it is a "special" ethnicity, you can be interesting or elite, but nevertheless you must have something. And if, like Ted Jackson, the identity you have to hold on to is being part Irish, French, Scottish, German, and English, you celebrate and hold on to that identity. In Ted's case he says he feels closest to the French part, but it is the maintenance of an identity, any identity, that people strive for. Again Liz Field describes why her ethnicity, even though it is not of a rich culture, is so important to her:

> While I don't feel that my ethnic heritage needs to be dominant in my awareness, I do have an awareness of it and I am encouraged to learn a bit more about the type of people I may have come from. The type of traditions that I might have way back there somehow gotten exposed to. By knowing OK, I am X and X, or XY and Z. Then I don't have to pay any more attention to it. If you know what I mean. It's like OK, there, that is solved now. And you move on. It's important to be something. I need an awful lot of help in defining myself and that is a tool. A piece of information that puts a boundary on things.

Symbolic ethnicity is thus not something that will easily or quickly disappear, while at the same time it does not need very much to sustain it. The choice itself – a community without cost and a specialness that comes to you just by virtue of being born – is a potent combination.

SYMBOLIC ETHNICITY AND RACE

But what of the consequences of this symbolic ethnicity? Is it a harmless way for Saturday suburban ethnics to feel connected and special? Is it a useful way to unite Americans by reminding us that we are all descended from immigrants who had a hard time and sacrificed a bit? Is it a lovely way to show that all cultures can coexist and that the pluralist values of diversity and tolerance are alive and well in the United States?

The answer is yes and maybe no. Because aside from all of the positive, amusing, and creative aspects to this celebration of roots and ethnicity, there is a subtle way in which this ethnicity has consequences for American race relations. After all, in much of this discussion the implicit and sometimes explicit comparison for this symbolic ethnicity has been the social reality of racial and ethnic identities of America's minority groups. For the ways in which ethnicity is flexible and symbolic and voluntary for white middle-class Americans are the very ways in which it is not so for non-white and Hispanic Americans.

Thus the discussions of the influence of looks and surname on ethnic choice would look very different if one were describing a person who was one-quarter Italian and three-quarters African-American or a woman whose married name changed from O'Connell to Martinez. The social and political consequences of being Asian or Hispanic or black are not symbolic for the most part, or voluntary. They are real and often hurtful.

So for all of the ways in which I have shown that ethnicity does not matter for white Americans, I could show how it does still matter very much for non-whites. Who your ancestors are does affect your choice of spouse, where you live, what job you have, who your friends are, and what your chances are for success in American society, if those ancestors happen not to have been from Europe. Whether this is a temporary situation, and the experience of non-whites in America will follow the same progression as the experience of these white ethnic groups, has been one of the central questions in American social science writing on this subject. The question, then, of whether ethnic groups such as Italians and Poles are in some way the same as minority groups such as Chicanos and blacks is a complicated one – both analytically and politically. Analytically, social scientists have tried to assess the assimilation process of white ethnics and non-white groups to ascertain whether the American opportunity structure will open up for non-whites. Politically, this issue is also an important one – especially with the development of affirmative action legislation and the Voting Rights Act, which moved to provide legal protection and special attention to what were defined as "minority groups" subject to discrimination, as opposed to ethnic groups who were not. Stephen Steinberg (1981) and others writing on the ethnic revival of the 1970s argue quite strongly that the self-conscious organization of white ethnics on the basis of their ethnicity was a racist response to the civil rights movement of the 1960s and 1970s and to celebrations of racial and ethnic identities by non-white groups.

Michael Novak, author of *The Rise of the Unmeltable Ethnics*, was the conservative leader of the white ethnic movement of the 1970s. He tries to answer the criticism that white ethnics are anti-black and "going back to their ethnicity" in order to oppose the black power movement. He writes: "The new ethnicity is the nation's best hope for confronting racial hatred. A Pole who knows he is a Pole, who is proud to be a Pole, who knows the social costs and possibilities of being a Polish worker in America, who knows where he stands in power, status and integrity – such a Pole can face a black militant eye to eye" (Novak 1973, 294). Novak really could not have been more wrong here, but not only for the most obvious reason. In the context of the content of the rest of his book and the debates of the early 1970s, Novak was wrong because the "new white ethnics" *were* in opposition to the black power movement, and various other developments that came out of the civil rights movement. And Novak's own work was read then and can be read now as fanning the flames of racial division at the time.

But the other sense in which Novak is wrong in this passage is in part a result of some of the developments of the new ethnicity movement of the 1970s. A Polish-American who "knows he is a Pole, who is proud to be a Pole, who knows the social costs and possibilities of being a Polish worker" is less able to understand the experience of being black in America precisely because of being "in touch with his own ethnicity." That is because the nature of being a Pole in America is lacking in social costs, providing enjoyment, and chosen voluntarily.

A major point is the disparity between the idea and the reality of ethnicity for white ethnics. The reality is that white ethnics have a lot more choice and room for maneuver than they themselves think they do. The situation is very different for members of racial minorities, whose lives are strongly influenced by their race or national origin regardless of how much they may choose not to identify themselves in ethnic or racial terms. Yet my respondents did not make a distinction between their own experience of ethnicity as a personal choice and the experience of being a member of a racial minority.

People who assert a symbolic ethnicity do not give much attention to the ease with which they are able to slip in and out of their ethnic roles. It is quite natural to them that in the greater part of their lives, their ethnicity does not matter. They also take for granted that when it does matter, it is largely a matter of personal choice and a source of pleasure.

The fact that ethnicity is something that is enjoyed and will not cause problems for the individual is something people just accept. This also leads to the belief that all ancestries are equal, more or less interchangeable, but that you should be proud of and enjoy the one you have. Louise Taylor articulated this attitude:

You have to be something. I am sure I would be happy with whatever I was. It is like matter, mass, you have to come from somewhere. I could not imagine myself being unhappy with anything...I am sure if I was Swedish and Japanese combination...the feelings of happiness and self-esteem would be the same.

The sentiment among my respondents was that people should be proud of their heritage, whatever it is. And because they happened to be Irish or Polish or Italian, they were proud to be Irish or Italian or Polish. But they could just as easily have been something different. Ellen Albert:

Q: Would you say that being Irish is important to you now?
A: Well, I don't know. I have fun being it. I would not know what to say. I have never been anything else. I am proud of it, but I am not really 100 percent anyway. And my husband, he doesn't have a drop in him and you should see him on Saint Patrick's Day.

This approach to their own ethnicity leads to a situation where whites with a symbolic ethnicity are unable to understand the everyday influence and importance of skin color and racial minority status for members of minority groups in the United States. This lack of understanding of the difference between the experience of ethnicity for white Americans and the implications of ethnicity for members of racial minorities was made quite clear in an interchange in the "Dear Abby" newspaper column. The following debate is between two Irish-Americans and two Asian-Americans on the issue of whether or not it is polite to inquire about an individual's ethnic background. The Irish-Americans cannot understand why the Asian-Americans are offended:

Dear Abby,
    Regarding "100 Percent American," the American of Oriental descent who complained that within five minutes of being introduced to a Caucasian, he was asked, "What are you?": You replied that it was rude to ask personal questions at any time, but because the average Caucasian doesn't know a Chinese from a Japanese, Cambodian, Vietnamese, Korean or a Thai, the question seemed reasonable – but it was still rude.
    Rude? I disagree. Inquiries about a person's roots are not necessarily rude. It shows a sincere interest in their heritage.
    The Orient is a rich and diverse geography. The face of an Oriental reveals his heritage. His looks tell of a passage through

villages, cultures and languages – but which ones? His story is probably quite fascinating. I don't think it is rude to observe that such a face has a rich ancestry. I think it is a positive component of international understanding.

AN AMERICAN NAMED FINN

Abby replied:

My mail was heavy on this one. Without exception, all writers of Oriental descent resented being asked, "What are you?" shortly after being introduced. A typical letter:

Dear Abby,

I, too, am 100 percent American and because I am of Asian ancestry, I am often asked, "What are you?" It's not the personal nature of this question that bothers me, it's the question itself. This query seems to question my very humanity. "What am I?" Why I am a person like everyone else!

Another question I am frequently asked is, "Where did you come from?" This would be an innocent question, when one Caucasian asks it of another, but when it is asked of an Asian, it takes on a different tone...

A REAL AMERICAN

Dear Abby,

Why do people resent being asked what they are? The Irish are so proud of being Irish, they tell you before you even ask. Tip O'Neill has never tried to hide his Irish ancestry.

JIMMY

(*San Francisco Chronicle*, February 28, 1986)

I was struck when I read this by how well it summarized the ways in which I found that the symbolic ethnicity of my respondents related to their ideas about racial minorities in our society. "An American Named Finn" cannot understand why Asians are not as happy to be asked about their ancestry as he is because he understands his ethnicity and theirs to be separate but equal. Everyone has to come from somewhere – his family from Ireland, another's family from Asia – each has a history and each should be proud of it. But the reason he cannot understand the perspective of the Asian-American is that all ethnicities are not equal, all are not symbolic, costless, and voluntary. And that is where the subtle effect of symbolic ethnicity on American race relations develops.

The people I interviewed were not involved in ethnic organizations and were not self-consciously organized on the basis of their ethnicity. However, I do think that the way they experience their ethnicity creates a climate leading to a lack of understanding of the ethnic or racial experience of others. People equated their European ancestral background with the backgrounds of people from minority groups and saw them as interchangeable.

Thus respondents told me they just did not see why blacks and Mexican-Americans were always blaming things on their race or their ethnicity. For instance, Bill McGowan:

A lot of people have problems that they bring on themselves. I don't care what religion or what nationality they are. The Mexicans, a lot of times they will say, "Well, it is because I am Mexican that it is much harder." But if they were Irish they might have the same problems. People are people.

Barbara Richter:

I think black people still do face discrimination to a point. But when other people come to this country with half a brain in their head and some industrious energy and they make it on their own after a while, I just think the opportunities are there for everyone.

Sean O'Brien:

I think everybody has the same opportunity. It doesn't matter what their background is. The education is there and if they have the gumption to go after it, they can do anything they damn well please. It doesn't make any difference if they are Irish, German, Jewish, Italian, or black. There are all different groups who are multi-millionaries. They have the same opportunities. I think a black kid has the same opportunity as one of my own.

Tim McDaniel:

I think black people and Hispanic people face discrimination. Definitely. I think a lot of it they bring on themselves. They talk too much about it. If they would let it go it would be better.

Others denied, especially, that blacks were experiencing discrimination, citing examples of when affirmative action policies had hurt them or their families as "reverse discrimination." Megan O'Keefe:

I never saw blacks being discriminated against at all. Now whether they are or not, maybe it is true. But I have seen a lot of the reverse. I have seen a lot of reverse discrimination.

Part of the tradition handed down as part of an ethnic ancestry are the family stories about ancestors having faced discrimination in the past. In fact, a large part of what people want to pass on to their children is the history of discrimination and struggle that ancestors faced when first arriving in the United States. All of my respondents were sure that their ancestors had faced discrimination when they first came to the United States. Many had heard stories about it within their families, some had read about it in history books, but all were sure it had happened. It was also one of the most important things mentioned to me by parents when they talked about what they wanted their children to know about their ethnic ancestry. For instance, Elaine Williams wanted her children to know about the hardships associated with their Italian ancestry:

I just want them to know who they are and appreciate where they came from. I like them to talk to my older aunts. Sometimes they will tell them stories about when they were in Italy. Things like that. Because I don't think my kids know any hardship. Not that I know a lot, but I think it is nice to know the things people went through to put you where you are.

This is interesting, because Elaine herself did not think that her family had experienced much hardship until her father told her some stories one day at dinner:

About four or five months ago we had a discussion at dinner about this. I had said that I never thought I had been prejudiced against because I was Italian. My dad went into a tirade about how back then it was much more common. He told us about different things that happened to him and just the general attitude toward Italians. It kind of stunned me because I had never experienced that. But my dad says that just because I didn't live through it, I should know that there was more anti-Italian feelings back when he was younger.

Most people had heard stories about how their ancestors had faced discrimination in the past. Rich Cahill, a 29-year-old policeman, described what he had heard in his family: "I know my grandmother used to tell me that there used to be signs in different places saying 'Irish need not apply.' In Philadelphia and down at the shore."

Judy Gilligan spoke of the problem faced by her Serbian ancestors: "They talked about fights they had with other kids on the street, and being called guinea, honky. Those kinds of names. My grandparents told me the stories about how during the depression their milk box would be raided. People would come steal their milk."

People were all aware of the fact that their ancestors had come here as immigrants to make a better life and that they had faced adversity to do it – and they often pointed to the similarities between the experience of their ancestors and the discrimination experienced by non-whites now. Carol Davis's image of what it used to be like for the Irish is perhaps the most affected by being seen through the prism of the civil rights movement:

Q: Did your ancestors face discrimination when they first came here?
A: Yes, from what I was told they were. I know that Irish people were treated almost like blacks for a while. They weren't allowed in certain buildings. They were discriminated against. From what my mother says there were even signs in Philadelphia for Irish people not to come into the restaurants. I think they were even forced to ride in the back of the bus for a while there.

This type of interpretation of history contributes to the problems middle-class Americans of European origin have in understanding the experiences of their contemporary non-white fellow citizens.[3] The idea that the Irish were forced to sit at the back of a bus (when, in 1840?) in a sense could be seen to bring people together. The message of such a belief is that all ethnicities are similar and all will eventually end up successful. If the Irish had to sit at the back of the bus sometime in the past, and now being Irish just means having fun at funerals, then there is hope for all groups facing discrimination now. But, of course, if the Irish did not need legislation to allow them into the front of the bus, then why do blacks? If the Irish could triumph over hardships and discrimination through individual initiative and hard work, then why the need for affirmative action and civil rights legislation?

It is clear that people have a sense that being an immigrant was hard, that society did not accept their groups, and that now discrimination and prejudice is much less than it was before. People also believe that blacks, Hispanics, and Asians are still in a somewhat earlier stage. But, on the other hand, beliefs that the discrimination faced by Irish, Italians, and Serbs was the same both in degree and in kind as that faced by non-whites sets the stage for resentment of any policies that single out racial minorities.

The way in which they think about their own ethnicity – the voluntary, enjoyable aspects of it – makes it difficult to understand the contemporary position of non-whites. Thus some people made it a point to assert their ethnic identity on forms or in situations where forms or institutions were trying to determine minority status. For instance, Patrick O'Connor answered that he would put "Irish" as his answer to the ancestry question on the census form. But then he volunteered that that is not the only place he puts "Irish": "In fact, I put 'Irish' on all sorts of forms when they ask for racial identity. They want black or white, I always put 'Irish.' Let them figure out what it means." Lisa Paulo also gives her ethnicity on forms she knows are not specifically asking for it:

> On those forms it usually is, "Oh, you are Portuguese," therefore you have to be white Caucasian and so it usually gets pushed aside. And I usually feel more upset that it gets pushed aside than anything else. If you have a special category for Afro-American and for Filipino-American why can't you have one for Portuguese? I will mark "Other" and then just write in "Portuguese," because I get tired of being white Caucasian.

But most respondents no longer saw their ethnicity as having that much influence on their lives anymore. For most people I spoke with, ethnicity is something everyone has to have, but why would people be particularly proud of their ethnic ancestry or ashamed of it? It is just something you have, not something that really influences your life. Most respondents would admit that there was something different about blacks, Hispanics, and Asians, that they had faced some societal discrimination, especially in the past, but in another sense the individualistic approach to ethnicity was a much stronger influence. Some people stressed that they thought all societal discrimination against blacks and Hispanics had lessened to the point where they should just start forgetting about it and act as individuals, not as groups. In short, if your own ethnicity is a voluntaristic personal matter, it is sometimes difficult to understand that race or ethnicity for others is influenced by societal and political components.

In this sense the process and content of symbolic ethnicity tend to reinforce one another. If invoking an ethnic background is increasingly a voluntary, individual decision, and if it is understood that invoking that background is done for the enjoyment of the personality traits or rituals that one associates with one's ethnicity, then ethnicity itself takes on certain individual and positive connotations. The process and content of a symbolic ethnicity then make it increasingly difficult for white ethnics to sympathize with or understand the experience of a non-symbolic ethnicity – the experience of racial minorities in the United States.

THE FUTURE OF SYMBOLIC ETHNICITY

This analysis suggests both that symbolic ethnicity persists because it meets a need Americans have for community without individual cost and that a potential societal cost of this symbolic ethnicity is in its subtle reinforcement of racism. Perhaps this is an inherent danger in any pluralist society. The celebration of the fact that we all have heritages implies an equality among those heritages. This would obscure the fact that the experiences of non-whites have been qualitatively and quantitatively different from those of whites.

It is true that at the turn of the century Italians were considered by some to be non-whites. It is also true that there were signs in many East Coast cities prohibiting the Irish from applying for jobs or entering establishments. The discrimination faced by Jews was even greater. They were excluded from certain neighborhoods, organizations, and occupations. Yet the degree of discrimination against white European immigrants and their children never matched the systematic, legal and official discrimination and violence experienced by blacks, Hispanics, and Asians in America. The fact that whites of European ancestry today can enjoy an ethnicity that gives them options and brings them enjoyment with little or no social cost is no small accomplishment. But does it mean that in time we shall have a pluralist society with symbolic ethnicity for all Americans?

The respondents described in this study are socially mobile, middle-class whites, and their type of ethnic identity is specific to their social situation. As the description of the experiences of southern and eastern European immigrants at the beginning of the book suggests, the experience of ethnicity would have been very different at the turn of the century. This is a crucial aspect of ethnicity that is important to remember – ethnicity is historically variable. In the past it had social costs associated with it for these white groups. It has few, if any, now.

However, this symbolic ethnicity is not just something associated with generational movement. It is also very much dependent on social mobility. As long as racial or ethnic identity is associated with class stratification, or as long as ascriptive characteristics are used to assign reward in society, ethnic identity will be much more complex than individual choice and selective personal and familial enjoyment of tradition.

The effects of changes in American immigration law make it difficult at times to distinguish developments owing to generational mobility from those owing to social and economic mobility. This is because the social and economic mobility of white ethnics in the twentieth century coincided with the drastic reduction in immigration from European sources – which means that the cohorts of Poles and Italians advancing socially and generationally have not been followed by large numbers of fresh immigrants who take over unskilled jobs and populate ethnic ghettos. Thus when the socially mobile children and grandchildren of the original immigrants left the urban ghettos and unskilled jobs for college and the suburbs in the 1950s and 1960s, blacks, Hispanics, and Asians took their places. The social mobility that makes a symbolic ethnicity possible for these whites might have looked very different if the supply of new immigrants from Europe had not been drastically curtailed.

This also makes it difficult to generalize from the experience of these white ethnic groups to the experiences of the largely non-European immigrants arriving since the 1965 immigration law. There is definitely evidence of social mobility and increasing intermarriage among the second- and among the small number of third-generation Asian-Americans. There is also evidence of social mobility and intermarriage among Hispanics. However, both of these groups are different from groups of European origin in that there is a continuing supply of new immigrants who take the place of the older generations in the ethnic neighborhoods and occupations. Middle-class third-generation Mexican-Americans may enjoy some of the same intermittent and voluntary aspects of ethnic identity as Italian-Americans, but the existence of a strong first-generation ethnic community, as well as of continued discrimination in housing and employment against Hispanics, would probably impose constraints on such upwardly mobile third-generation Mexican-Americans that it would not on Italian-Americans.

Aside from the very crucial issue of eradicating racial discrimination – which is still an inescapable fact of life for those of non-European descent in the United States – the question of the development of this type of symbolic ethnicity among these new immigrant groups is open because of the fact that they are at the forefront of a still-active immigrant stream. As these new groups – such as Chinese, Koreans, Jamaicans, and Filipinos – move into the third generation and into middle-class suburbs, more studies such as this one should be done on the later-generation form of ethnicity.

Given the fact that the structural conditions and trends that give rise to symbolic ethnicity are continuing, I would expect that symbolic ethnicity will continue to characterize the ethnicity of later-generation whites. The individual and familial construction of the substance of that ethnicity, along with increasing intermarriage, means that the shared content of any one ethnicity will become even more diluted. Consequently there will be increased dependence on the mass media, ethnic stereotypes, and popular culture to tell people how to be Irish or Italian or Polish.

But that dilution of the content of ethnicity does not necessarily mean that there will be a decline in the personal satisfaction associated with having a symbolic ethnicity. Partly this is because the contentless nature of this ethnicity enables it to provide the feeling of community with no cost to the individuality we Americans value so highly. But it is also because this ethnicity is associated by people with close and intimate ties in their nuclear families, in fragments of their extended families, and with close friends and neighbors. The Saint Patrick's Day parties I attended with my respondents may not have had too much to do with being Irish, and the people giving them may have had very little Irish in their complicated family trees, but the parties were warm and rich celebrations, which embody traditions for the people who gather each year. The "community" that gathers for these celebrations is not necessarily illusory, but it is a voluntary, personally constructed, American creation.

The paradox of symbolic ethnicity is that it depends upon the ultimate goal of a pluralist society and at the same time makes it more difficult to achieve that ultimate goal. It is dependent upon the concept that all ethnicities mean the same thing – that enjoying the traditions of one's heritage is an option available to a group or individual – but that such a heritage should not have any social costs associated with it. The options of symbolic ethnicity involve choosing among elements in one's ancestry and choosing when and if voluntarily to enjoy the traditions of that ancestry. However, the interviews presented here show that the individuals who enjoy a symbolic ethnicity for themselves do not always recognize the options they enjoy or the ways in which their own concepts of ethnicity and uses of those concepts constrain and deny choice to others.

Americans who have a symbolic ethnicity continue to think of ethnicity, as well as race, as being biologically rooted. They enjoy many choices themselves, but they continue to ascribe identities to others, especially those they can identify by skin color. Thus a person with a black skin who had some Irish ancestry would have to work very hard to decide to present him or herself as Irish – and in many important ways he/she would be denied that option. The discussion of racial intermarriage makes this point clearly – racial identity is understood by these respondents as an inherited physical aspect of an individual, not as a social construct. Thus respondents exhibit contradictory ideas about minorities in American society – they are clear that there is a fundamental difference between a white ethnic and a black person when the issue is intermarriage in their own families. On the other hand, they do not understand why blacks seem to make such a big deal about their ethnicity. They see an equivalence between the African-American and, say, Polish-American heritages.

So symbolic ethnicity only works for some ancestries – the pluralist ideal of an equality of heritages is far from a reality in American life. But at the same time, as I have argued, the legacy of symbolic ethincity is to imply that this equality exists. The political result of that ideological legacy is a backlash against affirmative action programs that recognize and try to redress the inequalities in our society.

The ultimate goal of a pluralist society should be a situation of symbolic ethnicity for all Americans. If all Americans were free to exercise their "ethnic option" with the certainty that there would be no costs associated with it, we could all enjoy the voluntary, pleasurable aspects of ethnic traditions in the way my respondents describe their own enjoyments. It is important not to romanticize the traditional white ethnic group. In addition to its positive aspects, it was experienced as extremely constricting and narrow by many people. There are parts of these past ethnic traditions that are sexist, racist, clannish, and narrow-minded. With a symbolic ethnic identity an individual can choose to celebrate an ethnic holiday and refuse to perpetuate a sexist tradition that values boys over girls or that channels girls into domestic roles without their consent. The selective aspects of a symbolic ethnicity are in part what make it so enjoyable to so many individuals.

Currently, however, we are far removed from a position where this freedom is available for all. As the Asian-Americans who wrote to

Dear Abby make clear, there are many societal issues and involuntary ascriptions associated with non-white identities. The developments necessary for this to change are not individual but societal in nature. Social mobility and declining racial and ethnic sensitivity are closely associated. The legacy and the present reality of discrimination on the basis of race or ethnicity must be overcome before the ideal of a pluralist society where all heritages are treated equally and are equally available for individuals to choose or discard at will is realized. It is a sad irony that the enjoyment and individual character of their own ethnicity contributes to the thinking that makes these middle-class whites oppose the very programs designed to achieve that reality.

NOTES

1. Wilkinson cites recent works such as Bellah et al.'s *Habits of the Heart*, Yankelovich's *New Rules: Searching for Self-Fulfillment in a World Turned Upside Down*, and Slater's *The Pursuit of Loneliness: American Culture at the Breaking Point*.

2. If Americans cannot have that type of community, the authors of *Habits of the Heart* suggest, the next best thing for people to do is to go back to church. Wilkinson notes that Bellah et al. do not tell their readers that "such communities can be oppressive, snoopy, and stultifying. Conversely, they underestimate the satisfactions of being able to create and select one's social networks, and the sheer vitality of association that comes from working at it out of a fear of being isolated" (Wilkinson 1988, 44). Wilkinson's direct answer to such solutions is, I think, absolutely correct and is also echoed in the remarks just quoted from Liz Field.

3. I do not want to minimize the Irish experience of discrimination and hostility in America in the mid-to-late nineteenth century. There was a great deal of anti-Irish feeling and discrimination, especially in Boston, New York, and other East Coast cities. However, the negative experiences of the Irish were never as extreme or as long lived as the discrimination and violence experienced by blacks and American Indians. (For detailed discussions of the different experiences of America's white and non-white groups see Lieberson 1980 and Blauner 1972.) In the case of Carol Davis's understanding of this situation, it is clear that she is interpreting her knowledge of the experiences of discrimination of the American Irish through her experience of the civil rights movement of American blacks.

REFERENCES

Beeman, William O. 1986. "Freedom to Choose: Symbols and Values in American Advertising." In *Symbolizing America*, ed. Herve Varenne, 52–65. Lincoln: University of Nebraska Press.

Bellah, Robert, Richard Madsen, William M. Sullivan, Ann Swidler, and Steven M. Tipton. 1985. *Habits of the Heart: Individualism and Commitment in American Life*. Berkeley: University of California Press.

Blauner, Robert. 1972. *Racial Oppression in America*. New York: Harper & Row.

Lieberson, Stanley. 1980. *A Piece of the Pie: Blacks and White Immigrants Since 1880*. Berkeley: University of California Press.

Novak, Michael. 1973. *The Rise of the Unmeltable Ethnics: Politics and Culture in the Seventies*. New York: Macmillan Co.

Steinberg, Stephen. 1981. *The Ethnic Myth: Race, Ethnicity and Class in America*. Boston: Beacon Press.

Tocqueville, Alexis de. 1835–39. *Democracy in America*. Translated by George Lawrence. Garden City, NY: Doubleday, 1969.

Wilkinson, Rupert. 1988. *The Pursuit of American Character*. New York: Harper & Row.

Williamson, Judith. 1978. *Decoding Advertisements: Ideology and Meaning in Advertising*. London: Marian Boyais.

Part III
A New World Disorder: International Dilemmas of Racial and Ethnic Pluralism

12 Multicultural Foreign Policy
Yossi Shain

A decade has passed since *Foreign Policy* published three essays that introduced its readers to the international agenda of America's "new ethnic voices" and their influence on US foreign affairs. The essays included an analysis of "Black American Demands" and an explication by two Arab American officials of "Arab American Grievances."[1] In light of the dramatic transformations world politics has undergone over the past ten years, it is time to re-evaluate the international and domestic effects of ethnicity in American foreign policy. Such an examination is particularly important today when the United States is searching for a new sense of purpose in its foreign relations, and multiculturalism has heightened concerns over the nature of the American identity.

Scholars, journalists, and political practitioners increasingly recognize the ability of American ethnic groups to influence US foreign policy. Yet very little has been said about how such influence bears on America's national interest abroad, on ethnic relations inside the United States, and on American civic culture in general. Do ethnic voices threaten to Balkanize US foreign policy, or are they constructive? What is the relationship between an ethnic group gaining an effective voice in US foreign policy and its adoption of American political ideals? What function do ethnic lobbies serve in America's global role as the champion of democratic ideals? And does ethnic commitment to ancestral countries impede US domestic cohesion and encourage subnational loyalties?

Undoubtedly, many ethnic groups have undergone a major transformation, changing from outsiders who struggle to penetrate the US foreign policy system to insiders who act in its service as exporters of American ideals. In fact, as the United States continues to concede a role to its ethnic groups in the formulation of foreign policy, it may recast them not only as marketers of the American creed abroad but also as America's own moral compass. Ethnic influences may thus help to keep US foreign policy true to Wilsonianism at a time when neo-isolationism is on the rise. The role of ethnicity in foreign affairs

299

has already begun to show its effect on ethnic relations inside America, with some surprising results that should lessen fears about multiculturalism.

This argument is underscored by tracing the evolution of the African and Arab American diasporas in the last decade. The term *diaspora*, as opposed to ethnicity, accentuates the bond between Americans and their countries of origin. US diasporas are Americans who maintain some affinity – be it cultural, religious, racial, or national – with their ancestral lands or their dispersed kinfolk elsewhere. The homeland may be a person's actual native country, or it may be a place that serves as a symbolic home, as Africa and the Caribbean are for many blacks in America and as Israel is for American Jews.

Diasporas in the United States have long been dedicated to political causes in their homeland. Some diasporas have been involved in the struggle for the political independence of their stateless nations. Others have taken an active role in securing the well-being of their independent home countries.

US diasporas have also devoted their efforts to the well-being of members of their dispersed kinfolk in other countries. Jewish Americans have been the driving force behind the transnational effort to liberate Jews in Syria, Ethiopia, and the former Soviet Union. The US Armenian community has provided critical support to Armenians struggling for independence in Nagorno-Karabakh. Other mobilized diasporas such as Cubans, Filipinos, Haitians, Koreans, and East Europeans, have contributed to the weakening of dictatorial rule and the advent of democracy in their ancestral countries or symbolic homelands. The efforts of many Cuban Americans to unseat Fidel Castro have generally concurred with US objectives. As a result, the Cuban American lobby has usually been well received in Washington, and its influence has grown. Other diasporic campaigns against authoritarian or communist home-governments that did not coincide with the US Cold War design were ignored or even obstructed by the US government, such as the Filipino American opposition to Ferdinand Marcos.

The American melting-pot concept, which stresses assimilation into a Protestant Anglo-Saxon culture, has given way to a pluralist creed that recognizes ethnicity as integral to American life. Thus, immigrants are no longer required to give up their ethnic identity, language, or attachment to country of origin to become Americans. Hyphenation is well respected. Since they are less and less subjected to charges of disloyalty, ethnic officials and their constituencies are more inclined to reconstitute and strengthen their ties with their ancestral countries. In fact, many ethnic elites have discovered that by focusing on political causes in their homelands they are better positioned to mobilize their communities for domestic empowerment in America. Moreover, efforts on behalf of ancestral countries are widely recognized as legitimate political practices, licensed and encouraged by the nature of the American party system and the power of each congressional representative.

By influencing state and local governments, diasporas may also have an impact on foreign policy. This was best demonstrated during the campaign by African Americans for comprehensive sanctions against South Africa. The federal government opposed trade sanctions against South Africa for many years, so activists persuaded institutions at the local level to divest. With ties to home countries reinforced by modern modes of transportation and communication, many home-governments (or their opposition) now make direct patriotic appeals to their diasporas, courting them to influence US policy. For example, the Mexican government urged Mexican Americans to lobby Congress for passage of the North American Free Trade Agreement.

DIASPORA POLITICS

Diaspora politics has been bolstered by the collapse of the Soviet Union, which resulted in a decline in the influence of traditional political elites, who dominated US foreign affairs throughout the Cold War. In fact, the growing influence of diaspora politics on foreign policy has led many to question whether America's national interest is undermined by such partisan forces and whether the commitment of ethnic Americans to their ancestral countries impedes US domestic cohesion by encouraging subnational loyalties. Some have wondered how far American leaders are willing to go in order to earn the support of the newly organized ethnic elements of the American electorate. Such concerns are compounded by the uncertainty regarding America's future international role. As US strategic interests become less clear than they once were, and as US decision makers appear unable to articulate or execute a coherent global strategy, foreign policy becomes more susceptible to pressures by diasporic lobbies.

Khachig Tölölyan, editor of the journal *Diaspora*, recently dismissed the possibility that an ethnic group might become the decisive force in prompting American military intervention in its ancestral country:

> Whether the issue is borders or regimes, the US is likely to commit troops only when the foreign policy elites in government, business, the armed forces, the media and the academy are convinced that American national interests overlap or coincide with those of a specific ethnic group whose support for such a commitment would then be welcomed.

Yet the political dynamic leading to US intervention in Haiti in September 1994 demonstrated that such a broad consensus was not in place before (or after) President Bill Clinton committed American troops to reinstate Haiti's president-in-exile, Jean-Bertrand Aristide. In fact, US intervention in Haiti is probably the most dramatic demonstration of the power of newly mobilized diasporas: Many observers assert that Clinton acted more in response to the organized elements of the African American electorate, primarily the Congressional Black Caucus and the African American international lobby TransAfrica, than to a broader national consensus. The episode that apparently tilted the balance toward an invasion was the hunger strike of TransAfrica's executive director, Randall Robinson.

The potency of ethnicity and race in American society has alarmed many observers who caution against the tendency toward Balkanization. Critics of the growing "cult of ethnicity" in American education and civic culture are also rearticulating an old American anxiety that the devotion to ancestral homelands undermines national cohesiveness by exacerbating ethnic strains. They point to many instances of ethnic rivalries inside the United States that are prompted or fueled by diaspora relations with ancestral lands, such as the feuds between American Turks and Greeks, between blacks and Jews over such issues as Israel's relations with South Africa during apartheid and black support for the Palestinians, and between American Serbs and Croats. Another example is the tension between Cuban and African Americans in Miami, which grew primarily out of local struggles over economics and political power and was heightened in 1990, when Cubans in Miami snubbed visiting South African leader Nelson Mandela over his embrace of Castro. In retaliation, black leaders declared a tourism boycott that cost Miami's economy about $50 million.

According to Harvard professor Samuel Huntington, demographic trends indicate that ethnic conflicts in the United States will grow more common since "kin-country" loyalties run much deeper than liberal assimilationists are willing to admit. By 2050, whites are expected to lose their majority status in America, and as other groups grow in number so will both their cultural and political clout and, consequently, the likelihood of clashes among them. As a growing number of scholars and political observers point out, internal divisions also confuse US external interests. Indeed, if America is becoming a multicultural society with powerful ethnic influences, one should expect to see strong ramifications in US foreign affairs, including a redefinition of US national interests.

Some political observers, such as Michael Clough, a senior fellow at the Council on Foreign Relations, have concluded that the reality of the growing number of ethnic groups creating their own foreign policy is at the core of Washington's failure to articulate a more coherent national interest. Others, however, reverse the causal order and argue that the exacerbation of US domestic divisions is rooted in America's new international posture. Accordingly, America's loss of its Cold War enemies has undermined political leaders' ability to rally the nation around a unifying cause. In the absence of well-defined foreign policy challenges, Americans are turning inward to debate domestic problems. It is a process that encourages the flare-up of dormant culture wars and the renouncement of a common national identity. Many, therefore, worry that the fragmentation witnessed abroad is also affecting the United States.[2]

As a re-examination of the foreign policy roles of African and Arab Americans indicates, however, these fears are at least partially unfounded. African Americans, who since the mid-1980s have emerged as one of the strongest voices on US policy toward Africa and the Caribbean, have been converted from outsiders trying to penetrate the system into mainstream foreign policy players. This metamorphosis, with all its advantages, has also brought new responsibilities and has already yielded dramatic changes in terms of African American international orientations. Whereas in his 1985 *Foreign Policy* article, Kenneth Longmyer described the attitude of blacks toward US foreign policy as essentially "non-interventionist," today the African American lobby's is one of the leading forces behind US interventionism. The lobby's new status also affects domestic alignments. It has strengthened the bond between mainstream blacks and whites while fracturing relations between black integrationists and black separatists. It has also eased tensions between blacks and Haitian immigrants as African American leaders have championed a return to democracy in Haiti.

Arab Americans have also recently gained a more respected voice in US foreign policy. For decades the Arab American agenda was consumed by the Palestinian cause. Arab American organizations' support of Palestinian independence and of the Palestine Liberation Organization (PLO) helped them build a domestic constituency. At the same time, however, it hindered their lobbying effectiveness because of the PLO's low standing in Washington. Yet, in the aftermath of the PLO-Israeli accords, mainstream Arab American organizations have been transformed from stigmatized "anti-Israel" ethnic lobbies into recognized promoters of peace. This new role has provided their officials with greater opportunities for domestic empowerment and with a voice in US foreign affairs. The Middle East peace process has improved Arab Americans' relations with American Jews. This new posture, however, has produced a crisis of identity and purpose. Mainstream activists have felt pressured to assume a greater role in democratizing autocratic Arab regimes and have been forced to contend with the rise of Islamism among their diaspora kinfolk. Indeed, just as it seemed to reach its apex, the Arab American lobby finds itself in a deep crisis.

INTEGRATIONISTS VERSUS ISOLATIONISTS

Both African and Arab Americans have long been excluded from central roles in American politics and society. In order to confront their marginalization, members of the two communities face a choice between two strategies: isolationism or integrationism. Isolationists consider their culture, religion, or tradition as alien – and often superior – to American culture. They deliberately avoid acculturation, reject assimilation, and at times promote a cultural war against the dominance of European heritage in the United States. Some even promote irredentism. In many respects, isolationists are the silent allies of Anglo-Saxon nativists, as they confirm the nativist position that membership in American society should be limited to those who are part of a particular Anglo-Saxon culture.

Black Power separatists of the late 1960s advocated national liberation and rejected the civil rights movement's vision of a color blind, integrated America. Their crusade was bolstered by the successful struggle for independence of African states and by the rise of Third World ideology. Conversion to Islam was a reaction to the perception of Christianity as "a slave religion." Yet by the early 1970s, black separatism was already waning, as more and more black leaders, including Martin Luther King, Jr., and Roy Wilkins, the former executive director of the National Association for the Advancement of Colored People, preached the gospel of power-sharing and pluralism and denounced Black Power as reverse racism. Moderate black leaders realized that only by playing an insiders' game and embracing the American electoral system and its democratic values could they hope to become equal participants in American society.

Isolationism was also a strong force in the Arab American community in the late 1960s. The ethnic identity of US Arabs was mostly dormant until the 1967 Six-Day War. With no ideological core, political organization, or funding, Arab Americans – chiefly second-and third-generation Christians of Lebanese origin – retained little homeland affinity and remained politically inactive. The traumatic defeat of the Arabs in 1967, Israel's occupation of the West Bank and Gaza, and the spread of anti-Arab sentiment in the United States, roused the Arab American community. As the Middle East conflict intensified and the US – Israeli alliance grew stronger, Arab Americans began to organize. The first diaspora organizers were mostly Palestinian American students and professors, who in 1967 established the Association of Arab American University Graduates (AAUG). The group preached against assimilation and soon discovered sympathizers in the Black Power movement. The black nationalists who dominated black political dialogue in the late 1960s characterized Israel as an extension of American imperialism and racism and condemned black leaders who supported the Zionist state as collaborators in the oppression of "our Palestinian brothers and sisters." The Black Panther Party, the Student Nonviolent Coordinating Committee, and the Nation of Islam (Black Muslims) all drew a parallel between Israeli treatment of Palestinians and South Africa's apartheid policy. They also denounced Zionism as racism and equated the exploitation of blacks in America with the mistreatment of Arabs by Israel. It was in this context that the civil rights alliance between blacks and Jews began to disintegrate.

Arab American isolationists, like many black radicals, regarded the United States as an imperialist and racist country seeking to dominate the Arab world. Christians and Muslims alike immersed themselves in pan-Arab and Third World ideologies that came to denote the struggle of the Palestinians. Palestinian American scholar and PLO activist

Edward Said provided the intellectual leadership when he explicated the notion of "orientalism." Said charged the West with an "unbending desire to discredit and thus debunk the Arabs as a people and as a society." Isolationists repudiated the United States in a manner that combined attacks on America's imperialist policies and its anti-Islamic bigotry. By the early 1990s, however, the old Arab American Left had lost its allure. While some of its followers have remained hostile to the idea of becoming Americans and are irritated by the actions of Arab American integrationists, they are increasingly outnumbered by the moderate voices. Left-leaning isolationists are also outnumbered by the wave of Islamic revivalism. Even the AAUG has moved closer to the center: It has given greater attention to the issue of Arab dictatorial regimes and has denounced the mistreatment of women throughout the Arab world. In his 1994 address to the AAUG's annual convention, AAUG president Ziad Asali called upon his colleagues to re-examine their old convictions:

> It will not do to lay the blame solely on imperialism and Zionism to explain away the current state of disarray and degradation across the Arab world. It will not do to formulate slogans and generalizations as a substitute for realistic strategies and thought out tactics.... The suppression of free expression across the Arab world adds an extra measure of responsibility on the shoulders of the Arab intellectuals in the West who are not encumbered by government or violent censorship.

Today, the isolationists among Arab Americans are mainly orthodox Muslims who reject, in principle, the idea of Muslims building a minority life in a non-Islamic country. While some of them may advocate the transformation of American society by attracting Americans to Islam through religious outreach (*Da'awa*), the militants consider the United States to be Islam's greatest enemy. Often led by exiled Muslim preachers (*imams*), Islamists tend to adopt a theology that construes their life in the United States as a transitional phase, a modern form of *Hijra* similar to the Prophet Muhammad's retreat to Medina, which marked the beginning of a Muslim community (*umma*), superseding a world of tribal kinship. Accordingly, the United States provides these exiles a temporary haven from which they can launch their campaign to return to a land conquered by so-called infidels. In recent years, there have been many reports about the growing number of militant Islamic groups that have established bases among Arab Americans.

In contrast to their isolationist kinfolk, the majority of African and Arab Americans seek integration. Although they may protest their exclusion, they still identify themselves as Americans. Even so, their political and intellectual elites encourage them to cling to ancestral identities. Yet, while they may resist assimilation into a dominant Anglo-Saxon culture, integrationists still endorse the vision of a pluralist democracy. They believe that American culture is dynamic, that it does not have a European essence, and that it may be utilized to address their own cultural affinities. In other words, while they reject the notion that every community in the United States has already achieved a cultural identity sufficient to enable it to blend into a multicultural society, integrationists still seek to achieve such an accommodation. Accordingly, they demand cultural and political recognition from mainstream US institutions.

When it comes to foreign affairs, diaspora integrationists present their case in terms of "America's best national interest" and establish political lobbies to compete for their own interpretation of that interest. In the African American community, the integrationists' mode in foreign affairs is best represented by TransAfrica. From its inception, TransAfrica considered African American involvement in African and Caribbean affairs to be an additional mechanism for domestic empowerment. In the crusade to reverse America's posture toward South Africa, TransAfrica endeavored to apply Martin Luther King's domestic strategy of challenging Americans to live up to their democratic creed. When TransAfrica opened its foreign policy institute in Washington, DC, in June 1993, Randall Robinson said: "This town produces policy as a result of a competition of policy ideas.... We have never competed evenly institutionally in the area of foreign affairs. That's why we wanted a fully fleshed out think tank to grind out the analysis that represents the interests of our community."

In the Arab American community, the integrationist organizations that focus on foreign affairs, and primarily on the Palestinian cause, have been the National Association of Arab Americans (NAAA), which endeavored to counter the impact of the American Israel Public Affairs Committee, the pro-Israel lobby; the Arab American Institute (AAI), which officially concentrates on empowering Arab Americans in the electoral system; and the American-Arab Anti-Discrimination Committee (ADC), the initial goal of which has been to combat "anti-Arab racism." In their 1985 *Foreign Policy* article, David Sadd and Neal Lendenmann of the NAAA described their organization's goals in this way:

Arab Americans are deeply proud of their culture and heritage. They seek to promote the closest possible relations between the United States and the Arab world.... They are Americans first, last, and always. Their approach to lobbying, therefore, is to identify America's national interests in the Middle East and to promote those interests through advocacy and education.

Interestingly, all of the above groups, each of which has often expressed its resentment of Jewish American lobbying power, deliberately established themselves in the image of parallel Jewish groups. Yet while American Jewish organizations have been thriving by drawing on the energies and resources of their constituency, Arab American groups – which claim to speak on behalf of between 2 and 3 million Americans of Arab descent – have failed at grassroots mobilization. In 1995, the NAAA's staff was cut dramatically to three because its Arab benefactors slashed its funding. Khalil Jahshan, NAAA's executive director, expressed agony, saying that "Arab-American organizations lack the cementing factors." Jahshan acknowledges that Arab American organizations failed to connect with their own constituency, and he concedes that the NAAA's role in foreign affairs has ended: "When [Israeli prime minister Yitzhak] Rabin lobbies Washington for money for the PLO and when Arab governments ignore our existence, we must turn our energies [from foreign affairs] to the community."

For years, African and Arab Americans attributed their failure to affect US external affairs to Jewish American hegemony over the public and institutional discourse in this field. The 1979 Andrew Young affair was a turning point in blacks' struggle to gain influence over US foreign policy. Young, then the most influential African American in President Jimmy Carter's administration, was forced out of his post as ambassador to the United Nations after it was revealed that he negotiated with the PLO observer at the UN despite official US policy barring such dialogue. The incident embellished the mythology of secret Jewish power and of black powerlessness. Young's removal was stamped as a form of Jewish racism that suggested that blacks were unqualified to participate in the realm of international diplomacy.

In a similar manner, Arab American activists have long argued that their exclusion radiates primarily from the Arab-Israeli conflict. It is a result, they claim, of associating them with Americans' twisted images of their Arab and Palestinian compatriots in the Middle East.

These activists also held the pro-Israeli lobby responsible for the lack of access to the American political system. Thus, Arab American integrationists have drawn a direct link between their domestic empowerment and the ebbing of the Middle East conflict.

NO TO APARTHEID, YES TO PALESTINIAN RIGHTS

In the Summer 1974 issue of *Foreign Policy*, Martin Weil wrote an article titled, "Can The Blacks Do For Africa What The Jews Did For Israel?" He predicted that sooner or later the United States would face a powerful black lobby that would challenge American policy in Africa. He further argued that

> to be successful, a black movement for reform of American policy toward Africa must be perceived as a vehicle for exporting *American* ideals. It must be an affirmation of black faith in the United States and a demonstration of black ability to manipulate the fine structure of American politics with the astuteness and finesse of previous practitioners. Blacks as blacks may identify with Africa, but it is only as Americans that they can change United States policy in Africa. If Afro-Americans ever gain leverage in foreign policy, it will be those black politicians who are most successful *within* the system who will do so – those who can command the respect of their black constituents and reassure white America at the same time.

Weil's projection began to come true in the mid-1970s with the sharp decline in black extremism. During the 1976 presidential campaign, blacks first made their mark on the Democratic party's platform by pushing the issue of independence for the white minority-ruled states of southern Africa. The establishment of TransAfrica in 1977 furthered the institutionalization of black political power in the US foreign policy arena. The link between the black domestic agenda and the anti-apartheid struggle was reinforced during the Reagan administration, with many African American leaders believing that President Ronald Reagan was insensitive to civil rights issues in general and uncaring on apartheid in particular. Apartheid became a rallying cry for the rejuvenation of the political activism of the 1960s, as black Americans organized as insiders to set the American conscience back on track. As much as Reagan wanted to argue that support for the African National Congress fortified communism, his

administration's rhetoric rang hollow in the face of such clear violations of American ideals. The wave of protests, sit-ins, and voluntary
arrests orchestrated by TransAfrica spread across the nation, helping
to make apartheid a principal political concern for local governments,
towns, media, and universities. The political momentum paved the
way for an unprecedented coalition in the House and Senate, which
approved sanctions against South Africa over Reagan's veto. The
"domestication" of apartheid was complete; then Senate majority
leader Bob Dole even acknowledged that the issue of sanctions had
"now become a domestic civil rights issue."

The mobilization of the black community against apartheid coincided with a renewed search for black identity in the United States,
which eventually manifested itself in the campaign to change the
group appellation from "black" to "African American." The campaign for "African American" at that juncture represented a strong
perception that integration and political power in the United States
have much to do with an affiliation with a country and culture
abroad. In late 1988, the Reverend Jesse Jackson declared: "Every
ethnic group in this country has a reference to some land base, some
historical, cultural base. African-Americans have hit that level of
cultural maturity." Ultimately, the identification with black South
Africa emerged as one of the critical factors by which politicians'
allegiance to domestic black causes was measured.

By 1990, Arab American integrationists had already established
high visibility in US politics and media. They did so primarily by
drawing upon Palestinian suffering during the *intifada*, and by rebuk-
ing the pro-Israeli lobby for what it called an abusive use of money to
pressure Congress. Arab Americans made the Palestinian issue their
ideological core, a cause portrayed as an extension of "America's
most cherished ideals – Wilsonian self-determination, human rights,
[and] freedom," as Gregory Orfalea, an Arab American activist and
writer, said. The AAI, for example, considered its most meaningful
political accomplishment up to that point the breaking open of the
debate on Palestinian rights and the Middle East peace process on the
floor of the 1988 Democratic National Convention in Atlanta. In this
debate, AAI president James Zogby announced: "Today we respond
to the Palestinian people. We address ... the violation of their basic
human rights, the killings and the beatings, and agonizing expulsions,
the daily humiliations of being a people without a state." The event
was recognized by some Jewish American officials as "the Arab
American *intifada*."

Regardless of their accomplishments, however, Arab Americans' entry into the American political arena remained circumscribed by events in the Middle East and by the negative publicity garnered by extreme elements in the diaspora. During the Persian Gulf war, Arab Americans were torn between their desire to express their American loyalty and their concern for Arabs abroad. The NAAA and the AAJ moved uneasily between supporting US intervention to restore Kuwait and requiring American "consistency" when it comes to Israel and the Palestinians. Too often, as was evident in the immediate aftermath of the April 1995 bombing in Oklahoma City and in the wake of the February 1993 bombing of New York's World Trade Center by a small group of Islamists residing in the United States, the diaspora has been collectively held accountable for the repudiation of America in Arab and Muslim countries and for the terrorist activities of Islamists in the United States. This collective stain has frustrated the foreign policy efforts of Arab Americans even when their cause was consistent with American values; the United States's failure to respond to the brutal assault on Bosnian Muslims demonstrates the inability of Arabs and Muslims in America to promote such a cause through the mechanisms of US foreign policy.

Following the Gulf war, Arab American integrationists concluded that their domestic political empowerment could no longer remain in the sole service of Palestinian interests: They could not settle for a showdown with American Jews. In reality, some forms of Arab and Jewish American cooperation had already appeared in the 1980s, as more and more Israelis and American Jews called for a "two-state solution" to the Israeli Palestinian conflict. Adopting the American jargon of opportunity and fair play, Zogby, a Lebanese Christian born in the United States, called in 1988 for reconciliation and cooperation with American Jews. "We do understand Jewish fears and the need for security felt so deeply by Israelis. Now I urge you to understand realities like Palestinian nationalism and the emergence of an Arab American political constituency." By 1991, Jewish Americans' habit of providing uncritical support for Israeli policies had begun to fade. The repercussions of the new geopolitical posture on US-Israeli relations became apparent when President George Bush linked financial assistance to Israel with the halting of settlement practices in the West Bank and Gaza. Caught between the Israeli government's expectation that it would use all its political influence in Congress to reverse the president's decision and the administration's position that such a showdown was equivalent to an act of disloyalty, the pro-Israeli lobby retreated. Indeed, in the 1992 election, Bush was supported by many Arab Americans who rewarded him despite their opposition to his policies in the Gulf.

After the signing of the Israeli-PLO accords on the White House lawn on September 13, 1993, Arab American integrationists expressed a huge sigh of relief. The AAI declared that the accords provide an opportunity for Arab Americans "to achieve full empowerment and assimilation into the mainstream of American culture and life." The ADC, which failed to endorse the accords, was soon marginalized. Ray Hanania, a leading ADC activist, recently wrote that the organization "was governed by a board consisting of old-fashioned thinking Arabs who had yet to understand what being an American is all about." Zogby's partnership with Jewish American leaders in the White House's "Builders for Peace" initiative – a joint venture aimed at developing the private sector economy in the West Bank and Gaza – is something of an American story of overcoming mistrust between two ethnic communities.

MARKETING THE AMERICAN CREED ABROAD

The African American anti-apartheid campaign largely parallels the Arab American crusade for Palestinian statehood. Both diasporas have built their foreign policy agendas around American ideals of democracy, pluralism, self-determination, and human rights. Yet in order to sustain their "democratic" reputation, they must now continually demonstrate their hostility to non-democratic practices in their native countries or symbolic homelands. They must also be ready to challenge unequivocally their radical kinfolk inside the United States. Their responsibility to become "marketers" of the American creed abroad has been reinforced since the end of the Cold War by the greater emphasis on America's mission of spreading democracy and human rights abroad. This new posture marks a change from previous US approval of "authoritarian" dictatorships friendly to the United States and opposed to communism.

Thus, in recent years, one can observe symbiotic relationships between the makers of US foreign policy and the roles assumed by US diasporas. The more the diasporas are harnessed by the American government to promote democracy abroad, the more likely they are to improve their influence on US foreign policy. In fact, since American policymakers may still try to retreat from their neo-Wilsonian pledge to traditional realism, as demonstrated by Clinton's friendly overtures toward China and his lengthy indecisiveness on Bosnia, diasporas may assume the role of a moral compass in US foreign policy. Their pressure on policymakers to follow through on their commitment to promote democracy and human rights, even when such policies seem to hinder *ad hoc* strategic interests, are bound to create strains on US relations with repressive regimes and to help ensure that oppressed groups cannot be ignored by US policymakers.

During the Cold War, mainstream African Americans could vindicate their support of non-democratic African governments as a way of countering US "imperialist intervention" via authoritarian proxies. Arab American organizations could similarly overlook the autocratic quality of Arab regimes by focusing on Israeli violations of Palestinian national rights, a unifying cause that also bridged religious and national divisions within the diverse Arab American community. However, with the collapse of communism, and with improving prospects for Palestinian statehood, the pretense and motivation for siding with or acquiescing to black or Arab transgressions disappeared. As a result, African American leaders have moved steadily to redefine their pro-Africa crusade along the democratic theme of urging the US government to get serious about promoting democracy and human rights in Africa. In his testimony before the Senate Foreign Relations Committee in May 1991, TransAfrica's Robinson called for a new US foreign policy in Africa "contingent on respect for human rights and progress toward political and economic reform." Bolstered by its striking success in influencing American policy on Haiti, TransAfrica recently launched a national campaign to restore democracy in Nigeria, urging the White House to take a more confrontational posture toward the military junta by refusing to buy Nigerian oil. This latest campaign is the first display of a strong African American protest against the abuses of a black African regime. The campaign has been applauded by some Nigerian opposition leaders, such as former foreign minister Bolaji Akinyemi. The Nigerian government and some Nigerian interest groups in the United States, however, charged Robinson with exploiting the Nigerian political tragedy to promote TransAfrica's fundraising and warned that Robinson's crusade "will ultimately batter our national pride, and cause harm to the image of the black man," as one such group stated.

Similarly, with the unfolding of the peace process in the Middle East, Arab Americans began to speak about the need for democratic reforms in the Arab world. NAAA executive director Jahshan has written that "Palestinian chaotic democracy or 'the democracy of the guns'... must be transformed into genuine democracy, in which basic and universal civil, human and political rights are respected and protected." In January 1994, the AAI held a conference titled "Challenge '94: Making Democracy Work at Home and Abroad." Zogby warned that if the diaspora remains mute on the issue of spreading democracy into the Middle East, then it will compromise its political credibility:

> I feel deeply that this period requires a new way of thinking – a new paradigm. If the peace accords are to bear fruit then we must make every effort to begin to develop new priorities.... [While] we are committed to Palestinian statehood... [and] are opposed to Israeli occupation of any Arab land... we [also] want to see human rights and democracy in the Arab world.

More recently, Zogby has restrained his pro-democracy oratory. He is now calling for an Arab American alliance with pro-American Arab regimes, regardless of their internal practices. This position may still fall within the Clinton administration's foreign policy formula of "pragmatic Wilsonianism," to use Harvard professor Stanley Hoffmann's phrase, but it is unlikely to impress the many in the Arab American community who have heard allegations that the AAI has become dependent on Saudi money.

The transformation of the African and Arab American foreign lobbies from outsiders seeking to penetrate the American system into insiders helping to shape its course or being mobilized in its service is a testimony to the positive value of including ethnicity in US foreign policy. The increasing involvement of these diasporas in foreign policy has already contributed to the decline of ethnic tensions inside the United States, especially between integrationist members of the two diasporas and moderates among American Jews. Thus, one may consider the recent reconciliation between Jewish Americans and mainstream African American leaders on international matters as the first stage in the healing process. Jesse Jackson, whose rhetoric and deeds have long epitomized the shared nature of the internal and external rift between Jews and blacks, took it upon himself to become a domestic and international healer. While in the past Jackson described Zionism as "a kind of poisonous weed," in a 1992 speech to the World Jewish Congress he identified it as a "liberation movement." Jackson has also called for the rebuilding of the civil rights alliance. He and other black leaders have expressed hope that the

Middle East peace will bring peace between Jews and African Americans in the United States.

Thus, the dedication of diasporas to democratic causes abroad may also energize liberal discourse inside the United States in a manner that can temper the fear of American disunity. Just as the openness of American government to the influence of ethnicity has guided diasporic groups to champion the creed of democracy and human rights around the globe, it also forces them to be more committed to liberal pluralism domestically. As ethnic elites gradually find their way into the American mainstream via the diaspora channel, their affinity with isolationists and extreme multiculturalists in their own community becomes awkward. Many African-American leaders, for example, have distanced themselves from extreme Afrocentrists and the anti-Semitic rhetoric of the Nation of Islam. Zogby was among the signatories of the American Jewish Committee ads against the profanities of Louis Farrakhan's aide Khalid Abdul Muhammad: "We are Americans, whose diversity of faith, ethnicity and race unites us in a common campaign against bigotry." Edward Said seems to have undergone an intellectual metamorphosis as he called on the Arab American diaspora to capitalize on its freedom in the United States and to rescue the Arab culture from Arab leaders and governments: "It is now left to the Arab diaspora on its own to do for the Arabs what leaders and governments in the Arab world will not or cannot do for their people."

The damaging impact of ethnic influences in US foreign affairs has been overstated. Ethnic involvement in US foreign affairs may be seen as an important vehicle through which disenfranchised groups may win an entry ticket into American society and politics. Indeed, one of the signs that an ethnic group has achieved a respectable position in American life is its acquisition of a meaningful voice in US foreign affairs. Yet in order to obtain such a role, ethnic officials must first demonstrate their determination to advocate the principles of pluralism, democracy, and human rights abroad. In fact, in the aftermath of the Cold War and with the advent of a more unipolar, ideological world order that favors democracy and the free market economy, ethnic lobbies are likely to become mobilized diasporas. They are "commissioned" by American decision makers to export and safeguard American values abroad and are expected to become the moral conscience of new democracies or newly established states in their homelands. Such commissioning, in turn, further legitimates the ethnic voice in America's external affairs and enables diasporas to push

American policymakers to adhere to America's neo-Wilsonian values of promoting democracy and openness around the globe, even when such policies seem to obstruct *ad hoc* strategic interests.

Finally, the new foreign policy role of ethnic groups is likely to reflect positively in American civic culture by reinforcing the values of democracy and pluralism at home. Contrary to conventional wisdom, diaspora politics has the potential to temper, rather than exacerbate, domestic ethnic conflicts, because it discourages tendencies toward Balkanization at home. In many ways, then, the participation of ethnic diasporas in shaping US foreign policy is a truly positive phenomenon.

NOTES

1. See Kenneth Longmyer, "Black American Demands," and David J. Sadd & G. Neal Lendenmann, "Arab American Grievances," *Foreign Policy* 60, Fall 1985.
2. See Bruce D. Porter, "Can American Democracy Survive?" *Commentary*, November 1993, pp. 37–40. See also Morris Dickstein, "After the Cold War: Culture as Politics, Politics as Culture," *Social Research*, Fall 1993, pp. 531–44.

13 Racial and Ethnic Conflicts: A Global Perspective

Rita Jalali and Seymour Martin Lipset

Race and ethnicity provide the most striking example of a general failure among experts to anticipate social developments in varying types of societies. Until recently, there was considerable consensus among many Marxist and non-Marxist scholars that ethnicity reflected the conditions of traditional society, in which people lived in small communities isolated from one another and in which mass communications and transportation were limited. Many expected that industrialization, urbanization, and the spread of education would reduce ethnic consciousness, and that universalism would replace particularism. Marxists were certain that socialism would mean the end of the ethnic tension and consciousness that existed in pre-socialist societies. Non-Marxists sociologists in western countries assumed that industialization and modernization would do the same. Assimilation of minorities into a large integrated whole was viewed as the inevitable future.

It is now clearly established that the assimilationist assumptions are not valid. Most parts of the globe have been touched by ethnic conflict. While the post-colonial countries continue to experience the effects of ethnic polarization, ethnic passions have now engulfed regions of the world that until recently were thought to have solved the "nationality" problem. Ethnic conflict now threatens most former communist countries and has led to the political fragmentation of Yugoslavia and Soviet Union. From the movements for autonomy in Canada, the United Kingdom, Spain, and France to the strivings for a more formally pluralistic society in the United States, ethnic and racial cleavages have become a part of the political landscape of many of the western industrialized countries.

Ethnic movements have emerged under a variety of circumstance and encompassed many forms. They have emerged among large minority groups (Quebec and East Pakistan), and among small ones (Frisians in Holland, Jurassians in Switzerland, and Gorkhas in

317

India). They encompass both cultural and economic components. For example, in Wales and Scotland the issues are more economic, while in the Basque country and Quebec they are more cultural. Within the same country, for example, India, ethnic protest has emerged in backward, poor regions as in Nagaland and in the advanced regions like Punjab. Ethnic political mobilization has occurred in democracies (India and Belgium) and in authoritarian systems (Franco's Spain and Uganda); in centralized states (France and Senegal) and in federal systems (the former Yugoslavia and India).

A variety of cultural markers have provided the basis for ethnic mobilization: the use of skin color in the United States, language in Canada, tribal loyalties in much of Africa, religion in Sudan and Northern Ireland. Some movements demand outright secession, others aim for cultural autonomy, while still others pursue equal rights within the prevailing political system. In all instances, the movements are powerful expressions of group identity and a desire for a more equitable distribution of political and economic resources.

The problems that ethnic diversity pose for efforts at nation-building have, as Walker Connor points out, been largely ignored by social scientists concerned with the topic. The territorial boundaries of states rarely coincide with ethnic boundaries.

> Of a total of 132 contemporary states, only 12 (9.1 percent) can be described as essentially homogenous from an ethnic viewpoint . . . In some instances, the number of groups within a state runs into the hundreds, and in 53 states (40.2 percent of the total), the population is divided into more than five significant groups.[1]

Conversely, there are ethnic groups widely dispersed over various states. Thus, although there is a Jewish state, Israeli Jews form only 16 percent of all Jews. They are dispersed over 39 other countries, with the largest number (44 percent of all Jews) residing in the United States.[2] There are other examples, including the Arabs who may be found in more than 37 states, Malays in over seven, and Kurds in over six.[3] In Europe, 40 percent of Albanians live outside of Albania, and 23 percent of Hungarians reside outside Hungary.[4]

The interaction of groups from diverse ethnic backgrounds often is accompanied by intolerance and conflict. The costs to society of such conflicts are enormous: denial of human rights, breakdown of political order, decline of economic performance, and escalation into civil and regional wars. Ethnically driven violence has ravaged many regions of the Third World and created an exodus of refugees. By one estimate, "more than half the world's thirty million refugees at the beginning of 1990 were fleeing from civil wars and repression which were the result of communally-based conflicts."[5]

Such tensions have also had an enormous impact on the economic development of countries. The poor performance of the Sri Lankan economy since the mid-1980s can be traced largely to ethnically driven conflicts.[6] They have created famine conditions in African countries like Ethiopia and Sudan, where millions have faced starvation as interethnic warfare has prevented farmers from growing food.

Ethnic conflicts also entail international complications as they repeatedly provoke military intervention by outside powers. Libya, for example, was in part motivated by ethnic considerations when it got involved in the Chadian civil war, as was India in Bangladesh (earlier East Pakistan) and in Sri Lanka.

The political instability prevailing in many parts of the Third World can also be traced in large part to interethnic conflict. In Sri Lanka, for example, there was a deterioration of democracy mainly because of an "explosion of ethnic conflict into violent insurgency, which... polarized the polity, embittered all groups, and provided an excuse for increasingly authoritarian measures."[7]

The effects of ethnic cleavages on prospects for peace and democracy, however, vary with the pattern of cleavage and the way they articulate with political structures. Where ethnic identities are cross-cutting, they are less likely to threaten political stability. In India, because

> major religious communities are split into many language communities which in turn are stratified into caste and class formations ... an eagerness to utilize one affinity by a political leadership that seeks an easy constituency of popular support may encourage other leaders to exploit the other affinities of the same individual. Thus, for example, the easier course of exclusive Hindu mobilization, by seizing upon the Hindi language loyalty in northern India, created negative political reactions among Hindus who spoke other languages.[8]

On the other hand, ethnic cleavages in Sri Lanka and Malaysia are cumulative (with linguistic, religious, regional, racial, and class cleavages overlapping) and thus a threat to democracy. In this article, we seek to deal with some of the causes of interethnic conflict and the strategies adopted by countries to manage such conflict.

THE THIRD WORLD

Latin American scholars have argued that their societies are not racist and that class rather than ethnic cleavages predominate. Yet in spite of racial and ethnic pluralism, stratification correlates with racial ancestry in almost all of the nations of the region. The privileged classes are largely of European background and/or are lighter skin-colored than the less affluent strata. "Money whitens" in these societies, in that those darker-skinned persons who manage to succeed economically do not face overt social discrimination, and they and their offspring frequently marry whites. In general though,

> the closer the relationship to European stock, the more apt a population cohort is to have a high income level, land, and education; the closer the relationship to indigenous [Indian] or African stock, the more apt the group is to lack land, to have a low income level and little schooling, and to suffer discrimination in the workplace, in schools, and at sites where public services are dispensed.[9]

A 1989 US State Department report states that racial minorities suffer from discrimination in Bolivia, Brazil, Ecuador, Guatemala, Mexico, and Peru. In Brazil, where the government denies the existence of prejudice, the report notes that blacks and mulattos receive less income and education than whites and encounter discrimination in housing and services.[10] The 1980s have exacerbated the conditions of these racial groups as the countries have had to reduce public budgets for health and other social services in order to repay the foreign debt.

Ethnic-based antagonisms have severely disrupted many African and Asian polities. Most of the countries in these two regions are multiethnic societies, many of which do not even have one numerically dominant ethnic group. According to one study, of the 230 minorities at risk globally, 72 groups were found to inhabit Africa south of the Sahara, forming about 41 percent of the region's total population and 49 groups were in Asia, estimated to constitute nearly 12 percent of the continent's population.[11]

Tensions stemming from this situation add considerably to the task of creating and maintaining democratic, or at least non-coercive, politics. Not only must these countries seek to allocate resources and foster policies seen as equitable by diverse social strata, they must also find ways of securing the loyalty of ethnic groupings that constitute sub or embryonic nations whose initial loyalties and sense of group consciousness, of "we versus them," is to themselves rather than to the nation-state. And since the economic resources of these countries are low, it is not surprising that ethnic conflict often bodes to tear them asunder, to produce outcomes in which dominant groups and sometimes minorities discriminate against others in the pursuit of access to political power and economic and social advantages.[12]

A proper understanding of ethnic politics in the regions of the Third World also requires an examination of the role the colonial powers played in shaping interethnic relations. Ethnic heterogeneity in the countries of Africa, for example, is often the result of national boundaries drawn by foreign powers, which for the most part ignored tribal cultural patterns in the subjugated societies:

> The vagaries of European diplomacy and military campaigns, possibly influenced by alliance with local African political forces, determined the boundary outcomes. A particular precolonial African state might by treaty or alliance, or by calculation (or miscalculation) of advantage, assign itself to a given colonial domain. However, almost no one on the European side cared whether a particular language group was united or divided by colonial partition.[13]

The need to institutionalize dominance also required counting and classifying peoples into discrete, bounded groups whereas before, as Aidan Southall observes, the cultural identities were only "interlocking, overlapping, multiple."[14] In extreme cases, this created new categories of identity, particularly in Anglophone Africa. "Ethnonyms in East Africa such as Teso, Gisu, Acholi, Kiga, Sukuma, or Luhya would hardly have been encountered at all a century ago."[15]

Ethnic relations were also profoundly affected by colonial state policies, which actively promoted differential treatment of ethnic groups. Over time such policies created widespread economic and social disparities between ethnic groups.[16] Certain ethnic groups were selected as collaborators or channels for the transmission of government patronage. In Sudan, as A. E. A. Abdallah notes, the longstanding feud between the north and the south can be traced, among other factors, to "the British conception of a future for the South separate from the North. Systematic policies of divide-and-rule were instituted, ensuring very little interaction between ethnic groups."[17] Economic development in the south was neglected. During negotiations over independence, southerners were not included in the discussions, prompting the creation of a southern Sudanese political movement. Other examples include the British preference for northern

Nigerians in Nigeria and Tamils in Sri Lanka. The British also pursued different policies toward Malays and non-Malays in Malaysia. The Malays were accorded a special position when land rights were granted to them, and a separate college was granted for their aristocratic sons, who were later recruited into public service positions.[18] After independence the system of quotas and privileged access was continued, creating severe ethnic conflicts. As Neil Nevitte and Charles Kennedy note, "the selection of one group over others...in effect constituted an incipient policy of preference during the colonial phase,"[19] setting a precedent for ethnic preference policies in the post-colonial period.

Modernization under colonialism also exacerbated interethnic tensions as it widened ethnic group disparities. It upset traditional relationships between groups as some groups more than others were able to utilize the opportunities for social mobility.[20]

WESTERN EUROPE

Asia and Africa are ethnically more heterogeneous than Europe, because much of Europe's nationality problem was "solved" by wars and population transfers over the span of several centuries. Nationalism, an ideological movement for self-determination, emerged with the French revolution and spread over the whole of Europe. As Walker Connor has pointed out, the dogma that "alien rule is illegitimate rule" proved to be a potent challenge to the legitimacy of multinational structures and ultimately led to their disintegration.[21]

The peace settlements that followed World War I brought about an extensive redrawing of boundaries in favor of ethnically homogenous nations leading to a decrease in the percentage of population belonging to ethnic peoples without a state or self-government-by one count, from about 26 percent in 1910 to only about 7 percent in 1930.[22] Adjustments after World War II further reduced the problem of ethnic minorities throughout Europe. Both benign (assimilation, voluntary, or otherwise) and brutal methods (forcible transfer of population and genocide) were used to achieve the nationalist principle. Jaroslav Krejci and Vitezslav Velimsky estimate that about 20 million people moved and permanently settled in new homelands.[23]

The changes in the ethnopolitical relationships over a century and a half are striking.

In 1820 more than half the population of Europe belonged to ethnic nations who either lacked a territorial political status of their own (state or autonomy) or [who] were scattered amongst several dynastic states uninterested in their national aspirations. By 1920, the share of such ethnic groups (whole nations or their fragments) declined to about 7 percent. As result of the Second World War, the share of ethnic minorities without an autonomy status dropped to 3 percent only.[24]

However, as the prevalence of numerous ethnic movements in Western Europe illustrate, not all ethnic aspirations were satisfied. Especially notable are the problems in the United Kingdom with Northern Ireland, Scotland, and Wales; in Spain with the Basques and Catalans; and in France with Bretons, Corsicans, and also with the Basques. While such ethnonational aspirations continue to dominate the political arena, new sources of interethnic conflict have also emerged in Europe. One has to do with the rise in the guest-worker and immigrant populations in Western Europe and the other with the breakdown of Soviet and Yugoslav polities.

The large scale migration of guest-workers who come from countries not sharing the predominant cultures or language has created new ethnic tensions in Western Europe. They constitute about 5 to 15 percent of the total population of most Western European countries.[25] Over half of the foreign workers and their dependents are located in France, Switzerland, and West Germany. Rising unemployment in host countries has heightened tensions between the local and foreign populations, particularly in Germany, where the problem has reached explosive levels. Racist attacks on foreign workers occur every day in the country with over 600 attacks reported in one year, 1989. Fully half of these attacks have taken place in western Germany, although the reincorporated eastern section is now the center of the most vicious ones. There is increased support for extreme right-wing political groups campaigning on anti-immigrant platforms.[26] In France, the National Front Party has increased its standing by basing its campaigns on fears about North African immigration.

In Britain, the dissolution of the empire created an inflow of migrants from former colonies. The country now has immigrants from diverse religious, language, and regional backgrounds. There are, for example, about one million Muslims who have migrated from South Asia and Middle Eastern countries. In recent years they have become organized, insisting that they be subject to Islamic rather than British family law.

ETHNIC CONFLICT IN THE FORMER SOVIET UNION

The dismemberment of the last of the great multinational empires also threatens to create chaos and disorder in Eastern Europe and beyond. Starting with the conquest of Kazan in 1552, the growth of the Russian empire took place over 360 years.[27] As a result of this expansion, the empire dominated over people from several different language, religious, and ethnic backgrounds.[28] During this period Russian treatment of the minorities changed frequently – from tolerance to forced assimilation and discrimination. By the late nineteenth century, Orthodoxy had become the state religion. Other non-Christian and non-Orthodox religions were discriminated against, particularly if their spiritual centers were located outside the territory of the empire like the Catholic and Muslim faiths.[29]

Before the revolution, conversion to Orthodoxy was the chief means for assimilating minorities. Later, Marxism became the instrument of fusion. The original Marxist theory considered ethnic minorities an unnecessary distraction, if not inhibitors, to economic and political progress. Classic Marxist reasoning justified historically the ethnic domination over economically less productive peoples by developed groups because it was considered to be a historically useful mission: the integration of less productive cultures – such as Mexicans, Algerians, and Asian Indians – into industrially advanced ones helped to produce capitalism in stable agrarian societies. As Carlos Moore points out, Marx's systematic condemnation of "inferior races" included a belief that their nationalist movements could easily become obstacles for agrarian societies in the process of becoming industrialized.[30] To Marx and Engels the struggles of the then politically oppressed blacks, Asians, Slavs, and Latins were distractions from the "real" issue of class struggle.[31]

Marx and Engels lashed out against Bohemia and Croatia for seeking freedom from German (Austrian) imperialism. Writing about the situation in the Austro-Hungarian Empire, Engels recognized three of its peoples as destined for a progressive role – Germans, Poles, and Magyars. Then, in an unfortunate turn of phrase, he emphasized "the chief vocation of all the other races and peoples, great and small, is to perish in the revolutionary holocaust."[32]

On the formal ideological level, the communist regimes that had come to power since 1917 rejected Marx's and Engel's idea of absorbing minority and backward peoples into the cultures of more advanced societies. Lenin proposed that national minorities in the Soviet Union should have as much autonomy as possible and the right to secede. Lenin suffered a disabling stroke before he could elaborate on the "nationality" policy. When Stalin came to power, he ignored Lenins' views on this subject.[33] Although he claimed to support the development of cultures that were "national in form, socialist in content," under his rule the rights of the national minorities, guaranteed under the Soviet constitution, were frequently violated.

While the nationalism of the majority with its state-building and unifying potential was treated with empathy, the nationalisms of the minorities were considered divisive and, therefore, suppressed.[34] The republics were subjected to brutal, colonial Russification. Linguistic and cultural assimilation were promoted through Russian schools. Whole ethnic groups were deported – the Tatars of the Crimea, the Germans of the Volga, the Chechentsy of the Caucasus.[35] Terror managed to keep the lid on ethnic aspirations for several decades. Under Nikita Khrushchev and Leonid Brezhnev, Stalin's nationality policy was implicitly dropped. "The live-and-let-live practices placated many officials of non-Russian ethnic groups. Lobbies representing native interests became increasingly entrenched."[36]

The advent of *glasnost* under Mikhail Gorbachev unleashed movements for secession. The Union of Soviet Republics is dead and the fourteen non-Russian republics are now independent, although most have joined a loose commonwealth. However, since many of the republics contain ethnic minorities, independence has not ended ethnic tensions in the region.

EASTERN EUROPE

Ethnic problems have reached explosive levels in other previously socialist countries of Europe, particularly the former Yugoslavia. No single group formed a majority within it, although Serbian influence tended to predominate. Four of the country's republics have so far declared independence (Slovenia, Croatia, Bosnia-Herzegovina, and Macedonia). Croatia's declaration in June 1991 sparked an uprising by the republic's minority Serbs, who constitute about 11 percent of

Croatia's population. Serbian insurgents have since seized about one-third of the territory of Croatia and about two-thirds of Bosnia-Herzegovina, with help from the Republic of Serbia and the Serb-dominated federal army.

Czechs and Slovaks have agreed to partition the former Czechoslo-vakia into its respective parts; the Hungarian minority in Romania faces discrimination, as does the one million Turkish minority in Bulgaria, who until recently was not allowed to keep Turkish names, speak its language, or practice its Muslim faith; and there is an increased persecution in Eastern Europe against Jews and Gypsies and other foreigners, such as refugees from the former Yugoslavia.

The resurgence of ethnicity worldwide raises several important questions. What factors explain the timing and nature of modern ethnic conflicts? Why do some cases of interethnic contact generate conflict and others do not? For instance, while the presence of many foreigners has created ethnic tensions in France and Germany, in Luxembourg and Sweden large numbers of immigrants have resulted in only a few cases of interethnic hostility. Luxembourg has the largest proportion of semisettled aliens in Europe (out of 370,000 people, 100,000 are foreigners, most of whom are culturally and racially different from the locals.)[37] Similarly, Sweden in recent decades has incorporated more than 400,000 foreign-born immigrants without much difficulty. In the developing world, Tanzania has a large number of relatively small tribal groups but little intertribal conflict.[38] In societies where ethnic tensions are high, what can be done to minimize these conflicts? How have countries like Switzerland or Papua New Guinea (with 700 different language groups) managed relatively peaceful ethnic relations in a culturally heterogeneous environment?[39] What is the consequence of ethnic fragmentation for the stability of nation-states? Is the next century going to witness a Balkanization of large states or will the move be in the other direction toward integration of ethnic units into suprastate governments? Will it be a world of ECs (European Communities), OASs (Organizations of American States), ASEANs (Association of South East Asian Nations), UNs (United Nations), or one of Latvias, Croatias, Kashmirs, and Eritreas?

ETHNIC MOBILIZATION

Contrary to the expectations of many Marxist and non-Marxist scholars, the process of modernization itself brought about an increase in ethnic consciousness. As Connor has pointed out, while the notion of popular sovereignty legitimated demands for national self-determination, modernization acted as a catalyst for ethnonationally inspired demands. In Europe, prior to World War II, when there were fewer roads and cars, local radio rather than state-wide television was in operation, and income and education levels were much lower than today. "Brittany's culture appeared safe from French encro-achment.... [M]ost Walloons and Flemings seldom came into con-tact...with members of the other group."[40] With substantial increases in communication and intergroup contact the divisive sense of ethnonational uniqueness has been reinforced rather than dis-sipated.

Most theories of ethnic mobilization assume that modernization has played an important role in stimulating the ethnic movements of recent times. They diverge in the factors they identify as causally more significant in the development and persistence of ethnically based movements. Thus Michael Hechter, puzzled with the rise of national-ist movements in the industrialized West, argues that capitalist forms of development create economic disparities between core and peri-pheral regions and produce "...a cultural division of labor: a system of stratification where objective cultural distinctions are superimposed upon class lines. High status occupations tend to be reserved for those of metropolitan culture; while those of indigenous culture cluster at the bottom of the stratification system."[41] This type of a stratification system ultimately gives rise to nationalist movements in the periphery. However, the evidence of stronger nationalist movements in relatively prosperous, peripheral regions of some countries, like Quebec, the Basque region, Catalonia, Flanders, and to a lesser extent, Estonia and Slovenia, casts serious doubts on Hechter's internal colonial thesis.[42]

A model of ethnic mobilization that has enjoyed much popularity in recent years is economic competition. The basic arguments are derived from the ecological theories of Frederick Barth and his associates[43] and Michael Hannan.[44] Proponents of the economic competition model argue that "modernization increases levels of competition for jobs, housing, and other valued resources among ethnic groups" and that "*ethnic conflict and social movements based on ethnic (rather than some other) boundaries occur when ethnic competition increases.*"[45] Studies using this approach have found that ethnic party support is much higher in developed, urbanized, and industrial regions than in underdeveloped ones.[46] Development leads to a rise rather than a decline in ethnic mobilization, because it provides resources to ethnic groups in the periphery, increasing their bargaining position and organizational capacity for action. The literature on the class basis of ethnic movements is also supportive of the theory, for it shows that movement activists tend to be more educated, are more well-to-do, and have higher occupational status than others among their ethnic groups.[47]

The economic competition model has also been applied to explain the rise of national consciousness in the Ukraine. In a book written before the ethnic turmoil of the Gorbachev era, Bohdan Krawchenko notes "the question of competition is crucial in explaining the rise of national consciousness" in Ukraine following the economic growth of the 1950s and 1960s. "With mobilized individuals, expectations race ahead of the real possibilities. These were the same people who had to compete with Russians for employment, and the rivalry led to an exacerbation of ethnic tensions."[48]

Similarly, Teodar Shanin in a more recent article implies that economic growth in the Soviet Union's ethnic peripheries created more opportunity to amass individual fortunes, both legally and through corruption. All this facilitated the formation of ethnic lobbies in the post-Stalin era. Industrialization and urbanization led to an increase in the number of local non-Russian cadres and intelligentsia who had to compete with the Russian workers. "As a result nationalist tensions were building up."[49]

The economic competition model is, however, not without its weaknesses. First, as Sarah Belanger and Maurice Pinard point out, theories with this perspective "fail to compare countries experiencing conflict with others experiencing accommodation."[50] They cannot explain why Switzerland, a highly developed country, has little ethnic tension between the French and German-speaking Swiss, although the competition between these two groups should be very high as their socioeconomic positions are equal. It also cannot explain the escalation of ethnic conflict in Sri Lanka and its decline in Malaysia. Cases like these bring up the most prominent defect in all models of ethnic processes that focus primarily on economic explanations – their neglect of political variables.[51] In many ethnic movements, institutional structures and state policies play a major role in shaping and conditioning the emergence of such movements.

In the case of Ukrainian dissent, for example, Alexander Motyl argues that the rise of nationalist sentiments in the pre-*glasnost* era was primarily the product of political circumstances, foremost of them being Khrushchev's de-Stalinization and Brezhnev's partial re-Stalinization of Soviet state and society.[52] Others have similarly observed that by implementing policies that recognized and institutionalized ethnic differences – "creating administrative units along national lines, giving national languages official status, and recruiting local political elites from the indigenous populations" – the Soviet authorities unwittingly helped to establish the infrastructure for nationalism during the post-Stalinist era.[53]

The cases of Switzerland, Sri Lanka, and Malaysia also illustrate that specific political mechanisms chosen to regulate ethnic conflict can often affect the likelihood and intensity of such conflicts. Before the nineteenth century the relations among the three major language groups in Switzerland (German, French, and Italian) were characterized by conflict.[54] If ethnic tension is now muted, this may be because the Swiss have a political system that has institutionalized ethnic pluralism, allowing each of the three major language groups proportional equivalence in power sharing extending from the Federal Council to the bureaucracy and the armed forces.[55]

Before the period of ethnic violence began in Sri Lanka, interethnic relations appeared far more tolerant there than in Malaysia. Malaysia has so far succeeded where Sri Lanka failed, partly because of the differences in political structures. In Malaysia, these structures provided incentives for parties to seek multiethnic bases.[56] Malaysia has a simple majority voting system, and voting districts are drawn so that no ethnic group has a majority. In contrast, in most of the voting districts of Sri Lanka, the Sinhalese have an automatic majority so that their parties do not need to seek Tamil support. Incentives to form interethnic coalitions are now also built into the Sri Lankan electoral arrangements, but as Donald Horowitz argues, "in the formative period of Sinhalese exclusiveness and Tamil separatism, all of the incentives were the other way."[57]

The political system, however, not only responds to existing ethnic differences but often creates "new ethnic groups out of extant,... unorganized ethnocultural categories,... and [promotes] ethnic awareness and action among formerly mobilized, recently inactive, ethnic groups."[58] It does so in several different ways. First, the expansion of political authority over a long list of functions creates a competitive arena for distribution of state resources; moreover, in developing countries the state itself is a resource over which ethnic groups engage in a continuous struggle.[59] Second, when the state's administrative structures and legal institutions distribute resources based on ethnicity, they further encourage political mobilization linked to ethnic differences.[60] Scheduled Castes, a historically disadvantaged group in India, has been given special encouragement for political participation and other benefits in education and government service. Although they are diverse culturally, linguistically, and geographically, such benefits have created a common sense of identity and increased their political mobilization.[61]

In the United States, where the preference for individual rights as opposed to group rights made demands based on ethnicity less legitimate, in recent years affirmative action policies have legitimized and encouraged such claims. A study of Latino mobilization in the city of Chicago found that affirmative action policy provided the critical base for the organizational development and growth of a Latino identity and agenda.[62]

Census categories have facilitated this process by redrawing ethnic boundaries. For example, the US census puts diverse ethnic groups like Koreans, Chinese, Japanese, and Asian Indians under the broader category of "Asian and Pacific Islanders." Similarly, since 1980, Mexican-Americans, Puerto Ricans, and other Spanish speaking groups have been classified as Hispanics. Because the government uses these artificial categories as units in allocating political and economic resources, over time such diverse groups begin to act collectively as they see themselves sharing common interests and experiences of oppression and also benefits.[63] As William Petersen has argued, few things facilitate a category to coalesce into a group as readily as its designation as such by an official body.[64]

Third, the state, for its own administrative convenience and in order to improve control over local elites, may select certain ethnic elites and organizations as collaborators or channels for the transmission of government patronage. This situation is common in many colonized countries (British preference for Tamils in Sri Lanka and Sikhs in India) and now also frequently occurs in many developing countries engaged in the task of nation-building, thereby affecting the identity and political mobilization of particular ethnic groups.[65] The late Indian Prime Minister Rajiv Gandhi, in order to undermine the ruling Communist party in West Bengal, expressed his sympathy for the demand of the Nepalis to form a separate state in the northern part of West Bengal.

Fourth, ethnic processes are also often shaped by state policies with regard to military recruitment. "Military and police forces are rarely neutral actors in ethnic conflicts. They are typically ethnically imbalanced as a result of both historical socioeconomic maldistribution of opportunities and of deliberate recruitment strategies pursued by central governmentalities."[66] Thus, Yugoslavia's army, whose officer corps is 85 percent Serbian, has openly supported Serb guerrillas in the civil war in Croatia.

Given the variety of ethnic conflicts and their dynamic and fluid qualities, no one factor can provide a comprehensive explanation. What has been clearly established, however, is that ethnicity derives its strength not only from the symbolic and affective aspects of primordial ties but also from its use as an instrument for economic and political advantage.[67]

MULTIETHNICITY AND FORMS OF GOVERNMENT

The proposition that no nation in the world is free from some form of violation of human rights in the form of ethnic, religious, or racial discrimination (unless it is one of the few totally homogeneous in these terms, such as Iceland) is by now accepted as a fact. Much more often than not, people resist and resent those who differ from themselves in race, culture, and religion. Many have sought to institutionalize privileges for members of their groups. In modern times, both rulers and the masses have turned to virulent expressions of bigotry in response to social tensions, to threats perceived by those in power, and to insecurity stemming from economic or status uncertainty. The most extreme racist effort, the Holocaust of European Jewry, occurred in modern times. Anti-Semitism was also the policy of some communist states which, like the former Soviet Union, restricted the rights of Jewish citizens. Racism still prevails in many African states, where the politics of ethnicity continue to determine who rules. Uganda eliminated East Indian minorities, among others.

The white-dominated society of South Africa began to dismantle its segregation and other discrimination policies against the majority black population only after international pressure was brought to bear on it. Ethnic divisions have also undermined the apparent unity of countries as diverse as Belgium, Canada, the United Kingdom, Spain, Cyprus, Pakistan, Malaysia, Lebanon, Nigeria, and Zaire.

What steps have proved effective in containing these divisive forces? How has ethnic conflict been managed in multiethnic polities? Some scholars have argued that consociational democracies provide a model of conflict management for segmented societies. In such democracies the political leaders of the major subcultures "cooperate in a grand coalition to govern the country."[68] Such coalitions have been successfully formed in Austria, Belgium, the Netherlands, and Switzerland.

Dependence on elite conciliation makes consociationalism less effective in Third World countries.[69] Federalism, on the other hand, has proved to be a useful device to reduce ethnic conflicts in many countries – from economically advanced countries like Switzerland to developing ones like India. Federalism works because it transfers the target of political mobilization from the national to the provincial centers, shifts conflicts in homogeneous provinces to intraethnic divisions, and gives ethnic groups local autonomy. Papua New Guinea managed to resolve its most serious conflict arising out of secessionist-based demands by decentralization of power and the establishment of nineteen provincial governments.[70]

For federalism to work, however, it must be properly balanced with the pattern of ethnic cleavages. In Nigeria, the original division of the country in 1960 into three tribally distinctive regions – with their own parliaments, police forces, universities, and budgets derived from local revenues – failed to prevent serious tribal conflict. By creating a nineteen-state federal structure, Nigeria's Second Republic crosscut ethnicity to some extent and dispersed the stakes in electoral competition.[71]

In India, a federal system gives control over cultural, educational, and linguistic policies to state governments whose boundary lines were drawn largely to correspond to ethnic variations in response to collective protest. But federalism also works in India because the social system is highly segmented, "enabling the center to intervene in crisis situation in individual states without necessarily creating a national issue."[72] Electoral reforms (like heterogenous constituencies and incentives to pool votes across ethnic lines) that force ethnic parties to form coalitions with rival groups are also techniques that help to maintain peace between ethnic groups as the earlier discussion of Malaysia and Sri Lanka illustrated. In India, ethnically based parties have difficulty winning elections at the national level because many of the country's electoral constituencies are heterogenous. The key, as Donald Horowitz notes, is to have institutional arrangements that provide political incentives for accommodation and that penalize extremism.[73]

Secession or partition is rarely an adequate solution, because most regions of a country are ethnically heterogenous and partition can involve a costly process of exchanging populations and dividing land

and natural resources, often resulting in loss of many human lives and continuing border conflicts. The partition of British India illustrated that separation can lead to an orgy of interethnic violence, even when carried out under peaceful conditions. Secession also introduces ethnic problems in a "sharper form on a narrower scale, with smaller and smaller nationalisms oppressing smaller and smaller minorities."[74] Serbs in an independent Croatia, as Mihajlo Mihajlov points out, would be an even more vulnerable minority than Croats in Yugoslavia. The problem is further complicated by the fluid quality of ethnic identities. When Pakistan was founded, the Muslim religion formed the base of ethnic solidarity that united Muslims in the eastern regions with those in the western parts. Several decades later the eastern region demanded and secured a separate state, Bangladesh, on grounds of language discrimination. Now the Pakistan government faces secessionist demands from Pathans and Baluchs.

In the former Soviet Union, where deportations, industrialization, and Moscow's settlement policies made most republics ethnically mixed, secession and independence may not be the solution to the ethnic problems. The ethnic and national groups in the Soviet Union were not always confined to the titular political administrative unit. Nor was the titular nationality necessarily a majority in its administrative unit, a fact that creates major tensions in the newly independent republics.[75]

In Georgia, the first non-Baltic Soviet republic to formally declare independence, 30 percent of the population belong to a wide variety of minorities. In recent years conflicts have developed with Abkazians and Ossetians.[76] The dispute with the Ossetian minority has often turned violent. In 1990, the Georgian legislature formally declared an end to the longstanding local autonomy of South Ossetia after the Ossetian assembly voted to remain part of the former Soviet Union.

In the Moldavian republic (where only 64 percent of the population is Moldavian), the Turkic-speaking Gagauz proclaimed independence, claiming they were being discriminated against by the Romanian speaking Moldavian majority. In Azerbaijan, Armenians want the Nagorna-Karabakh region to be united with Armenia. Since some of these republics are now under the control of authoritarian leaders, minorities are likely to encounter further repression.

The independence of the Baltic republics could not result in a clean ethnic break. With Moscow's encouragement many Russians settled in the Baltic areas, altering their ethnic makeup. Russian minorities usually occupied a disproportionate number of the better jobs and housing, creating resentment among the indigenous population. In Estonia, 61 percent of the population is Estonian. In Latvia, only 52 percent of the population is Latvian.[77]

Except for Slovenia in the northwest, most republics in the former Yugoslavia are ethnically mixed. Over a third of all Serbs and 22 percent of all Croatians live outside their republics. Even if the Croatian republic is able to resolve the dispute with its Serbian minorities, the problem of the republic of Bosnia- Herzegovina looks insoluble. This republic is 40 percent Muslim, 32 percent Serbian, and 18 percent Croatian. Since it lies between Serbia and Croatia, both lay claims to portions of it and "there is no way to partition it."[78]

Many countries have adopted preferential or affirmative action policies to reduce ethnic conflict arising out of economic disparities between groups. Preferences are granted most often in education, employment, and land. Malaysia, Fiji, and Indonesia have policies that favor their indigenous populations. Many nations in Africa have adopted regional equalization, policies which in reality favor the ethnic groups concentrated in some regions and not others (some examples are Zaire, Tanzania, and Nigeria). India has fixed quotas in education and civil service and reserved seats in the legislature for Scheduled Castes and Tribes, who together form 22 percent of the population. Many Indian states have also extended preferential treatment to other lower status castes and to the indigenous populations.

Preferential programs are sometimes instituted by politically dominant groups against another ethnic group – usually an immigrant minority – which holds a disproportionate share of economic power. Preferential policies in such cases are designed to enhance the economic position of those who govern the polity. Currently, this pattern exists in Malaysia, Indonesia, Fiji, Sri Lanka, several African countries, and many states in India.

In some countries, preferential policies have been instituted by the ethnic groups in power for the benefit of historically disadvantaged minority groups. The most notable cases are India's preferential programs for the Scheduled Castes and Tribes mentioned earlier and the affirmative action quota programs for blacks in the United States. Other examples, all from democratic countries, include benefits for Maoris in New Zealand, aborigines in Australia, Sephardim in Israel, and some minority groups in Canada.

In countries like Malaysia, India, and the United States such policies have been vigorously pursued and have provided educational and job opportunities to some in the targeted groups.[79] However, such policies have also created a wave of resentment among the privileged groups. It is easier to measure progress towards interethnic equality than it is to assess improvements in ethnic harmony. Have preferential policies accentuated ethnic conflict or have they helped to reduce it? While sweeping statements on this issue are abundant, more studies are needed to carefully evaluate the policies' impact on interethnic relations before a definite answer can be reached.[80]

Is democracy viable in a multiethnic society? There is plenty of evidence from African and Asian countries that demonstrates that intense ethnic loyalties endanger democracy. Yet many ethnically heterogenous societies have succeeded in managing conflict within a democratic framework. Ethnic cleavages do not necessarily lead to violence. Indeed, one could argue that they can be a source of democratic strength and renewal, for "ethnic peace may require greater decentralization, distribution, rotation, and representation of power than authoritarian regimes have been able to provide."[81] Masipula Sithole notes that the heterogeneity of the Zimbabwean social milieu is one factor that has helped to sustain pluralist democracy in that country. "In a real sense, continued Ndebele [tribal] support for Nkomo's ZAPU [opposition] has slowed down ZANU's [government party] speed toward countryside hegemony and the one-party state."[82] Similarly in Nigeria, Larry Diamond argues that although democratic stability has often been threatened by ethnic divisions, authoritarian systems also have been hamstrung in managing ethnic conflicts.[83]

As a comparative study of the democratic experience in 26 developing nations concludes, "when ethnic leaders are allowed to share power, they generally act according to the rules of the game, but when the state responds to ethnic mobilization with exclusion and repression, violence festers."[84] Indeed, the fact that interethnic relations are more peaceful in the West than in the Third World does not result from differences in ethnic groups in the different regions. The differences appear to rest in the nature of the western political structures, which have incorporated multiple ethnic expressions and channeled ethnic conflict into more peaceful and constructive directions.[85]

CONCLUSION

Does the drive toward supranational organizations and the economic and political integration of European countries signify a trend away from ethnic fragmentation? There are several reasons why this is unlikely. First, the principle of self-determination is now viewed the world over as one of the basic rights of all peoples and as a legitimate basis for governance. Second, with a myriad of human rights organizations (Amnesty International, Middle East Watch, the Minority Rights Group, America Watch, Asia Watch, and Cultural Survival) monitoring discriminatory and repressive practices of regimes, it is likely that the problems of minorities will receive greater world attention and support, encouraging ethnic mobilization by previously quiescent minorities.

Third, the independence movements in the former Soviet regions also provides precedents for other parts of the world. As John Lewis Gaddis points out, "If the boundaries of the dying Soviet empire are to be revised, then why should boundaries established by empires long since dead be preserved?"[86]

Recent world reaction to the Kurdish massacres and the Yugoslav internationality conflicts suggests that there is now greater support than at any time since World War II for international intervention to aid movements for autonomy. In the words of French Foreign Minister Roland Dumas, "This break in the longstanding and rigid doctrine (of noninterference in the internal affairs of states) permits the hope today that the international community will find the means to intervene in similar cases, and first of all the Kurds."[87] Under the threat of international economic sanctions, Iraq finally agreed to the presence of UN peacekeeping forces for the protection of Kurds, and the Yugoslavs (Serbs) have accepted a peacekeeping role for the UN forces.

However, if history is any guide, it is unlikely that international bodies can offer effective protection to minorities. In 1919, the League of Nations adopted treaties to protect minorities in new states against nationalist forces. The treaties guaranteed traditional minority rights dealing with religion, language, and cultural activities. But the treaties were imposed only on weak or defeated states and were largely ignored after they regained their legitimacy. Similarly, now the world bodies have imposed minority protection conditions only on Iraq and Yugoslavia, while Turkey's treatment of Kurds, Indonesia's of the peoples of East Timor and Irian Jaya, or China's repressive practices toward Tibetans receive little attention. In the past, as now, almost all countries including the Great Powers and the former colonies are afraid that international recognition of minority rights will encourage separatism and lead to interference in the internal affairs of states. A memorandum prepared for the British government during the Paris Peace treaty negotiations after World War I warned:

efforts will doubtless be made to embody provisions in the [Paris Peace] treaty safeguarding the rights of racial, religious and other minorities and further, to interpret the doctrine of "national self-determination" as entitling such minorities, if they can claim to be nations, to present their case to the Peace Conference and to subsequent Inter-State Conferences. On both these points the best course would seem to be to leave as much discretion as possible in the hands of each of the Associated Powers. It would clearly be inadvisable to go even the smallest distance in the direction of admitting the claim of the American negroes, or the Southern Irish, or the Flemings or Catalans, to appeal to an Inter-State Conference over the head of their own Government. Yet if a right of appeal is granted to the Macedonians or the German Bohemians it will be difficult to refuse it in the case of other nationalist movements.[88]

Such concerns have also dictated the US and EC reactions to nationalist movements in the former Soviet Union. Interethnic tensions are, however, moving far beyond the ability of the world bodies to contain them. Threats to withdraw aid, imposing an oil and arms embargo, and suspending trade preferences have had little effect on multiethnic republics in the former Soviet empire. Whether other countries in Central and Eastern Europe go the way of Yugoslavia will be determined more by the political beliefs and attitudes of the popularly elected leadership than by any pressure the world bodies can bring to bear on the nationalists.

NOTES

1   Walker Connor, "Nation-building or Nation-destroying?" *World Politics* 24 (April 1972): 320.
2   Gunnar Nielsson, "States and 'Nation-Groups' a Global Taxonomy" in Edward A. Tiryakian and Ronald Rogowski, eds., *New Nationalisms of the Developed West: Toward Explanation* (Boston: Allen & Unwin, 1985), 35.
3   Ibid., 37.
4   Jaroslav Krejci and Vitezslav Velimsky, *Ethnic and Political Nations in Europe* (New York: St. Martin's Press, 1981), 79.
5   Ted Robert Gurr, "Third World Minorities at Risk Since 1945" (Background paper prepared for the Conference on Conflict Resolution in Post-Cold War Third World, U.S. Institute of Peace, October 1990), 7.

6   L. Kenneth Hubbell, "Political and Economic Discrimination in Sri Lanka" in Michael L. Wyzan, ed., *The Political Economy of Ethnic Discrimination and Affirmative Action: A Comparative Perspective* (New York: Praeger, 1990).

7   Larry Diamond, Juan J. Linz, and Seymour Martin Lipset, eds., *Democracy in Developing Countries: Comparing Experiences with Democracy* (Boulder, CO: Lynn Rienner, 1990).

8   Jyotirindra Das Gupta, "India: Democratic Becoming and Combined Development" in Diamond, Linz, and Lipset, eds., *Politics in Developing Countries* (Bouldese, Co: Lynn Rienner, 1990).

9   William C. Thiesenhussen, "Human Rights, Affirmative Action, and Land Reforms in Latin America," in Wyzan ed., *The Political Economy*, 26.

10   Ibid., 28.

11   Gurr, "Third World Minorities at Risk," 8.

12   S. M. Lipset, "Racial and Ethnic Tensions in the Third World" in W. Scott Thompson, ed., *The Third World: Premises of U.S. Policy* (San Francisco: Institute of Contemporary Studies, 1978), 123–148.

13   Crawford Young, "Patterns of Social Conflict: State, Class, and Ethnicity," *Daedalus* 111 (Spring 1982): 75.

14   Aidan Southall, "The Illusion of Tribe," *Journal of Asian and African Studies* 5 (January-April 1970): 36.

15   Young, "Patterns of Social Conflict," 79.

16   Michael L. Wyzan, "Introduction" in Wyzan, ed., *The Political Economy*; Neil Nevitte and Charles H. Kennedy, "The Analysis of Policies of Ethnic Preference in Developing States" in Nevitte and Kennedy, eds., *Ethnic Preference and Public Policy in Developing States* (Boulder, CO: Westview Press, 1986); Young, "Patterns of Social Conflict"; Donald Horowitz, *Ethnic Groups in Conflict* (Berkeley: University of California Press, 1985).

17   A. E. A. Abdallah, "Ethnic Conflict in Sudan" in Wyzan, ed., *The Political Economy*, 145.

18   Horowtiz, *Ethnic Groups*; Michael L. Wyzan, "Ethnic Relations and the New Economic Policy in Malaysia" in Wyzan, ed., *The Political Economy*.

19   Nevitte and Kennedy, "The Analysis of Policies," 10.

20   Young, "Patterns of Social Conflict." Also see Horowitz, *Ethnic Groups*.

21   Walker Connor, "Ethnonationalism in the First World: The Present in Historical Perspective" in Milton J. Esman, ed., *Ethnic Conflict in the Western World* (Ithaca, NY: Cornell University Press, 1977), 19–45.

22   Krejci and Velimsky, *Ethnic and Political Nations in Europe*, 63.

23   Ibid., 64.

24   Ibid., 69–70.

25   Mark J. Miller, *Foreign Workers in Western Europe: An Emerging Political Force* (New York: Praeger, 1981).

26   Philip N. Jones, "West Germany's Declining Guestworker Population: Spatial Change and Economic Trends in the 1980s," *Regional Studies: Journal of the Regional Studies Association* 24 (Spring 1990): 223–233.

27 Alexander Bennigsen, "Soviet Minority Nationalism in Historical Perspective" in Robert Conquest, ed., *The Last Empire: Nationality and the Soviet Future* (Stanford, CA: Hoover Institution Press, 1986), 133.

28 The 1979 Census identified 104 nationalities. Prior to its dissolution, ethnic Rusians had ceased to form the majority of Soviet Union's population. By one estimate Russians probably did not exceed 48.5 percent of the Soviet population. See Mikhail S. Bernstam, "The Demography of Soviet Ethnic Groups in World Perspective" in Conquest, ed., *The Last Empire*, 320. In the USSR one was required to choose an official nationality at the age of 16, (Nathan Glazer and Daniel P. Moynihan, eds., *Ethnicity: Theory and Experience*, [Cambridge, MA: Harvard University Press, 1975], 17). Because choosing Russian as a nationality had long-lasting economic and political benefits, it is estimated that four million people reidentified themselves as Russians in the census of 1979.

29 Benningsen, "Soviet Minority Nationalism." 136. For more information about the Russian empire's treatment of minorities also see V. Kozlov, *The Peoples of Soviet Union* (Bloomington, IN: Indiana University Press, 1988).

30 Carlos Moore, "Were Marx and Engels Racists?: The Prolet-Aryan Outlook of Marxism," *Berkeley Journal of Sociology* 19 (1974–75): 125–156.

31 Lipset, "Racial and Ethnic Tensions," 138.

32 Quoted in Helen d'Encausse and Stuart Schram, *Marxism and Asia* (London: Allen Lane Penguin Press, 1969), 10.

33 Teodar Shanin, "Ethnicity in the Soviet Union: Analytical Perceptions and Political Strategies," *Comparative Studies in Society and History* 31 (July 1989): 409–424; Martha B. Olcott, "Official Soviet Policy and the 'National Problem'" in Olcott, ed., *The Soviet Multinational State: Readings and Documents* (New York: M. E. Sharpe, Inc., 1990).

34 Shanin, "Ethnicity in the Soviet Union."

35 Ibid., 419.

36 Ibid., 421.

37 Martin O. Heisler, "Ethnicity and Ethnic Relations in the Modern West" in Joseph V. Montville, ed., *Conflict and Peacemaking in Multiethnic Societies* (Toronto: Lexington Books, 1990), 22.

38 Ted Robert Gurr, "Ethnic Warfare and the Changing Priorities of Global Security," *Mediterranean Quarterly: A Journal of Global Issues* 1 (Winter 1990): 82–98.

39 The latter have problems in the offshore Solomon Islands.

40 Connor, "Ethnonationalism in the First World," 330–331.

41 Michael Hecher, *Internal Colonialism: The Celtic Fringe in British National Development 1536–1966* (London: Routledge and Kegan Paul, 1975), 30.

42 Anthony D. Smith, *The Ethnic Revival* (Cambridge, England: Cambridge University Press, 1981); Ken Medurst, "Basques and Basque Nationalism" in Colin H. Williams, ed., *National Separatism* (Vancouver: University of British Columbia Press, 1982). Hechter later recognized

this problem in his theory. See his "Internal Colonialism Revisited" in Tiryakian and Rogowski, eds., *New Nationalisms*, 17–26.

43 Frederick Barth, *Ethnic Groups and Boundaries* (Boston: Little, Brown, 1969).

44 Michael T. Hannan, "The Dynamics of Ethnic Boundaries in Modern States" in J. Meyer and M. T. Hannan, eds., *National Development and the World System* (Chicago: University of Chicago Press, 1979), 253–275.

45 Susan Olzak and Joane Nagel, "Introduction" in Olzak and Nagel, eds., *Competitive Ethnic Relations* (Boston: Academic Press, 1986), 2. (Emphasis in original.)

46 Susan Olzak, "Ethnic Mobilization in Quebec," *Ethnic and Racial Studies* 5 (July 1982): 253–297; Eric Leifer, "Competing Models of Political Mobilization: The Role of Ethnic Ties," *American Journal of Sociology* 87 (July 1981): 23–47; Francois Nielsen, "The Flemish Movement in Belgium After World War II: A Dynamic Analysis," *American Sociological Review* 45 (February 1980): 76–94; Charles Ragin, "Ethnic Political Mobilization: The Welsh Case," *American Sociological Review* 44 (August 1979): 619–635.

47 William R. Beer, "The Social Class of Ethnic Activists in Contemporary France" in Esman, ed., *Ethnic Conflict*; William R. Beer, *The Unexpected Rebellion: Ethnic Activism in Contemporary France* (New York: New York University Press, 1980); Maurice Pinard and Richard Hamilton, "The Parti Quebecois Comes to Power: An Analysis of the 1976 Quebec Election," *Canadian Journal of Political Science* 11 (December 1978): 739–775; Ragin, "Ethnic Political Mobilization"; Nielsen, "The Flemish Movement"; Olzak, "Ethnic Mobilization in Quebec"; S. M. Lipset, "The Revolt Against Modernity" in Per Torsvik, ed., *Mobilization, Center-Periphery Structures and Nation Building* (Bergen, Norway: Universitet Forlaget, 1981), 451–500.

48 Bohdan Krawchenko, *Social Change and National Consciousness in Twentieth-Century Ukraine* (New York: St. Martin's Press, 1985), 184–85, 198.

49 Shanin, "Ethnicity in the Soviet Union," 420.

50 Sarah Belanger and Maurice Pinard, "Ethnic Movements and the Competition Model," *Working Papers on Social Behavior* (Department of Sociology, McGill University, Montreal, 1989), 7.

51 For an attempt to introduce political variables into an Ethnic competition model see François Nielsen, "Structural Conduciveness and Ethnic Mobilization: The Flemish Movement in Belgium" in Olzak and Nagel, eds., *Competitive Ethnic Relations*, 173–198.

52 Alexander J. Motyl, *Will the Non-Russians Rebel? State, Ethnicity, and Stability in the USSR* (Ithaca, NY: Cornell University Press, 1987).

53 Michael Mandelbaum and Christian A. Herter, "The Roots of Nationalism in the Soviet Union," *Council Briefings* (New York: Council on Foreign Relations, no. 21, May 1991), 2.

54 Jaroslav and Velimsky, *Ethnic and Political Nations*, 91.

55 Jurg Steiner, "Power-sharing: Another Swiss 'Export Product'?" in Montville, ed., *Conflict and Peacemaking*, 107–114.

56 Donald Horowtiz, "Ethnic Conflict Management for Policymakers" in Montville, ed., *Conflict and Peacemaking*, 115–130.

57 Donald Horowitz, "Making Moderation Pay: The Comparative Politics of Ethnic Conflict Management" in Montville, ed., *Conflict and Peacemaking*, 465. In presidential elections now the entire country has become one large heterogeneous constituency and "Sinhalese divisions make it likely that the election will be decided on second preferences, including Tamil second preferences." In parliamentary elections the change was made from first-past-the-post in mostly single-member constituencies to a party list system of proportional representation in multimember constituencies. According to Horowitz these changes in the electoral system came too late to foster interethnic accommodation (ibid., 463, 465).

58 Joane Nagel, "The Ethnic Revolution: Emergence of Ethnic Nationalism" in Leo Driedger, ed., *Ethnic Canada: Identities and Inequalities* (Toronto: Copp Clark Pitman, 1987), 40.

59 Daniel Bell, "Ethnicity and Social Change" in N. Glazer and D. P. Moynihan, eds., *Ethnicity: Theory and Experience* (Cambridge, MA: Harvard University Press, 1975), 141–166; Anthony Smith, "The Diffusion of Nationalism: Some Historical and Sociological Perspectives," *British Journal of Sociology* 29 (June 1978): 234–48; Anthony Smith, *The Ethnic Revival* (Cambridge, England: Cambridge University Press, 1981); Paul R. Brass, *Ethnic Groups and the State* (Totawa, NJ: Barnes and Noble Books, 1985); Young, "Patterns of Social Conflict."

60 Cynthia Enloe, "The Growth of the State and Ethnic Mobilization: The American Experience," *Ethnic and Racial Studies* 4 (April 1981): 123–36; Joane Nagel, "The Political Construction of Ethnicity," in Olzak and Nagel, eds., *Competitive Ethnic Relations*, 93–112.

61 Rita Jalali, "Preferential Policies and The Movement of The Disadvantaged: The Case of the scheduled Caste in India," *Ethnic and Racial Studies* 16 (June 1993): 95–121.

62 Felix and Padilla, "Latino Ethnicity in the City of Chicago" in Olzak and Nagel, eds., *Competitive Ethnic Relations*, 153–172.

63 Enloe, "The Growth of the State," 123–136; Espiritu, "The Census and Ethnic Enumeration: Playing the Numbers Game" (Paper presented at the 84th Annual Meeting of the American Sociological Association, San Francisco, 9–13 August 1989).

64 William Petersen, "Politics and the Measurement of Ethnicity" in William Alonso and Paul Starr, eds., *The Politics of Numbers* (New York: Russell Sage Foundation, 1986), 187–234.

65 David D. Laitin, "Hegemony and Religious Conflict" in Peter Evans, D. Rueschemeyer, and Theda Skocpol, eds., *Bringing the State Back In* (New York: Cambridge University Press, 1985), 285–316; Brass, *Ethnic Groups and the State*.

66 Cynthia Enloe, "Police and Military in the Resolution of Ethnic Conflict," *The Annals of the American Academy of Political and Social Science* 433 (1977): 137; also see W. L. Young, *Minorities and the Military: A Cross-National Study in World Perspective*, (Madison: University of Wisconsin Press, 1982).

67   For example, the decision of the Indian government to have elections in 1983 changed the Assamese movement from a language-based unity that was supposed to be shared by Hindu and Muslim members of the same speech community to a movement that excluded many Muslim speakers of the language on the grounds that they were illegal immigrants from neighboring Bangladesh. (See Das Gupta, "India; Democratic Becoming and Combined Development," 241). In Eritrea, as Ted Gurr notes, "nearly three decades of rebellion and repression have by now formed a viable sense of national identity that cuts across historically divisive lines of tribal, linguistic, and Christian-Muslim cleavage." See his "Ethnic Warfare," 86.

68   The other three basic elements of consociational democracy according to Lijphart are "(1) the mutual veto or 'concurrent majority rule,' which serves as an additional protection of vital minority interests, (2) proportionality as the principal standard of political representation, civil service appointment, and allocation of public funds, and (3) a high degree of autonomy for each segment to run its own internal affairs." Arend Lijphart, *Democracy in Plural Societies: A Comparative Exploration* (New Haven: Yale University Press, 1977), 25.

69   Horowitz, "Ethnic Conflict Management," 115–130.

70   David M. Lipset, "Papua New Guinea: the Melanisian Ethic and the Spirit of Capitalism" in Larry Diamond, J. Linz, and S. M. Lipset, eds., *Democracy in Developing Countries: Asia* III (Boulder, CO: Lynne Rienner, 1989), 383–422.

71   Horowitz, *Ethnic Groups in Conflict*; Larry Diamond, "Nigeria: Pluralism, Statism, and the Struggles for Democracy" in Diamond, Linz, and Lipset, eds., *Democracy in Developing Countries: Africa* II (Boulder, CO: Lynne Rienner, 1988), 65.

72   Myron Weiner, *The Indian Paradox* (Newbury Park, CA: Sage Publications, 1989), 36.

73   Horowitz, "Making Moderation Pay."

74   Mihajlo Mihajlov, "Can Yugoslavia Survive," *Journal of Democracy* 2 (Spring 1991): 90.

75   In two out of fifteen republics the nationals form less than 50 percent of the population; in Kazakstan the nationals are 36 percent and in Kirghizia they form 48 percent.

76   For conflict with Abkazians see Ernest Gellner, "Ethnicity and Faith in Eastern Europe," *Daedalus* 119 (Winter 1990): 286.

77   *A Map of Ethnicity and Political Boundaries in the Soviet Union* (Washington, DC: Office of the Geographer, US Department of State, 1990).

78   Mihajlov, "Can Yugoslavia Survive?" 84.

79   For Malaysia see Horowitz, *Ethnic Groups in Conflict*. Also see Milton Esman, "Ethnic Politics and Economic Power," *Comparative Politics* 19 (July 1987): 395–418. For India see Jalali, "Preferential Policies and the Movement of the Disadvantaged." For the United States see Lawrence Fuchs, *The American Kaleidoscope: Race, Ethnicity and the Civic Culture* (Middletown, CT: Wesleyan University Press, 1990).

80   Horowitz's comparative study of such policies in developing countries concludes that in the short run preferential policies tend to accentuate ethnic conflict (see his *Ethnic Groups in Conflict*). On the other hand, Fuchs in a book that examines race relations in the United States reports that after several years of affirmative action programs "whites who worked directly with blacks were significantly freer of prejudice than those who did not. Overall, the percentage of whites who indicated strong personal antagonisms to having black neighbors dropped from 47 to 14 between 1963 and 1978, and the percentage of those who said they were either already living in proximity to black neighbors or would have no objection to doing so rose from 36 to 60 percent." See Fuchs, *The American Kaleidoscope*, 444. Also see Seymour Martin Lipset, "Equal Chances Versus Equal Results," *The Annals of the American Academy of Political and Social Science* 523 (September 1992): 63–74.

81   Larry Diamond, Juan J. Linz, and Seymour Martin Lipset, *Democracy in Developing Countries: Persistence, Failure, and Renewal* (Boulder, CO: Lynn Rienner, forthcoming).

82   Masipula Sithole, "Zimbabwe: In Search of a Stable Democracy" in Diamond, Linz, and Lipset, eds., *Democracy in Developing Countries: Africa*, 243.

83   Diamond, "Nigeria" in Diamond, Linz, and Lipset, eds., *Democracy in Developing Countries: Africa*. Ethnic homogeneity does not necessarily produce democratic societies. Countries like North Korea and Haiti have homogenous populations and yet were nondemocratic.

84   Diamond, Linz, and Lipset, eds., *Politics in Developing Countries*, 29.

85   Heisler, "Ethnicity and Ethnic Relations," 21–52.0

86   John Lewis Gaddis, "Toward the Post-Cold War World," *Foreign Affairs* 70 (Spring 1991): 110.

87   Jim Hoagland, "What Price Unity?" *Washington Post*, 14 May 1991.

88   Hurst Hannum, *Autonomy, Sovereignty, and Self-Determination: The Accommodation of Conflicting Rights* (Philadelphia: University of Pennsylvania Press, 1990), 52. The author has reprinted the quote from L. C. Green, "Protection of Minorities in the League of Nations and the United Nations" in Allan Gotlieb, ed., *Human Rights, Federalism and Minorities* (Toronto: Canadian Institute of International Affairs, 1970), 193.

14 Ethnic Nationalism: Politics, Ideology, and the World Order

Joane Nagel

INTRODUCTION

The twentieth century has taught us to respect the power and durability of ethnic differences, that is, divisions among populations according to language, religion, culture, national origin, even appearance. Researchers have catalogued an enormous amount of ethnic conflict among the world's nearly 200 states to such an extent that ethnic antagonism, ethnic violence, and ethnic mobilization may comprise the one common ground shared by the world's diverse population of independent countries.

Perhaps most notable about the ubiquity of ethnic conflict is the diversity of settings in which it occurs. Ethnic conflict and particularly ethnic political claimsmaking, occur around the world in industrial as well as in developing states, in one-party and in multi-party systems, posing challenges to civilian and to military governments, taxing the resources of both the rich and the poor.

The widespread prevalence of ethnic conflict suggests that systemic processes are at work, processes that span national borders and that produce the impetus to ethnic mobilization in many states. The question arises: What is it about the modern world system, particularly since the close of the Second World War, that has produced ever increasing numbers of ethnic nationalist movements?[1] Put another way, the question becomes: What could there possibly be in common among such diverse movements as the Kurdish movements in Iraq, Iran, and Turkey; the Basque and Catalan movements in Spain; the conflict in northern Ireland; the Angolan civil war; Scottish nationalism; the Polisario movement in the Western Sahara; the Lithuanian independence movement; the Puerto Rican nationalist movement; Quebec nationalism; the Lebanese civil war; or the Eritrean independence movement, to mention but a few?

The answers presented here rest on the premise that ethnic nationalism occurs within an international context, and that the extent and outcome of ethnic nationalist movements depend on the stance of powerful international actors as well as the position taken by the symbolic institutions of the world system (e.g., the United Nations). Where ethnic movements are supported by world system forces, they will endure and sometimes succeed. Where such movements are not externally supported and legitimated, they will languish and fail.

There are two common factors which unite the many instances of ethnic mobilization cited above, and both are properties of the world system: ideology and politics. Ideology refers to the international ideological system that supports the global order. This legitimating ideational system simultaneously upholds *and* challenges the current configuration of the world state system. Politics refers to political competition at two levels, local political competition for self-rule and politically-controlled resources (of lesser interest here), and international political competition until quite recently organized into an East-West struggle for global alignment. Ethnic conflict and ethnic nationalism arise out of both forms of competition – national and international.

The next sections discuss the ideological and political competitive forces that continue to fuel both historical ethnic conflicts as well as a new wave of ethnic nationalism following the break up of the Eastern Bloc. The paper concludes with a discussion of the implications of the international realignment currently underway and the ongoing pressures for decentralization and devolution in the Soviet Union.

THE NATIONALIST-SUBNATIONALIST DIALECTIC

Despite the certain truth contained in the expression, "All politics is local," too myopic a view of ethnic nationalism produces a reductionist understanding of a phenomenon whose worldwide occurrence might better be understood from a more cosmopolitan vantage point. The bulk of literature on ethnic nationalism focuses on particular movements and the unique historical, economic, political, and cultural circumstances that led to their development (see Horowitz, 1985). However, recent world history is clearly marked by waves of ethnic nationalism, particularly during the period since the end of the Second World War.[2]

The first wave of ethnic nationalism began right after the war ended and occurred in the European colonies, mainly in Africa and Asia. Strictly speaking, these were instances of nationalism, though in most cases they represented a form of *new* nationalism not based on historical identities. This wave of nationalism was mainly organized according to colonial designations, such as Nigerian nationalism, Ghanian nationalism, Sri Lankan nationalism, and Indian nationalism (Melson and Wolpe, 1971: Illife, 1979; Schermerhorn, 1978).

Most of these nationalist movements were comprised of ethnically quite diverse sub-populations. The constitution of these nationalist movements into sovereign states led to the second wave of sub-nationalist movements which began not long after independence in many of the new states, and extended throughout the 1960s and 1970s; many continuing into the 1980s. These included the Muslim secession from India that created Pakistan, the Bengali secession from Pakistan that created Bangladesh, the unsuccessful Biafran secession from Nigeria, ethnic conflict in Somalia, Ethiopia, Indonesia, India, Sri Lanka, Malaysia, Sudan, Angola, Mozambique, and many more (see Young, 1976; and Horowitz, 1985).

Ethnic nationalism, particularly during this second wave, was not limited to former colonies but occurred in the more established states of Europe and the Middle East as well: the Kurdish conflicts in Iraq, Iran, Turkey, the escalation of violence in Northern Ireland, nationalist movements in Canada, Britain, France, Spain, and the resurgence of ethnic identity in the United States.

The most recent, third wave of ethnic nationalism has occurred in the last few years, particularly since November 1989, when the Berlin Wall was breached and the Soviet Union reversed its interventionist stance toward Eastern Europe, freeing Eastern European states to embark on a course of self-determination. The overthrow of Communist governments in Eastern Europe was simultaneously accompanied by demands for self-rule and independence among the Soviet republics and among minority populations in Eastern European states, e.g., Hungarians in Romania and Czechoslovakia, and Serbs, Croats, and Slovenes in Yugoslavia.

These waves of ethnic nationalism can be tied to both constant and shifting dimensions of the international state system. The constant factor is two-part. The first part is ideological, comprising the principles of sovereignty, representative government, and self-determination. The second constant factor promoting ethnic nationalism is geopolitical, namely, the East-West political and economic competition which dominated the world system from the end of the Second World War until only recently.

The shifting factor contributing to these waves of ethnic nationalism might best be characterized as "hiccups in hegemony" – moments when the major powers shifted their grasp on land and labor, and reorganized the international system. There have been two such hiccups during the past half-century. Both occurred as colonial empires dissolved. Both took the form of state-making windows which opened as empires collapsed. The first such state-making window opened just after the Second World War, in the late 1940s, when European colonial territories mobilized for independence and were recognized by the international system as sovereign states. The second state-making window, I believe, is opening now, as the Soviet empire reconstitutes itself.

There is an interesting dialectic that these state-making interregna set into motion. The nationalist movements which ascended to power to head the independent states created by the first state-making window became targets of sub-nationalist movements organized by the ethnic minorities enclosed within the boundaries of the new states. This process is quite likely to recur during the next decade, as the nationalist movements currently achieving sovereign independence face separatist challenges from sub-national subject populations.

The events in the Soviet republic of Azerbaijan beginning in 1990, involving ethnic conflicts between the Armenian minority and the Azeri majority, reflect this dialect. The conflict in Yugoslavia between the Serbian-controlled national army and various ethno-nationalist independence movements in Croatia and Bosnia represents another instance of this process. While Yugoslavia was not directly colonized by the Soviet Union, the country was loosened from several decades of Soviet control in the late 1980s. The Balkanization underway there illustrates the dialectic of nationalism (against Soviet domination) followed by sub-nationalism (against Serbian domination).

The dialectic of nationalism arises out of the combination of interests and ideology that props up the world state system. The next two sections examine the role of these two factors in ethnic nationalism and ethnic conflict.

IDEOLOGICAL ORIGINS OF ETHNIC NATIONALISM

In 1861, John Stuart Mill wrote the following in his work, *Representative Government*:

Where the sentiment of nationality exists in any force, there is a
prima facie case for uniting all members of the nationality under the
same government, and a government to themselves apart. This is
merely saying that the question of government ought to be decided
by the governed. One hardly knows what any division of the human
race should be free to do, if not to determine with which of the
various collective bodies of human beings they choose to associate
themselves   (Mill, 1955).

This strikingly current pronouncement echoes from the last century
– the ideational precursor to the twentieth century principle of self-
determination. It joins complementary notions of territorial sovereignty, representative government, and rule-by-consent to form the
philosophical foundations of the modern state system. This system of
organizing the world's land and population into sovereign states has
grown rapidly during the last century, expanding from around 50
states in 1900, to 75 on the eve of World War II, and to 160 before
the disintegration of the Soviet Union (Crawford, 1979), to nearly 200
today.

For the majority of the new states established since 1945, the march
toward independence stepped to the rhythm of anti-colonial nationalism. And while there was great variation in the length and difficulty
of the various independence struggles, all rallied around the banner of
self-determination and home rule. However, the exuberance of independence was short-lived in many states as the nationalist consensus
began to disintegrate. The harmony of interests that combined to
form various nationalist movements fractured into a cacophony of
sub-national challenges to new state boundaries. And as the new
states set about the business of administering independence, the
undercurrent of cultural and regional interests once submerged in
the hopes and rhetoric of independence, increased in volume and
intensity. One voice became many and the fictive unity of the new
nationalism was shattered.

The shift from nationalism to sub-nationalism should not have been
surprising. The relevance of the principles that launched the new
states had not been lost on the linguistic, cultural, and religious
minorities who found themselves enclosed within newly-erected state
boundaries. Demands for recognition, autonomy, and sovereignty re-
sounded across Asia and Africa: Biafra, Bangladesh, Kurdistan, Eritrea,
South Molucca, and Tamil Nadu. The forces of self-determination
and self-rule once wielded by nationalist alloys forged in the fires of

common opposition, had come full circle and turned inward to confront their former champions, many of whom were now the political elites of the new states.

Thus, the same principles which fashioned out of European colonialism many Third World independent states, became the platform upon which challenges to those state boundaries were mounted. Nationalism against colonialism became sub-nationalism against the new states. This confrontation between nationalism and ethnic sub-nationalism was a predictable outcome clearly implied in anti-colonialist argumentation. In its articulation, the self-determination recipe for a new world order contained deadly ingredients. United Nations Resolution 1514 declared:

> The subjection of peoples to alien subjugation, domination, and exploitation constitutes a denial of fundamental human rights ... All people have the right to self-determination; ... any attempt aimed at the partial or total disruption of the national unity and territorial integrity of a country is incompatible with the purposes and principles of the Charter of the United Nations
>
> (Emerson 1964, pp. 28–29).

We see here two principles in opposition: self-determination and national unity. In 1960, it might have seemed reasonable for the new nationalists to hold these two positions simultaneously when advocating self-determination in opposition to colonial rule. However, balance between the sanctity of state boundaries and the right of peoples to rule themselves became increasingly precarious *within* the borders of the new states.

In fact, the rush to self-rule which produced the largest proliferation of sovereign states in world history, inevitably lay bare the opposing premises upon which rested the edifice of modern state power. Thus, the independent government – in so many states, structural evidence of liberation from alien domination – came to be seen by many under its rule as a mechanism of internal subjugation. In response to sub-national unrest, governments, born of anti-colonial nationalism, became principled advocates of sovereignty and territoriality.

Thus, when the government of Somalia objected to the 1960 design for Somali independence which had resulted in the partition of the Somali nomadic population into three states (Somalia, Ethiopia, Kenya), the Kenyan delegation to the 1960 Addis Ababa African Summit Conference, asserted the following:

The principle of self-determination has relevance where *Foreign Domination* is the issue. It has no relevance where the issue is territorial disintegration by dissident citizens (Emerson 1964, pp. 35–36).

While this position was rather oddly taken by a former subject state, the Kenyan delegation was by no means unique in such advocacy. The resiliency of the international system of state boundaries in the face of continuous pressures for dissolution confirms the popularity of the Kenyan position and underlines the strength of the forces of unity both within and without sovereign states.

Nonetheless, at particular moments in history, the tensions imbedded in the global ideology of sovereignty and self-determination cannot be contained. The concepts are both compelling and contradictory. On the one hand, who can argue against a people's right to self-determination? Thus, self-determination, sovereignty, and representative government are unassailable principles upon which to build a modern state. On the other hand, these same principles of state-building provide an equally sturdy platform from which to launch an attack on the integrity of modern states. After all, who can argue against a state-enclosed minority's right to self-determination?

INTERNATIONAL COMPETITION AND ETHNIC NATIONALISM

Given the tension inherent in the current world system-legitimating ideology, the impetus to ethnic nationalism is not surprising. This ideological impetus has flourished in the post-Second World War geopolitical environment. The Cold War fueled ethnic nationalism in many countries around the world. East-West competition for markets, resources, and geopolitical dominance led the superpowers and their allies to interfere and intervene in numerous states during the last half-century. Given the universal presence of dissident minorities in the world's states, this international meddling often provided support for ethnic conflict and ethnic nationalist mobilization.

The United States and its allies and the Soviet Union and its allies exploited ethnic antagonisms and supported ethnic minorities for a variety of purposes: to destabilize regimes, to install regimes, and to gain advantages in war. The cases abound: the Atlantic Coast of Nicaragua, with its Afro-Indian and Indian minorities, the best known case: the Miskito Indians (Dozier 1985; Hale 1987); the indigenous mountain peoples of Indochina, the best-known case: the Hmong of Laos (Stockwell 1978); the Kurds in Iraq, and to a lesser extent in Turkey and Iran (Gunter 1989; Malek 1989); various ethno-political contenders for state power in Africa and Latin America, most notably in Nicaragua and El Salvador and in Angola and Mozambique. In all of these cases, American-Soviet competition led to arms transfers, material support, promises of support in international forums, aid by proxies or allies such as Cuba and South Africa, and, in some cases, direct military intervention.

The contest among industrial states, particularly the superpowers, to complete a network of international alliances in such a way as to maximize the number and wealth of allies and trading partners, tremendously enriched and inflated ethnic movements, particularly in the Third World. The injection of external resources into domestic ethnic conflicts resulted in larger, better organized, and more violent ethnic movements. The consequences for ethnic movements of international involvement were a lengthening and escalating of conflict, often resulting in civil wars, and a decreased likelihood of negotiated settlements.

The international arms trade, in which the United States currently holds the distinction of being the world's largest exporter (Sivard 1991), is a good example of how international competition translated itself into the militarization of ethnic movements. Arms exports to the Third World contributed to the level of violence in domestic, often ethnic, conflicts, resulting, in an escalation of many conflicts and a reduced likelihood of negotiated settlements (Mullins 1987; Neuman 1985).

Not all ethnic movements have attracted international support, however. Third World movements are much more likely targets due to their economic dependence, and their officially non-aligned status which makes them open arenas for major power competition. Nonetheless, the support of ethnic movements in the Third World has combined with the international ideology favoring ethnic self-determination, to create a climate which legitimates ethnic nationalism in all states, First, Second, or Third World.

GLOBAL REALIGNMENT AND ETHNIC NATIONALISM

In light of the impact on ethnic nationalism of international competition organized historically along East-West lines, the recent decline of Soviet-American competition raises an interesting and important question: Does the new Soviet-American cooperation in international affairs mean a decline in ethnic nationalism and ethnic conflict around the world?

Recent shifts in the international balance of power favoring unchallenged American military dominance appear to have mixed results for externally-driven ethnic conflict. On the one hand, the decline of American-Soviet military competition makes proxy intervention and the arming of opposing contenders less likely, and, thus, suggests a reduced level of domestic ethnic conflict. An example of this can be found in Angola. Since the 1970s, ethnically aligned conflict in Angola has been supported both by the United States (supporting ethnic opposition movements, most notably Jonas Savimbi's UNITA), and by the Soviet Union (supporting the ruling MPLA Party), as well as involvement by a number of outside powers including Cuba, China, and South Africa (Marcum 1978, 1986, 1989; David 1985; Clute 1989). The conflict has been long, violent, and inconclusive. Only when the United States and the Soviet Union agreed to stop supporting the various sides was a negotiated end to the conflict possible. In May 1991, UNITA and the MPLA signed a peace accord and the last Cuban troops departed from Angola. Renewed conflict among Angolan Contendus for power following the 1992 elections reflects more a "Cold War hangover" of arms and animosities, than an influx of international support for opposing sides.

While Angola points the path toward one set of possible outcomes for ethnic nationalism and ethnic conflict, the path revealed by the case of Iraq leads in quite a different direction.[3] Here, the decline in American-Soviet competition has produced a situation where American military dominance and interventionism is unchallenged. The United States has had a long history of supporting Kurdish nationalism in Iraq, mainly to destabilize the Soviet-aligned Iraqi government (Malek 1989; Mark 1985; Olson 1989). The decline in Soviet-American competition has not resulted in a quelling of Iraqi-Kurdish tension. In fact, just the opposite has occurred. As a result of the 1991 American-orchestrated Gulf War, the United States has moved from being an external sponsor of ethnic nationalism to being more directly entangled in the Kurdish-Iraqi conflict. Given the ubiquity of ethnic nationalism, continued American interventionism carries with it the potential to increase ethnic rebellions and autonomy or secessionist conflict. The precedent set with the Kurds may strongly influence the shape and extent of ethnic nationalist claims throughout the Third World.

Despite American involvement in Iraq's Kurdish problem, American and international reluctance to establish an independent Kurdish or Palestinian or Eritrean homeland in order to reduce ethnic conflict, reveals the continued sanctity of the world state system. The disintegration of the Soviet Union and the wave of independence declarations and international recognitions following the August 1991 attempted Soviet coup, suggests some international willingness to redraw the world map, at least in Eastern Europe.

The prospects for ethnic independence movements outside the former sphere of Soviet influence remain unclear. Movements for autonomy or federation may fit better into the current international blueprint for rule than do movements of secession. However, the new global realaignment underway following the breakup of the Soviet empire is too recent and too dynamic to determine its consequences for the future shape of the entire world map.

CONCLUSION

The ambivalency of industrial states to violate the principles of sovereignty and territorial integrity in favor of ethnic self-determination could be seen in the case of the internal war in the former state of Yugoslavia. Serbian military opposition in the 1990s to the independence movements of various ethnic and regional minorities resulted in massive destruction, dislocation, and starvation in the secessionist republics. European Community and American failure to respond to the war and its consequences reflected the problematic definition of the principles upon which the "new world order" was to rest: sovereignty or self-determination.[4]

The collapse of European colonialism after the Second World War opened a window of opportunity for state creation. The result was the emergence of the new status of Africa and Asia-colonies and ruled territories transformed into sovereign states. The events which began in November 1989, with the fall of the Berlin Wall, appear to represent the beginning of another state-making era. Whether the entire world map will be revised, or only the boundaries of the former Soviet-controlled states and territories, remains to be seen. However, the forces of nationalism set loose upon the landscape of the former Soviet empire will not be easily subdued. The tensions and contradictions of the world state system remain firmly in place despite changes in its configuration.

NOTES

1. Ethnic nationalism refers to subnational movements for autonomy or independence organized along linguistic, religious, or cultural lines. Ethnic nationalism can be seen as one form of ethnic mobilization, one strategy pursued by ethnic groups as they seek to improve their minority status situation. Other forms of ethnic mobilization include ethnic rights movements, movements for autonomy, interethnic conflict, and civil war (see Connor 1991, for a discussion of nations and nationalism).

2   There was a wave of nationalist mobilizations following the end of the first World War as well (see Hohsbawm 1990).

3. See Nagel and Whorton (1992) for further discussion of these two cases.

4. American inaction in Yugoslavia stands in clear contrast to its eager intervention in Kuwait after Iraq's 1990 invasion. The difference appears to reside in the calculation of interests as articulated by Secretary of State Howard Baker:

    We're looking at the first time since the 1930s that the United States deliberately stayed out of a European conflict . . . our vital interests are not what they used to be (Binder 1992, p. A4).

REFERENCES

BINDER, David 1992 "The Yugoslav Crisis: Why U.S. is Bearing Down on Belgrade." *New York Times*, May 27: A4.

CLUTE, Robert E. 1989 "The American-Soviet Confrontation in Africa: Its Impact on the Politics of Africa." *Journal of Asian and African Studies* 24: 159–69.

CONNOR, Walker 1991 "When is a Nation?" *Ethnic and Racial Studies* 13 (1, January): 92–103.

CRAWFORD, James 1979 *The Creation of States in International Law*, Oxford: Clarendon Press.

DAVID, Steven R. 1985 "The Use of Proxy Forces by Major Powers in the Third World." p. 199–226 in S. G. Neuman and R. E. Harkavy (eds.), *The Lessons of Recent Wars in the Third World*, Volume II. Lexington, MA: Lexington Books.

DOZIER, Graig 1985 *Vicaragua's Mosquito Shore*: Birmingham: University of Alabama Press.

EMERSON, Rupert 1964 *Self-Determination Revisited in an Era of Decolonization*. Cambridge: Harvard University Press.

GUNTER, Michael 1989 "The Kurdish Problem in Turkey." *Middle East Journal* 42 3, Summer; 389–406.

HALE, Charles 1987 "Institutional Struggle, Conflict, and Reconciliation: Miskitu Indians and the Nicaraguan State, (1979–1985)". p. 101–128 in *Ethnic Groups and the Nation State: The Case of the Atlantic Coast in Nicaragua*. Stockholm: University of Stockholm, Department of Social Anthropology, CIDCA/Development Study Unit.

HOBSBAWM, Eric 1990 *Nations and Nationalism since 1780*. London: Cambridge University Press.

HOROWITZ, Donald 1985 *Ethnic Groups in Conflict*. Berkeley: University of California Press.

ILLIFE, John 1979 *A Modern History of Tanganyika*. Cambridge: Cambridge University Press.

MALEK, Mohammed H. 1989 "Kurdistan and the Middle East Conflict." *New Left Review* (May/June): 79–94.

MARCUM, John A. 1978 *The Angolan Revolution, Volume 2: Exile Politics and Guerrilla Warfare, 1962–1976*. Cambridge: MIT Press.

—— 1986 "Bipolar Dependency: The People's Republic of Angola." In M. Clough (ed.), *Reassessing the Soviet Challenge in Africa*. Berkeley: Institute of International Studies.

—— 1989 "The People's Republic of Angola: A Radical Vision Frustrated." p. 67–83 in E. J. Keller and D. Rothchild eds., *Afro-Marxist Regimes: Ideology and Public Policy*. Boulder: Lynne Rienner Publications.

MARR, Phoebe 1985 *The Modern History of Iraq*. Boulder, CO: Westview.

MELSON, Robert, and Howard WOLPE 1971 *Nigena: Modernization and the Politics of Communalism*. East Lansing: Michigan State University Press.

MILL, John Stuart 1955 *Representative Government*, Chicago: Encyclopedia Press.

MULLINS, A. F., Jr. 1987 *Born Arming Development and Military Power in New States*, Stanford: Stanford University Press.

NAGEL, Joane, and Brad WHORTON 1992 "Ethnic Conflict and the World System: International Competition in Iraq (1961–1991) and Angola (1974–1991)" *Journal of Political and Military Sociology* 20 (1): 1–35.

NEUMAN, Stephanie G. 1985 "The Role of Military Assistance in Recent Wars." p. 115–149 in S. G. Neuman and R. E. Harkavy (eds.), *The Lessons of Recent Wars in the Third World, Volume II*. Lexington, MA: Lexington Books.

OLSON, Robert W. 1989 *The Emergence of Kurdish Nationalism*. Austin: University of Texas Press.

SCHERMERHORN, Richard A. 1978 *Ethnic Plurality in India*. Tusion: University of Arizona Press.

SIVARD Ruth L. 1991 *World Military and Social Expenditures, 1991*. Washington, DC: World Priorities.

STOCKWELL, John 1978 *In Search of Enemies: A CIA Story*. New York: Norton.

YOUNG, Crawford 1976 *The Politics of Cultural Pluralism*. Madison: University of Wisconsin Press.

15 Nationalism Reborn
Robert Wistrich

The demise of Communism and the fall of the Iron Curtain in 1989 presented Europe with a golden opportunity to unite and become a great stabilizing force in the world today. Across the Continent, from East to West, a new consensus had emerged in favor of democracy, pluralism, human rights and the rule of law. For a brief, euphoric moment there was a high tide in favor of the idea of European integration, the hope that a common European purpose might yet assert itself beyond the selfish interests of the individual nation-states. With the collapse of the Berlin Wall, the common ideals of peace, security, freedom, and prosperity suddenly seemed within reach of millions in the eastern half of the Continent who had been denied this promise. Yet only four years later, the idea of Europe is floundering in both East and West.

Let me quote the perceptive words of Czechoslovakia's President Vaclav Havel, in an address to the Council of Europe:

> Europe today lacks an ethos; it lacks imagination, it lacks generosity, it lacks the ability to see beyond the horizon of its own particular interests, be they partisan or otherwise, and to resist the pressure from various lobbying groups. There is no real identification in Europe with the meaning and purpose of integration.

Instead of a new dawn, we are seeing before our eyes how in the whole of the former Yugoslavia an internationally recognized multinational state has been subdivided according to the dictates of fanatical warlords. To quote Haval again: "We talk and talk, we drown in compromises, we redraw the maps, we read the lips of the ethnic cleansers, and, with increasingly serious consequences, we forget the fundamental values upon which we would like to shape the future of our continent." In its first great test since the end of the Cold War, Europe seems not only to have failed miserably but to be opening its back door to the demons of nationalist collectivism.

A new specter is haunting not only former Yugoslavia but all of post-totalitarian Europe: the sanctification of the "ethnically pure state." The quest for self-determination, in itself a noble and irreproachable ideal, is beginning to threaten the integrity of individual

356

states, the inviolability of their borders and even the validity of all post-war treaties. The bloody ethnic, tribal, and religious warfare in Georgia, Armenia, Azerbaijan, the Balkans, and Northern Ireland has produced the nightmare of controlling ethnic groups and aggressive majorities or minorities seeking to eliminate other groups.

The new ethnic nationalism proclaims, as in ex-Yugoslavia, that people are born with ethnic identities which they can never change – you are a Serb, a Croat, or an Albanian because your father was one before you. This primary identity is a reaction to the leveling and homogenizing tendencies of modernity and, in the case of ex-Communist states, a reaction against the totalitarian experience. But the erasure of the Soviet past has not brought with it a true sense of unity, freedom, or the mutual recognition of self-determination by the ethnically mixed populations of Eastern or Southeastern Europe. We are witnessing there, at one and the same time, a post-Communist predicament and a throwback to the pre-war past, whether in the Baltic States, Transcaucasia, Slovakia, Romania, Hungary or ex-Yugoslavia; a return to history, against a modern backdrop of decentralization and fragmentation, instead of against the monstrously tyrannical unity and centralization which characterized the Fascist and Communist experiments.

Today, in the former Soviet Russian Empire, in the Balkans and Eastern Europe, neither military force, state terror, nor Marxist-Leninist ideology can hold the center. What has happened since 1989 recalls in many ways the centrifugal forces that disintegrated four empires in 1918 – that of the Romanovs in Tsarist Russia, the Ottoman Turks in the Middle East, the Hapsburg dynasty in Austria-Hungary, and the Hohenzollerns in Imperial Germany.

It was war and revolution which brought down these multi-ethnic empires in the maelstrom events of 1917–18. In the name of national self-determination, East-Central Europe after 1918 was to be made safe for Western-style democracy. But the new map of Europe which restored Poland, reduced Germany, Austria and Hungary, enlarged Romania, and created new states in the Baltic region, Czechoslovakia and Yugoslavia, did not result in peace. The multinational empires became multi-ethnic states masquerading as homogeneous nation-states, discriminating against their ethnic minorities. Worse still, they rapidly became, with the exception of Czechoslovakia, authoritarian and quasi-fascist states. Their fate was to be sandwiched between a revanchist Germany – embittered by the Versailles Treaty – and a Communist Russia driven by a messianic ideology of revolutionary expansion. Neither Britain nor France was strong enough in the interwar period to guarantee the independence of Eastern Europe against the pressure of such powerful neighbors, themselves in the grip of Nazism and Stalinism.

Since 1989, as East-Central Europe has struggled painfully to make the transition to market capitalism and pluralist democracy, the echoes of this past still haunt the present. Just as the fiction of *Homo Sovieticus* has given way in the ex-USSR to the primary ethnic identities of Russians, Ukrainians, Balts, Georgians or Armenians, so too, the Yugoslav identity has been erased in favor of Croat or Serb nationality.

Ex-Czechoslovakia has split into Czech and Slovak republics, while in Slovakia itself there has been a revival of the interwar intolerance towards Hungarians, Gypsies, and Jews. There have been moves to rehabilitate its wartime clerico-fascist leader, Monsignor Tiso, who collaborated with the Germans in the genocide of Slovakia's Jewish population. Similarly, in Romania, there is a renewed cult of the wartime fascist dictator and Hitler ally, Marshal Antonescu, and to some extent of the prewar Iron Guard, whose mystical, religious nationalism had such devastating consequences. The downfall of the Communist dictator Ceaucescu has not prevented Romania from pursuing the harassment of Hungarians in Transylvania, of the large Gypsy minority, or from renewing the anti-Semitic traditions of the interwar period. As in other East European countries, Jews find themselves retrospectively scapegoated by the nationalist press for all the evils of post-war Communist misrule. The xenophobic, populist discourse of the authoritarian nationalists with its paranoid hatred of ethnic minorities, Gypsies (surely, the pariah people of Eastern Europe today), and Jews is the darker face of the return to the past. In countries like Romania, Slovakia, and Croatia it has been further nourished by the return of virulently anti-Communist exiles from the Western diasporas, where their pre-war ideology remained frozen in a strangely distorted time-warp. Even the more economically successful, nationally homogeneous and self-confident nations like Poland and Hungary are not free of this misplaced nostalgia for an authoritarian, ethnocentric nationalism.

The reassertion of national consciousness in East-Central or Southeastern Europe is not surprising when set against the effects of four decades of virtual slavery and an economic deprivation whose end is not yet in sight. The Communist repression of the national past and of cherished religious symbols was bound to produce some kind of backlash, as was the disappointment of exaggerated expectations that there would be a rapid rise in the standard of living. But Western and Central Europe are also experiencing, from a very different starting-point, the re-emergence of the politics of an authoritarian right. While incomparably more affluent, Western societies are far from basking in the prosperous, contented boredom imagined by visionaries of a global Common Market. The effects of recession, of significantly high unemployment and homelessness, of urban decay and rootlessness, not to mention a growing anomie and moral confusion, have created a new reservoir for the illiberal politics of the radical right. Disaffection with established parties and elected politicians is rife, calling into question the liberal democratic consensus and encouraging a powerful challenge from those national-populist movements which voice the discontent from below. The Front National of Jean-Marie Le Pen in France, the Republikaner in Germany, the increasingly successful Freedom Party in Austria under the photogenic Jörg Haider, the Lombard League and the neo-fascists in the Italian government, and the Vlaams Blok in Belgium all express in their different ways the present crisis of confidence. While in Russia, the ultra-nationalism of Vladimir Zhirinovsky casts a huge shadow over that country's future.

The most visible target of the new populist politics has been the influx of immigrants and asylum-seekers from the Third World, or more recently from Eastern and Southeast Europe, into the European community. Almost every Western industrial society in the past two decades has to some extent become multi-ethnic, with significant minority communities in most of its major cities. This has exacerbated fears and anxieties about law and order, jobs, housing and education, not to mention the more irrational reflexes aroused by differences of culture, religion and race. In France, Germany, Britain, Italy, Austria, Belgium, and parts of East Europe, it has led to a resurgence of radically motivated violence and resentment against the very existence of a multi-ethnic society. Opinion polls over the past few years across the European continent consistently show high levels of prejudice towards immigrants, foreign workers, asylum-seekers, refugees, and Gypsies. In France, the main targets are Arabs from the Maghreb and to a lesser extent Africans; in Germany they are Turks; in Britain, Asians (especially Pakistanis), and Afro-Caribbean people; in Italy they are primarily Africans; in Austria they tend to be Slavs; and in Eastern Europe, Gypsies are a specially favored scapegoat. Alongside this general xenophobia there is also some anti-Semitism – less intense than it used to be in the prewar period – but still ideologically central to the agenda of the far right.

The new populism and its leaders (most of them fairly articulate and intent on maintaining a respectable façade) abide by the democratic rules of the game in playing to the xenophobic gallery. Their slogans of "Germany for the Germans," "France for the French," "Austria for the Austrians" or "Russia for the Russians" offer simplistic, reassuring answers for these beleaguered citizens who feel abandoned, lost or betrayed by the established parties; and for all those who feel angry at the influx of foreigners which has changed the character of their local habitat. Sometimes, as in Italy, it is not so much against foreigners but fellow citizens – in this case Southern Italians – that the xenophobic stereotypes are directed. The more prosperous Italians of the North, disgusted by the political corruption of the establishment in Rome, flock to the populist Lombard League. In West Germany, alongside the backlash against immigrants and guest-workers, there is unexpectedly deep resentment towards East Germans, blamed for the costs of unification and a temporary decline in the standard of living.

The populist demagogues flourish, as always, in a climate of fear – fear of unemployment and recession, fear of the alien and different, fear for the future. In France, Le Pen's Front National has consistently won between 12 and 14 percent of the vote in regional, cantonal, and national elections. With 60,000 members and 239 regional councillors (out of a total of 1,829), with strong bases in Province, Alpes, Côte d'Azur and Ile de France, the radical right in France is solidly implanted. Its campaign against immigration has played no small role in bringing the present French government of the conservative right to adopt draconian legislation whose declared aim is zero-immigration in what was traditionally Europe's most hospitable country.

In Germany, the Republikaner did not do well in the recent national elections, due to internal divisions, but they have a potential support base of around 10 percent of the electorate. The pressure of the radical right forced the German government to drastically modify its liberal asylum laws. In Austria, Jörg Haider's Freedom Party enjoys the support of nearly 25 percent of the electorate and is threatening to replace the Conservatives as the second largest party. Its rhetoric about the threat of *Umvolkung* (ethnic transformation) resulting from further immigration from the South or East is redolent of the vocabulary of the Third Reich. In Belgium, too, the far-right Vlaams Block, which adopts an extreme anti-immigrant stance, is well-positioned. In Antwerp in 1991 it won 25 percent of the vote in the last general elections and this could increase the next time around. Significantly, as in some other European countries, the populist right is openly supported by neo-Nazi groups.

It is tempting to dismiss the neo-Nazi movements and violent skin-head gangs who have envenomed race relations in Europe in recent years as politically insignificant in view of their small size, their lack of leadership, coherent organization or ideology. Apart from Germany, their numbers are small in most individual European countries (they are generally in the age 14 to 25 group) – and they have no influence on electoral politics. But the wave of racist violence in Germany in the last few years – with brutal attacks on Turks, Third World immig-rants, handicapped people, as well as the desecration of Jewish ceme-teries and Holocaust sites – has been a chilling reminder of the fascist potential still lurking in the lower depths of European society. In 1992 alone, there were over 2,000 racist attacks (nearly double the previous year), over 600 cases of arson, and 17 deaths caused by neo-Nazi skinheads in Germany. Their message of hate is relayed through a skinhead music scene (a pattern pioneered by racist rock bands in Britain) and computer games as well as racist literature. The denial of the Holocaust is a consistent feature of their propaganda, as it is of equivalent neo-Nazi groups in Britain, France, Italy, and other Euro-pean countries. The light penalties given by German courts for their criminal activities and the relative passivity of the government and police (somewhat corrected in recent months) suggests more than an echo of Weimar. The ill-fated Republic was notoriously blind in the right eye, when it came to responding to extremist violence from the right. Historical analogies can be misleading, but many Germans themselves draw the parallel with late Weimar conditions. These parallels are even more striking when we look at Russia where a devastated economy, national humiliation, and a crisis of identity make some version of fascism a growing temptation. Similarly, in what was formerly East Germany, which knew only Nazi and Com-munist dictatorship between 1933 and 1989, the prognosis is not encouraging.

Not only have the so-called "Ossies" been living in an ideological vacuum since 1989, but they have seen their industrial base and collective self-esteem progressively eroded. But the fact is that there are even more organized neo-Nazis in Western Germany, which until recently never had it so good. Hitler's great-grandchildren (if that is who they are) are no less the products of an economic miracle shaped by the Bonn Republic than the misfits of Communist totalitarianism. Moreover, at its core the resurgence of nationalist xenophobia, with its echoes of a genocidal past, is much more than simply a German problem.

We are dealing here with a general European and perhaps even a planetary malaise, involving a fundamental breakdown in moral and societal values. The ghosts of Europe's past will not be exorcised by the facile search for scapegoats in the present nor by futile exercises in normalizing the collective traumas of history. The search for roots and for a secure national identity can often be liberating experiences – especially in the service of freedom from tyranny, oppression, and humiliation. But even the noblest patriotic sentiments are liable to become the "last refuge of the scoundrel" unless they are also balanced by an elementary respect for dignity, solidarity, and universal human rights.

Acknowledgements

I thank Kamille Rath for technical assistance during the preparation of this volume.

The essays appearing in this volume are printed with the permission of their original publishers.

Chapter 1, "Race and Ethnicity" by Max Weber, reprinted with the permission of J.C.B. Mohr from *Wirtschaft und Gesellschaft: Grundriss der verstehenden Soziologie*, 4th German edition, Johannes Winckelmann (ed.), 1954; and Max Weber, *Economy and Society*, translated by Guenther Roth and Claus Wittich. Copyright © 1978, The Regents of the University of California.

Chapter 3, "Beyond Reason: The Nature of the Ethnonational Bond" by Walker Connor, reprinted with the permission of Routledge from *Ethnic and Racial Studies*, Vol. 16, No. 3 (1993). Copyright © 1993, Routledge.

Chapter 4, "An American Dilemma" by Gunnar Myrdal is reprinted by permission of Harper Collins Publishers, Inc. from Gunnar Myrdal, *An American Dilemma: The Negro Problem and Modern Democracy*. Copyright © 1944, 1962, Harper Collins Publishers, Inc.

Chapter 5, "Americanism and Its Discontents: Protestantism, Nativism, and Political Heresy in America" by Michael W. Hughey is reprinted by permission of Human Sciences Press from *The International Journal of Politics, Culture, and Society*, Vol. 5, No. 4 (1992). Copyright © 1992, Human Sciences Press.

Chapter 6, "The Race Question and Liberalism: Casuistries in American Constitutional Law" by Stanford M. Lyman is reprinted by permission of Human Sciences Press from *The International Journal of Politics, Culture, and Society*, Vol. 5, No. 2 (1991). Copyright © 1991, Human Sciences Press.

Chapter 7, "The New American Pluralism: Racial and Ethnic Sodalities and Their Sociological Implications" by Michael W. Hughey and

Arthur J. Vidich is reprinted by permission of Human Sciences Press from *The International Journal of Politics, Culture, and Society*, Vol. 6, No. 2 (1992). Copyright © 1992, Human Sciences Press.

Chapter 8, "Contesting the Meaning of Race in the Post-Civil Rights Period" by Howard Winant is reprinted by permission of the University of Minnesota Press from Howard Winant, *Racial Conditions: Politics, Theory, Comparisons*. Copyright © 1994, by Howard Winant.

Chapter 9, "Multiculturalism and Universalism: A History and Critique" by John Higham is reprinted by permission of The Johns Hopkins University Press from *American Quarterly*, Vol. 45, No. 2 (1993). Copyright © 1993, Johns Hopkins University Press.

Chapter 10, "Constructing Ethnicity: Creating and Recreating Ethnic Identity and Culture" by Joane Nagel is reprinted by permission of The University of California Press from *Social Problems*, Vol. 41, No. 1 (1994). Copyright © 1994, the Society for the Study of Social Problems.

Chapter 11, "The Costs of a Costless Community" by Mary C. Waters is reprinted by permission of the University of California Press from Mary C. Waters, *Ethnic Options: Choosing Identities in America*. Copyright © 1990, The Regents of the University of California.

Chapter 12, "Multicultural Foreign Policy" by Yossi Shain is reprinted by permission from *Foreign Policy*, Vol. 100 (1995). Copyright © 1995, The Carnegie Endowment for International Peace.

Chapter 13, "Racial and Ethnic Conflicts: A Global Perspective" by Rita Jalali and Seymour Martin Lipset is reprinted by permission of the Academy of Political Science from *The Political Science Quarterly*, Vol. 107, No. 4 (1992–93). Copyright © 1992, the Academy of Political Science.

Chapter 14, "Ethnic Nationalism: Politics, Ideology, and the World Order" by Joane Nagel is reprinted by permission of E. J. Brill from *The International Journal of Comparative Sociology*, Vol. XXXIV, No. 1–2 (1993). Copyright © 1993, E.J. Brill.

Chapter 15, "Nationalism Reborn" by Robert Wistrich is reprinted by permission of the author from *Partisan Review*, Vol. LXII, No. 1 (1995). Copyright © 1995, Robert Wistrich.

Notes on the Contributors

Herbert Blumer (1900–1987) was one of sociology's most innovative voices and sharpest critics. His works include *Symbolic Interactionism: Perspective and Method* (1969) and *Movies, Delinquency, and Crime.* (1933) In 1983, Blumer was honored by the American Sociological Association as a recipient of its award for a Career of Distinguished Scholarship.

Walker Connor is John R. Reitemeyer Professor of Political Science at Trinity College in Hartford, CT. His works include *Ethnonationalism: The Quest for Understanding* (1994) and *Mexican-Americans in Comparative Perspective* (1985).

John Higham, a historian, is Professor Emeritus at Johns Hopkins University. Among his many works are *Strangers in the Land: Patterns of American Nativism, 1860–1925* (1963) and *Send These to Me: Immigrants in Urban America* (1984).

Michael W. Hughey is Professor of Sociology, Moorhead State University, Moorhead, MN. He is the author of *Civil Religion and Moral Order: Theoretical and Historical Dimensions* (1983) and co-editor of a volume of essays entitled *The Ethnic Quest for Community: Searching for Roots in the Lonely Crowd* (1993).

Rita Jalali is Assistant Professor of Sociology at Michigan State University. Her research interests include the womens' movement in developing nations and the impact of affirmative action and multiculturalism on minorities in North America. She has published in the areas of race and ethnicity, caste conflict in India, and social movements.

Seymour Martin Lipset is the Virginia E. Hazel and John T. Hazel Chair of Public Policy at George Mason University and Senior Fellow at the Hoover Institution at Stanford University. He is a past president of the American Sociological Association. Among his recent books is *Jews and the New American Scene* (1997).

Stanford M. Lyman is Robert J. Morrow Eminent Scholar and Professor of Social Science at Florida Atlantic University, Boca Raton,

366

Florida. He is the author of numerous books and essays, many of which deal with aspects of race and ethnicity. Some of the latter include *Civilization: Contents, Discontents, Malcontents, and Other Essays in Social Theory; Militarism, Imperialism, and Racial Accommodation: An Analysis and Interpretation of the Early Writings of Robert E. Park* (1990); and *Color, Culture, Civilization: Race and Minority Issues in American Society* (1994).

Gunnar Myrdal (1898–1987) was an influential Swedish social scientist and a 1977 Nobel Laureate in Economics. His major works include *An American Dilemma: The Negro Problem and Modern Democracy* (1944) and *Asian Drama: An Inquiry Into the Poverty of Nations* (1968).

Joane Nagel is a political sociologist at the University of Kansas. Her most recent book is *American Indian Ethnic Renewal: Red Power and the Resurgence of Identity and Culture* (1996).

Yossi Shain teaches political science at Tel Aviv University and is a visiting fellow at St Antony's College, Oxford. His latest book (with Juan J. Linz) is *Between States: Interim Governments and Democratic Transitions* (1995).

Arthur J. Vidich is Senior Lecturer and Professor Emeritus of Sociology and Anthropology at the Graduate Faculty of the New School for Social Research. His works include *Small Town in Mass Society (1968); American Society: The Welfare State and Beyond* (1986); and *American Sociology: Worldly Rejections of Religion and Their Directions* (1985).

Mary C. Waters is Professor of Sociology at Harvard University. She is the author of *Ethnic Options: Choosing Identities in America* (1990) and "Immigration and Ethnic and Racial Inequality in the United States" (1995).

Max Weber (1864–1920) was a highly influential German sociologist, historian, and philosopher. His works include *The Protestant Ethnic and the Spirit of Capitalism (1997); Economy and Society* (1979); and *General Economic History* (1981).

Howard Winant is Professor of Sociology at Temple University. His books include *Racial Conditions* (1994) and *Racial Formation in the United States from the 1960's to the 1980's* (1994).

Robert Wistrich is Professor of Modern Jewish History at Hebrew University of Jerusalem. He is the author of *Weekend in Munich: Art, Propaganda and Terror in the Third Reich* (1996).

Index